Murder on the Common

Murder on the Common

Keith Pedder

BLAKE'S
TRUE
CRIME
LIBRARY

Published by John Blake Publishing Ltd,
3, Bramber Court, 2 Bramber Road,
London W14 9PB, England

www.blake.co.uk

First published in paperback in 2004

ISBN 184454 057 X

British Library Cataloguing-in-Publication Data:

A catalogue record for this book is available from the British Library.

Design by www.envydesign.co.uk

Printed in Great Britain by BookMarque

3 5 7 9 10 8 6 4 2

For legal reasons, the names of certain individuals have been changed.

Glossary

ACPO	Association of Chief Police Officers
ACTO	Assistant Commissioner Territorial Operations
AMIP	Area Major Investigation Pool
Book 40	police record ledger
BSU	Behavioural Science Unit
CAD	Computer Aided Despatch
CLO	Community liaison Officer
CM	home address
CPS	Crown Prosecution Service
CRO	Criminal Records Office
DACTO	Deputy Assistant Commissioner Territorial Operations
DCI	Detective Chief Inspector
DCS	Detective Chief Superintendent
DIO	Deputy Investigating Officer
ESDA	Electrostatic Document Analysis
FIB	Force Intelligence Bureau
HA	home address

HOLMES	Home Office Large Major Enquiry System
IC1	Identity Code 1
IIMAC	information, intention, method, administration and commurncation
the Job	police force
LIO	Local Intelligence Officer
MO	*modus operandi*
NCAVC	National Centre for the Analysis of Violent Crime
OP	observation point
PACE	Police and Criminal Evidence Bill
PCR	Polymerise Chain Reaction
PDF	personal description forms
PM	post mortem
PRSU	Police Resource Support Unit Ree
Ree-Gee	Regional Crime Squad
RV	rendezvous point
SIO	Senior Investigating Officer
SO1O	covert operations unit
SO11	Criminal Intelligence
SO9	Regional Crime Squad
SOCOs	Scene of Crime Officers
TI	Trainee Investigator
TIE	trace, interview and eliminate
TSG	Territorial Support Group
TSU	Technical Support Unit
UC operation	undercover operation
VICAP	Violent Criminal Apprehension Program

Prologue

The tragic events of the morning of Wednesday, 15 July 1992 were to spark one of the most intensive and controversial murder inquiries this country has ever seen.

The appaling and callous murder of 23-year-old Rachel Nickell in front of her young son, Alex, had a profound effect, not only on the detectives and uniform officers who attended the scene and investigated her death, but it also sent a shudder throughout the entire country. There was shock and outrage at the sheer brutality of this senseless offence. It also served to emphasise the ever-present and increasing fear of violent crime and posed the question: 'Is anybody safe?'

This offence had not been committed in some dark alleyway in the dead of night, nor had it occurred in an area renowned for its high crime rate. The horror of this most vicious of crimes was compounded by the fact that the killer had struck as Rachel and her young son were enjoying the warmth of the summer sun as they walked with their mongrel puppy, Molly, in a famous London beauty spot. The cruellest irony was that Rachel had only recently begun to visit Wimbledon Common as she felt it was safer than Tooting Common, which was closer to home, but where she had been the victim of an incident involving indecent exposure.

Over the course of my career as a CID officer, I have investigated many violent and sexual offences and have noted, as have my colleagues, the increasing resignation of the female victims to the fact that the confidence to walk alone after dark was fast becoming a thing of the past. Our violent society is making women of all ages think twice about the clothes they wear, for fear of being judged as provocative, or about embarking on a journey that would take them to less salubrious areas of town. I have witnessed the terror in the eyes of these women as they have recalled the details of their ordeals, and have seen the long-term damage which has left them shadows of their former selves. All the time and counselling in the world cannot totally remove the mental scars or stop the nightmares. The murder of Rachel Nickell was the embodiment of the worst of those nightmares.

As the inquiry began to unfold, it quickly became apparent that this would be a protracted and complex investigation. We had no forensic evidence to speak of and the only eye-witness to the killing was Rachel's son, Alex, who was not quite three years of age at the time. There were in excess of 500 people on the common when Rachel was killed, yet it seemed the killer had struck then slipped away unnoticed.

There was a driving determination amongst the investigating team to solve this particular murder. The tragedy of Rachel's death really seemed to have struck a nerve. The more we dug, the greater the sense of outrage became. With all murder inquiries, the strategy is to start with the victim, the centre, and work outwards. In the majority of cases, there is a connection between the victim and the suspect and normally a clearly identifiable motive as a result of that connection. However, as time went on, it became apparent that this crime was an attack by a stranger. Rachel Nickell had been a blameless victim of opportunity; she died simply because she was in the wrong place at the wrong time.

It is now a matter of common knowledge that following an

appeal on the BBC's *Crimewatch* programme, Colin Stagg was identified as a potential suspect. Stagg was arrested on 18 September 1992 and interviewed over the course of three days. As a result of the answers provided by Colin Stagg in those interviews, it became clear that his account of his movements on the morning of the murder was at variance with the evidence provided by three witnesses who placed him on Wimbledon Common at, or very close to, the time of the murder and, according to one of those witnesses, he had been acting suspiciously.

We were clearly faced with a dilemma – Stagg had, by his own behaviour, made himself a compelling suspect. That being said, it was also recognised that there may be an explanation which could eliminate him from suspicion. Our problem was how to establish the truth of the matter. Traditional policing methods had run their course, and, in the absence of an eyewitness to the killing, or forensic or material evidence, how could we resolve this issue? It was essential that we did something. With the spectre of a killer striking apparently at random and seeking victims of opportunity, no stone could be left unturned. If there was an explanation for Mr Stagg's apparent lies, then we needed to find it. But more importantly, we needed to find the killer. The urgency of this was reinforced by consultant clinical psychologist Mr Paul Britton's chilling warning about the probability of another offenc and, if Mr Stagg was not our man, we needed to clear him and concentrate our efforts on other lines of enquiry.

It was against this background that the undercover operation was begun. The purpose was either to eliminate Mr Stagg from our enquiries or further the case against him. Our other lines of enquiry were extensive and varied. The result of the undercover operation is also now well known; Mr Stagg was re-arrested on 17 August 1993, charged with the murder of Rachel Nickell, and following an eleven-day, contested committal he was sent for trial at the Old Bailey.

'Thoroughly reprehensible' and 'deceptive conduct of the grossest kind' were just two of the expressions which heralded the collapse of the prosecution case against Mr Colin Stagg. His

Lordship Mr Justice Ognall was fulsome in his condemnation of police action in his judgment delivered to a packed Old Bailey courtroom on the morning of 14 September 1994. The manner in which the case was unceremoniously thrown out of court only served to add to the bitter blow already dealt to Rachel's family. As I listened to Andrew Nickell's dignified and very controlled press statement, I struggled to make sense of the sequence of events which had led to their hopes being raised and then dashed with respect to resolving the question: 'Who killed Rachel?' I felt then, and indeed still feel, a deep personal responsibility for their continued suffering.

In the days that followed Mr Stagg's discharge from court I often asked myself, 'How could we have got it so wrong?' The furore caused by the failure of this tragic case heightened the need to re-examine the investigation and to come up with some answers.

The murder inquiry was re-opened following the collapse of the trial and a new team was brought in to reinvestigate. That inquiry has now been completed. The investigation and reinvestigation have resulted in the taking of 2,893 statements, 1,676 interviews, a total of 6,761 potential witnesses being seen and 33 persons being arrested. The new investigation took officers to New Zealand in 1996 to interview a former barman who had emigrated from Britain, but he was cleared of any involvement. The new team was headed by Detective Superintendent Brian Tompkins, who at the announcement of the closure of his reinvestigation said, 'The job is to seek evidence and at the end of the day we don't have the evidence to charge anyone. There is disappointment.' I echo his sentiments.

It is no coincidence that nine years have elapsed since the offence before I have produced this book. I realised that earlier publication could have jeopardised the new investigation and my most fervent hope was that they would succeed where I had failed.

The purpose of this book is not to point accusing fingers at Colin Stagg, nor to criticise the decision made by an experienced and highly regarded judge. Colin Stagg walked from the court a free and innocent man. I accept and respect the law. My intention is explain our actions and procedures to a concerned public who have been subjected to much sensationalist and misleading media coverage. The nature of Paul Britton's designed operation was extremely complex and the issues have since become blurred by over-simplification.

I wish to highlight that these unusual steps were not embarked upon lightly. My hope is to communicate to the reader that this was not a vindictive witch hunt against one man, but an inquiry conducted with professionalism and dedication by a staff who worked long and hard, very often without being paid.

My goal is to explain these unusual and innovative steps. Yes, they are radical even by today's standards, but the law and criminal investigation are dynamic things. Fingerprints, one of the most powerful weapons in the detective's armoury, were initially treated with derision and suspicion. It took from 1879, when Dr Henry Faulds, a Scottish physiologist, was credited with the first crime to be solved by fingerprints, to 1905 for fingerprints to be accepted grudgingly by an English court. And 30 years, on palm print evidence was brought before a British court. In addition, the controversy still rages as to the reliability of DNA evidence, so it may be many years before the use of psychology is accepted as having evidential value rather than being an investigative tool. That's if it ever is – only time will tell.

Our entire operation was based on clinical and forensic psychology and not 'offender profiling' as the press reported. It was recognised that the prosecution took its use into uncharted waters. There is diverse expert opinion as to its value, and the adversarial system and the court hearings have certainly polarised opinion on the subject. In the light of the Colin Stagg case, such evidence is clearly held to be inadmissible. The debate as to its psychological worth rumbles on, and I hope that this book will widen the debate.

In conclusion, I hope that this book will underline the thoroughness of the investigation and the reasons for the undercover operation, which was a search for the truth and designed as much to eliminate as to incriminate. It is intended to be an objective account which will offer the reader an opportunity to reflect on the dilemma which faced the police and the prosecuting authorities. They may then, if they so choose, form their own views as to the correctness or otherwise of the action taken. Whatever decision they come to, it will be based upon what is intended to be a frank explanation which recognises both the strengths and weaknesses of the prosecution and defence cases, and may give a clearer picture of the events of this tragic case

Chapter 1

The traffic had been nose-to-bumper all the way out of South London on that warm July evening, but by the time I had negotiated the back-doubles to avoid Sydenham High Street, the going became a little easier. I estimated that I had about another half-hour's drive to reach my home in Kent.

It was 8.30pm, and I switched on the radio just in time for the news. The main story concerned the discovery, earlier in the day, of the body of a young mother on Wimbledon Common. Her child, a two-year-old boy, had been found clinging to the corpse. The newsreader said that the victim's name was being withheld, and a Scotland Yard spokesman was quoted as saying that a man had been taken into custody and was helping police with their enquiries.

I turned off the radio and lit a cigarette. Wimbledon was a bit of an unexpected location for a murder, I thought. To my mind, this up-market corner of suburban South-West London was best known for lawn tennis and cuddly Wombles, and not exactly what you'd call a high-crime area. If a young mother wasn't safe on its famous common, I wondered, was anyone, anywhere?

I didn't really think too much more about it, except that the crime was probably a domestic. In something like 98 per cent of murder cases, the suspect is either known to the victim, or connected in some way; it's very rare indeed for a total stranger to attack somebody out of the blue and kill them in a motiveless crime. And they'd said that somebody had already been arrested, so that was that – case solved, done and dusted.

My mind turned to more pleasant matters as I thought about my wife and two young boys. I wondered, too, if there'd be a cold bottle of wine or a few beers waiting for me in the fridge. I had been sitting at my desk at Brixton Police Station since 7.30am that morning and I could do with a drink. Newly promoted to the rank of Detective Inspector after 17 years with the Met, five-and-a-half of those in the Flying Squad, I'd taken up the new posting just a day or two before. The first case I'd been presented with concerned an allegation of rape that had been reported three months post-offence, and after several hours of scratching my head I was still none the wiser as to how on earth I could take the investigation any further.

As I walked into the house, Debbie called to me from the living room. 'I'm just watching the news – that poor girl murdered in Wimbledon.'

'Somebody's been nicked, haven't they?' I said as I went through and joined her.

The reporter confirmed that a man was in custody, and that the girl's name was still being withheld until next of kin had been notified. All very routine stuff as far as I was concerned, and not enough to distract me as I sank into my favourite armchair and accepted the glass of cold wine Debbie was offering me.

But then a face I recognised appeared on the television screen, and it looked so uncharacteristically strained and tight-lipped that I couldn't help sitting bolt upright.

I had known Mick Wickerson a long time. Now a Detective Chief Inspector, with postings that included some of the more stressful areas such as Peckham and Brixton, he was a veteran of the Flying Squad and had spent 12 months in Hong Kong attached to the anti-corruption commission. At 5ft 11in and with the build of an athlete, Wicko was a shrewd and experienced investigator, but his voice was charged with emotion as he faced the TV cameras.

'She was just an innocent young mother walking her little boy in a public park,' he said in obvious distress. 'It's quite horrific ... so tragic.'

What had he seen, I suddenly wondered, that had had such an effect on a normally very laid-back detective?

I had lost count of the number of murder cases I had worked on myself. They all tended to merge and blur into one another, though I remembered the first one, partly because I was just a young PC, partly because you always remember your first body.

A young girl had been pushed from the 19th floor of a block of flats; a hell of a mess, and quite a shock, but I had already learned that you cope with the moment and get on with what you have to do; when you've finished, that's when you go round the corner and throw up into your helmet. Since then, I had been involved in so many cases that they all became part of one continuum, which wasn't indicative of the fact that I was uncaring, it was just that unless there's a specifically good reason for remembering, they simply fade into the dim and distant past.

It made me think all the more about the look on Mick Wickerson's face and the way his head shook slowly from side to side, as if in disbelief at what he had seen.

Over the next few days, I learned in the newspapers that the victim was a 23-year-old girl called Rachel Nickell, and her 2-year, 11-month-old son was called Alex. They lived with Andre Hanscombe, her partner and the child's father, at a flat in Elmfield Road, Balham. I also gathered that the victim's parents, Andrew and Monica Nickell, were in the USA on holiday. Her brother and two officers from Scotland Yard had flown out to break the news to them.

Other than that, none of the details stuck in my mind and I didn't think much more about it until the following Monday morning, five days after the murder, when I received a telephone call from Detective Chief Superintendent Bob Chapman, head of the 4 AMIP (Area Major Investigation Pool) at Croydon.

Coming straight to the point, he said, 'I need a DI for the Wimbledon murder, Keith – can you get down there?'

'I thought they'd nicked someone.'

'They did, but he's been eliminated from the inquiry. It's back to square one, and it looks like being a sticker. There's half-a-dozen Regional Crime Squad DCs arriving this morning to deal with the suspect enquiries and you'll be in charge of them. Get down here as quick as you can.'

'Ree-Gee? That's a bit unusual, isn't it?'

'It's an unusual job.'

Wimbledon Police Station is an Edwardian building that has been renovated and extended. Most of the new building work was completed in a similar architectural style to the original parts which faced the street, but the structure hidden away at the rear was no more than a functional, box-like, single-storey extension. It was in here that the incident room had been set up.

Opening the door and stepping inside, I was hit by the sheer number of officers, telephones and computer terminals crammed into a space not much larger than my own living room. White boards lined the walls, listing the names of investigating officers and linking them to reference numbers to show which leads they were following up. A large map of Wimbledon Common was covered with yellow Post-Its. The flurry of activity and deafening level of noise reminded me more of a dealing room in the City.

I had been on many major inquiries but the sight of no fewer than nine HOLMES (Home Office Large Major Enquiry System) computer terminals and indexers (operators) quite threw me. HOLMES is a facility for classifying, storing and cross-referencing the tens of thousands of pieces of information collected during a major inquiry. The system had only been available since 1987 when the hunt for the Yorkshire Ripper had exposed the dangers of important information being buried under a mountain of paperwork. It became clear that the Ripper, Peter Sutcliffe, would have come to light as a strong suspect much earlier if there had been a computer system that signposted the numerous points at which his name appeared in relation to the murders.

It was normal to have perhaps two or three operators, and very rarely four, but to have nine was way beyond what I was used to. In addition to the indexers, there also appeared to be two receivers, officers whose job it is to assess information and pass it on to the indexers to process on to the computer. Again, a solitary receiver was the norm.

It struck me immediately that this inquiry was being given preferential treatment. A quick glance at the action board also confirmed that there were unusually large outside teams and research teams – nearly 50 in total. In my experience, this was an unprecedented number for a Metropolitan Police major inquiry, 15 or 16 being considered well staffed.

Most of all, however, it was the presence of computer terminals at all which surprised me. Wimbledon was situated in 4 Area, and their HOLMES suites were located at Croydon and Thornton Heath. Wimbledon was not a HOLMES site so it was obvious that MS22 (Management Services 22 branch) had been asked to install all the hardware especially for this incident – and they must have complied very rapidly. Again, not something I had encountered before.

I went over to a couple of faces I recognised. Bob Ritzo, a dark-haired, heavy-set DC in his early forties, looked up from the terminal as I approached.

'Hello, Keith, what are you doing here? Still on the Squad?'

'No, I've been posted to this murder. Is the boss around?'

'First floor – up the stairs, follow the corridor all the way and it's the last door on the left. You can't miss it.'

I made my way up the stairs to John Bassett's office. It was a while since I had worked with the Detective Superintendent, better known in the Job (police force) as JB or Bertie, and I was aware that this might well be the last occasion, since he was only a little over a year away from retirement.

I had only gone halfway along the corridor when I encountered Mick Wickerson rushing in the opposite direction.

'Late for court,' he said, running for the stairs. 'JB's in my office – he'll fill you in.'

I smiled at Wickerson's disappearing back. I had known him since 1978, when he was a DS at Peckham and East Dulwich police stations, and my impression of him even then was that he was always in a rush. At the time, I was a lowly Crime Squad PC with aspirations of joining the CID. We worked together on many jobs and he had been one of the formative influences on my detective career, a formidable investigator who had been more than willing to pass on the tricks of the trade. I became the sorcerer's apprentice.

I found the Superintendent sitting behind Wickerson's desk, pen in hand, leafing through a stack of statements and making notes. He looked up and smiled as he removed his glasses. Hand outstretched, he said, 'Keith – welcome to chaos.'

JB offered me a seat. With whitish-grey hair that was slightly receding, black bushy eyebrows, and an almost permanent smile on his face, the senior officer had always reminded me of everybody's favourite uncle.

'It can't be that bad,' I said, 'can it?'

'Things are a little hectic. Have you been into the incident room yet?'

'Looks very impressive. How did you manage to get all the hardware?'

'No choice, really. A manual system wouldn't have coped with an inquiry this size and all the Area HOLMES suites are being used. And the fact that the Commissioner's wife, Lady Imbert, was on Wimbledon Common at the time of the murder may have helped just a little.'

I returned his smile, then it was time to get down to business.

'How much do you know already?' he asked.

'Only what I've picked up from the news. I know that the victim was young, white and single, and that she was stabbed to death in front of her son.'

'Correct. Rachel Nickell was 23 and lived with her boyfriend, Andre Hanscombe, in a two-bedroom flat in Elmfield Mansions, Balham. He's a motorcycle messenger. Andre left for work at

8.30am on Wednesday the 15th. We know that Rachel left the flat 15 minutes later for a walk on Wimbledon Common, and arrived just before 10.00am. She was with her two-year-old son, Alex, and their black-and-white mongrel dog, Molly. We have a last sighting of them at about 10.20am, when a cyclist saw them heading towards the woods near to where Rachel was found. Then, at 10.30am, a retired architect called Michael Murray, out walking his dog, found Alex clinging to Rachel's body.'

JB explained that Rachel had been provisionally identified through the registration number of her silver Volvo estate car which she had left in the Windmill car park before she set off on her walk with Alex and Molly.

Later that morning, Andre had stopped at a phone box in North London to make a call home to say hello to Rachel and Alex. A police officer answered, and when Andre insisted on knowing what had happened to Rachel, he was told the terrible news.

'According to the officer, he howled like a wounded animal at the roadside, Keith,' JB said.

As soon as Andre had arrived at Wimbledon station, DCs Sparshatt and Miller were assigned to take him back to the flat to pick up all the things he'd need to spend the night at his mother's house in Hampstead. The press pack was already on the doorstep and he had to be smuggled past them. Andre's flatmate was also there; he'd come home to find the door broken down and the flat full of officers, and reporters outside who, unbelievably, shouted offers of money to take photographs of the inside of the flat.

Rachel's brother Mark, a merchant banker, arrived soon afterwards, having travelled by Tube from his office in the City.

Sparshatt and Miller explained to Andre all they knew, as quickly and clearly as they could. They explained that they had to take bundles of Andre's and Alex's clothing to be examined forensically, so that any fibres which belonged to them could be ruled out as evidence, and anything else categorised as unknown. While that was happening, a police surgeon arrived at the flat to take a blood sample from Andre.

Andre was then taken to collect Alex from the hospital, where some minor cuts and bruises on his face were being attended to. A child psychologist was on hand to explain to Andre that he mustn't lie to Alex; he had to tell him that there had been a terrible accident and that his mummy was never coming back. It must be very clear-cut in the toddler's mind that she had gone for ever.

Andre's mother had remarried and changed her name, which meant the media hadn't got to her yet. The television news and *Evening Standard*, however, were already full of the story. Reporters had tried to question parents who were collecting children from Alex's nursery that afternoon. When they were ignored, they ran down the road shouting questions. That was how many parents learned of Rachel's death.

Mark went to his parents' house in Ampthill in Bedfordshire. His elderly grandmother had been staying alone in the house, there to feed the cats while the Nickells were away. Officers warned him to make sure there was always someone on the premises from now on; if the press ran true to form, there was a good chance they would try to break in and steal family photographs. Mark arrived to find reporters already ringing the front doorbell and jamming the telephone with calls. Mark didn't dare disconnect it in case the Nickells, who still hadn't been contacted, happened to call.

JB told me that later that night, while Alex slept, Sparshatt and Miller started their questions. As I've stated, in any murder inquiry, you start from the centre and work out. Our transatlantic cousins refer to it as 'victimology'; to us, it's just good old-fashioned detective expertise. You research. You dig. You want to know about the mother, the father, the brother, the sister, the aunt, the uncle by marriage twice removed – an obvious procedure when you bear in mind the statistics. However, there was no need to ask Andre to provide an alibi for his movements that morning. His employers had already been questioned and were able to establish his whereabouts in North London at the time of the murder.

I didn't have to ask JB what the two officers would have asked Andre. Who did they know? Who did Rachel see? When had he left the house? Did they owe anybody any money? Did they have any enemies? Did Rachel have any life insurance? Was she wearing any jewellery?

Many of the questions would have focused on trying to establish what Rachel and Alex had done that morning. The squad needed to know who she was in the habit of talking to, who she might have seen. Did Andre know what Rachel's movements were that morning? What did she normally do? Who did Rachel see? What had she done the day before? When was the last time she and Andre had gone to the common together? Had he seen anything that made him suspicious? Sparshatt and Miller had offered to stop and resume the next day, but Andre wanted to carry on and give them all the help he could.

Andre said that when he had left her that morning, Rachel had been intending to run a few errands to the shops. She and Alex were then going to go for a walk on the common. He said that the week before, they had run around looking for lost golf balls in the bushes, so it was possible they would be somewhere near the golf course. Almost certainly, she would have parked in the Windmill car park, and would have aimed to be home by lunch.

Andre wondered why Rachel's body had been found so far off their usual route. Maybe the dog had got lost, he ventured. Or maybe Alex had been looking for something? Or maybe she had been talking with someone else she knew? One other thing was discussed many times – no one had heard Rachel scream, and yet the attack had taken place within hearing distance of the car park which was full of people. Only Alex could provide answers, and so far there had been no specific information from him about what had happened, and no certainty that there ever would be. So the officers concentrated on tying in what Andre was able to tell them with the times of sightings by witnesses at the car park and then walking with Alex.

Sparshatt and Miller asked also for the couples diaries and address books so the investigating team could speak to everyone Andre and Rachel knew, and took details of their bank accounts and other seemingly irrelevant personal information. Most murder cases are solved by a small piece of evidence which comes to light as a result of 'routine' police work. Often, cases have turned on the smallest of details which lead to more and more evidence.

Then, as gently as they could, they had asked the intimate questions that cannot be avoided in cases of sexual assault. When had Rachel and Andre last made love? What contraceptives had they used? What had they done and not done? The police have to know these things because the defence can always blame any signs found on the victim's body on the partner or husband.

JB said to me, 'Rachel had only recently started using Wimbledon Common because she'd been flashed at by men on Clapham Common and Tooting Bec which are closer to her home. She thought Wimbledon would be safer.' The irony in his voice was obvious. 'She went there about four times a week, letting Alex play outdoors and giving the dog some exercise. On the morning of the 15th she was wearing blue jeans, a grey T-shirt and brown boots.'

I said, 'The papers mentioned that a man had been nicked and was helping police with their enquiries, but I understand from Mr Chapman that he's not in the frame any more. Who was he; any relation to the victim?'

JB shook his head. 'No, just a local sad-case – and he's in the clear.'

The suspect, he explained, had been arrested within an hour or two of the body being discovered. He'd been seen begging for cigarettes outside the Asda superstore on the A3 and someone had reported him, mentioning that he had blood-stained clothing.

'We spent three days interviewing him, whilst carrying on other enquiries,' JB said. 'He had to be considered a suspect, but begging for fags outside Asda shortly after committing a murder was more than a little unlikely.'

They had forensically examined the man, his flat and it all came back negative. No weapon, no nothing; he was just in the wrong place at the wrong time.

'No other suspects at this stage?'

JB said that he believed Rachel's murder was the work of a local man. 'We get flashers and nuisances, but nothing like this ... not until now. We're looking at the usual categories – indecent assaults, peeping toms, flashers. Also any complaints from the common and sex offenders with a history of using the park who might recently have been released from prison.'

He added that when a criminal records check had been run on known sex offenders who might be suspects in the murder, it threw up the fact that over 100 convicted sex attackers lived within a radius of a mile or two of the common.

From the huge number of interviews already conducted by officers on and around the common, it was clear that no one had actually seen the killer attack Rachel – apart from young Alex. Nor had any suspects been observed running from the scene. The best early leads appeared to be the sighting of a short-haired man crouching to wash his hands in a ditch close to the murder scene, and a man with a pony-tail seen leaving the common in a hurry shortly after the body was discovered. As yet, however, neither had produced a positive line of enquiry.

'So you're not treating it as a domestic, then?'

Even as I said it, I realised that the presence of so many staff and computers made it a silly question.

'Andre's alibied,' JB said. 'But apart from that, you only have to see him with Alex and listen to him talking about Rachel to realise that he worshipped the ground she walked on, and absolutely idolises his son.

'Besides that, one of the ladies who looked after Alex after Michael Murray had discovered the body asked him who he had come to the common with and he replied, "Mummy and Molly." If his father had been there, I'm sure Alex would have mentioned it. We have quite naturally looked at Rachel's nearest and dearest but at the moment all we can say is that Andre is in the clear, as are other members of her immediate family. Friends and former boyfriends are being checked.'

I said, 'Look, Guv, rather than me sitting here asking questions off the top of my head it might be better if you just ran me through it.'

JB leaned back in his chair and steepled his fingers thoughtfully. Intelligent, compassionate, quietly spoken, the papers were later to draw a comparison between him and television's Inspector Morse.

However, there was something distinctly unusual about his manner this morning that, at first, I couldn't quite put my finger on. There seemed to be an air of sadness about him, not the detachedness you would expect from a man of his length of service. Then it dawned on me; here was a 30-year detective who had dealt with many major inquiries, yet in the space of less than a couple of minutes he had referred to the deceased not as the ,'victim', 'the dead girl' or simply the 'body', but by her Christian name, Rachel. It was extremely unusual.

'It would probably be better if you went up there to see the layout for yourself,' he went on, 'otherwise you'll never make head nor tail of what went on. Mick will give you a guided tour. There were about 500 people on the common at the time and the public response has been overwhelming – the major problem is keeping up with the new messages and information coming in and at the same time coping with the back record conversion.'

JB said that on 17 July, DCs Sparshatt and Miller had accompanied Andre to the mortuary to undertake a formal identification of the body. From the hospital, Andre had been driven to a press conference at New Scotland Yard. He said only a few words but, while he spoke, something completely unprecedented happened. Nearly everyone in the room was crying, male as well as female. Andre pleaded for anybody who knew anything at all that could help to come forward. This person had to be found before someone else was killed and another family destroyed. Throughout the interview, Nick Sparshatt held Andre's hand.

'As a result of the press conference, even more witnesses came forward,' JB said.

Apparently, it had taken the best part of 72 hours for the terminals to be installed, and, as a result, there were some 700 messages outstanding.

'Then the *News of the World* offered a reward of £15,000 yesterday for information leading to the arrest and conviction of the killer. Even more calls are flooding in.'

'What did the PM reveal?' I asked. 'Any forensic?'

JB brightened at the question. 'Doc Shepherd found traces of what he thinks is semen on Rachel's legs, so once we've identified our man, we've got him.'

'The media said she'd been stabbed – any luck with the weapon yet?'

JB's brief smile vanished. 'Not yet. There are 1,100 acres of common and woodland where Rachel was killed; it's like looking for a needle in a haystack. And as for the injuries, they were horrific – 49 stab wounds.'

He pushed a set of photographs across the desk. I picked up the folder and looked through them. JB was right, they were stomach-churning. I was glad that I hadn't been at the scene.

The colour prints ran in a sequence, starting with long range shots of the copse. Rachel's body was only just visible, showing up as a splash of white amongst the trees that could have been a discarded piece of litter or clothing.

Then the lens moved closer. The victim was lying on her left side, with her hips and knees slightly flexed. She was almost decapitated. Her arms and hands were raised and lay adjacent to her face. There were numerous stab wounds to the back, chest, neck and left hand. Her blue jeans and pants had been pulled downwards to the ankles, the jeans being inverted over the shoes. There was extensive blood-staining of the T-shirt and of the ground adjacent to the body. There were other areas of blood-staining adjacent to the body, and disturbance of the ground around the body. The cup of the left side of the bra had been displaced slightly downwards, exposing part of the breast. There were numerous cuts in both the T-shirt and bra.

I studied the pictures for a few minutes, making myself apply a detached investigative eye to the images, pushing to the back of my mind the sadness and revulsion that this type of offence always made me feel. It was particularly difficult in this case because Photographic Branch had included a picture of Rachel's son Alex at the back of the binder. The little lad had been found clinging to his mother's body and had also sustained some superficial physical injuries. This meant that he had to be considered as a secondary major crime scene and as such had to be photographed and forensically examined. I studied his small, innocent face; such big brown eyes, filled with fear and confusion. Even then, something told me that I would never forget their injured stare.

'She was last seen alive by Roger McKern, an actor, who was cycling along the Queen's Ride,' JB said. 'He was able to pinpoint the time and place exactly because he was running late and had stopped his bike to check the time. He said he saw this very attractive blonde woman with a young child and small black dog heading across the open space of ground in front of the mound and adjacent to where her body was eventually found. He checked his watch as he reached the Windmill car park and it said 10.20am.

'Doc Shepherd estimates that it would have taken a very minimum of three minutes to inflict so many wounds.'

I had attended enough post mortems to know the procedure, and to know that in the absence of witnesses, Rachel became the most important piece of evidence in the investigation. Every square inch of her body would have been photographed, scraped, swabbed or cut open. Body fluids, fingernail dirt and pubic hair would have been sealed in plastic or glass; in time, they would be passed along the evidential chain from pathologist to the laboratory, to the prosecution, to the court and to the jury. There is no dignity in death, especially once the investigative arms of law and order become involved.

The pathologist's preliminary investigation suggested that even after Rachel was dead, the horrific assault on her body continued, the knife being driven into her body with such force that an outline of the hilt was imprinted on her flesh. Bruising on Alex's cheek suggested that he had probably been struck a glancing blow by the killer sometime during the attack.

'Perhaps Alex was threatened first in order to make his mother comply,' JB said. 'Maybe he tried to help her. It's all conjecture. We do, however, think the murder happened at about 10.30am. We can time that by Michael Murray, who found the body at 10.35am; we can tell by the direction that he came from and his line of sight that it couldn't have been any later than 10.30am, otherwise he would have seen the attacker. She was last seen alive at 10.20am, found dead at 10.35am – so we have a window of opportunity of 15 minutes.

'Now we also know that she was meandering quite slowly, so what we think has happened is the killer has seen her walking across the open space, probably from the summit of the mound. We're not sure where she entered the wooded area, but what might have happened is he's seen her go into the woods at a point, and then moved down the right-hand side of the mound and sat there in some long grass waiting for her to appear along the bridle path.

'If the scene of the murder was the trees, then we know that she got some ten, fifteen, perhaps even twenty yards past there, by virtue of the fact that she was carrying Alex's T-shirt. As she walked past the scene where her body was found, we think she was confronted on the footpath twenty yards further on. The little boy has told us that he was disposed of almost immediately by being thrown into some brambles. Rachel was obviously confronted because she'd dropped the T-shirt, which was found on the footpath, and we think that perhaps she was a little bit unsteady on her feet and was perhaps forced back, because there was a footprint found on the T-shirt. We can't say with 100 per cent accuracy that it's her footprint, but the lab is of the opinion that it is of a very similar tread pattern to that of her shoes.'

'What about the injuries?' I said.

'There are three wounds on Rachel's body that are not stab wounds as such; they're what can only be described as prod marks. There are two on her chest and one on her back, so what we think happened is the little boy has been thrown into the undergrowth, she has been controlled by the prod marks of the knife, she's been turned around and prodded back towards the tree, and it's at that point that the first blow was struck.'

I looked again at the photographs. Rachel had a massive injury that looked like two oval, separate wounds on either side of the throat. 'We think he struck her so hard that the knife has actually gone through the larynx,' JB said. 'But in order for him to remove the knife, he's had to wrench it up and down. There were then another 47 knife wounds inflicted.'

'Any defence wounds?'

'Strangely enough, only one, on her left hand, which penetrated the knuckle of her little finger – though whether it was a defence wound or whether it was something that happened in the frenzy of the attack, we're not sure. Then of course there's the indecent assault aspect,' he added. 'She was interfered with anally.'

The album of photographs was open at one particular picture taken in the mortuary which clearly indicated the sexual nature of the attack. The lab sergeant was holding apart the buttocks to show that her anus was about 1.5cm dilated.

'What did Doc Shepherd make of this?' I asked.

JB said that whatever the sex act was that the killer had inflicted on Rachel, it was carried out literally at the point of death or just after. Doc Shepherd was of the opinion that Rachel had either been subjected to anal rape or had been violated with the handle of a knife or some similar implement. 'We're keeping quiet about that specific aspect of the murder, by the way,' he added, 'as well as one or two other things.'

It is normal police practice to keep certain details of the crime confidential to enable the investigators to assess the veracity of informants and suspects in the event of a confession. If the informant or the suspect is able to give details of how the offence was committed and those details include information that we know to be confidential, then we know we're on the right track. Conversely, if the information or confession does not include those details we have a pretty good idea that we're dealing with a time-waster. It's surprisingly common for people to confess falsely or give deliberately misleading information concerning crimes, especially high profile ones. In this particular case, there were only three ways that anybody could ever know about the injury to Rachel's anus: if we told them, if they had been present at the post mortem, or if they were the killer.

'What else are we keeping quiet about?'

'A bit of a strange one – this piece of paper on Rachel's head.'

JB indicated a photograph in the album which showed Rachel lying at the foot of a silver birch tree. I could quite clearly see a folded piece of paper which appeared to have been deliberately placed on her head.

'What was on it?'

'Notification of her new Halifax cashcard PIN number.'

'It couldn't have just blown there?'

'Not when you consider how it was folded – it would have been too heavy.'

'As you say, very strange. Why would the killer want to put it on her head? It's not possible that one of the first people at the scene could have picked it up and then dropped it?'

'Anything's possible, Keith, but look how precariously it's balanced. What are the chances of it dropping on Rachel's head and staying there?'

'I take your point. What else?'

JB began leafing through the photographs. 'There's Alex's T shirt.'

He stopped at a shot taken looking away from the body and along the path leading towards the direction of the A3, around the left-hand side of the mound. It was difficult to judge the distance from the picture, but about 10 yards further on from the tree I could see the outline of a blue T-shirt trodden into the mud.

'Did the killer undress the child?'

JB shook his head. 'No, we have a sighting of Rachel carrying the T-shirt.'

He pointed to a map on the wall beside him. 'That's where she was last seen alive; she was heading in this direction.'

I looked closely at the map. 'The X marks the spot where she was found?'

'Yes.'

'So she was coming from this direction?'

Bassett nodded.

'So if I've got this right,' I said, my finger moving across the map, 'she came across here, was found here, and the T-shirt was found here?'

'Correct.'

'So she must have been accosted near where the T-shirt was found, and taken back along the path to the tree?'

'We think so. It's only conjecture but we think whoever killed Rachel may have seen her from the top of the mound as she crossed the open space here,' he pointed. 'We think he must have seen her enter the wooded area and waited for her to come along the path.'

'Why do you think that? Has the boy said something?'

What would the poor child remember after such a terrible ordeal? I wondered. Might something he can tell us be the key to finding his mother's murderer?

JB said that within hours of being found, Alex was in the care of experts whose job was to minimise the emotional damage he must have suffered, and, it was hoped, gently elicit from him any piece of information which might assist us in identifying the killer.

'When Mr Murray found him, he was clinging to his mother's body, saying, "Get up, Mummy, get my Mummy." They were the last words Alex spoke for more than 24 hours.'

JB looked down at the desktop for a moment, as if to compose himself. 'We can only imagine the nightmare the little lad's suffered,' he said. 'It was an awful scene, Keith. Rachel lying there and the little boy, caked in his mother's blood, sitting shocked in the back of a police van.'

Alex had been so traumatised that he formed an instant bond with the WPC who cuddled him while they waited for an ambulance. He had clung on to her tightly, just as he had held on to his mummy earlier, refusing to let go.

The WPC had gone with him to the hospital, her uniform soiled by the blood and mud covering his little body. JB said, 'Wickerson saw him later and said the little boy was totally silent, just staring into space. He said it was his worst experience in 26 years in the Job.'

'Is the boy still in shock?'

'He's said very little, but that's hardly surprising considering his age and the trauma he must be suffering.'

Perhaps in time, JB said, Alex may be able to help. But in truth the prospect of him being able to give anything of evidential value was remote. 'And anyway, we owe it to him and his family to place his immediate needs before those of the inquiry.'

I nodded. For the little child, therapy had to take precedence over investigation.

'So what's my role, Guv? Mr Chapman said something about the Ree-Gee supplying staff?'

'We've got six DCs to deal with suspect enquiries and act as an arrest team. You're in charge of them.'

'Are they bringing their own vehicles with them?'

I wanted to know, because the RCS had covert cars equipped with all sorts of radio equipment which would be extremely useful for surveillance on potential suspects. Their equipment, like the Flying Squad's, was far more sophisticated than anything readily available on Area.

JB shook his head. 'I'm afraid not – but I've agreed to pay them mileage for using their private vehicles.'

'Do I have an overtime budget for these officers?'

'The Regional Crime Squad have kindly agreed to fund them up to 32 hours each a month, and anything over that will come out of our budget. Your specific terms of reference are quite simply to TIE (trace, investigate, and eliminate) all suspects that are actioned to you – and that will involve any surveillance and searches which you deem necessary.'

'Will we be expected to research these suspects ourselves?'

'Hopefully, no. I've got a team of four researchers who will do most of the preliminary checks before you get the actions.'

'Well, if there's nothing else, perhaps it might be an idea if I started reading through the statements to try and get a feel for the job.'

'There's the office manager's copy downstairs. Ask Paul Penrose, I'm sure he'll get you anything you need. Oh, and Keith – there's a scene-of-crime video which you might find useful. It gives you more of a feel for the scene than these photographs. Paul will show you.'

'Only other thing I need to know – when's the next office meeting?'

'Four o'clock,' JB said, and with that he returned to his pile of statements.

The office meeting is an important part of any murder inquiry; it's the time for everybody to sit down and disseminate information, and it's not unusual for such a meeting to last three hours. It's also not unusual to have an office meeting in the morning to discuss any developments which might have occurred overnight, since the previous meeting, and also an office meeting last thing at night to see what developments and information has been gleaned during the intervening eight or ten hours.

As I started to leave, JB suddenly looked up again. 'Keith,' he said quietly, 'we've got to catch this man. Whoever killed Rachel Nickell is a very sick man. We've got to get to him before he has the chance to do this again ...'

Chapter 2

The moving images were even more powerful than the stills. I noticed the minutest details, like how the flies had already begun to infest Rachel's wounds, their frantic activity in stark contrast to her stillness. And the location – by walking through the scene the cameraman had managed to give a sense of distance and perspective that was missing from the photographs. I was shocked that the place where Rachel was found was no more than 20–30ft from open parkland and safety. It seemed incredible that such horrendous damage to a person could have been inflicted in such a relatively exposed area of the common, without anything being seen or heard. I could see why JB had said that any one of a dozen individual wounds would have killed her. These were savage injuries, suggesting violence for violence's sake, the work of a very sick, damaged or sadistic mind.

The team, all of them case-hardened officers, had sat in stunned silence as they took in the full horror of the events of 15 July, and after the video had finished it took a long time for conversation and activity to resume.

For the next few hours, we busied ourselves reading through the bundle of 100 or so statements which had so far been gathered by officers on and around the common and 'put on to the box' (filed on computer).

It was clear, unfortunately, that no one had seen the killer attacking Rachel – apart from Alex. Nor had any suspects been observed running from the scene. The best early leads, as JB had said, appeared to be the sighting of a short-haired man crouching to wash his hands in a ditch close to the murder scene, and a man with a ponytail seen leaving the common in a hurry shortly after the body was discovered, heading towards a council estate at Norstead Place. As yet, however, neither had produced a positive line of enquiry.

I had already had a quick skim through the material, and was intending to take the papers home with me later for a more detailed study. However, I was really still none the wiser after my second reading. I had built up a rough picture of the sequence of events and the character and lifestyle of the victim, but was finding it difficult to pinpoint the 500 people who had been on the common – both geographically and temporally, and also in relation both to each other and the offence. Regular users of the common would obviously be familiar with the different landmarks I was hearing about and the general lie of the land, but to us uninitiated investigators it was more or less impossible to make sense of what they were saying.

It was also beginning to dawn on me that a lot of the times given by the various potential witnesses were approximations. The common was used by people for recreational purposes and as such they would hardly have been clock-watching as they meandered along the paths. The only saving grace was the fact that the majority of them at least knew what time they had arrived and what time they'd left.

When Mick Wickerson returned from court, he and Bill Lyle took us on a conducted tour of the common. I'd known Bill since about 1987 when he was on the Regional Crime Squad at East Dulwich. When we were short of firearms officers at Tower Bridge we'd often borrow authorised shots from the Ree-Gee to assist with our armed operations. Invariably, Bill would be one of the officers deputed to help. He was now in his mid-thirties, 6ft tall and quite heavily set, but he carried his weight well. He had left the Job for a couple of years to try his luck in the outside world and then rejoined – not because he was unsuccessful but because he missed the people. In fact, Bill was so successful in the field of private security that he had a large house, convertible Mercedes sports car and big-dollar lifestyle to prove it. It said something about his dedication to the Job that he left the private sector to rejoin with a considerable drop in salary.

Bill was the exhibits officer on this case, one of the most important roles in any major investigation. To him would fall the job of documenting every piece of property or evidence that was recovered or seized, and ensuring that a full and accurate record of the movements of those exhibits was kept. If an exhibit was sent for forensic examination, for example, he would have to record to whom the exhibit was handed and where it is was being taken. For legal reasons, the chain of continuity of all exhibits must be capable of being proved, and the prosecution have to be able to show that the 'bloody knife' taken from the body was the same knife on which the defendant's fingerprints were found. I had attended trials where we had had to call dozens of witnesses to prove that chain of continuity. A meticulous attention to detail is required, for on the ability and actions of the exhibits officer can depend the success or failure of an entire prosecution.

It was only a ten-minute drive through Wimbledon village from the police station to the common. Mick explained that its 1,100 acres were bordered by five main roads: Parkside and Wimbledon Parkside to the east, Kingston Road and Roehampton Vale (the A3) to the north, Robin Hood Way to the west and a maze of minor roads to the south.

The best access to the scene was via Windmill Road, which leads from Parkside to the Windmill car park, a distance of about 500 yards. As we drove along it, directly ahead of us were the windmill with its giant white sails made famous by Baden Powell, the cafe, and the Royal Wimbledon Golf Club. Turning right at a small roundabout, we approached the large, loose shale car park. There was a police sign appealing for witnesses. The adjustable date had been set at 15 July.

As Mick pulled in on the right-hand side and switched off the engine, he said quietly, 'This is the exact spot where Rachel parked on that morning.' He seemed lost in thought, and it took a moment or two before he snapped out of it.

He indicated that directly in front of us was a large open area leading to Queensmere Lake; off to the north-east corner of the car park was a large wooded area, and it was within these woods, he said, that Rachel had died.

A mobile incident room fitted with hot-line phones was located in the car park, co-ordinating the actions of scores of officers trying to trace witnesses, tracker dogs searching the woods and scrubland, even divers dredging the ponds. A police helicopter rattled overhead. Nearby, and providing an almost surreal backdrop to all the police activity, was a brightly striped marquee, erected by Tesco to entertain the 160 players who had been taking part in a charity golf contest the morning of the murder.

'We asked everyone to abandon the game and assemble in the clubhouse to assist in identifying the victim's car,' Mick said. 'We then got everybody to go and stand by their own vehicle.'

Each car had been claimed, until there was just a silver Volvo left unattended. A registration check matched the name and address on documents found on Rachel's body.

Wickerson said, 'We also had a witness come forward later that evening – an acquaintance of Rachel's called Eric Roberts [this is not his real name]. Their boys are at the same nursery school. He rang the incident room at about 6.00pm and said he'd recognised Rachel's car from the news footage of it being towed away. We hadn't released her details at that stage because we hadn't informed her parents. He came in for a chat but he's not in the frame.'

Mick explained that the tour of the common would have to be limited to the tree and various different landmarks. The TSG (Territorial Support Group) were still in the process of searching a route from the scene which ran alongside the drainage ditch where the man had been seen rinsing his hands and ended abruptly 200 yards away at the walls of the Putney Vale cemetery located on the north-western edge of the common. On the day of the murder, a police dog had picked up a scent and followed it along this path. It would not have been difficult for a fit man to have climbed the railings at the edge of the cemetery and made his escape through the graveyard, and indeed two witnesses in the cemetery reported hearing the sound of somebody crashing through the undergrowth on the common side of the cemetery fence.

Mick had taken the view that an area of 30 yards each side of the route should be searched as this was about the distance a knife could have been thrown by the escaping killer. A team was scanning with metal detectors in case a knife had been thrown away or hidden. They were finding old knives and other metal bits and pieces, but nothing that matched the imprint that had been left on Rachel's body.

'Doc Shepherd said that all of the stab wounds are consistent with infliction by a single weapon,' Mick said. 'However, he can't say for sure the handedness of the assailant, nor his height.'

It appeared that the injuries were consistent with infliction by a knife or knives with a single cutting edge, approximately one-and-a-half centimetres in width at the hilt and nine centimetres in length. From marks left on Rachel's body, it was also possible to say that the hilt of the weapon had a squared lower margin about half a centimetre wide adjacent to the cutting edge, and extended about half a centimetre beneath the bottom margin of the blade.

We followed Mick from the north-east corner of the car park down a small dirt path which led to a fork by the top of the drainage ditch. At this junction stood an oak tree, at the foot of which were a large number of bouquets of flowers. I was puzzled by this, because the area had been sealed when Rachel and Alex were found so it would not be generally known exactly where it happened.

Mick obviously noticed my expression. 'For some reason, people have assumed that this is where Rachel was murdered,' he said. 'I don't know why, and we haven't informed them otherwise.'

As I examined the flowers, I realised from the messages on the cards that these expressions of sympathy were almost entirely from people who hadn't even known Rachel Nickell, yet had been touched by her death. One note read, 'Hope they find the animal that did this to you and your son. God bless you and your child.' One offering in particular, however, caught my eye – not for its magnificence, for it was only a small posy of hand-picked wild flowers lying at the foot of the oak. In fact, they looked rather pathetic when compared to the grander tributes, but the obvious spontaneity of the emotion behind the gesture made them stand out. The impact that the offence had had on the local community was brought home to me and I sensed that my own detachedness was fading fast.

Mick led us past the oak tree and along the right-hand path for about 60 or 70 yards. The silver birch came into view and we approached it in silence. The scene-of-crime photographs of Rachel's mutilated body still filled my mind.

As the team and I stood in front of the tree, Mick began his explanation of what he had found on the day of the murder. Wickerson was an extremely experienced investigator and was renowned for his laid-back approach, and also his ability to remain light-hearted even when faced with the most appalling crimes. It wasn't that he was callous, it was just his way of dealing with things and maintaining his sanity. However, as he talked us through the scene and the pathologist's findings, there was no trace of his characteristic levity. His grasp of the facts was as impressive as ever, but he was exceptionally business-like and there was a grim determination about his manner which I'd never seen before.

'Rachel, as you'll remember from the video, was found here,' he said, indicating a point 4–5ft from the base of the tree. She'd been discovered, he went on, by retired architect Michael Murray as he walked his white Samoyed dog. It had been a warm and sunny day, and Mr Murray was at first embarrassed by what he saw, thinking he'd stumbled on someone sunbathing privately a few yards off the main path. However, as he neared the motionless figure, he saw that the half-naked woman had been horribly injured. As he got even closer, he realised that she was dead. A tearful, distraught little boy, dressed only in navy-blue tracksuit bottoms and trainers, was gripping tightly to her arm, and a black mongrel dog was whimpering nearby. So tight, in fact, was Alex's grip on his mother's arm that Mr Murray had had to prise the boy's fingers free before he would let go. Mr Murray then lifted the blood-soaked toddler into his arms, handed him to two women, Emma Brooks and Penny Horne, who had also been walking nearby, and ran to the park rangers' office, some 300 yards away.

The two women had attracted the attention of a jogger, Sean Beckett, and he ran and found a mounted park ranger, Steven Francis, who summoned assistance on his radio. At about the same time, John and Janet Marshall also came across Rachel's body. Mrs Marshall instinctively looked at her watch, which said 10.45am. The first call received by the police was timed at 10.44am. Three PCs responded and arrived at the scene at 10.56am. They met with Francis and the scene was preserved for the benefit of the investigating officers.

'We found three significant areas of blood-staining, the largest area being over there,' Wickerson continued, pointing to a spot about 10ft from where Rachel's body had been discovered. The second, and smallest, area of blood was adjacent to the tree close to the body, and the third was beneath the body itself.

The degree of blood-staining in any area will depend on the nature of the injuries that are bleeding, the victim's heart-rate and blood pressure at that time, and the length of time that they are lying at that site. The distribution of blood-staining to Rachel's jeans had been almost exclusively confined to the upper portion of the front of the jeans, with some distribution around the buttock and right upper thigh at the back, and significant spotting and blood-staining to the back of the lower legs of the jeans. There was also some mud-staining of the lower front areas of the jeans.

'All of which leads Doc Shepherd to believe that the only injuries that would have bled to any significant degree externally at the time of infliction were the injuries to the neck,' Mick said. 'Most of the other injuries would have bled internally for the most part, only producing minimal seepage of blood through the external skin wounds until the body was in a lying position. Consideration of the blood-staining at the scene, the pattern of the blood-staining of the clothing, and the injuries themselves, led him to his conclusions.'

Mick repeated what JB had already told me. The killer had pounced, it was thought, after watching Rachel's progress across the common from the top of the mound made years before from the spoil of the A3 London to Guildford road. From his vantage point, he would have been able to see Rachel and Alex as they wandered slowly across a piece of open land and then wound their way down into the copse. He would also have been able to eyeball the area to check that no one else was in the vicinity to be able to witness, or prevent, the attack he was about to carry out. Seeing that the coast was clear, he'd probably come down a little-used path at the side of the mound, and had confronted her with a knife.

One of the features of sexual murders is the need to control the victim. This may be achieved by direct threats to the victim, threats to a third party or the infliction of immobilising wounds.

It was believed that the two prods to Rachel's chest drew blood, and she had been guided at knife-point away from the footpath and into the protective shelter of the copse. The thickness of the foliage where we were standing made this part of the woods quite dark, contrasting with the brilliant sunlit area of the open space just 20 or so feet away. I wandered briefly out into the open and looked back towards the silver birch. It was impossible to see the tree.

The pathologist believed that the first phase of the actual assault occurred at or near the large area of blood-staining which lay away from the body and the tree. The relative absence of blood-staining of the lower front portions of the jeans combined with the mud-staining of these areas was strongly indicative that Rachel was kneeling at the time of infliction of injuries that had bled significantly.

Mick said, 'The neck injuries were the only injuries associated with this type of external haemorrhage. The stab wounds to the heart and left lung resulted in internal haemorrhage and must have been inflicted during life. The injuries to the right lung and liver were not associated with haemorrhage and must have been inflicted after death.'

Wickerson went to the position where the large area of blood had been found. 'Doc Shepherd thinks that this is where the assault proper began, probably with the injuries to the neck; Rachel was probably in a kneeling position at this stage. She would have fallen to the ground and, because of the nature of the injuries to the muscles of the neck and to the cartilages of the larynx, wouldn't have been able to cry out, and would very quickly have lost the ability to fend off further blows.'

As I stood quietly absorbing the information, deeply impressed at the pathologist's detailed interpretation of the physical evidence, I suddenly realised why it was that no one on the common that morning had heard any screams from the copse where the young mother met such a violent end.

Mick went on to say that, in Doc Shepherd's opinion, the most likely position of the assailant was behind Rachel with the knife in his right hand. He also thought that at this point Rachel's jeans and pants were still in place, though he couldn't exclude the possibility that some of the stabbing injuries to the trunk had occurred at this point.

He thought that Rachel then moved, or was moved, to a point adjacent to the tree where the smaller area of blood-staining had been noted. We followed Wickerson to the place. 'She would have been lying on her back at this stage and was still fully clothed.'

'How can we be certain of that?' I asked.

'If you remember the video, Keith, you will recall that there was quite a large amount of leaf mould on the back of the T-shirt and Rachel's back. Its presence is consistent with her lying on her back at this point and the position of the area of blood-staining suggests that her head was adjacent to the tree at this time. Because of the clear delineation of stained and unstained portions of the T-shirt, the doc thinks that at least some of these injuries must have occurred before the removal of the lower clothing.

'We believe that it was at this point that Rachel's jeans and pants were pulled down and inverted over her shoes; the leaf mould found on her buttocks indicates she must have been lying on her back when this occurred. Either during, or after the partial removal of the clothing, Rachel's body was turned and pulled away from the tree to the position in which she was finally discovered.'

Mick's voice then dropped, the sadness redolent in every syllable: 'The sexual assault then took place. The doc thinks that this would have been right at, or just after, the point of death ...'

He paused for a second as if composing himself, then said, 'At least she wouldn't have known anything about that part of her ordeal.'

I was already aware of the assault because of my chat with JB, but the others hadn't yet been told this piece of information. DC Martin Long was the one to ask the obvious question: 'What exactly was the nature of the sexual attack?'

The question was obvious because the video had not contained the same specific detail as the stills taken in the mortuary, and these were not in general circulation amongst the squad. Therefore the nature of the sexual aspect of the attack was not readily apparent and I had not explained it to my team at this stage.

'We'll go into that later,' I said.

'No problem, Guv.' This ready acceptance by Martin was a strong indication that I had been given an experienced and shrewd team. Lesser detectives might well not have realised the reason for my reticence to answer and pressed the point.

The tour of the common continued for another half-hour or so as we tried to get to grips with the topography and apply our new knowledge to the information we had gleaned from reading the statements. This was easier said than done. As with any large open area, it is always difficult to be precise as to locations of sightings and events which have taken place. Wimbledon Common was no exception. Admittedly, there were various landmarks which could assist, but you would have had to be very familiar with the geography of the place in order to decipher what the witnesses were talking about.

The common was an investigator's nightmare. Its entire 1,100 acres had to be considered as the crime scene, because no one was sure of the escape route used or whether or not the murder weapon had been secreted in the grounds. The sheer size presented the suspect with endless opportunities to hide or dispose of evidence in the knowledge that it wouldn't be easily found. The lush foliage in the wooded areas only served to make things more difficult. I guessed it would take numerous visits to the scene to orientate ourselves.

Descriptions of a sighting by a witness which included a reference to the 'big silver birch' or the 'large oak', or for that matter, such and such a 'memorial bench', meant nothing to us at this stage. I discovered that just by walking the common it was not easy to put things into perspective; the dense undergrowth and heavy leaf cover made it difficult to place landmarks accurately in relation to each other. Apart from the main footpaths, there was a maze of smaller tracks criss-crossing the whole area.

Over the next few days, it would not be unusual for three or four of us to be seen wandering around the common with statements in one hand, maps in the other, trying to make sense of what a particular witness was saying.

[illegible] the [illegible] used [illegible] weapon had been secured [illegible] [illegible] [illegible] [illegible] [illegible] [illegible] [illegible] [illegible] [illegible]

[illegible]

Chapter 3

The first 72 hours of a murder investigation are usually the most important, but when the killer is a stranger to the victim, or his planning has been particularly complex or cunning, the search is often fated to be more difficult and drawn out. In Job parlance, it becomes a 'sticker'.

Five days had now passed since Rachel's murder, and the officers on the inquiry might have been forgiven for letting up a little as they began to pace themselves for a long haul. Yet amongst the 50 or so men and women who assembled in the main CID room for the 4.00pm office meeting, there was an almost palpable sense of purpose.

It is essential in the early stages of an investigation to hold full squad meetings at the start and finish of each day. Everybody, not just the SIO (Senior Investigating Officer) and DIO (Deputy Investigating Officer), has to be kept up to speed with the latest developments, otherwise they might pick up a seemingly worthless piece of information and ignore it, when with the benefit of the full picture that information might have assumed great importance.

Mick Wickerson was not looking at all happy as he entered the room, and he continued to sit broodingly on the edge of a desk as JB started his update. Andrew and Monica Nickell had been on a three-week touring holiday in the USA and Canada, and JB had been eager to get to them before the press did. However, neither Andre, nor Rachel's brother Mark, knew precisely where they were staying. It had taken all this time to trace the couple to Ontario, where they had been staying with relations. JB said that Mr and Mrs Nickell had returned from a day's sightseeing over the border in the USA to find a note pinned to the door asking them to go to the local police station in connection with a 'serious family matter'. There they were told that there had been a death in the family, and that they should wait and talk to their son for a fuller explanation. However, the Nickells insisted on being told there and then what had happened. Three thousand miles from where it had happened, they learned that their daughter was dead, but the Canadian police were able to give them only the sketchiest of details.

Meanwhile, Mark Nickell had caught a flight from Gatwick and he arrived in Canada soon afterwards, accompanied by two detectives from Wimbledon. He could obviously have informed his parents on his own, but JB felt that the officers should also to be there to answer, as well as they could, the many questions that any grieving parent would be asking in the circumstances. The group, we were told, were booked on the first available flight back to London, and would be returning the following morning.

'Ladies and gentlemen,' JB said with a change of tone, 'I would like to thank you all for the very hard work you have put in over the last five days.' He smiled in that familiar, avuncular fashion, then went on, 'However, before Mr Wickerson gets down to the nitty-gritty, I want to say that I know how much we all want to solve this dreadful murder, but the question of overtime has also to be considered. I can tell you that the expenditure for the last week came to ...' he consulted his notes, '... £22,234. Now there is no suggestion at this stage that the funding will dry up, but I would ask you to be sensible. If you have an Action that can only be done in the evenings perhaps you should consider booking on duty an hour or two later in the morning. There will be red ink time over next weekend but it will be split, half of you working the Saturday and the other half Sunday.'

'Red ink time' is the time-and-a-half rate that officers are paid for working their rest days. 'Black ink time' is the time-and-a-third rate paid for over eight hours worked on a scheduled working day.

'So much for the financial admin. I'll now let Mr Wickerson bring you up to date on the other events of the day.'

Mick looked up as his name was mentioned. He was still unhappy about something, and we were about to find out what it was.

'I'm afraid the main news is from the laboratory,' he said gloomily, 'and it doesn't look good. As you all know, Doc Shepherd thought we had found traces of semen when he took swabs at the scene. Unfortunately, the lab have been unable to find any trace of a DNA-able substance on that particular swab.' He looked round the room and his gaze settled on the exhibits officer. 'Have I got that right, Bill?'

'Yes, Guv. The biologist, Ray Chapman, said that there was definitely some biological or cellular material present but they can't DNA it.'

No wonder Mick was downcast. DNA analysis or 'genetic fingerprinting' had been used to solve hundreds of murders and rapes since it had been pioneered by Professor Alec Jeffreys of Leicester University ten years earlier. Every human cell contains the blueprint of the entire human body carried as coded information in the form of DNA (deoxyribonucleic acid) arranged into groups called genes. Since genes govern heredity, Jeffreys found that DNA material isolated from a cell and presented as an image will be as unique to an individual as a fingerprint. The discovery that no two people, except for identical twins, have the same DNA cell pattern was one of the most important developments in crimefighting techniques this century, and had revolutionised the forensic detection of killers and sex attackers worldwide. A single hair root could give a complete genetic profile, and the odds against a DNA 'fingerprint' being wrong were more than 30 million to one. The technology had enormous possibilities, and in 1986 a murder suspect in the Midlands became the first alleged killer to be set free as a result of DNA testing.

Wickerson continued, 'So whatever the material is, it would appear not to be semen. We'll have to ask the doc to do another post mortem to go back for another look. Sorry, Bill, but can you get on to the mortuary and arrange another PM?'

He had good reason to apologise. Post mortems at the best of times are unpleasant, but second or subsequent PMs tend to be even more harrowing because the processes of decomposition are even further advanced.

I felt dismayed, and so did everyone else in that room. The fingertip search at the murder scene had failed to yield any sign of a murder weapon or any other significant evidence. Now it seemed that the SOCOs (Scene of Crime Officers) had also found nothing that the lab could work with – no blood, no saliva, skin tissue, hair samples or semen; in other words, nothing which could be from the killer, either on Rachel's body or Alex's, or at the scene of the crime. And without such vital samples, there would be no chance of producing a DNA genetic fingerprint to help to trap the killer. My mind was ticking over. It was extremely unusual for there to be neither forensic evidence nor fingerprints. Did it mean that the killer was just lucky, I wondered, or was he clever or cunning enough to have deliberately ensured that he left no clues behind?

The next part of the meeting was largely unexceptional and consisted of the usual round robin from the various teams, giving details of their progress in the preceding 24 hours. The outside inquiry team had been split between house-to-house enquiries and common enquiries, the latter being further sub-divided into teams responsible for the estimated 500 rangers, golfers, dog-walkers and joggers present at the time of the murder. All these people had to be traced and spoken to.

A good office meeting should be held on democratic lines. That is to say, regardless of rank or experience, every officer should be encouraged to express his or her views and ideas, like a sort of think-tank or brains trust. Sometimes, the suggestions can be a little outlandish, but a good SIO, if he's wise, won't dismiss these out of hand.

The inside teams – research and office management – also had their say as to how they were progressing with the back record conversion and anything else which they considered to be important, and it was now that one of the indexers, WPC Janet Smith, voiced an opinion held by herself and some of her colleagues.

Jan was one of the few office staff I already knew. We had been at training school together back in 1975 and she had helped me subsequently as an indexer on a supergrass operation. She was a sensible and straight-talking lady and not prone to flights of fancy, which made the bombshell she was about to drop even more powerful.

'If we haven't got semen,' she said, 'and I know we don't know that for certain … but if we haven't – what is there to say that the killer wasn't a woman?'

You could have heard a pin drop.

Then there was a small ripple of uneasy laughter, but this soon died away as the words sank in. In reality, this wasn't such a silly question. I had certainly assumed that the killer was a man, but in the absence of any semen there was nothing to exclude the possibility of the offence having been committed by a woman. After all, at this stage little Alex hadn't said anything and he was, to our knowledge, the only eye-witness.

Mick considered the question. 'What makes you think that?'

'It's just that – well, the indexers have been talking about the injuries and it seems to us that there is something very female about that number of stab wounds. You know, hell hath no fury …'

'So what are you suggesting? Rachel had a secret lover, and his wife or girlfriend found out and murdered her?'

'That could be one explanation, sir. Another could be that the killer was a lesbian.'

The implications of this suggestion took a while to sink in. It raised the question of Rachel's sexuality, or the prospect of a lesbian stranger attack.

'I suppose it's possible,' Wickerson conceded, 'and we will

certainly bear it in mind. But I think we will keep this one under our hats for the time being.'

As he looked around the office to reinforce the point, his expression gave the clear signal that this was not to be the subject of speculation or conversation outside these four walls. If the press got a hint of it, they'd have a field day.

By now it was 7.30pm and the meeting had run its course. The squad began to drift away to go about their evening calls, although as this was my team's first day we hadn't as yet been issued with any Actions – these were in the process of being allocated to me and I would delegate them to the team the next day. Before an officer goes out to do anything, he has to have an 'Action', a form which gives him instructions. For example: 'Take a statement from Fred Smith re his movements on such and such a day,' or 'TIE (trace, interview and eliminate) Fred Smith.' Actions can be raised from messages received by phone, or from information received by officers from informants or members of the public. I'd decided I would work out my own issuing system so that all paperwork came back through me before being returned to the main incident room. This way I could keep track of what was being done and maintain quality control of our part of the operation.

I made a bee-line for Mick Wickerson's office. WPC Smith's suggestion had brought home to me the fact that, after five days of exhaustive investigation, the squad was unable to state with any degree of certainty even the gender of the killer, let alone what he or she might look like, and I was eager to discuss how we could move things along.

Chapter 4

I followed Mick and JB into Wickerson's office and sat myself down. 'That was quite lively,' I said. 'Especially Jan Smith's theory.'

Wickerson said, 'It's an interesting idea but I think we should keep it on the back-burner, don't you? Can you imagine what the press would make of it if they got wind that we'd even discussed the possibility? Anyway, we've still got the second post mortem. With any luck we'll find something we can DNA and that'll be the end of the homicidal lesbian theory.'

I said, 'I must admit I'm a bit confused about this disappearing sperm.'

'All I know is that Dick Shepherd swabbed Rachel's body in situ last Wednesday and the ultraviolet seemed to show something on the back of her thigh. I thought, great, we've got the bastard. So God knows what's happened.'

JB said, 'Let's just keep our fingers crossed, shall we? As for the other business, an open mind will have to be kept.'

'Can you fill me in on this Eric Roberts?' I said. 'What's he all about?'

'He's a bit of a puzzle,' Mick said. 'As I told you, he rang the incident room at about 6.00pm on the day of the murder. He reckoned he'd recognised Rachel's car from the news footage of it being towed away. We hadn't released her details at that stage because we hadn't informed her parents.'

It is standard procedure not to release a victim's details until the next-of-kin have been informed. We would rather the relatives heard from us first than have them face a barrage of reporters.

Wickerson went on, 'So Roberts reckons he knows the car, and who the victim is, and he offers to come down and identify the body.'

'And did he? What did we do?'

'We asked him to pop along for a chat. Nothing official, just a voluntary visit to help with our enquiries. He turned up and a couple of the blokes interviewed him, all very low-key. He provided an alibi for the relevant time.'

'Which was?'

'Not the best – he claims he was at home in bed, and his common-law wife verifies his story. Apparently, they take it in turns to have a lie in, and Wednesday was his turn. His wife claims she went out just after 10.00am and he was still in bed when she returned about 45 minutes later. I know what you're going to ask, but if she's telling the truth he wouldn't have had enough time to get from his home to Wimbledon and back again. We've done local enquiries but can't find anyone who can say whether or not his car was outside the address; certainly there aren't any sightings of either him or his motor at this end.'

'Tell me about his connection with Rachel.'

'According to him, they were just friends. They met when he used to take his son Dave to the sandpit on Tooting Common. Dave is about the same age as Alex. It's a bit strange; Roberts doesn't strike me as the sort who would have had much in common with someone like Rachel. But he says that they regularly took the kids to Wimbledon Common for walks.'

I had to ask the obvious question: 'Was there anything going on between them?'

'I can't see that as being a serious possibility. Rachel was absolutely gorgeous and, with the best will in the world, Roberts couldn't be described as being an attractive man, either physically or personality-wise. He's pleasant enough, though. It appears that both Andre and this Margaret knew about the walks on the common but neither seemed to be concerned about it.'

'Really? I couldn't see my other half being exactly philosophical if I were to go walking in the woods with an attractive girl.'

'Roberts was adamant that their relationship was purely platonic. He was quite candid about it. He admitted that he was attracted to Rachel but he knew that she wouldn't have been interested in him in that way, and he didn't want to make a fool of himself and risk losing her friendship.'

'Doesn't sound kosher to me,' I said.

'We're still digging, so he's not entirely out of the frame yet. We've had a look at his clothing and taken his trainers for the lab to have a look at.'

'So it really is looking more and more like a sticker,' I said.

'The joke of it is, it didn't even happen on our ground.'

'So why are we dealing with it?'

'Because we didn't bloody realise until after we were up and running and the Asda suspect was already in the nick.'

'We've started so we'll finish?'

'When 5 Area found out they didn't seem too worried.'

'I bet they didn't! It's a good wheeze, isn't it? Getting 4 Area to investigate 5 Area's crimes and at our expense.'

'Not entirely. 5 Area have given us some staff and five grand from their budget.'

JB, who had been sitting quietly, not seeming to be taking too much notice of my conversation with Mick, suddenly joined in. 'Despite my comments back there about overtime, it's not the money that's my primary concern, Keith – it's obviously a consideration, but if the outside team keep generating work from their existing Actions and the public keep coming forward with information, it's all got to go on the system. The truth is, as fast as we clear one lot, another lot is there waiting to take its place. We've not even made a dent in the back record conversion, and that's with the office staff working 16-plus hours a day.'

'So what's the answer, Guv?'

'We've got to have more computer operators – the only trouble is, we haven't got any spare capacity on this Area, or 5 Area. I've asked DACTO (Deputy Assistant Commissioner Territorial Operations) for a trawl to be made of the rest of the Met for extra operators.'

'What are our chances?'

'Put it this way – if we don't get them, God alone knows what we're going to do. Despite the fact that I seconded indexers and terminals from other major inquiries over the weekend and all our staff worked flat out, I've still got a massive backlog – add that to what came in today and I calculate that even with twice the indexing staff working in two 12-hour shifts, we might be lucky to clear the backlog in a week. Once the backlog's dealt with, we should be able to cope even if the work keeps coming in at the same rate.'

I could sympathise with JB's dilemma. In any investigation, however large or small, a methodical approach is essential. You have to document and cross-reference everything that comes into the incident room to minimise the chances of missing something important. There has to be a structured approach; you can't have officers going off and acting on their own initiative; that road leads to chaos.

Once a statement has been taken it is entered on the box and is read by the office manager and the receiver, then by the senior and deputy investigating officers. From that statement other Actions might be raised. The statement and new Action instructions are then handed to the indexers who type it on to the system. The indexers will also create files on the person's name (formally termed the 'nominal index'), their address, phone number and, if appropriate, their vehicle. All of these files are numbered and cross-referenced with each other as well as the statement. Any new Actions raised from the statement will also be cross-referenced with the original Action and each other.

Each individual Action is dealt with on its own merits and the amount of time and resources spent on each one depends on the individual circumstances. Some are dealt with exhaustively, others can be disposed of following a single visit to the potential suspect. The basic rule of thumb is to look at the information, assess the source and then research the suspect. Has he got any form? What is the connection between the informant and the suspect? Is there any history of aggravation between them? All normal police procedure. If there is any doubt as to whether a line of enquiry should be actioned, the SIO or DIO have the final say. Every Action is consecutively numbered in its appropriate category and cross-referenced. Then the whole process begins again.

It may seem a complicated business but the HOLMES system is remarkably successful, especially on protracted and complicated inquiries. HOLMES is basically a computerised retrieval system. It uses the same categories as a card carousel system but is obviously more efficient. Both systems use the following basic categories: Nominal, Address, Telephone, Vehicles, Actions and Other Documents and, dependent on the type of inquiry, other special categories may be created.

There are certain advantages to the computer system, such as a search facility known as SB, which is a word search. This comes into its own on large and complex inquiries when information is processed and its importance is not realised at the time, but as the investigation progresses it may be necessary to retrace certain specific pieces of information. For example, information about a vehicle such as the make, model, registration, colour and the fact that there was damage to the offside passenger door might have been entered on the box. Two or three months later, a vital witness might come forward with information about a suspect who drove a dark-coloured saloon car which had damage to the offside passenger door. In the absence of a car number, make or model, an SB search on the words 'damage' or 'offside passenger door' may throw up the vital missing piece of information. The computer could complete this task in a matter of seconds but a manual search of a card index system could take weeks and still come up with a negative result. The human mind is fallible, the box isn't – provided the system has been used properly. The adage 'rubbish in, rubbish out,' definitely applies.

The problem of not using the HOLMES system from the outset is that having started on a manual system you then have to transfer all the data on to the box, back record conversion and, of course, while you're doing this there is a flood of new stuff coming in. It's rather like swimming against the tide – lots of hard work and effort but you never seem to get anywhere.

The system could not be efficiently searched if a quarter of its paper flow was awaiting input. The danger was that vital pieces of the jigsaw puzzle might be missing.

'When can we expect an answer?' I continued.

JB was smiling again. 'How long's a piece of string? I put in an urgent report today – at least the response in providing the initial equipment was encouraging.'

Another point had been raised at the meeting that I didn't fully understand. 'These tyre marks and footprints that Dave Perry was talking about – where were these found?' Dave Perry was a salty old DS with nearly 30 years' service; part of his responsibilities in this inquiry included tracing cyclists on the common.

Wickerson said, 'Mainly on the path running beside the tree and a footprint close to the area of flattened grass.'

'Anything unusual?'

'Not really: a few trainer marks, a couple of boot marks and some mountain bike tyre marks. But we can say that they must have been made on the morning of the murder.'

That intrigued me; from what I'd seen on the video and from my visit to the scene, the paths were like quagmires. 'How do we know these prints were made on the day of the murder? The paths are obviously well used and were extremely muddy and I assume they have been in that condition for some time judging from the way they were churned up.'

Wickerson smiled. 'It rained very heavily during the night of Tuesday the 14th, so any marks which weren't filled with water must have been left after the last rain, which, as I say, was Tuesday night.'

People had often made the mistake of being misled by Mick's laid-back attitude, but underneath his flippancy lay a serious talent for his work.

'Any marks by the tree?'

'No.'

'So now that the DNA has blown out, we haven't physically got anything in our possession to tie a suspect to Rachel?'

'Not unless Fingerprints come back with anything on the piece of paper.'

'But other than that?'

'Not a bean.'

This was obviously a major problem. It appeared that the killer had left no trace of himself on the victim or at the immediate scene, but there was still a possibility of trace evidence from Rachel or on Alex or his clothing. However, five days had now passed and experience said that the chances of having found such evidence by the time we eventually found our man were dwindling by the hour.

One of the basic theories of forensic science is Lockhart's Principle of Interchange. This states that when two objects touch there will be an exchange of matter from one to the other. So, for example, fibres from Rachel's or Alex's clothing would have transferred to the killer, and vice versa. Rachel's body was forensically examined at the scene; i.e. she was taped to lift any fibres which might have been present on her skin, and her clothing was also checked. The method is very useful for proving a connection between a suspect and his victim, but – and there is always a but – within about 48 hours most fibres would have fallen off the recipient's clothing and certainly after 96 hours none would remain. Obviously, if we had fibres from a suspect, the lab would be able to find and identify them, but at this stage we wouldn't have found any from Rachel on him. A two-way exchange is much better evidence.

The next hurdle to be overcome is the rarity of the type of fibre. If the fibre found is an unusual fabric with an unusual dye, the probative value is much increased. But if the fibres are from chain store clothing, it won't be worth a light. Denim jeans such as Rachel was wearing don't shed many fibres and there must be millions of pairs of denim jeans in the country – the same went for the cotton top she was wearing.

Fibre evidence was therefore not, in reality, going to be of much use in positively establishing a link between victim and suspect. At best, this type of evidence is used as an extra, but tenuous, link, and is supportive rather than conclusive evidence. In twenty years, I had only ever encountered one case where this type of evidence was of paramount importance. It involved an offence of armed robbery where cashmere fibres were found in the getaway car and on overalls worn by one of the suspects. The lab discovered that the dye was extremely rare and only used by a particular French fashion house. Enquiries in France paid dividends when it was found that this particular dye was only used in the manufacture of extremely expensive designer jumpers of which only 27 had ever been made. All the retail outlets were checked and one of these jumpers was traced back to the prime suspect who had very kindly paid for it using his credit card. Things like that happen once in a career and I had a funny feeling that the gods were not smiling on this particular investigation. 'Right,' I said. 'So if we end up drawing a blank with fingerprints and the second PM what are we going to use as evidence when we get this man?'

'Good question. What we need is a bit of luck – an eye-witness or the weapon would be handy.'

'To be honest, Mick, I wouldn't hold my breath for getting an eye-witness. With all the media attention they must be from another planet if they haven't come forward by now. But I agree that we could do with finding the weapon. Have we got any idea what sort of knife we're looking for?'

'Dick Shepherd says it was a single-edged blade and about 5–5½in length. But he's got some new system which he thinks might give us more details. It's something to do with an MRI scanner but he'll let us know. You can take a copy of the pathology report away with you.'

I said, 'Whoever did this, someone must have seen him – if not committing the murder, then at least either going to or from the scene. One point that occurs to me is about how he'd be looking. In the photographs and video, I didn't see any evidence of blood-splashing. Did I miss it, or wasn't there any?'

The degree of staining of an assailant depends on the closeness of contact between him and his victim; if no significant close contact occurs, then it is entirely possible that the only easily visible areas of blood-staining of the assailant will be his hands. It is quite likely that forensic examination of clothing will reveal small spots of blood on his clothing, but these would not be apparent to the casual observer.

Wickerson shook his head. 'Believe it or not, no. None of the 49 wounds actually severed any main arteries, so according to Dick there wouldn't have been spurting as such. He thinks there were probably only small blood splashes to the attacker, caused when the blood-stained or blood-smeared knife was moved quickly, causing tiny drops of blood to be flicked off the blade. The phases of the assault would not have resulted in him necessarily coming into close contact with a heavily blood-stained body or clothing.

'What we're talking about is the blood seeping back into the body cavities rather than spraying the assailant. Dick also said that blood pressure would have been a critical factor.'

'But Rachel's blood pressure would have been sky high: she must have been terrified.'

'Right, but any one of about 12 wounds was potentially fatal and as a consequence her blood pressure would have fallen rapidly.'

'You're not telling me there's a chance this bastard might not have had any blood on him?'

'No, but there is a strong possibility that he wouldn't exactly have been drenched.'

'Jesus Christ, Mick! So we've got this bloke, he attacks Rachel in broad daylight, a few feet away from a well-used footpath and clearly visible to anybody who might have come along, yards from a wide open space where God knows how many people are wandering about. He inflicts 49 vicious stab wounds, but misses all the major arteries and escapes possibly unsullied by his activities. Nobody appears to have seen him during or after the attack. He's got the luck of the devil – either that, or he's the invisible man.'

'On the face of it, he's been damned lucky, but there's no way he won't have got some of Rachel's blood on him; it just might not be that blatantly obvious to a person who saw him leaving the scene. So we're maybe looking for something a little more subtle than the screamingly obvious blood-soaked suspect.'

JB had busied himself with the statements again and was deeply engrossed in his work. I looked at Mick and said, 'Unless there's anything else I ought to know, I think I'll take a copy of the path report and statements home and have another look through. See you in the morning then. Office meeting at ten o'clock?'

I left Wickerson and Bassett and went down to my new office to retrieve the binder of statements. It was 8.30pm but the incident room was still buzzing. There was a constant tap-tapping of indexers' fingers on keyboards and a low hum of conversation. I said goodnight to Ritzo and Paul Penrose, who were up to their elbows in Actions and messages. They all had a long evening ahead of them.

As I drove out of the station yard, my mind was full of the facts, names and places I had learned about that day. But there was more to it than cold, hard data – I was as shaken as everybody else by the tragedy and sadness of a wasted and viciously curtailed young life. Rachel Nickell had been just 23 years old, a devoted and caring mother, happily settled in a loving relationship. It had taken just three or so minutes for all that to be destroyed and, in the process, so many other lives were shattered.

Had it been a purely random killing by a stranger, I wondered – a beautiful girl with long blonde hair and a bright, toothy smile in the wrong place at the wrong time? Or had the killer singled Rachel out as a specific target?

So many other things didn't make sense. The piece of paper on her forehead, for example – even if it had fallen out of Rachel's jeans during the struggle, how did it get on her face? The attack would have been so frenetic and violent, it was almost impossible for it to have landed there by accident. It had to be a deliberate act, but why?

I drove home, my mind full of unanswered questions. I knew

only one thing for sure – that we were looking for a maniac, and we had to find him quickly.

It was 11.30pm as I sat myself down at the dining room table and began to read. The first document I picked up was Doc Shepherd's pathology report. I knew Dick reasonably well; a very tall, chain-smoking, affable man, about whom the most noticeable thing was the smell of death that followed him into a room. Death does have a smell, and if you go to a post mortem it will stay with you for days. As a leading Home Office pathologist, Doc Shepherd did all the horrible ones, and had investigated more than 750 suspicious deaths over the past ten years.

Doc Shepherd had arrived at Wimbledon Common at 12.18pm on 15 July 1992, to be told by Mick Wickerson at the murder scene, 'It's a nasty one, Doc.' Nothing had been moved. Rachel lay exactly as the killer had left her. SOCOs were just finishing a video film of the body and the surrounding area for future use in the investigation.

The result of the pathologist's investigation that I was about to read was a stark, dispassionate chronicle of the horror that Rachel must have endured.

At 1218hrs on Wednesday 15-07-92, I attended at Wimbledon Common where DI Wickerson and Det Supt Bassett showed me the body of a young Caucasian female, later identified as RACHEL JANE NICKELL aged 23 yrs lying in a small copse.

Following still and video photography, I examined the body in situ and noted that rigor mortis was present only in the jaw. Body temperature taken through a skin incision (marked with a black circle) at 13.50 was 76 degrees F. the ambient temperature at the scene was noted to be 65 degrees F.

I noted that the anus was widely patent but no evidence of injury or of bleeding was noted in the anal or genital area. Some strands of black material were noted adherent to the skin in the perianal region. Swabs from the anus and vagina were taken at the scene. I noted numerous stab marks to the body but further examination was deferred until arrival at the mortuary.

The body was transferred to St George's Hospital mortuary where at 1530hrs on the same day, I performed a post mortem examination.

The body was that of a well-nourished, young Caucasian female, weighing 58kg and 5'4" in height. The clothing from the lower body had been removed at the scene to prevent contamination by blood during transportation to the mortuary. The remaining clothing, comprising of T-shirt and bra, were removed in the mortuary; both were heavily blood-stained. The cup of the left side of the bra had been displaced slightly downward, exposing the left nipple. Numerous cuts were noted in both the T-shirt and the bra.

Rigor mortis was noted to involve all muscle groups at this time and the body temperature at 1545 was noted to be 70 degrees F. Dilatation of the anus to approximately 1.5cm was confirmed and numerous stab injuries were noted to the back, chest, neck and hand.

Doc Shephered went on to list each of the 49 stab wounds and, as standard in a PM report, to describe, in turn, the distance of each from the heel, its relation to the mid-line, its angle, length and track.

There were 19 stab wounds to Rachel's back, 26 in her chest, 3 in her neck, one to her hand. An area of abrasion 6cm x 1cm was noted on the right side of the chin. No other significant external abnormalities were noted at the time.

The pathologist's conclusions were as follows:

1. Rachel Nickell was a well-nourished young girl, with no evidence of natural disease that could have caused or contributed to her death at the time.

2. *The injuries are consistent with infliction by a knife or knives with a single cutting margin, approximately 1.5cm in width at the hilt and approximately 9cm in length. The hilt has a squared lower margin approximately 0.5cm wide adjacent to the cutting edge and extends approximately 0.5cm beneath the bottom margin of the blade.*
3. *Many of the stab wounds have penetrated into the cavities of the body and stabbing injuries to both lungs, the heart and the liver were identified.*
4. *The stabbing injuries to the heart and left lung show evidence of adjacent haemorrhage and were inflicted ante mortem. The stabbing injuries to the right lung and the liver are not associated with significant haemorrhage and are of peri-mortem or post-mortem origin.*
5. *The through-and-through stab wound of the left hand (injury 49) is consistent with a defensive injury.*
6. *The variation in site and angle of track of the injuries is consistent with relative movement of the victim and assailant during stabbing.*
7. *I give as cause of death: multiple stab wounds.*

Next, I wanted to go through the various witness statements and used my *London Geographia* to check locations as they cropped up. The first priority, as far as I was concerned, was to put to the back of my mind what I had seen and learned during the day and start from scratch. An open mind is essential; experience has taught me that this is the only safe way to progress. If you come into an investigation late it is essential, in my view, to start from square one and not to rely on the views and conclusions of other officers. That was not to say that I didn't trust or value the opinions of others, but it is always safer to do the groundwork yourself and, if by happy chance your conclusions coincide with the others, then all well and good – but if there are areas of uncertainty then there is an opportunity to discuss them. It's all about checks and balances.

Start from the centre and work out.

I began by looking at Statement 36, that of Rachel's partner, Andre Hanscombe, then the statements of neighbours. To all intents and purposes, it looked as if 15 July 1992 had been just another ordinary day, beginning early for the happy little family who were up and about long before 7am.

Andre Hanscombe was the result of a mixed marriage, with a white mother and black father. During his youth, he had shown a tremendous talent for tennis which took him into the professional circuit as a player in Europe and the United States. In latter years, he had various jobs, interspersed with periods of unemployment, but was currently working as a dispatch rider for A–Z Couriers.

In order to help make ends meet, Andre and Rachel had taken in a lodger to help with the mortgage. I immediately made a mental note: Check up on lodger, Steven Gardner.

The statements showed that Andre left for his job between 8.45am and 9.00am, and Gardner much earlier, at around 7.10am. The evidence of a Gas Board employee, Thomas Gerachty, verified roughly the time Andre left for work. Gerachty remembered a silver Volvo parked outside Elmfield Mansions. He made enquiries as to who owned the vehicle because it had to be moved in order for him to carry out his work. The gas man spoke to a neighbour, possibly Mr Smith; Gerachty stated that whilst speaking with the neighbour, Andre appeared and said that the car would be moved in five to ten minutes.

The early movements of Rachel and Andre on 15 July appeared to be unexceptional. There were obviously discrepancies between various witnesses as to the exact timing of different events, but that was to be expected. I would have been surprised and more than a little uncomfortable if everything had dovetailed perfectly.

I then turned my attention to Rachel's arrival at the common. What time did she leave home? Had any one seen her leave home? Did anyone see her arrive at the Windmill car park? And, more importantly, was she with anyone? The evidence on this aspect appeared to be contradictory and confusing. Gerachty stated that he saw the Volvo drive off at around 9am. but he didn't notice who was driving. Was this Rachel just repositioning the vehicle or was she heading off towards the common? Mr Smith, the neighbour, stated that she normally left home between 9.00am and half-past, but he hadn't seen her leave on this particular morning.

There were several potential sightings at the common between 9.05am. and 9.20am. First, a man named Woolas claimed to have seen a silver Volvo, driven by a young blonde woman, edging out of a side-turning into Parkside; there was a child in a rear child seat. This was at about 9.05am. Could this have been Rachel? If so, the gas man's timing must have been out or Woolas had to be wrong about the time. I wasn't particularly familiar with south-west London but I would have estimated that the journey from Elmfield Road to the common was about five miles and at that time of day would have taken about 20 to 30 minutes. Another mental note: Get an officer to time the trip.

9.10–9.15am: Janet Goodson recalls seeing a woman, a toddler and a black dog in the area of Bluegate gravel pit. She was a bit vague and no description was given. Goodson thought there may have been a pushchair. I didn't remember any mention being made of Rachel having had a pushchair. Certainly there wasn't a pushchair in the scene-of- crime photos. I made another note: Check with Wickerson – pushchair?

Two more possible sightings were revealed in the statements of Ian Brown and Julianna Warren.

9.20am: Brown claims to have seen a blonde walking northwards towards the direction of Bluegate gravel pit. She was wearing a light top and light trousers and was with a young child and a small black dog. Most interestingly, he also mentions that there was a dark-haired man talking to the child.

9.25–9.30am: Warren sees a woman of the same description with a toddler walking north along the Parkside edge of the common. No mention was made of the dog or the man.

I must have been reading for about an hour or so and I was beginning to feel tired and groggy. I put the kettle on and went into the garden for a cigarette and to stretch my legs. The night was warm and the sky was clear. I looked at the stars and tried to make some sense of what I had seen and learned during the previous 15 or 16 hours. It was peaceful standing there under the heavens, until I realised with a jolt that the same stars were shining down on the person or persons who had murdered Rachel, wherever and whoever they might be.

I stubbed out my cigarette on the patio and returned to the kitchen to make myself a big jug of black coffee.

I settled back down to my reading. Although the descriptions varied, Goodson, Brown and Warren had probably seen the same woman. The question was, was it Rachel? I had to keep an open mind, but my instincts told me that it wasn't. The clothing was wrong; Rachel had been wearing blue jeans and a grey T-shirt. Descriptions almost always vary from witness to witness and there have been occasions when three or four people witnessing the same offence have given such differing accounts that you begin to wonder whether they are talking about the same event. But here, both Brown and Warren had described the light-coloured top.

The location of the three sightings tended to corroborate the fact that they had all seen the same person, but Brown's mention of the man and the dog did not appear in Warren's recollection. Still, I reasoned, if this were a family group, Dad and the dog could have been off in the bushes and Warren might have missed them. If it was a family, it obviously couldn't have been Rachel, as Andre was at work. Unless, of course, she was with another man.

I remembered JB's reasoning about what Alex had said to Brooks and Horne, the two women who looked after him until the police arrived. He had said that he'd been with Mummy and Molly. OK, he was obviously in shock, but he made no mention of anyone else. If Dad or someone else had been with them, then he surely would have said so.

Something else came back to me. Mick had said something about Alex being shy with strangers, so if this group was Rachel and Alex, the fact that Brown had said that the toddler was talking to the man made it seem unlikely that this man was a stranger. Note: Check with Wickerson – Alex shyness.

Of course, it could have been Rachel, but the timing and the direction in which they were walking would tend to suggest otherwise – but I had to keep that open mind. As I ploughed on through the other statements, I came across one made by Antonia Alafouza, who saw a silver Volvo drive into the Windmill car park and park in the right-hand corner. This was some time between 9.40am and 9.45am. She further claimed that a young blonde woman with her hair up got out of the car. She also had a little boy with her, and had a dog lead looped through her belt. Alafouza described the woman as wearing tight jeans and a brownish top and the child as wearing a green T-shirt. Again, the clothing was not right, but the position of the car would strongly suggest that this was Rachel arriving.

Another sighting at about two or three minutes before 10.00am was reported by a couple named Corsan who were returning to the car park. They described a young blonde woman with a dark child and a black dog heading away from the car park in roughly the direction of Windmill Ride. Again, I noticed the discrepancies in the descriptions given by Ann and Jonathan Corsan concerning Rachel's hair – another example of two people seeing the same thing but having differing recollections.

Five days into the inquiry, it still appeared that the last person to have seen Rachel alive, other than the killer, was the cyclist named Roger McKern, who just before reaching the windmill saw the little group walking towards the open area in front of the mound. Mr McKern was adamant that this sighting was at 10.19am, as he had checked his watch when he reached the windmill and the time was 10.20am. Furthermore, he said he had arrived at his place of work, the Wimbledon Theatre, at between 10.32am and 10.33am. Another note: Distance from the common to the theatre? Could Mr McKern have made the journey in the time he claimed? What do we know about him? Have we checked tyres of his bike against those found near the scene?

I would have been very surprised if these enquiries hadn't already been undertaken but I was trying to catch up on five days of investigation and I had always been taught never to assume anything – otherwise you are likely to end up with the 'everybody, somebody and nobody' syndrome, where everybody thinks somebody else has done the task and it transpires that nobody has.

My eyelids were drooping and I checked my watch. It was past 3.30am. I looked at the pile of statements still to be read and decided that more coffee was needed. As I got up to go into the kitchen, I noticed the overflowing ashtray. Had I really smoked that much? I really had to do something about stopping, but I had a funny feeling that giving up was going to have to be put off until after this investigation had been sorted out. How long would that be? Even if we didn't solve it, I knew that there were guidelines as to how long a sticker is allowed to run – three to four months normally being the limit. Files on unsolved murders are always kept open, but the investigative teams are scaled right down. Sometimes a single officer will keep the file and follow up any new information as, when and if it comes in, but these offences are not proactively pursued.

I sat down again at the table with a new jug of coffee and continued reading. It seemed that there was a gap of 15 minutes during which no one had seen Rachel or Alex, until Michael Murray discovered Alex clinging to the lifeless body of his mummy. As I already knew, Mr Murray was out walking with his Samoyed dog when, at about 10.35am, as he was approaching the silver birch along the main footpath from the Parkside direction, he noticed what he initially thought was a sunbather lying on the ground. As he got closer, the realisation struck him and he noticed that this person was naked from the waist down. Murray also noticed the horrific wounds to Rachel's throat. His next observation, even though I was already aware of it, brought a tear to my eye: 'The little boy was holding on to the woman by her arm; he was crying, covered in blood, and saying, "Get up, Mummy, get my Mummy".'

I flicked through to find the statements of Emma Brooks and Penny Horne, the two women to whom Murray had handed Alex whilst he went off to get help, then recapped on what I had discovered of Rachel's movements. She had arrived at the common some time between 9.05am and 9.45am, was seen walking away from the car park at two or three minutes to ten, and was last seen alive at 10.20am. Her body was found at 10.35am.

My initial thoughts were that more enquiries needed to be made to establish Rachel's time of departure from Elmfield Road and to firm up on her arrival at the car park. Note: Time the journey from Elmfield to Wimbledon. Check out McKern and Murray.

There were various mentions made of men on the common. I would need to speak to the office manager concerning the steps taken to identify them, but I was too tired to think about these potential suspects at this time of night. My priority had been to get the sequence of Rachel's last movements clear in my mind.

As I put the statements away and started to think about going to bed, there was one question still burning away at the back of my mind concerning the vicious death inflicted upon this beautiful woman, who was a loving mother, partner and friend, and of whom no one appeared to have a single bad word to say.

The question was – *why?*

Chapter 5

Rachel Jane Nickell was born on 23 November 1968. Her father, Andrew, had served for many years as an army officer, and now made a successful living as an importer. Rachel and her older brother, Mark, grew up in an atmosphere of middle-class security in the Essex village of Great Totham, near Colchester.

Rachel was a popular pupil at Great Totham Primary School. After sailing through her 11-plus, she won a place at Colchester High School for Girls, a selective grammar school and, according to teachers, she was equally talented in and out of the classroom. A natural at dancing, acting and singing, Rachel had been a star pupil with the Essex Dance Theatre in Chelmsford. The principal stated, 'She could easily have made it in the West End. She had the ability and the looks. She passed all her exams with ease. It is so tragic to think so much has gone to waste.'

Rachel was also an exceptionally kind person, both to animals and to her fellow human beings, organising Christmas parties for the elderly and for disabled children. All in all, according to neighbours who had been interviewed, the Nickells were 'the perfect family'.

Monica Nickell, for example, became a swimming coach at a nearby club in order to encourage her children to enjoy the water. Yet again, Rachel had excelled, going on to become a particularly good diver and passing lifeguard exams with distinction.

Rachel's striking good looks brought offers of modelling work before she was 16, but she turned them down to concentrate on her studies. Dr Aline Black, headmistress during the five years Rachel spent at Colchester High, described Rachel as 'a lovely and active young woman who had great potential and a wonderful future ahead of her'.

Rachel finally left Colchester High with four As and five Bs at O-level. She began studying for a degree in English and History, working between terms as a lifeguard at a pool in Richmond, Surrey. It was while on duty one Saturday, in September 1988, that she met Andre Hanscombe, then a 24-year-old dispatch rider with a courier firm. Rachel was only 19, but from that day on they were inseparable, soon afterwards moving into Andre's two-bedroom, second-floor flat in a Victorian house at 29 Elmfield Road, Balham. When she became pregnant with Alex, Rachel abandoned her university education to become a full-time mother.

Alex was born in August 1989 and Rachel soon began passing on her swimming skills to him at mother and toddler sessions at the Balham Leisure Centre, close to their flat. She was anxious that Alex should feel safe in the water and enjoy swimming just as much as she herself had done as a child.

At roughly the same time, her parents left Great Totham and moved to Ampthill in Bedfordshire. Rachel, Andre and baby Alex were regular visitors to the house. 'Such a lovely family,' yet another neighbour had said, 'always doing things together.'

Andre and Rachel, however, were not entirely happy with their impecunious circumstances. According to Andre, they had often talked of moving from London to the countryside or even to France, or somewhere near the sea at least, and tentatively approached estate agents about putting their flat on the market. Andre had said he saw working as a motorbike courier as purely a temporary measure to pay the mortgage while he pursued his ambition of becoming a tennis professional. He had played semi-professionally and had coached at the Roger Taylor Tennis School in Portugal.

Just before she became pregnant, according to Andre, Rachel had let her studies drop, and began to have thoughts that, maybe, when Alex was a little older, she could break into children's television. She set about researching how to achieve that aim and was in the middle of drawing up a CV, together with some pictures and an audio tape.

I was still struck by the very personal nature of the response that the investigating officers were taking to this particular crime, my surprise being due not to of the personalities of the Nickell team, but because of the actual mechanics of the AMIP murder squad system in operation at that time. Officers from all over the Area, which covered about a fifth of the Metropolitan Police District, were drafted in to augment the SIO's small permanent squad, which meant that strangers from widely differing policing environments were brought together to work as a team to investigate the most serious of offences and, once the job had been completed, they returned to their own stations. The system was effective and efficient almost to the point of being clinical; the temporary nature of AMIP squads ensures intense and totally focused investigations, a '*Blitzkrieg*' approach which concentrates enormous resources over a relatively short period.

That wasn't to say that other murders weren't dealt with sympathetically. Anger and disgust at the killer, and compassion and grief for the victim are common emotions experienced by detectives. But Rachel's case was different; there seemed to be an unusually intense feeling of loss, determination and outrage in the Wimbledon incident room. This manifested itself with the warmth which was apparent when people were talking about her; she wasn't just an identity-less victim who had brought us all together, and as we began to find out more about her background, parents and family, that feeling of affinity and affection towards her only seemed to increase.

A few days after Rachel's murder, somebody had cut out and pinned to a board in the incident room a paragraph from an article in the *Daily Express*. It read, 'The whole country has been jolted by Rachel's murder. She stood for qualities of honesty and goodness that are supposed to triumph over dark and violent forces. This week, on a lonely stretch of Wimbledon Common, evil won.'

It is all too easy for police officers' emotions to become blunted, dealing as often as we do with man's inhumanities to his fellow man. But we were husbands, wives, mothers and fathers as well as detectives, and each new personal detail we learned about Rachel only served to reinforce our determination to hunt down the man who had taken so much away.

I was at the incident room by 8.00am that Tuesday morning and, despite the fact that I'd been up reading until after 4.00am, I wasn't feeling particularly tired. I had thrown up quite a few questions as I ploughed through the binder of statements and was keen to get on with finding answers.

Even at this time of the morning, the guys in the incident room were working flat out, each incoming phone call first being taken down in long-hand, and then typed in as data into the computer terminals linked to HOLMES.

The morning's first coffee mugs and bacon sandwiches were jockeying for room with the night shift's overflowing ashtrays and empty paper plates from the canteen. Bizarrely, amid all this activity and clutter, sat a large cuddly toy with red ears, a red nose and a yellow hat. I looked at the label around its neck. It had been sent 'From a granny for the little boy whose mother was murdered.' Somebody told me that upstairs was a room full of toys, teddy bears and books that had been flooding in from all over the country, all sent by people whose hearts had been touched by Alex's tragedy.

The office meeting at 10.00am didn't throw up anything new, so I assembled the Ree-Gee boys in our office and allocated the first batch of TIE Actions. Any TIE is dealt with on its own merits, the amount of time and resources spent on each one depending on the individual circumstances. Some might be dealt with exhaustively, others can be disposed of following a single visit to the potential suspect. The basic rule of thumb with a TIE is to look at the information, assess the source and then research the suspect. Has the suspect got any form? What's the connection between the informant and the suspect? Is there any history of aggravation between them? Normal routine police procedure.

I had decided I wanted the Ree-Gee boys to work in pairs. Obviously, if they worked alone then, in theory, twice the volume of Actions could be shifted, but from the point of view of safety and morale, the 'buck' system was preferable – 'buck' being the expression used in the Job to refer to one's operational partner. I split the team up into DCs Garlinge and Long, Richardson and Costello, Palmer and Bailey.

'Right, chaps,' I said, calling them to order. 'I have a feeling that this is going to be a long job. I've no doubt that in the next few weeks we're going to be seeing an awful lot of these Actions, so we might as well start with a system. First, all Actions will be allocated to me; they will then be entered in this Book 40 (police record ledger) and issued to you. Once they're completed, they must come back to me to be recorded in the Book 40 and I will return them to the system. Paul Penrose has asked me to remind you that a PDF must be completed with each Action.' (Personal Descriptive Forms are a record of what a person looks like, together with their vehicle details. All persons involved with an inquiry, whether they're witnesses or suspects, should have a PDF.)

Martin Long looked thoughtful. I had never met him before – or any of the other Ree-Gee guys for that matter – but I knew 'Longy' by reputation as a shrewd, straight-talking Cockney in his mid-thirties who did not suffer fools easily, and who was rarely seen without a cigarette in his mouth.

'What about prem (premises) search records, Guv?' he asked, exhaling a cloud of smoke.

'Good point. I think just for the sake of completeness we ought to keep a copy of all documentation. So photocopy all custody records, arrest notes, exhibits books and prem search warrants and we'll start a binder. The originals will go into the main incident room but we'll have a copy in here. That way I'll have an independent record of what we've done.

'I've no doubt that a lot of these Actions won't actually justify feeling collars, so you'll have to use your discretion. If you can eliminate someone without recourse to taking them to the local nick, all well and good. If you can't, or you're in any way unhappy with someone, or you get any crap from them, then you've got no choice but to bring them in.'

'What about interview tapes?' asked Andy Palmer in a West Country burr.

'The originals will stay at the nick but we'll keep a copy here, so don't forget to run off an extra copy.'

The established system with interview tapes is that the master tape is sealed in the presence of the suspect, and the seal cannot then be broken without the authority of a judge. The master tape seal number is entered on the custody record and the tape is stored at the station where the prisoner was interviewed. Each tape machine holds two tapes and at the end of the interrogation the suspect is given the choice as to which one he wants as the 'master'. The second tape is then copied and the suspect, if he's charged, is offered a copy and the officer keeps a working copy, which he can then summarise or get transcribed for the CPS (Crown Prosecution Service) file. On the grounds of cost, only in major cases will authority be given for a full transcript to be made.

'And what about intimate samples?' Keith Richardson asked. He looked to me to be aged in his early to mid-thirties, 6ft 2in tall and a little overweight. He had collar-length, straight brown hair and wore metal-framed glasses. There was something about his appearance which put me in mind of the record producer Jonathan King.

'Good question. We won't know until after the second PM whether we've got anything to compare it against, and probably for some considerable time after that. Until the lab put it in writing that we've got nothing, if we've got a good suspect we should still request blood or saliva. Failing the suspect's co-operation, we should go for a non-intimate of head hair without his consent. I'll speak to Mick Wickerson and get a policy decision on it. Any other questions?'

Martin Long was sitting in an armchair, leafing through the pile of the dozen or so Actions which I had just given him. 'Some of these are a bit vague, Guv'nor ... look at this one: "Mrs Smith reports seeing man aged 35 to 40 years looking strangely at women in Kingston Hill on 17 July. Speak with Mrs Smith and TIE unknown male." '

'They're not all like that – you've got some good ones to get your teeth into.'

Long still looked unconvinced. 'Talk about looking for needles in haystacks,' he muttered as he re-read the Action. Then he added with a grin, 'And judging from the date and location, I'm not even sure we've got the right haystack!'

I looked around the office at the unsympathetic faces of his colleagues. 'I don't know why you lot are smiling. If you look towards the bottom of your Actions you'll find you've all got a couple like that one.'

The major problem we were to encounter was the use to which most people put the common, and that was recreational. Whilst most witnesses could tell us what time they arrived and what time they left, they had problems with their movements and progress between those two points and their exact locations at any given time; what was more, to the casual user one tree looks very much like another and one footpath looks very much like another, unless you are totally familiar with the ground. It was very difficult to identify which person was in what position, and whether the person that Witness A saw at a certain point was the same person that Witness B saw at a different point.

It was one of the research team, DC Roger Lane, who came up with an answer that, like the corkscrew, was blindingly obvious once you'd invented it. His solution was simply to use a gridded map of the common and to get each witness to mark their route and any sightings on it. Whilst the maps weren't a perfect answer, they probably offered the best result we were going to get.

We also encountered the usual problems we are faced with in any investigation. It can be surprisingly difficult, for example, to get witnesses to give accurate descriptions. Height is a notoriously unreliable measure, since one person's perception of 'tall' may not necessarily coincide with somebody else's. Perception can be so subjective that sometimes it's possible to have six people see the same incident and appear to be describing six totally different events.

Nonetheless, suspects were being nominated and in these early stages we couldn't afford to discount a single scrap of information for fear of missing something important. ACPO (Association of Chief Police Officers) guidelines state that officers on major inquiries should only be allocated two Actions at a time; this would have gone by the board within the first couple of days, with most officers carrying a workload of between 40 to 50 Actions each.

Many members of the public were ringing in with information which appeared to be tenuous to say the least. But the country had been shocked by Rachel's death and everyone seemed keen to impart information which, to them at least, seemed to be important. For the most part, these people were acting out of the best possible motives but some, albeit a very small minority, had motives other than public-spiritedness – the settling of old scores, a dislike of the police or full-blown delusions being quite popular. All lines of enquiry had to be pursued as far as possible or until they were proved to be malicious.

I was in my office at about midday that Tuesday when the telephone rang. Keith Richardson answered it.

'Suspect Team, DI Pedder's office.' He listened for a few seconds and said, 'Right, I'll tell him.'

Surrey police had arrested a suspect. He was in one of the interview rooms and his mother was at the front desk demanding to see him.

My heart sank. 'Our suspect is a juvenile?'

Juvenile prisoners are difficult to handle because of all the safeguards written into the Police and Criminal Evidence Act concerning their treatment and detention. Appropriate adults have to be present when they're interviewed, and you're not allowed to detain them in cells. Nine times out of ten they know the system better than you do, and know they can take the mickey and get away with it.

It turned out that the prisoner, in fact, wasn't a juvenile, just one of the most sadly inadequate 18-year-olds I'd ever encountered.

Jimmy was slightly built, shy, spotty and painfully inarticulate. It appeared that during the evening prior to Jimmy's arrival at Wimbledon, there had been a bit of a family dispute during which he had lost his temper and started waving a knife around and smashing up the home. The police had been called and Jimmy was taken into custody. It was then that his mother had decided to add fuel to the fire by accusing her son of involvement in the Nickell murder. This was all too much for Jimmy, who had another flare-up and subsequently, perhaps due to his limited mental capacity, found himself unable to account for his movements on 15 July.

There was no evidence to connect Jimmy to the murder but an open mind had to be kept. We waited until a social worker had arrived before interviewing him. The thought of this pathetic lad being able to inflict the sort of injuries which Rachel had suffered was almost beyond belief, but his clothing was blood-stained and his knife was immediately submitted to the laboratory for examination. His alibi took some sorting out, but eventually we were able to establish that he had been attending a counselling session at the time to help him cope with his not inconsiderable problems. He was to be bailed to return pending the results of the test on the knife and, hopefully, on his DNA, should the second PM throw up anything to compare it against.

I spoke at great length to Jimmy 's mother and her boyfriend, who had also turned up to lend his support. The bottom line was that Mum and Jimmy lived in very cramped accommodation and the arrival of a live-in lover meant there wasn't enough room for the three of them. It appeared that she had decided that Jimmy had to go, and that the best method was to get him locked up out of the way. She was not pleased with the news that Jimmy was to be bailed. She produced a cassette tape that contained, according to her, irrefutable proof that Jimmy had killed Rachel. I had the feeling I would regret the question as I sat opposite her in an interview room a few minutes later, but I heard myself asking it anyway.

'Can you describe to me what is on this tape?'

'It's proof that he killed that girl.'

'What do you mean proof? Has Jimmy confessed?'

'It's better than that ... they actually told me he done it, they told me how he done it.'

'Who are "they"?'

'I have these dreams and the people in them tell me all about it. You'll have to lock him up now.'

'You recorded what they said, did you?'

'Yes, I woke up and switched on the tape recorder. They were still there telling me.'

'And it's all on this tape?'

'Listen to it and then you'll have to do something about it.'

After she had gone I took the tape out to my car and put it into the cassette player. I didn't know what I was expecting to hear, but apart from one isolated bout of coughing the silence on the tape was deafening.

The lab results came back negative and I sent one of the local PCs round to Jimmy 's address to cancel his bail. He reported back to me that the boyfriend had gone and Jimmy and his mum looked as happy as newly-weds.

The incident had taken several precious hours to sort out, and even after it was over I had to go and see the office manager to get a retrospective Action issued to TIE Jimmy, and follow the paperwork through. That's the way the system works.

Thank goodness that in amongst the dross there were nuggets of gold. I looked again at some of the statements that suggested possible sightings.

Amanda Phelan reported the sighting of a man acting suspiciously near the stream or drainage ditch which runs more or less from the memorial tree in a north-westerly direction towards the edge of Putney Vale Cemetery. She noticed the man from a distance of about 100 yards. On her approach, he suddenly turned and ducked down into the stream as if he was washing his hands. He then walked off in the direction of the cemetery. This man was described as white, 20 to 30 years old, 6ft tall with short, collar-length hair, and wearing a cream, lightweight sweater, blue loose jeans or trousers. He was also carrying a black bag, which might have been a carrier bag. This sighting was at about 10.40am, approximately five minutes after Mr Murray had discovered Rachel's body.

There was also another man seen swishing both his hands quite violently in the water of Queensmere Pond. This person was described as in his teens, white, of medium build with short, dark, tidy hair. The witness, Valerie Hunt, stated that his face was red but she couldn't say whether this was his natural colouring or caused by exertion. He was wearing dark, casual clothing. The major problem with this sighting was the vagueness of the timing, which was 'around 10.00am'.

At between 10.02 and 10.07am, however, Margaret Kemp saw a white man with long, brown, unkempt hair, 5ft 8in tall with a wide nose and thick top lip wearing jeans and a white crew-necked T-shirt. Ms Kemp stated that the jeans were saturated from mid-thigh down. This person had run across the junction of Inner Park Road and Parkside, causing Ms Kemp to do an emergency stop.

A family named Harriman reported sightings of a suspicious white male on three occasions between 10.17 and 10.23am This man was wearing a white shirt and dark trousers, had short, dark hair and was carrying a black bag, possibly an Adidas sports bag.

In a nutshell, suspicious males were being sighted all over the common and on its outskirts. The problem was to time these sightings accurately and assess their importance to the investigation and, in the absence of an eye-witness to the offence, it was going to be a difficult task to sort the wheat from the chaff. I still pinned my hopes on the statistic that in only one in fifty murders are the suspect and victim unknown to each other, but an open mind had to be kept nonetheless.

As well as sifting through information from the public, we had other areas of investigation to look at. The first priority was to TIE every man who had been on the common that morning. Second, we were still in the process of going through Rachel's and Andre's address books and diaries and speaking to everyone they knew. We were also interviewing every past offender who lived in the local area, specifically those who had been involved in crimes of a sexual or violent nature. On top of that, police forces up and down the country had been contacted to see if there had been other similar attacks recorded elsewhere.

A week before Rachel's murder, another young woman, Katie Ratcliffe, had been stabbed to death in Hampshire, and the details of that inquiry were also on the HOLMES system. Purely for an exchange of information, not for any other specific reason, our two computer systems were linked – or rather, they would have been linked had the computers been compatible. As luck would have it, they weren't, which rather defeated the object of HOLMES, which was supposed to be designed to link one major inquiry with another – great in theory, until the various police authorities decided to go out and buy their own hardware, which included Hewlett Packard and IBM and various other systems that turned out to be incompatible. So instead, what was happening was that at the end of each 24-hour period, all the new information was put on a disk that was compatible with our computer and vice versa, and information was swapped to see if any suspects' names threw up any common links.

The papers tried to make out that we were seriously linking these crimes, but there was no thorough foundation for wanting to do that, other than just completeness, to make sure that at this stage we weren't missing anything.

At the 6.00pm meeting, JB filled us in on the day's events. Andre, though shattered by grief, had asked to be taken to the spot where Rachel had been murdered. Alex had gone with him. He wanted to be able to understand what Alex had witnessed, and he wanted to show him that it wasn't the trees or the grass that were bad, just the man who had killed Mummy. A child psychiatrist suggested that it was part of the healing process that might one day help Alex to obliterate the horror once and for all from his mind.

Sadly, but predictably, the media pack had been waiting. Photographers jostled to get pictures of the father and son as they walked from the car park to the copse. Soon it became a stampede and Andre had to gather little Alex into his arms and run. Officers had had to force the journalists back like a crowd of football hooligans. It was a disgraceful spectacle, the British media at their very worst. Apparently, one young constable, close to tears, had shouted, 'Why don't you bastards leave them alone?'

As they got back to the car park, by total coincidence Andre and Alex were met by Eric Roberts. He was on the common with other officers, helping to retrace what he knew of Rachel's favourite routes. The two men stopped to talk together for a few moments, but all the time Alex was struggling to get out of his father's arms.

JB then told us that Andrew, Monica and Mark Nickell had arrived back in London earlier that morning. Rachel's father, Andrew, had given a press conference within hours of landing at Heathrow.

JB was a great believer in the power of the press and was of the opinion that the more media exposure there was, the better our chances of solving the murder. I was more dubious; it was already obvious that the media were building up a head of steam, and my experience had always been that if they are given too much, it becomes a bit of a habit and they want more and more, to the extent that the media can actually became intrusive and seriously undermine what we are trying to do. But who was to say that a public appeal for assistance might not provide the vital lead to Rachel's killer?

On other topics, JB said that the search of the common was still continuing but nothing resembling the murder weapon had been found. Problems were being encountered getting statements from all the people who were present on the common at the time. JB suggested that these persons should be invited to attend the police station over a weekend so that these statements could be obtained.

He also said that the following day, 22 July, he was going to try a public memory-jogging exercise. A friend of Rachel's had offered to help in a reconstruction of her last walk in the hope that it would spark a recollection by anyone who was in the area at the time of the killing, and who might unwittingly have a vital piece of information stored away.

Bill Lyle rounded off the meeting by telling us that the second PM had been arranged, and would be conducted on Thursday the 23rd.

'How was the press conference?' I asked Mick Wickerson in his office.

'He handled it brilliantly,' Mick said. 'A lot better than I could have in his position. If there are any witnesses out there who haven't come forward yet, I'm sure Andrew's appeal will jolt them to do something.'

'I've been reading the statements last night and today and a couple of thoughts occurred to me. You've probably already got them in hand, but I'm just double-checking. First, how certain are we of the time that Rachel arrived at the common?'

'Why do you ask?'

'The statements of Goodson, Brown and Warren referring to sightings of a woman and child near to the Bluegate gravel pit – could it have been Rachel?'

Wickerson thought for a moment. 'If I remember correctly, the clothing was wrong and wasn't there a mention of a pushchair?'

'Yes, but it was only a possible. I was going to ask whether Rachel had a pushchair. I didn't recall seeing one in the photos.'

'No, she didn't.'

'Right. But it struck me that all three of these people saw the same woman, and Brown claims that there was a dark-haired man talking to the child. If this was Rachel and Alex, who was the man?'

'If it was Rachel that's a bloody good question. But I think the sighting by Alafouza is the first sighting of Rachel arriving.'

'I'll admit the position of the car tends to suggest that Mrs Alafouza saw Rachel. But she could just have been repositioning the Volvo.'

'Anything's possible – but the clothing was wrong. I know descriptions can vary tremendously but two of them described her wearing similar types of clothing and those clothes aren't what Rachel was found in.'

'It was only a thought. Didn't you mention something about Alex being shy with strangers?'

'According to Andre.'

'Well, just suppose that this earlier sighting is Rachel. The fact that the child is speaking to this dark-haired man would tend to suggest that he wasn't a stranger.'

'I see your point but the clothing's the stumbling block.'

'But apart from the clothes, would it have been possible for her to have got from Balham to the common in time for these sightings, if she'd left for the common at the time Gerachty said he saw the Volvo drive off, which was 9.00am?'

'I've no idea – it would depend on the traffic. We could get the trip timed. It might be useful.'

'Just for the sake of completeness, it would be nice to find out exactly when she left for the common. Let's face it, top whack that journey's not going to take more than half-an-hour, so if both Gerachty and Alafouza are right, we've got a gap of 10 to 15 minutes, maybe more, where we can't account for her movements.'

'The house-to-house teams are still knocking on doors so we may get an answer to that question.'

'Talking about timing, what do we know about Mr McKern? He was the last person to see Rachel alive – could he have got from the windmill to the theatre in the time he says?'

'That's in hand. One of the skippers here, Tom Barr, is a bit of a cyclist and he's going to do the journey. Anything else?'

'Not really. It's just that having read through the statements and the messages it seems that we're chasing shadows. We haven't really got too much to go on, have we?'

'It could be worse.'

'Really? Let's hope this isn't a stranger attack. At least that way we know that there is a logical answer.'

'Have you still got a bee in you bonnet about Eric Roberts?'

'No, it's not just him, Mick, but you have to admit that his alibi isn't exactly the best. He must be worth another look. Apart from that, there might be an ex-boyfriend or someone lurking in Rachel's past.'

Much later that night, I sat in my living room and watched Andrew Nickell on television. He showed remarkable composure as he sat, with his son Mark close by, asking for help from the public in catching the monster who had robbed him of his daughter.

'Please don't let it happen again,' he said. 'Next time it could be someone else's daughter, or mother, or wife.' Rachel, he said, was 'a shining light, a bright star in my life and everyone else's who knew her. Her happiness with Andre was so real you could almost touch it. She can never be replaced in our lives and we can only hope to pick up the pieces. But our lives will always be less rich now that she has gone.'

He also made a plea for Alex to be left alone by the press so that those around him could try and help him somehow recover from his ordeal, and asked for their privacy as a family to be respected. Uppermost in his mind (although he didn't say so at the time) was the fact that Alex was the only witness to his mother's murder and the killer was still free. Alex's life could be in very real danger – kill the boy as well, and the only person who could identify the murderer would be safely out of the way.

Only one newspaper ignored the request. The following day, 22 July, the *Sun* ran a full-colour, full-face picture of Alex, the only living witness to a vicious murder, exposed for all to see.

With the murderer still at large, his state of mind unknown, the newspaper's action was beyond belief. But quite apart from the danger they had placed Alex in, it is a local requirement that children involved in, or witness to, any crime of a sexual nature are not allowed to be identified. The Press Complaints Commission was deluged with protests, and many weeks later Andrew Nickell received a phone call from the editor. He apologised, but said that the story had been 'too big to miss'.

Chapter 6

Very few children, if any, have ever undergone a similar ordeal to Alex's. There was virtually nothing with which to compare his experience, and nobody on the squad had any idea at that stage whether Alex was a bright little boy for nearly three, or totally incapable of communicating. Rather than risk further traumatising the poor little chap, the decision was therefore made that anything we did with Alex would be therapeutic rather than investigative. Nevertheless, if there was any help he could give us, we wanted to know.

While there is no strict age limit on a child being able to give evidence, a lot would obviously depend upon the circumstances under which the evidence was obtained, whether there was any question of it having been tainted, whether the questions were closed or open, and whether there was suggestion. In Alex's case, because he was so young, it seemed a reasonable assumption that he was going to be able to give us very little.

Two DCs from the squad, Nick Sparshatt and Paul Miller, had been deputed to look after Andre and Alex, who were staying with

Andre's mother in Hampstead, and find out as much as they could.

Nick Sparshatt, a veteran of the Brixton robbery squad, had a reputation for being a hard-nosed and determined detective. Tall, slim with short, dark hair, he was 40 but looked younger, and despite his reputation had a smiley, happy-go-lucky demeanour. He was a kind and generous man, had a good rapport with children, and was an ideal choice as Family Liaison Officer.

Paul Miller was early thirties, a little overweight and balding, with a personality the size of a mountain. He was on his first posting as a DC but, despite his inexperience, was extremely capable. Personal problems had left him to bring up his four-year-old son on his own, and he would always go out of his way to help others.

In the first few days after the murder, Sparshatt and Miller had been wondering how to help Alex describe the killer, and came up with the idea of using dolls that were normally used in cases of suspected child abuse. The dolls were like big puppets, and anatomically complete. Some were black, some white, some even had grey hair to represent a certain age group. The dolls were fully clothed but could be undressed quite easily.

Andre, Alex and the detectives drove to Hampstead Heath for their daily walk. Alex was more or less totally at ease with them by now. He ran around letting off steam, then joined the grown-ups sitting on the grass. The 'tecs took out the dolls and put them on the grass, and Alex was interested.

Paul Miller said, 'We need your help, Alex. We weren't there that day, and your daddy wasn't, either. You're the only one who can help us.

'Remember, Nick and I are policemen, even though we don't wear uniforms. Our job is to catch the bad man who killed your mummy. We need you to tell us about him.'

Alex listened attentively and watched as the 'tecs began to show him various dolls.

Sparshatt started with the granny doll and said, 'Was it an old lady who killed Mummy?'

Alex giggled and said, 'No!'

'Was he an old man?'

Again, an emphatic, giggled, 'No!'

Going through the various dolls, they established from Alex that the man was young and white. He was very definite about his answers, and even if the dolls were swapped around and the questions repeated, he was consistent and definite in what he said.

'There's no doubt,' Paul said to me, 'he remembers everything.'

The dolls only had grey or black hair, so they had decided to try again another day with a hairdressers' book of styles.

Then they moved on to clothing. 'What colour shirt was the man wearing, Alex?'

'A white shirt.'

'Was it a T-shirt like daddy's wearing, or did it have buttons and a collar like Paul's?'

'Like Paul's.'

As Sparshatt and Miller gently probed, Alex also revealed that the man had been wearing his shirt over his trousers, and that he had a belt over the outside of it.

'That sounds a strange arrangement,' I said.

'Alex was definite about it,' Paul said.

They had gone on to ask, 'What were his shoes like? Were they trainers like yours?'

Again, Alex was very clear. They were dark shoes.

'Was he wearing jeans?'

'No.'

'Shorts?'

'No. Trousers.'

'What kind of trousers?'

'Blue.'

Still playing with the puppets, Miller asked casually, 'And did the man take off his trousers, Alex?'

'No.'

'Did he even start to take them off?'

'No.'

Paul said to me, 'You should have seen his face – he was so pleased to have helped.'

I looked at him and said, 'I wonder if one day he'll be able to tell us the whole story.'

Just a few days later, Andre told us that he'd been walking on Hampstead Heath with Alex and an adult friend. They were in the middle of a wide open space with a view all the way down a hill. They were sitting on a bench talking when Alex suddenly became agitated. His face looked terrified, but there was no one near. Andre asked what was wrong, but Alex was speechless. When Andre looked in the direction Alex was pointing, he saw a middle-aged man walking a large dog. The man was wearing an overcoat and had what Andre described as a 'stooped over, almost crouching kind of walk. It was very distinctive – and it was this man that was frightening Alex.'

The friend steered the man in another direction and Alex relaxed again.

DI Wickerson told us of how he went to Andrew and Monica's house several days after the murder and, as soon as he walked in, despite the fact that Alex had seen him before, the little boy ran and hid and wouldn't come out.

The decision was made that Alex should be counselled by a child psychiatrist, and the name of a doctor called Jean Harris-Hendrix was put forward. In the first week of August, Dr Harris-Hendrix was visited by Andre and Alex, Rachel's parents, Andre's mother, and Sparshatt and Miller.

They were shown into the doctor's front room and invited to sit down. Paul said that the room was full of toys of every description, together with a little chair and coffee table at just the right height for a small child to draw or play on. All the adults sat down, except for the child psychologist, who knelt on the floor.

Dr Harris-Hendrix introduced herself and talked briefly about her work, which mainly concerned child trauma, accidents, violence and death. She said that even when her immediate work with some children was finished, they came back to see her regularly, maybe every year or so. She would often ask them to draw her a picture, she said. The drawing would have something to do with the original trauma, and it was interesting that on each subsequent visit, the story that the child told was always much more advanced. The original event was unchanged in the child's mind, she said, but the child was able to describe it with greater maturity, and the information was therefore more detailed. In other words, there was no reason why, one day, Alex should not be able to describe everything in perfect detail.

Alex sat at a little chair and table that were just at his level. Dr Harris-Hendrix knelt on the floor near him. He was listening as she explained to the adults that if Alex could speak about what had happened, it would actually be good for him. She'd found that children who'd gone through trauma could describe a lot of what had happened almost immediately, but were limited in what they could describe by their vocabulary and their understanding of the world at that particular time. At different stages of their progress through childhood, they would then often revisit the trauma, but with improved vocabulary and understanding of the world, which equipped them to describe it in more detail.

She said that these stages could happen at any time, and it might be many years before Alex was able give an accurate description of the killer. That wasn't to say that he wouldn't be able to recognise the man if he saw him now, just that with the fullness of time, he was more likely to produce details that would help pick someone out. Interestingly, she also said that it was very important for Alex to know that he had done his duty as a citizen, so that he would always look back and know that he'd done all that he could to help the police bring the killer to justice.

The psychologist suggested that a good way to start the session would be to ask each adult in turn to explain how they'd found out about Rachel's death.

Everybody spoke, and by the end everyone in the room was shedding tears – even Sparshatt and Miller, who might not have known Rachel before they arrived at the common, but had come to know her through the family.

Alex had been playing quietly and continued to do so as

everyone talked, but he was listening hard and taking everything in. As Paul said to me later, 'I think it was good for him to realise that everyone around him was still feeling terrible, too.'

Jean Harris-Hendrix started to talk more directly to Alex. She spoke kindly but firmly while he continued to play with the toys on the table.

She started saying things like, 'To think that you were there when that bad man killed your lovely mummy. It's a terrible thing to have seen; you must have been so scared, and you must have felt so angry that you couldn't do anything to help her.'

Alex was starting to bang things around on the table, making quite a lot of noise, obviously very tense, but at the same time he was looking at the psychologist with an expression of surprise on his face, as if he couldn't believe that an adult should understand how he felt. It was plain for all to see by the tension in his little body and the look on his face that Alex was reliving the events of 15 July. Andre said afterwards that it was agonising for him to watch, but it at least meant that Alex's memory of that day was not yet buried, and it meant that there was a good chance of him getting it all out of his system before it could fester and cause untold long-term damage.

She went on, 'But the bad man with the knife was so much bigger than you and so strong there was nothing that you could do. You were so small, there was really nothing you could have done, even though you must have so much wanted to help her, and stop him hurting your lovely mummy!'

The child psychologist put some little finger-dolls on the table. She gave Alex one which looked like a little boy with brown hair. 'Look,' she said, 'here's little Alex. Maybe one day, when you're ready, you might be able to tell us all about what happened to him on that very, very bad day. Your worst ever day. I'm sure that he remembers lots, because he's such a clever little boy.'

But it was clear that Alex's attention had gone. He had had enough for one day.

On the way back in the car, Paul drove and Miller was in the front passenger seat. Andre began to draw some cartoon figures with felt-tip on a sheet of paper. He drew a fat figure and a thin figure and showed them to Alex. He asked, 'Was the man who killed mummy a fat man or a thin man?' pointing at each drawing in turn.

'A thin man.'

Andre then drew two figures, both of them thin, one with a long pony-tail, the other with short hair. 'Did the man who killed mummy have very long hair like this, or short hair like Daddy, or ...' He pointed to Sparshatt. Andre had hardly any hair; Nick had a full head of hair.

Alex pointed at the sheet of paper and said, 'Short hair.'

After that, Alex lost interest in the game. It wasn't much, but it was a start.

[illegible] sheet of paper [illegible] figure and showed them to Alex [illegible]

[illegible]

A thin man.

Andre then drew two figures, both of a thin man, one with a long ponytail, the other with short hair. [illegible] have very long hair like the ponytail [illegible]

[illegible] full head of hair.

Alex pointed at the other and said, 'Short hair.'

After this, Alex's [illegible] the game [illegible] much, but it was a start.

[illegible]

Chapter 7

My first two days were over and the next few followed a similar pattern – in early to catch up on my reading of statements and messages, and checking the returned Actions. Then the morning office meeting, and out with different members of my team to TIE suspects, occasionally doing surveillance on one of the better prospects. Then back to Wimbledon for the evening meeting and a debrief with JB or Wickerson.

Some of the TIEs were better prospects than others, but eliminating people from the inquiry was not easy, and I knew from experience that it would only become more difficult as the days and weeks went by. In truth, we didn't really know who we were looking for, there being no eye-witness to the murder other than Alex.

Admittedly we had numerous photofit pictures provided by persons who had sighted suspicious lone males on or around the common, but this was a long way short of definite evidence of involvement in the offence. However good or bad the resemblance eventually turns out to be, you are usually in the happy position with a photofit of being able to link the person in the picture with the offence under investigation, so the investigator has somewhere to start from. Not so with the murder of Rachel Nickell.

An early policy decision had been made by JB to trawl the surrounding LIO (Local Intelligence Officer, the new title for collator) records for details of sex offenders. This encompassed the entire spectrum ranging from pathetic flashers to dangerous rapists and child molesters. General Registry and Method Index were also searched. The result of this line of enquiry was more than 100 potential suspects, all of whom needed to be researched, prioritised and TIEd. To the outsider, it might have seemed strange, bearing in mind the viciousness of Rachel's death, that flashers should be considered alongside the more virulent and violent sex offenders, but it is often the case that the sad, raincoated flasher will progress to more 'serious' offending.

I had the feeling of plenty of activity but not much progress. With our ever-increasing list of names, we were still really just chasing shadows. In a lot of cases, the nominees were unemployed, and one day to them was much like the next. Obviously, it took time to get through the list, and the more time that passed the vaguer people's recollections became as to their movements on 15 July.

The results of the second PM on 23 July came back negative, although Dr Michael Hill concurred with the findings of Doc Shepherd. It meant that we still hadn't a shred of forensic evidence that could link the killer to Rachel. There was still a chance, however, that the killer might have something in his possession that would link Rachel to him. The lab was kept busy examining mountains of clothing and knives taken from suspects in the hope that we would find something; anything that looked remotely suspicious was seized and submitted, especially from those men whose only account of their movements at the relevant time was, 'I was at home alone,' or 'I was probably in bed, I don't normally get up until gone midday,' or 'I've got no idea, I can't remember.'

My team was working flat-out, sometimes in their pairs, though at other times the entire team would be involved. The full team commitment usually came about when 'intelligence gathering' surveillance was required – in other words, when the suspect was followed to establish his habits, movements, other addresses and associates. This normally also involved the use of an SO11 team, and this was an expensive exercise since any overtime for SO11 would have to be paid for out of the 4 Area AMIP budget.

One such example was the operation we carried out on a man we nicknamed 'Elvis'. A photofit of a fine-featured man with collar-length, black, swept-back hair was produced as the likeness of a man seen in Parkside at just after 10.00am. Elvis was suggested as being a ringer for this particular suspect, and a check on his form showed that he did, indeed, seem to have progressed from flashing to indecent assault. His MO (*modus operandi*) was to approach lone females in the street or a park, claiming that he had just been attacked by a man. In truth, this wasn't strictly an MO; it was what our American cousins call a 'signature', something which the offender does for his own special reasons. In this case, the prime intent offence was flashing; his approaching of the victims and telling his little story was a refinement which strictly speaking wasn't necessary to flash and therefore was an addition which was obviously done for his own reasons.

Elvis would appear distraught and dishevelled and would say that the assault had been of a sexual nature and that he had been injured as a result. The female victim in most cases would be sympathetic and concerned. Elvis would then offer to show her his supposed injuries which would inevitably involve him exposing himself and then decamping. This was a fairly unusual method and a step or two up the scale from the basic opening of the grubby raincoat.

The FIB (Force Intelligence Bureau) was the second tier in our three-tier intelligence system, comprising the LIOs, FIB and finally SO11. The first tier was a Divisional resource and fairly parochial, the second an Area resource, and the third was Met-wide and dealt with the more serious offenders and offences. The FIB had reported a fairly widespread occurrence of similar offences. Some of the latest ones had involved the victim being assaulted, and because of his MO or signature, Elvis, a local man, was strongly suspected of this latest spate of what I called 'aggravated flashings'.

For a couple of days, the Ree-Gee and SO11 teams followed Elvis up hill and down dale, but, as is often the way with surveillance, the sum total of our efforts was that we watched him fishing on Tooting Common and repairing his car.

We eventually did arrest Elvis as a suspect for the Nickell murder, and also for other outstanding offences. The upshot was that he was alibied up to the hilt for 15 July and all the lab tests were negative, but there were other victims who were more than happy that he'd been caught.

Very often the investigation of a murder will lead to the solving of other crimes, which is a testament to the thoroughness of the system. I remembered my early days on murder squads back in the late 1970s in and around the Peckham and Camberwell areas of South London. The hue and cry that would be put up following a murder would result in the arrest and charging of all and sundry for an amazing array of offences. Search warrants would be obtained and addresses turned over. A binder for charge sheets unconnected with the murder would be kept in every incident room. In short, the murder squad would upset the apple cart and generally disrupt their everyday 'honest' thieving. We would haunt their pubs and clubs and make thorough nuisances of ourselves. It never took long for someone to ring in and drop a name. The generous side of my nature would have liked to believe that this phone call would be made for public-spirited reasons, rather than an intense desire to put an end to the frenzied police activity, but experience was a harsh master and always overcame optimism. There might be cynics who would suggest that a shrewd SIO merely used to stir the pond and wait to see what surfaced.

The number of potential suspects was increasing by the hour and the resources of the research and suspect teams were being stretched to the limit.

Mick and I were having a meeting with JB one or two days further into the investigation when he said, 'You know, the problem we have is that just about any male in the country over the age of 13 could be responsible ... yet there has got to be some connection with either the common or Rachel that will help us narrow the field.'

'I'm beginning to think a crystal ball would be handy,' I said.

JB smiled. 'I think we can do better than that. ACPO have suggested to me that the inquiry might be helped by an offender profiler.'

JB was nobody's fool. He had worked his way up to the top levels of the CID with a reputation for shrewd judgement, but I couldn't help wondering if he'd lost the plot a bit on this one. To me, the idea of using a psychologist to help solve a crime was the stuff of movies like *Silence of the Lambs*, not your meat and two veg of criminal investigation.

'I had a couple of lectures on it when I did the senior CID course,' I said, 'but that was all to do with offences of rape. I must admit, from what I saw, it all seemed a lot of mumbo jumbo.'

'In my experience, it stretches a little further than that, and for offences other than just rape,' JB said.

He told us that he became interested in what was then a relatively new concept when he led the investigation into the kidnap of baby Alexandra Griffiths from St Thomas's Hospital in South London a few years earlier. He'd become convinced that the kidnapper had some personal connection with the hospital, rather than being someone who'd just walked in off the street and snatched the baby. Sure enough, when the baby was found in Burford, Oxfordshire, 17 days later, after a tip-off to a newspaper, the female kidnapper was found to be a former outpatient who had acquired bogus nursing qualifications, and who was obsessed with getting a baby of her own, just as the psychologists had predicted.

JB said that he was equally convinced now that the expertise of a profiler might hold the key to solving Rachel's murder.

'ACPO seem to be taking it quite seriously,' JB continued. 'Other enquiries have been using it to link offences, as well as to help with possible suspect parameters. It's the last bit, it strikes me, that could be useful to us in our present situation.'

There was certainly something to be said for a system that could help us sort the wheat from the chaff, but I was still a little sceptical.

'I still can't say that I can see how it works, Guv.'

'I don't pretend to understand it either, but that doesn't mean that it's not worth a try.'

The debate continued in this fashion for a while, but JB had the last word and it was decided that the assistance of an offender profiler would be sought. We contacted the ACPO sub-crime committee on offender profiling, and they recommended a man called Paul Britton, who lived and worked in Leicestershire.

A clinical and forensic psychologist and head of the Trent Regional Forensic Psychology Service since 1986, Paul Britton had, we were told, for a decade been assisting the police in building up offender profiles and planning strategies for catching sexually deviant criminals. Recently, he had been asked to join FBI specialists in designing and teaching at centres in the USA and Britain. He had also been the organiser of the 1992 Trevi conference on offender profiling.

While JB arranged for Mr Britton to come down to Wimbledon for a meeting, I took it upon myself to learn a little more about the subject it appeared we were going to get involved in, and the man who was one of its main pioneers.

From an afternoon's research at Scotland Yard, I discovered that in the mid-1980s, quite independently of each other, a number of psychologists and police investigators had paved the way for the procedure that was now being called offender profiling – quite simply, a system of tracing criminals from the way they behaved while committing their crimes. Even when a criminal left no forensic clues at a murder scene, early work in the UK showed that they still left a form of behavioural 'signature'. All that was needed was a means of deciphering that signature.

Basic profiling work began in 1983 when Paul Britton had been contacted by police to help in a hunt for a sadistic murderer. In July of that year, a 33-year-old pet beautician called Caroline Osborne, who had separated from her husband, failed to return home to Danvers Road, Leicester, after an evening walk in nearby Aylestone

Meadows. She had left with her own Labrador, and another belonging to a neighbour. Thirteen hours later, her mutilated body was found near a local footpath. Her neighbour's dog was still standing by her side and growled when anyone approached. Her own dog had wandered home.

The corpse had been found on waste land near the Grand Union Canal. She had not been sexually attacked or robbed, and there seemed no real motive to the attack. However, the severity and multiplicity of the stab wounds suggested that she might have been tortured.

The head of Leicestershire CID, David Baker, contacted Paul Britton, although the profile he produced was not of great use because they had no real suspects to test it against. It was only after a second murder, in April 1985, that it all became of particular value.

A 21-year-old nurse called Amanda Weedon was killed close to the hospital where she worked and lived. She was three months away from her wedding; it was a Saturday afternoon and she had arranged to pick up the keys of her new home while her husband-to-be was at a football match. Her body was found in a hedge at the side of a path next to the Groby Road Community Hospital in Leicester.

The murder was similar to that of Caroline Osborne. Amanda's body was severely mutilated, and again there had been no sexual attack. This time, however, a small amount of money and a cheque card had been stolen from her handbag.

David Baker wanted to know whether the crimes were connected, and Paul Britton again agreed to help. He was shown post-mortem reports and photographs, scene-of-crime pictures, and aerial photographs of the two murder scenes. Paul was convinced that the same man had killed twice, and that he would be a local man.

Paul Britton produced a profile of the offender that defined what he expected in terms of the killer's age, occupation, personal background and sexual history. Mr Britton said that the killer was an athletic, young, local man employed in a form of manual work, unmarried, sexually immature and sadistic. The profile did not give police enough to arrest anyone, but it highlighted one of their chief suspects, 19-year-old Paul Bostock.

Bostock lived near to both murder scenes, at Beaumont Leys in Leicester. He was a fanatical bodybuilder and had been known to take long walks on his own. He was also said to have an apparent morbid fascination with horror, the occult and black magic. He was 6ft 5in tall, a large youth who stood out wherever he went. When his grandmother read a police appeal for information in the local evening paper, she immediately recognised her grandson as one of the people detectives wanted to interview. There was a family conference about it, as a result of which they all turned up at Blackbird Road Police Station in Leicester to clear his name. After just a short while of questioning, however, it became obvious to officers that his story just didn't add up.

Bostock was detained, and Paul Britton was asked to come up with a strategy for the interview that would enable the youth to admit to the murders. At first, the suspect was very reluctant to say anything and completely denied the murders, but when questions were asked according to Paul Britton's suggestions, the officers eventually gained a full confession.

When officers visited Bostock's home, they discovered his bedroom to be filled with swords, knives, guns and kung fu martial arts stars. Among the hoard of weapons seized was a flick-knife that was covered in dried human blood. There were also numerous drawings that Bostock had made showing women in black magic rituals, or being bound and tortured. He had also kept a scrapbook of naked women in the bedroom.

Bostock told detectives that he was 16 and had just left school when he came across Caroline Osborne. He had gone out jogging, complete with a flick-knife and a black magic pentagram in his back pocket. He had stalked the woman with her dogs and then tortured and killed her. Later, when Caroline was buried, he visited the cemetery to stand over her grave.

DCS David Baker became a staunch supporter of offender profiling, although he added that, without Paul Britton's help, he would still have got his man – eventually. The problem was, Bostock might well have killed again before police were confident enough to arrest him.

Baker's view was that profiling had its place in some murder investigations, especially in the event of more than one killing. It would not lead you to a suspect's front door, but if you had a good suspect, then it gave the confidence to devote more time to him than any others.

At the same time that Baker was involved in the Osborne and Weedon murders, there was another double killing in Leicestershire, that of 15-year-olds Dawn Ashworth and Lynda Mann. Again, Paul Britton played a key role in targeting the offender, a bakery worker called Colin Pitchfork. It was a historic investigation, because Baker became the first policeman to use the new science of genetic fingerprinting as a means of proving that Pitchfork had raped and killed both girls.

ACPO reports said that since that first phone call from DCS Baker, Mr Britton had been asked on many occasions to assist the police, generally in three main areas: one, the deriving of offender profiles; two, advising on appropriate investigative strategies to minimise harm, loss or damage to the community and to enhance the opportunity of apprehension in those cases where an unidentified offender had made threats or demands; and three, the formulation of strategies for interviewing both suspects and witnesses where understanding the psychological process of the person concerned was essential, but would ordinarily be outside the knowledge of a non-specialist interviewer. An example might be significant sexual deviation, aggressive or grandiose fantasy life, or other factors which would be likely to lead a vulnerable interviewee into making an unreliable statement.

Paul Britton had also given both oral and written evidence for the Crown and the defence in the Crown Court and Court of Appeal, and had been recognised by the courts as being an expert witness.

It sounded a good enough CV to me.

Chapter 8

We assembled in JB's office a couple of days later to meet one of the world's leading exponents of offender profiling.

A large, confident, but quietly spoken and rather genial-looking man, Paul Britton began by explaining that, for at least 120 years, psychological experimentation had been carried out on an empirical basis, so that by now there had been tens of thousands of studies dealing with every aspect of human functioning and motivation. This had become specialised into different areas, including Paul's, which was forensic and clinical psychology.

Paul explained later that phorensic psychology had evolved from two different strands: from the prison system, where psychologists had worked for many years with individual prisoners; and from the sort of special hospitals and regional secure units where Paul worked, where offenders with a mental abnormality were detained, assessed and treated.

Paul said that quite early on in his career, he had developed an interest in understanding the broader psychological aspects of offending and offenders. What was it that could make a person abduct, rape, kill, torture or abuse, he wanted to know. By what developmental processes were such people moulded?

When Paul had first described to DCS David Baker the psychological characteristics that later proved to match those of Paul Bostock and Colin Pitchfork, his analysis was only possible because of an understanding of both sexual dysfunction and sexually deviant personalities. This understanding had been gained both from the literature and his own hands-on clinical experience.

Paul said that although sexual psychopaths are relatively rare in the general population, there are quite a number living in prisons, special hospitals and regional secure units. Some are child molesters, others are rapists; a few have even committed murder. Each time one of these offenders is caught, more is learned about their general backgrounds, psychopathology and, especially, their motivation.

It is the psychologist's job, in painstaking clinical interviews, to probe and dissect, over and over again, their childhood, schooling, employment, living conditions, hobbies, interests, sexuality, relationships and offending patterns. These accounts are cross-checked with other sources, such as family, social workers, teachers, friends and court and medical records, until eventually a series of snapshots emerges of the person at various points throughout the offender's life. These personality structures and motivations are then compared with those of others who might not yet have killed, but share many of the same worrying characteristics. Comparisons are also made with 'average' men and women, who have developed in an 'ordinary' way, so that psychologists can determine what factors might distinguish them. It was this vast database of knowledge, Paul said, that he drew on when compiling a psychological profile.

When he had set about profiling Rachel's killer, his investigation had followed an established pattern. He'd needed to know every detail of the crime – the location, timing, weapon, victim, ferocity of the attack and degree of planning – because all say something about the person responsible. Only then, he said, could he start piecing together the answers to the four questions he asked himself at the start of every investigation: what happened, how did it happen, who is the victim and why? Only when he had these answers could he tackle the most important question of all – who was responsible?

I wanted to know how Paul had come to be involved with police work in the first place. He said that, despite having advised in numerous cases, up until 1990 it had all been done in his spare time, unpaid. His only proviso to the police had been that he remain anonymous.

That changed when he was invited to attend a meeting at the Home Office hosted by the chairman of the ACPO Crime Sub-Committee on Offender Profiling. The Association of Chief Police Officers is one of the most powerful bodies in British policing, bringing together the most senior police officers from the 40 or so forces in England, Scotland, Wales and Northern Ireland.

The meeting had been called to explore the future development of offender profiling. It had been recognised that the early results looked promising and it was time to chart the way forward. By the time the meeting broke up, it had been agreed that a strategy should be developed for the future that would expand the understanding and use of offender profiling.

Paul heard nothing more about this until the following year, when he received a phone call from DS Ian Johnston of the PRSU (Police Research Support Unit). Set up originally as a link between the Home Office and the police service to ensure that the police had what they needed, the PRSU had also taken on a research and development role, looking at advances in law enforcement around the world in training, equipment and technology. One of the areas that had come under scrutiny was offender profiling.

Johnston said that the PRSU wanted to research and evaluate offender profiling and, in particular, he wanted to follow up all the work that had been done over recent years to see if it was proving useful to police. Paul advised on what quality checks would be needed and, in due course, was invited to carry out the review.

In June 1992, Paul delivered his report to the ACPO Crime Sub-Committee.

He made a series of formal recommendations, the major point being that any future offender-profiling service had to be entirely owned and guided by the police. No one with a financial or a reputation-enhancing interest should be involved in its management. Even then, each and every profile should be followed up for accuracy. Paul thought it unlikely that computers could ever replace experienced psychological profilers in crime analysis, but his blueprint also included a police-managed, computer-based support system that could save time by doing a lot of the spade work by looking for the presence of certain factors in a crime and drawing particular conclusions from them.

Having carefully explored the processes used by detectives in their investigations, Paul also said that police officers could be taught to look for psychological clues at a crime scene. Despite problems he'd found with the accuracy of some profiles, many senior officers were warmly enthusiastic about the guidance that profiling had brought their investigations, and the new perspective that officers could gain when they looked at a crime scene.

With very little discussion, ACPO had accepted every one of Paul's recommendations.

The most important part of a forensic psychologist's work was knowing where to look and knowing what was relevant. Rachel's killer would not be the first man to murder a stranger in a park. Neither would he be the last. As each of these killers was caught, more was learned about their backgrounds, motivation and pathology. It was on these psychological foundations, he said, that the art of offender profiling was built.

For the next hour or so, Mr Britton listened intently to a blow-by-blow account of the investigation, only occasionally interrupting. At the end, he said, 'He left no evidence of himself?'

Wickerson shrugged. 'There was a shoe-print in the mud that could be important; also a few interesting witness statements. There were about 500 people on the common at the time. We're working through them and so far two people recall seeing a man washing his hands in a stream about 150 yards from the scene.'

'What do you know about him? Not the physical details, that's your department. I want to know how he looked ... was he frightened, was he anxious?'

'From the two accounts, I'd say agitated,' said JB. 'He was carrying a bag and stooped to wash his hands. Another witness saw a man running towards a council estate in Norstead Place. Different description, possibly a jogger.'

'You have no shoe-prints matching Rachel or Alex?'

'No.'

'What about elsewhere – in the grass, for example? Are there any other prints that don't show up in the photographs?'

Wickerson shook his head.

'You said Alex wasn't hurt?'

'Not badly. He was covered in mud. He did have minor cuts and bruises to his face.'

'He's basically left us bugger all,' JB said. 'I'm always optimistic, but my pool of suspects is every male in the country over 12 years of age. We have to narrow the field.'

'I think I can help you,' Paul Britton said. 'But first, I need to learn everything there is to know about Rachel Nickell. Did she work? What were her routines? What sort of person was she? Was she aggressive, or perhaps likely to ridicule people? Was she streetwise, or naïve? When confronted by a stranger, would she be reserved, or would she smile and make eye-contact? If threatened or attacked, would she be likely to resist? What relationships did she have? Did she have any other boyfriends besides the one you told me about? Did any previous affairs end badly? Did she ever work as a prostitute, was she sexually promiscuous?'

JB cut in. 'Mr Britton, she was a lovely girl.' He said it almost defensively, as if it was his own daughter's reputation under scrutiny.

'Haven't we got enough in the statements we've already taken?' Wickerson asked.

Paul Britton shook his head. 'Gentlemen, I need to know Rachel as well as if she were sitting in the chair opposite. What's she going to say? What's she going to think? How's she going to respond to any given situation? Only when I know her that well, can I hope to move a step closer to knowing her killer.'

Wickerson and I exchanged a quick glance.

'Imagine, for example, a young woman who tends to be sexually provocative – not deliberately so, perhaps, just unwittingly. Her appearance and mannerisms might draw sexual attention to herself. She might rather enjoy the feeling this gives her, and when she walks past a strange man who takes an interest, maybe she giggles and says, "Hello." This scenario has very different implications than if the same young woman tends to be self-effacing, and tries not to attract attention to herself or make eye-contact.

'You see, different women present different levels of vulnerability. I need to find out whether Rachel was a high-level risk victim or a low-level risk victim. When I know that, then I can begin to know how particular the killer was being when he chose her.'

JB said, 'I'm afraid we haven't got all those answers right now.'

'Then please have someone talk to her family and friends – particularly her parents and her boyfriend. Beware of their bias; they will be thinking only of her good points, they will have filtered out any negatives. But I do want to know everything about her, and in fine detail – that's what makes the difference. And I'll also need copies of statements, maps, the post mortem, photographs, and that home video you showed me of Rachel.'

JB said, 'You list the questions, we'll get you the answers.'

We drove Mr Britton to the common to inspect the crime scene for himself. We indicated where Alex's T-shirt had been found, and also the shoe-print. Mr Britton said that because the toddler was barely three years old, he wouldn't suffer from 'total traumatic amnesia' which would mask his pain. 'He will remember his mother's screams and the sudden silence,' he said. 'But whether he will ever be able to retrieve this fully and put it into words is another matter. The danger in drawing it out of him is that it could do further damage to his little mind.'

He also said that the fact that Alex hadn't been killed or harmed was an important indicator. It demonstrated that Rachel had been the specific object of the attack.

Several times, Mr Britton walked down to the stream where witnesses had seen a man washing his hands. He got us to move through the copse. 'How soon does a person become lost in the trees, I'm wondering?' he said. 'I'm looking for the various potentials of the place; where the trees and undergrowth provided cover or vantage points.

'You see, depending on the motivation – be it the most innocent courting couple seeking privacy, or voyeurism, stalking, rape or murder – I can understand to what extent it was a suitable venue or otherwise. What I can't do – not yet, anyway – is to see it through the eyes of the killer and a terrified young woman about to die.'

We asked Mr Britton about the significance of the folded piece of paper on Rachel's temple. Why did he think it would have been placed there, and by whom? The psychologist was unable to shed any light on it. He said the Americans might want to say that it was a token covering of the face, and therefore might be indicative that the killer and victim were known to each other, but he didn't subscribe to that view. The significance of the piece of paper remained a mystery.

The biggest unknown, however, was whether we were dealing with a repeat killer who would strike again. Paul Britton said that the chances were high. He said that even without a detailed analysis, it didn't look like a disguised domestic murder or an argument gone wrong, nor a one-off event brought about by a psychotic disturbance that wouldn't occur again.

It was Paul Britton's considered view that we were dealing with a violent sexual psychopath. The only thing he couldn't tell us was when he would strike again.

We couriered Paul Britton the answers he needed, together with photographs Andre had lent us, taken of Rachel during a holiday at the seaside. She looked as she did in the home video, laughing as she tossed back her long blonde hair in the wind.

I had written, 'There's no doubt that Rachel had a natural poise, self-confidence and charm. She was attractive, but not provocative. She didn't flaunt it.' By the time we saw Mr Britton again a few days later, he was ready to share his findings.

'I know how this killer functioned,' he said, 'and I know what drove him. I have seen the same impulse in other people I've interviewed and treated over the years. I know that this killing was a decisive stage in a fantasy process that had been rehearsed for years before it ever became a reality.'

Very few people, Paul said, are born sex attackers. The overwhelming majority of us have a strong desire to be approved of and liked by others. As we grow up, most of us become more effective in forming relationships and more confident in ourselves; we come to feel that people value us and want to hear what we have to say, just as, in turn, we come to know and value them.

At the same time, our sexual needs, too, are growing and developing. The two elements usually evolve in tandem, so that our expression of sexual desire is a reflection of positive social values. Our fantasies and mental images, naturally evoked by sexual desire and arousal, will involve consensual sex where courting and intercourse are enjoyed by both partners.

Paul said that there is, however, a small number of people who have basic and strong sexual needs, but who haven't developed social confidence and self-esteem. Perhaps their early attempts to form sexual relationships have caused them to feel hurt, ridiculed or rejected. And that rejection does not have to be real; the important thing is that it is believed to be real. Either way, it can lead people into a life of sexual inadequacy and loneliness.

A smaller sub-group of these people will feel a sense of deep resentment, and a need to blame others for what has happened. They believe that people have hurt them, and for that those people must be punished – but how? In their real lives they know that they have little, if any, control or influence over others. They begin, therefore, to develop a private fantasy world, a place where they have power and control, where they dictate what happens.

When this is combined with a strong sexual need, Paul explained, the fantasies of being powerful might come to be based upon the sexual control or coercion of those with whom they are having imaginary relationships. They do not value others because they themselves are not valued. The bitterness, anger and resentment can become all-consuming.

As their powerful visual fantasy system develops, it requires more and more energy and increasingly specific detail for it to be as rewarding as it was in the beginning. The fantasies escalate. Where an imagined sexual act might once have involved just minor degradation of the other party, it will need to become more and more extreme in order to produce the same level of satisfaction. This usually means increasing the degree of control, sexual violence and detail. In the end, such a person will have in his or her mind a set of images and scenarios that are intensely clear.

Paul explained that within sado-sexual or sado-masochistic fantasies, the range of activities is actually quite narrow. Some focus on verbal interaction and degradation. Others include the use of constraints and bindings; others still, lashes or whips. Some might even involve weapons such as guns, clubs or knives. In the fantasy, these instruments will be used in a scenario involving a particular sort of victim and setting.

Ultimately, the fantasy alone will not suffice and he may begin to rehearse some aspects of it in the real world. A man might fantasise about raping a woman of a certain age, with brown hair and green eyes. In his mind, he follows her home, maybe watches her bedroom window as she undresses, then enters the house, usually in a particular way. In his fantasy scenario, he will then either violently rape her, or perhaps have her initially resist, then become sexually aroused and have consensual sex. The pleasure provided by this fantasy will begin to wane.

'He takes parts of it into the real world,' Mr Britton said, 'cruising the streets and rehearsing. It sexually arouses him and gets the adrenalin pumping.'

Soon, however, he needs more than this, and begins to follow women. They don't necessarily look exactly the same as they do in his fantasy, but at least they are there.

'He will follow them at a distance. If they are with someone such as a boyfriend or a child, he will simply blot out that person in his thinking.'

This process might go on for months or more as he cruises the streets, sneaks into back gardens or walks up and down the back of railway embankments looking into bedroom windows.

Eventually, he takes more and more risks. He might leave home with a tool with which to break into her house, a piece of rope to tie her up with, or a mask. He might even go through the initial phase of breaking into a house before running off.

Ultimately, he might act out the entire fantasy, and what happens next depends on how the victim reacts. It's the one thing he can't predict; he can control how she acts in his fantasy, but he can't control how she reacts in real life. A victim might be entirely passive, and this might save her life. It might just as easily lead him to kill her, because he has no reason to stop. Or maybe she resists, verbally and physically. This might make him kill her, or perhaps he had been going to kill her anyway – it all depends on the blend of what happens in his fantasy and what happens in real life.

'You're saying that Rachel's killer was just such a stranger?' I asked.

'I am almost certain. Alex wasn't harmed. If it was someone well known to Rachel, there is a reasonable chance that the boy would know him too, and would have been dealt with.

'The sexual fantasy element of the attack and the location also suggest that the killer was a stranger. If he had set out to kill a woman he knew, he would probably have known where she lived, worked, or would be at a given hour, so he could have selected a site that gave him more time with her.'

The copse was a risky place to take someone, Paul remarked. Although the foliage provided a shield, it was perfectly possible that at any moment someone could interrupt him – yet the killer was willing to take the risk.

'Equally, he couldn't have known exactly how Rachel would respond, what she would say or do, but to some extent that was irrelevant. What was important was that she fulfilled the role that he had assigned to her in his fantasy.'

He would have known that the only people likely to be on the common at that time of the day were joggers, horse-riders and people out walking their dogs.

'Young women would be among them, some with children. From his point of view, a few of them would be provocative and titillating. He wants them, but doesn't possess the skills to begin an ordinary conversation, or to chat them up.

'But this doesn't really matter any more. He's grown angry and embittered over the years and this has fuelled his sexual fantasies. He's been rehearsing, stalking women and taking home the images he collects.

'But 15 July is an exception, because today his overwhelming urge and the opportunity to enact his fantasy will collide and combine in the person of Rachel Nickell. To her, Wimbledon Common is somewhere she can take her dog and child in safety. For him, it is a place where victims are to be found, where he has hiding places and escape routes.'

'Is he likely to have seen Rachel before?' Wickerson asked.

'Perhaps. He might even have loosely followed her. More likely, on 15 July, he is simply cruising across the common to one of his favourite hiding places or observation posts. Then he sees her – a young woman, blonde, attractive, maybe wearing clothes he finds arousing. She's exactly what he wants. Not only is she compelling, but she has a self-assurance and naturalness about her.'

I remembered the photographs and videos of Rachel, and the comment I'd made to Paul: 'There's no doubt that Rachel had a natural poise, self-confidence and charm. She was attractive, but not provocative. She didn't flaunt it.' Ironically, Paul was saying, the very qualities that made her so popular with others, enhanced her as a victim in this man's mind.

'She brings all of his past into sharp relief, focusing his bitterness and rejection. As he leaves the trees and moves towards her, he has a sense of complete omnipotence. You see, she is going to pay the price for all of those other women.

'Rachel perhaps gives him a friendly smile, but that's not on his agenda. He's passed way beyond looking to start a friendship or a relationship. By the time Rachel realises what's happening, it's far too late. She may look round to see if there is someone there to help, but there is no one. She and her child are at risk from this man and she doesn't understand why. Her terror would have been absolute.

'She drops Alex's T-shirt; it marks the initial point of contact. He controls her with the knife, prodding at her chest. It draws blood and he pushes her where he wants her to go. She's already in shock; this is something completely outside her experience. She might have talked about what she would do if accosted by a stranger, but what she discovers at the moment of the attack is that she has absolutely no strength and no resistance. It's not a case of being paralysed by fear, it's a passivity that overwhelms her.

'For the killer, this is not enough. This woman has to be humiliated. He forces her away from the path, separating her from her child. He cuts her throat and she can no longer scream. He forces her down on to her knees so that she presents herself to him in the fulfilment of his fantasy as a woman wholly dominated, degraded and humiliated. Then he stabs her again and again and again, long after she ceases to struggle.

'Still this is not enough. He wants more than just her quick death. He pulls her jeans and pants down and either just before, or just as, she dies, he forces a smooth object into her anus. This is not a sexual act in the ordinary sense, it's an act of violation. In his fantasy, sex is inextricably linked with degradation and the defiling of the woman. Rachel, by now, has fulfilled this role. Her body is left with her buttocks prominently displayed, so that anyone coming across her will see her in the most degrading position the killer could manage in the circumstances.

'His exhilaration is enormous. He never knew that he could achieve anything like this outside of his fantasy. This is real; he doesn't have to put energy into holding it in his imagination, he can see the blood on his hands, he's holding the knife. Whatever else happens, no one can ever take from him the memory of his sense of fulfilment and completion at that moment.

'But then, as the arousal and exhilaration begin to decrease, so the anxiety starts to establish itself. He knows that he has changed himself in a way that he couldn't predict. Until now, everything has been in his imagination, but he has suddenly stepped across a threshold that separates him from most of mankind. Whatever else happens, he will always be a sexual murderer.

'It isn't remorse that he feels; it's the knowledge of the outcry that's coming; he will become a reviled and hunted person, using all his wits and resources to protect himself.'

As Paul Britton sat back in his chair, the rest of us exchanged glances. JB broke the silence by asking if Paul's examination of the evidence had produced any sort of description of the killer.

Paul said, 'The offender will be aged between 20 and 30 years. You see, most sexual attacks are committed by young men. This killer was well into the practising process, but probably early in the killing process. He'd had time to develop one, but not the other.'

I jotted this down, hoping that it wasn't the sum total of Mr Britton's deliberations.

'He will have poor heterosocial skills,' he went on. 'An inability to relate to women in ordinary conversation.

'He will have a history of failed or unsatisfactory relationships, if any. And in addition to his sexual deviation, it will be likely that he suffers from some form of sexual dysfunction, like difficulty with erection or ejaculatory control.'

Paul said that this could have been an early contributor to his poor heterosocial skills and failed relationships. Perhaps an early attempt at sexual intercourse failed because he couldn't get an erection, or ejaculated prematurely, and he had been ridiculed. If so, there was no reason to think that the dysfunction would have improved over time.

'He will be attracted to some form of pornography which will play a role in his sexual fantasy life. Some of it will be violent and he will fantasise about similar experiences.'

Paul said that research showed that killers with higher intelligence tend to be better organised and more methodical. They plan their crimes in detail and exert greater control over their victims. In Rachel's case the attack was brutal, frenzied and chaotic.

He said, 'The offender will be of not more than average intelligence and education. If he is employed he will work in an unskilled or labouring occupation. He will be single and have a relatively isolated lifestyle, living at home with a parent or alone in a flat or bedsit.

'He will have solitary hobbies and interests. These will be of an unusual nature and may include a low-level interest in martial arts or photography.

'He will live within easy walking distance to Wimbledon Common and will be thoroughly familiar with it. He is probably not currently a car user.'

He said that all of these conclusions were drawn from what clinical psychologists know about men who kill women in this way.

Having considered the chain of events, Paul said that he doubted that Rachel's killer had murdered before. 'Generally, you find that repeat killers get more and more experienced as they go on. They refine their techniques and behaviour, leaving an ever-clearer signature.'

Even if Rachel was her killer's first victim, there was, however, a significant probability that he had a history of sexual offending, perhaps minor offences like indecent exposure or stealing women's underwear. Paul put the probability of this at 50 per cent – he said he didn't want us relying on it, but neither should it be discounted.

He said that it might seem a big leap, physically and psychologically, from exposing his penis to a woman and murdering someone, but this killer would have made that journey in his mind long before he did it in reality.

'He rehearsed it in his fantasies ... not every detail, because he didn't have a precise victim or location in mind. Rachel was chosen by opportunity, and killed because of the strength of his impulse on that day. There was no caution, no sign of self-preservation, no place prepared.'

Paul said that after the killing, the offender would have been excited and agitated, but this would have passed within a few days.

'Mercifully, the combination of the sexual buzz together with the shock and fear of discovery is likely to keep him quiet for a while, but eventually his urges will return and he will be drawn out again.'

'So you really do think he might strike again?' I asked.

'As a result of the strong deviancy and aggressive fantasy urges I've already described, yes, in my view it is almost inevitable.'

'What more can you tell us about him?' I asked.

'What sets this man apart is the deviant sexual fantasy that drives him. I have written an analysis that I'll leave with you. I've never done this for an investigation before, but it seems logical and a positive step forward.'

My only thought was, if it'll help, it'll help – but to my mind, the value of offender profiles and sexual fantasy analysis remained to be seen.

Chapter 9

Paul Britton's definition of a psychological offender profile had been: 'A description of an unknown offender's characteristics – psychological and personal – which include, for example: residential location, age, race, sex, occupation, education, intellectual functioning, marital or family status, psychosexual functioning, beliefs and cultural interests, previous offending or deviant activities, emotional motivational and mental health functioning, and anticipated further offence-related behaviour, degree of familiarity with the victim, the scene of the offence and the general area in which the offence occurred and the relationship between the offender's residential location and the scene of the crime. The psychological offender profile is an investigative tool which is used by the police and other agencies for the generation of new lines of enquiry, the prioritisation of existing lines of enquiry and the appropriate allocation of resources.'

The profile he compiled of the killer of Rachel Nickell was as follows:

(1) The offender was a stranger.
(2) He would be aged between 20 and 30 years.
(3) He would have poor heterosocial skills.
(4) He would have a powerful, deviant sexual fantasy life.
(5) He would have a history of failed or unsatisfactory relationships, if any.
(6) It would be likely that, in addition to sexual deviation, he would suffer from some form of sexual dysfunction.
(7) It was likely that he would be attracted to or use some form of pornography.
(8) That there was a 50 per cent chance that he would have a previous history of offending, although this does not necessarily require previous convictions or equivalent seriousness.
(9) The offence will have been rehearsed in general terms in sexual fantasy, but the precise details and victims will have been chosen on the basis of opportunity and driven by the strength of the offender's impulse on the day.
(10) That the offender will have been of not more than average intelligence and education.
(11) That if he is employed, he will work in an unskilled or labouring occupation.
(12) He will live in a relatively isolated lifestyle. He will be single, living at home with parents or alone in a flat or bed-sitting room.
(13) He will live within easy walking distance of the common and will be thoroughly familiar with the common.
(14) Probably not a current car user.
(15) That the offender, in the few days immediately after the offence, will have been excited or upset, but it will have subsided to its normal level thereafter.
(16) He will have solitary hobbies or interests, these will be of an unusual nature, this may include a low-level interest in martial arts.
(17) It is almost inevitable that this person will kill another young woman at some point in the future, as a result of

the strong deviant sexual and aggressive fantasies and urges.

The second part of Paul's advice was in the form of a Sexual Fantasy Analysis. It was stated that the offender had a sexually deviant-based personality disturbance, the detailed characteristics of which would be extremely uncommon in the general population and would represent a very small sub-group within those men who suffer from more general sexual deviation. From the source materials Paul also stated that he would expect the offender's sexual fantasies to contain at least some of the following elements:

(1) Young adult women. The victim was a young adult woman who had been subjected to an attack which, in addition to the purpose of killing her, continued after her death to include very deliberate sexual interference. The victim's 3-year-old son was present during the attack, but was not himself incorporated into the stabbing, undressing or sexual assault. The murderer showed no functional interest in the child. Paul Britton regarded this as demonstrating that the young adult was the specific object of the murderer's intention and would reflect his fantasy victim.
(2) The women would be used significantly as a sexual object for the gratification of the offender. The sexual aspects of the attack did not require the female victim to consent to the sexual interaction or to actively participate in sexual intimacy. The offender clearly used the victim as an instrument of his sexual gratification. In doing this, he would be displaying one of the central features of his sexual fantasy.
(3) There would be little evidence of intimate relationship building. The assault was completed from initial contact to the assailant's escape within a very short period of time. If the offender's sexual fantasy had included features requiring the development of intimate or quasi-intimate relationships between himself and the victim, this would

have been reflected in the assault. The victim would have been taken in or to a place which permitted prolonged interpersonal contact which would facilitate the sexual fantasy element in reality.

(4) There would be sadistic content, involving a knife or knives, as well as physical control and verbal abuse. The assault upon Rachel included a number of small prodding or pricking injuries to her chest and back that were not consistent with vigorous stab wounds. These were most likely to have been used as part of the process to control her movements and to direct her from the site of initial contact on the muddy path, where the blue T-shirt was found, towards the site at which she was killed. These wounds would have been sufficient to cause fear and distress to the victim. Rachel's fear and distress did not deter the assailant from escalating his attack from simple control to violent murder, nor did it extinguish his sexual interest. Paul expected the assailant to use verbal directions and threats to the victim in order to direct her adequately to his preferred location and to encourage her to adopt whatever physical position he required. These are demonstrations of sadistic behaviour. A person gaining sexual pleasure from sadistic behaviour in this way would show such themes in his sexual fantasy. The prominent use of a knife as an integral part of the assault indicates the preference and importance of such a weapon in an elective sexual fantasy.

(5) The submission of the female participant. The means used to control Rachel referred to above combined with the degradation evident in the disposition of her clothing and body as found at the scene of the murder are consistent with a sense of power being an important experience for the murderer. Paul expected this to be reflected as a requirement for submissiveness by the female participant in the offender's sexual fantasies.

(6) It would involve anal and vaginal assault. Rachel's jeans

and pants were lowered as far as her ankles, other aspects of the assault indicate that she was moved or rolled during the assault in order to bring her into the position shown in the scene-of-crime photographs with her buttocks prominently displayed. This facilitated a deliberate and careful insertion of some implement into her anus. Given that the entire assault and murder were effected within a very short time, it is clear that the offender attached considerable importance to this aspect of the attack; consequently, Paul would have expected to find similar activity featuring prominently in the sexual fantasies of the offender.

Paul Britton also expected that the offender would regard the genitalia as a unitary aspect of the female body, especially if he himself has only limited experience of heterosexual intimacy, therefore the sexual fantasy would be equally likely to include anal and/or vaginal assault.

(7) It would involve the female participant exhibiting fear-based compliance. From the reasoning laid out in points (4) and (5) above, the offender would have been excited by Rachel's fear, submissiveness and acquiescence to or compliance with his instructions. This behaviour by the victim would be so sexually rewarding to the offender that it would be evident in his sexual fantasies.

(8) Paul Britton expected there to be elements of sexual frenzy which could culminate in the killing of the female participant. The assault upon and murder of Rachel involved a vigorous physical and sexual attack upon her which was completed within a very short time. The stabbing and, in particular, the assault upon her throat was more vigorous than was necessary to kill or to render her unable to resist other aspects of the assault. Paul concluded from this that the vigorous expenditure of considerable energy that was necessarily present in the actual assault would be a recognisable theme within the sexual fantasies of the offender.

Paul also emphasised that he expected the offender's fantasies to include some of the above points but it was not a necessity for them to contain all of them. He also stated that there was no reason why the offender's masturbatory fantasies should be confined solely to these points. He also felt it important to break down the manifestations of sadism in point (4) to include the 3 specific manifestations so it conforms to the single point format in each of the other numbered elements:

The sadistic content would involve:

(4)(i) A knife or knives.

(4)(ii) Physical control of the female participant.

(4)(iii) Verbal abuse towards the female participant.

The reason for such a precise specification was to inform me that, if it ever became necessary, I could discriminate between the deviant sexual fantasies of other people which might include sadism but lack the elements specifically relevant in the fantasy system of the murderer of Rachel.

The main purpose of Paul Britton's offender profile hadn't been to give us the name, address and telephone number of a suspect. It was to be used as a springboard from which to start an investigation – i.e. a method of prioritising actions and the best utilisation of limited resources. There was an element of risk, of course, because if it turned out to be totally inaccurate, we'd have launched our inquiry in totally the wrong direction.

But based upon the problem that we had – this vast inquiry with a mountain of information, an ever-increasing number of suspects that were being put up and named – we were going under, we couldn't cope with the amount of information that was coming in. So, rather than just use a basic policeman's instinct, it was decided to use a more scientific approach. We sought this external expert opinion, and he gave us various parameters within which to work.

We had to have some process of filtration to reduce the amount of stuff that we were looking at, because it was very labour-intensive to research each particular suspect and each particular line of enquiry, and unless we had some sense of direction the inquiry was going to turn into a headless chicken. That didn't mean that we just totally ignored all the suspects that fell outside of these particular guidelines, rather that they were put on the back burner and we concentrated on those who fell within Paul Britton's guidelines. Nor was that to say that we adhered strictly to what Paul Britton said, because we extended the age. Paul was quite specific – he gave an age of between 28 and 30 for the offender, which might seem an amazingly accurate and very small window of opportunity, but Paul had his reasons for being so specific. His research, and that conducted in the United States, showed that that is the most common age range in which these types of offenders begin to offend.

There were various other reasons why Paul thought that this was a first offence, so we extended the age to five years above and below the range, we didn't stick to that very tight age limit, but extended it further.

At the beginning of August, an ex-FBI agent named Robert Ressler arrived in London to publicise a recently published book of memoirs. Ressler, we read, had co-founded with John Douglas the Behavioural Science Unit at Quantico, the FBI academy, and had pioneered the use of offender profiling in the USA. More interesting still, he specialised in the murders of women and, in particular, murders which took place in woodland.

We spoke to Mr Ressler's publicists and discovered that it was he who had originally coined the phrase 'serial killer'. He had joined the FBI in 1970 and spent his professional lifetime hunting mass murderers and, as Paul Britton did with sex offenders, then interviewing them to find out what made them tick. A pioneer of offender profiling in America, he had used the technique to arrest more dangerous and disturbed sex killers than anyone in the FBI's history. He had interrogated some of America's most notorious criminals, including Charles Manson, Ted Bundy (who killed over 50 women) and John Wayne Gacy (who murdered 23 men and buried them under his house). His last interview was with Jeffrey

Dahmer, the Milwaukee murderer who butchered 15 young men and ate parts of them for dinner.

It had to be worth having a chat with him. In this country, offender profiling was the province of shrinks and academics; Ressler, however, was an investigator – or, at least, a retired investigator – and the FBI were no slouches when it came to serious crime.

JB visited Mr Ressler at his hotel. The former FBI agent generously offered to provide an offender profile, and the results were astounding. Robert Ressler and Paul Britton had worked separately, yet despite some differences of phraseology, had arrived at uncannily similar conclusions. The murderer, Ressler said, was a fantasy-crazed local man, a loner, white, in his mid-twenties and sexually inadequate. He was also, he predicted, a man obsessed with violence, and a man who was programmed to kill again.

Chapter 10

At the next session with the child psychologist, she was in her usual position on the floor. Alex was sitting at the low table playing with the toys.

'Little Alex is doing so well,' Mrs Harris-Hendrix said, 'being able to help the big detectives with their job. He's been able to tell us so much. And he's such a clever little boy, I'm sure there is more he can tell us, too.'

Alex pushed his shoulders back with pride.

The questions started right back at the point when Rachel and Alex left the Volvo in the car park and began their stroll.

'Do you remember getting out of the car with Mummy on that terrible, terrible day – the day you probably don't want to talk about at all?' the child psychologist asked.

'And Molly was there!' Alex piped.

Between answers, Alex continued to play busily with the toys on the table-top. But whenever the questions reached a point that he must have found more difficult to think about, his playing became noisier. Sometimes he would bang the toys around as hard as he could to drown the conversation. If the question had come from Andre, Alex would sometimes climb up on to his lap and put his hand across his father's mouth.

The child psychologist said that this type of noise generation was very typical of the children she worked with. It was always loudest when she was talking about the things that were the most difficult for the child to bear. The decision, she said, was whether to bow to the child's natural desire to stop the pain by ignoring it, or to continue to press in the hope of releasing the poison.

After still more sessions, the approximate sequence of events of 15 July became clearer. Then it became a matter of trying to fill in the gaps.

'Alex, did you see the knife that the bad man used to kill Mummy?' Paul Miller asked him.

'Yes.'

Remembering the success they had had with the dolls on Hampstead Heath, Sparshatt and Miller had been trying to think of a graphic means of helping Alex to give more evidence. They were looking into the possibility of having a three-dimensional model made of the location of the attack, in the hope that it would make it easier for Alex to understand what was being asked of him. They brought in a tray, and presented it to Alex as if it was a simple party game.

Miller said, 'We're going to show you some knives so you can tell us which one it looked like.'

Alex smiled as Miller put the tray down on the table. On it were some ordinary cutlery, a bread-knife, different kinds of large kitchen knives, a penknife, and a hunting knife. Without a moment's hesitation, Alex picked out the hunting knife. It had been carefully chosen because its blade matched the shape of the murder weapon as established by Doc Shepherd after examining Rachel's wounds.

'What did the bad man do after he had killed Mummy?'

'He lay down to look in the water. The bad man washed the blood off in the water.'

An adult witness had reported seeing a man leaning over the

stream, apparently washing his hands. She also described the man as being dressed in the same clothing that Alex had described.

Over the course of the next few days, Alex began to divulge more of what he remembered of the man who had hurt his mummy. With someone of such tender years as Alex, it is a matter of the utmost importance not to put ideas into their heads by asking 'closed' questions. Young children are highly susceptable to suggestion, and care must be taken to ensure that they are interviewed properly, otherwise the details they reveal cannot be relied on as being untainted.

Ideally, such debriefings should be done under controlled conditions to preserve the evidential integrity of the child's disclosure. However, in this particular instance, this was not done in accordance with Met policy. There were several reasons for this.

First, and most important, was the welfare of Alex. The decision had been made that our approach should be therapeutic rather than investigative. It was our hope that by adopting this approach we might be able to minimise the long-term damage and trauma which would be inevitable for a child who had witnessed the brutal slaying of his mother.

Second, the question had been raised of Alex being able to identify anyone in the conventional way, either through photographs or by an identity parade. We hoped it wouldn't be necessary; the more material evidence that was discovered to link a suspect to the crime, the less emphasis there would be on any evidence which came from Alex.

Third, we were coming round to the view that, due to his age, it was most unlikely that anything Alex disclosed could be evidentially viable in court. The law on how a child gave evidence had recently been changed. Up until more or less that time, a child's evidence had to be presented 'live' in a crowded courtroom. It was intimidating enough for an adult, so for a small child it must have been terrifying. And for that child to have to do so in the presence of the person they might be accusing would makes matters worse. It was now easier to admit videos taken of children talking about traumatic events instead of them having to be physically present themselves.

The law does not impose a minimum age for a child witness. A child of any age may be called as a witness in any criminal case provided that the child is possessed of sufficient intelligence to justify the reception of his or her evidence and understands the duty of speaking the truth. A child's competency depends not upon his or her age but upon understanding. (R v Williams [1835] 7 Carrington and Payne's reports.) This was also reinforced in the case of R v Moscovitch, 18 Criminal Appeal reports 37.

However, there was a precedent which appeared to make Alex an unlikely witness. This was in the form of R v Wallwork 42 Criminal Appeal Reports 153, 160 CCA, when it was said to be most undesirable that a child as young as five should be called as a witness. Also in R v Ormerod and Wright, 90 Criminal Appeal Reports 91 CA it was said that there must be quite exceptional circumstances to justify the reception of the evidence of a child of extremely tender years. This case concerned a child of six. It clearly did not look too hopeful that a boy one month short of his third birthday would be acceptable as a witness. There was no doubt that Alex was a very bright child and had an understanding of things beyond his years, and the circumstances were certainly exceptional. However, Lord Lane had said that the younger the child, the more care the judge had to take before he allowed the evidence to be received, but the statute laid down no minimum age and the matter remained in the discretion of the judge. This was a judgment in the case of R v Z [1990] 3 Weekly Law Reports 113 CA.

It seemed likely that anything Alex disclosed was destined to be purely 'intelligence' rather than evidence.

About three weeks into the inquiry, Martin Long came up with the idea of getting the TSU (Technical Support Unit S011(2)) – a highly secretive unit that specialises in the use and convert installation of very hi-tech surveillance equipment – to put the birch tree under surveillance in case the murderer decided to revisit the scene of his crime.

I had worked with this very secret organisation quite often in the past, being trained by SO11 officers on various courses in foot and vehicle surveillance techniques, and made the necessary calls.

Very early one morning, Martin set off to the common with one of their DCs and an engineer to carry out a feasibility study. On their return, they came into my office.

Chris Hardy, the DC, said, 'We should be able to sort something out for you. There are a few technical problems but nothing Eric here can't sort. Availability of kit will be a major deciding factor and I think we're going to need quite a bit. The location means we can't install a normal time-lapse camera or video set-up.'

'What's the alternative?'

'A miniature TV camera in one of the trees opposite the silver birch and infra-red lighting. But we'll still need to get the signal from the camera to a point where we can record what's going on. The only viable way would be to use cables from the camera to a point where we can use a microwave transmitter to send the images to a receiver where they can be recorded. The snag is the distance we can transmit the signal – or rather, the distance we can't. Is there any chance we could get access to that windmill?'

'Depends what you want to use it for. It's open to the public as a museum.'

He turned to Eric. 'What about mounting the receiving dish on the outside and running cables down to those outbuildings at the back?'

'At a push, but it's quite a distance.'

'Can you square it with the windmill people, boss? We've really got to have somewhere in direct line of sight from the edge of the woods. You can tell them the receiving dish isn't that big.'

'I'll see what I can do,' I said. 'What about the outbuildings?'

'They're something to do with the rangers,' Martin said. 'I'll give them a ring.'

Eric, the engineer, was shaking his head. 'There could be other problems. There's the cables for a start. We don't want some inquisitive dog digging the bloody things up! And then we've got to provide power for the camera, the infra-red and the microwave. But I expect we'll sort it.'

I asked, 'If we manage to get the windmill and the outbuildings, is there any chance that in addition to recording the activities around the tree we could also have a monitor installed so we can see what's going on?'

'No problem. You're planning to make this a manned OP?'

'The idea's just occurred to me. If our killer does go back, it might be beneficial to try and nick him at the scene rather than subsequently trying to identify him from the video.'

Chris Hardy said, 'It's an expensive exercise, providing 24-hour cover. Not to mention ball-achingly boring for the poor buggers who've got to sit with their eyes glued to the monitor.'

Eric said, 'What about putting some ground sensors in to give a warning that someone's approaching the tree? You bury them in the ground around the tree and on the approach paths and they pick up the vibrations of people walking. The sensors are activated and they transmit a signal to a monitor installed in the OP.'

'I like the sound of that. At least it'll give the guys in the OP the option of only having to watch the TV monitor when the sensors go off.'

Chris said, 'And in the event of a suspect doing a runner, it'll also tell us which way he went.'

Something had occurred to me. 'If we do get our man up there and he does do a runner, he's got plenty of opportunity to lose himself on the common. Unless we get him right at the tree or very close by, we could be faced with the "Not me, guv" syndrome. Can we mark the immediate area around the tree with some sort of chemical trap that'll show up on his shoes?'

'Good idea,' Chris said, 'but not our department. Have a word with Scenes of Crime.'

Over the next few days, I visited the TSU offices at Lambeth a number of times to finalise arrangements and obtain the requisite authorities to proceed. Eric and Chris were determined to solve the various logistical problems and whenever I turned up at Lambeth they were beavering away in the workshops.

At 3.30am the following Monday morning, I drove into the yard at Wimbledon ready to brief an assortment of officers on the installation of our surveillance equipment. Obviously, my team were there, together with a fairly large contingent from the TSU who were to perform the nuts and bolts of the installation. I had also arranged for two units from the TSG (Territorial Support Group) to be present, to seal off the area from the prying eyes of any members of the public.

We drove in convoy on to the common and parked as close as we could to the trees in order to avoid inquisitive eyes. We would have looked a strange sight as the mysterious equipment was surreptitiously unloaded – spades, metal equipment boxes, cables, heavy-duty batteries, ladders and, strangest of all, a crossbow.

We spent the next three-and-a-half hours crawling through the undergrowth burying batteries and other bits and pieces. Chris and his technicians got the slightly less grubby job of installing the miniature camera in the branch of a tree, and fitting the infra-red lighting and the microwave transmitter.

Connecting and powering the equipment in the woods obviously required cables to be laid. The distances between the various bits and pieces were not inconsiderable and to bury the cable would have been extremely time-consuming, and courting disaster from inquisitive dogs. The solution was therefore to run as many of the cables as possible over the top of the trees, and that was where the crossbow and several hundred yards of fishing line came in. Chris fixed the line to a bolt and fired it over the tree tops; the cable was then attached to the other end of the fishing line and hauled into position.

As a final touch, we put out chemical traps. If we challenged somebody at the scene and he legged it through the undergrowth, he could always say, 'It wasn't me.' But we could say, 'I don't think so, because the stuff on the bottom of your shoe is the stuff we put down to mark it.'

The installation on the common was completed by just after 7.30am; that just left the equipment that had to go in the windmill and the outbuildings, and this part of the task was completed over the next 48 hours. By the Wednesday evening, we were up and running.

The 'ops room' was about 10ft square. It contained just a table, a couple of old armchairs and an electric heater, but compared with some of the places that I'd had to use as OPs in the past, it wasn't too bad. It was to become a second home to the half-dozen young TIs (Trainee Investigators, all seconded from local nicks on the old 4 Area, and entirely separate from the main inquiry team) who were to man the post for the next month. As the days went by, the team started to bring in items like a portable TV, a microwave oven and a radio to make the long tours of duty more bearable.

The end result of the hundreds of man hours expended on the surveillance operation was that, several weeks later, in the early hours of the morning, the ground sensors went off, police officers descended on the area, and a group of people were apprehended near the tree. They turned out to be three students out of their brains on LSD. The incident was immediately reported by the *Sun*, and that put an end to any further covert surveillance.

Chapter 11

Over the course of the next couple of weeks, Alex began to talk still more about the day of the murder. Andre, as a caring and concerned father, was anxious to minimise further trauma and upset. This was totally understandable, and Nick and Paul were instructed to allow Andre to deal with things in his own way. This approach was not in accordance with Force policy, but it was deemed to be the best way forward.

A bombshell was dropped on the evening of Monday, 10 August. Nick had gone to see Andre at the North London address of his mother and I was sitting in my office late that afternoon going through the latest bunch of TIEs. The phone rang.

'Get up here quickly,' Wickerson said.

I took the stairs two and three at a time and opened his office door to find Sparshatt, Wickerson and JB in conference.

'Have a listen to this, Keith.'

Wickerson nodded for Sparshatt to repeat his story.

'I went over to Andre's mother's address today. It was just a routine visit to make sure they were all right.' Nick was grinning like a schoolboy who knew a secret that you didn't. He was clearly enjoying the moment. 'The bottom line is that Alex has named Eric as being the killer.'

'What? Eric Roberts?'

'Yeah.'

'Fucking hell! That's a turn-up for the books!'

I sat back to digest what he was saying. Eric Roberts had already been TIEd. I remembered that he lived with a woman called Margaret and they had a child of Alex's age called Dave. We had been contacted by different members of the public who remembered having seen a man answering his description in Rachel's company at the local swimming pool and at the children's playground on various occasions, and Andre had told us about Rachel's friendship with Roberts some time before.

Eric met Rachel at the sandpit at Clapham Common, and on his own admission was infatuated with Rachel Nickell. At the time, I'd had the alarm bells ring in my head, because of the policeman's instinct and the statistical probability that this was not a stranger attack.

Then we found out that Eric Roberts would occasionally come round and call for Rachel Nickell and they would take the kids and the dogs and go walking along Wimbledon Common together. He'd looked quite a good suspect, but he was very strongly alibied – albeit by his wife, but she would rather cut her arm off than tell a lie. She said Eric was in bed on the morning of the murder; she went out at ten past ten and was back in by just gone eleven. Eric was still in bed when she came back; she had the car, so he couldn't have driven to Wimbledon Common.

Now I suddenly also remembered the story of Roberts going up to Alex and Andre in the Windmill car park on the day that they had been taken back to the Common. He had been taken there to show us where he had walked on the one occasion that he and his son had gone there with Rachel and Alex. When Alex had seen Roberts that day, he had become visibly distressed. And if Alex was now saying ...

Various questions immediately started to pop into my head, and judging from the pensive expression on Wickerson's face, he was having similar thoughts.

'How did this bombshell come to light?' I asked.

'Andre said that Alex had named Roberts the day before. I asked him how the conversation had come about. He said that he had made a note of what he and Alex had said and he asked Alex the same questions this morning while I was there.'

'Come on, Nick, this is like pulling teeth – what did he say?'

Andre was trying to arrange social outings for Alex for the week ahead. 'Do you want to see Katie?' he asked, naming a little girl from Alex's class who had come and played with him a few days before.

'Yes,' said Alex, without looking up.

'Do you want to see Anna?' he mentioned the daughter of one of Rachel's friends.

'Yes,' said Alex, still not looking up.

Then Andre named the little boy that Alex and Rachel used to see during the day together with his father. 'Do you want to see Dave?' he asked.

Alex said, 'No.'

It occurred to Andre that the other little friends he had mentioned would be accompanied by their mothers or maybe a nanny. Alex was still fearful and mistrusting of all men that he did not know well, and Andre wondered if maybe it was the fact that they'd have to see Dave's father which was causing a problem.

'Are you afraid of Eric?' he asked Alex.

'Yes.'

Andre suddenly thought that perhaps the man who killed Rachel resembled Dave's father.

'Did the man who killed Mummy look like Eric?' he asked.

'Yes.'

'Do you think it was Eric?'

'Yes.'

The next day, Sparshatt was at Andre's mother's house on his own. Alex was in a particularly receptive mood and the house was quiet.

Andre explained what had happened in his conversation with Alex. He said he believed what his son was saying, but at the same time stressed that he might only have been describing someone who resembled the man who killed his mummy. It was natural enough that Alex wouldn't want to see the father of his friend if he 'thought' that he looked like the man who'd killed his mummy, but it was not the same as saying that this was the man himself.

While Andre was talking, Alex came over and joined them. He was smiling happily.

Andre asked Alex the same questions that he had the day before. Once again, this time in front of Nick Sparshatt, he came up with exactly the same answers.

Andre said, 'Alex, do you want to see Dave?'

Alex said, 'No.'

Sparshatt said the toddler's mood changed almost immediately and he lowered his head and stared at the table.

Andre said, 'Are you frightened of Eric?'

'Yes.'

'Does Eric look like the man who hurt Mummy?'

'Yes.'

'Do you think he's the man who hurt Mummy?'

'Yes.'

'Was it Eric?'

'Yes.'

I looked at Wickerson and we both winced. 'What did you make of Alex?' I asked.

'He seemed upset and he spoke very quietly, but I could hear him clearly.'

'Did you get a chance to ask him any questions?'

'No, as I said he seemed upset, so I didn't pursue the subject.'

Wickerson stood up and stretched. 'This is a real can of worms, isn't it?'

'How sure can we be about what Alex is saying?' I asked.

'Andre says he's totally confident about the detail of everything Alex has ever had to say,' Sparshatt replied.

'Yes, but does he believe him when he says that it's Eric?'

'He says that if he says he thinks it's Eric, then he has to believe him. However …' Sparshatt paused, looking thoughtful for a moment. 'I did ask him: "If you had a shotgun in your hand and Eric Roberts walked in front of you right now, would you pull the trigger?" '

'And he said …?'

'He said that to be 100 per cent sure, he needed someone else to come up with one piece of material evidence, no matter how small, to confirm what Alex was saying.'

I said, 'The question is, where do we go from here? Evidentially it's not worth a light; the questioning was hardly open, was it? The Child Protection Team would throw a blue fit about asking a three-year-old questions in that manner.'

'So what are we left with?' Wickerson said. 'Roberts is alibied, forensic isn't likely to be of much use and can we be sure that Alex actually means that it was Roberts, and not just someone who looks like, or reminds him of, Roberts?'

'Let's look at this logically. Let's assume that Alex is right. How do we go about proving it? If we go out and arrest him on the strength of what Nick has just told us he'll have to have a brief and we could end up with a no-reply interview.'

'Exactly, and that will take us no further forward,' Wickerson continued. 'Softly, softly, catchee monkey – we don't want to risk showing our hand too early.'

'What about his car, Guv?' asked Sparshatt. 'We haven't looked at that, and if he did it, chances are he'll have Rachel's blood somewhere on the inside.'

'Even if we found gallons of the stuff, he'd still have outers, wouldn't he?' I said.

'He'd have to explain how it got there.'

'He wouldn't have to utter a dickie bird. He could just wait till it got to court – if it ever did – and then say that Rachel was a regular passenger and on one occasion she had had a nose bleed, or had cut her herself on one of their walks, and we're back to square one. No, I think the only way forward is to have another crack at his alibi.'

'I agree with you, Keith,' said Wickerson. 'If we can find a chink in his armour that'll give us something to work on. We'll try again to see if we can find any sightings of his motor on the morning.'

'I've got to be truthful, Mick, I'm more than just a little unhappy with his version of events for the morning of the 15th.'

'Why?'

'He's got a dog, or a couple of dogs, hasn't he?'

'Yeah, one or two – he's certainly got a Doberman.'

'Well, I used to have an Alsatian, and the first thing she'd need in the morning was a run to answer a fairly urgent call of nature. Now if I've read Roberts's account correctly, he reckons that he took the dog walkies in the early evening of the 14th, and then not again until well after midday.'

'What's your point?'

'That he lives in a first-floor flat with no garden so the dog couldn't be just let out unsupervised for a crap. Which means the poor animal spent well over 12 hours locked up in the flat – my dog would have gone berserk and done a dirty protest all over the floor. Roberts doesn't make any mention of that, does he?'

'No, he doesn't – so what you're saying is that someone must have taken the dog for a walk?'

'Exactly. Margaret didn't do it, so that only leaves Eric. And if Eric did it, it means he was out of the flat during the morning and is therefore telling lies.'

'I can see what you're getting at, but how on earth do we adduce evidence of a Doberman's digestive system to prove someone's telling porkies?'

'I'm not talking about evidence, I'm talking about finding a chink in his armour which will help us prise him open a little bit. I reckon we should put an OP on Eric's flat and see exactly what his morning routine is. If it turns out that Rover gets his morning constitutional at the same time every morning and it contradicts his account for the 15th, then there's our chink.'

'Good thinking…'

'Then, of course, poor old Eric might just look like the killer,' I said, 'or little Alex might be totally wrong. So we're going to give the OP idea a run, yeah?'

'Seems like we haven't really got much choice under the circumstances,' said JB. 'But I think we should keep this Roberts thing as quiet as possible until we can either firm it up or discount it. If little Alex has got it wrong, disclosure is going to cause us one hell of a problem.'

This implication hadn't really occurred to me until JB mentioned it, but he was right. In the event that somebody else was responsible and was charged, Alex's comments concerning Eric would have to be disclosed to the defence team. Any defence barrister worth his salt would claim that his client must be innocent, based upon what Alex had said. The evidence of a 2-year, 11-month-old boy would suddenly become the ultimate truth. Ironically, were the prosecution to attempt to adduce such evidence, the defence would take entirely the opposite view. Still, despite the fact that Alex was so young and the circumstances under which he had named Roberts were questionable, we still had a duty to investigate thoroughly and effectively to resolve the issue.

In the sessions with Dr Harris-Hendrix that followed, they began to use the name of Eric Roberts. Instead of saying, 'Did the bad man speak to Mummy before she was killed?' the question would be phrased, 'Did Eric speak to Mummy before she was killed?'

Over a period of days, Alex was again taken through what had happened, from getting out of the car, to seeing the man approach them, and to his mother being attacked.

Alex answered readily enough but, significantly, he never used Eric Roberts 's name himself. Never once did he say specifically, 'Eric was wearing a white shirt,' or 'Eric had a knife.'

When the child psychologist asked, 'Alex, do you know the name of the man who killed your mummy?' he never gave an answer.

By now, Alex had confirmed that Rachel had exchanged some words with her killer before she died, but it was impossible to work out from Alex's answers whether this was one word or a conversation.

Alex had also confirmed that the killer was wearing the same clothing that he had previously described on Hampstead Heath: a white shirt with buttons and a collar, worn outside blue trousers which weren't jeans, and dark shoes.

He said that the man had a black bag, and Mrs Harriman, the witness who had seen an identically dressed man nearby only minutes before Rachel was killed, had also said that he was carrying a black bag. Everything Alex was saying had been confirmed by adult witnesses, and it was only his identification of Eric Roberts that was less than decisive. Why, everybody wondered, didn't he just come out with it and say, 'Eric killed my mummy.'?

In answer to another question, Alex again confirmed that the killer had walked away in the direction of the stream – but still without putting a name to him.

'Did Eric run away, or did he walk away?'

'Walked away.'

He said the killer had lain down to 'look' in the water, and from there had got up and walked away towards the cemetery.

The sessions with the child psychologist continued with our officers present. Alex seemed to respond best, they told me, when it was Andre who asked the questions. The pattern had therefore developed that once Andre understood what was being asked, he would take over, with Jean Harris-Hendrix occasionally guiding.

'I know how much you must remember your worst-ever day,' she said. 'The police are here to catch the bad man who killed your lovely mummy, and to put him in prison where he won't be able to harm anyone else again.'

Alex had watched her face as she spoke, and the last sentence provoked a nervous smile.

We still knew nothing of what happened in the minutes before the attack, so had agreed with Andre that he'd start with the most basic questions.

'Alex, who was with you the day that Mummy was killed?' he asked.

'Molly,' he replied, his attention more with the toys on the table. He looked very agitated, Nick said.

'Alex, did the man who killed Mummy have a dog with him?' Andre asked.

'No.' Alex didn't look up from his drawing.

'Did the man who killed Mummy have a bike?'

'No.'

'Was the man who killed Mummy carrying anything?'

'A bag.'

'Alex, do you remember what colour the bag was?'

'Black.'

'What was in the bag?'

'A knife.'

Andre had been briefed to avoid asking Alex questions that he could reply to with a simple 'Yes' or 'No'. He managed this well, and Alex's answers would often give a little more than was demanded by the question itself, which confirmed to all present that not only had he understood the question, but also that he could remember the small details of events.

In these first few sessions, it was often only possible for Alex to concentrate his mind for long enough to answer a handful of questions before he ran out of patience and simply clammed up.

On this occasion, while the child psychologist took over from Andre and was talking to him, Alex began stabbing hard with a pencil at the paper he had been drawing on. The officers described his movements as 'manic' and said there was a frighteningly glazed look in his eyes. Alex had become really violent.

Andre asked him to calm down, but the boy turned to his father and stabbed the pencil at his face. Andre told him to stop, which he eventually did, but the pieces of paper he had been drawing on were deeply indented with pencil stabs.

Dr Harris-Hendrix said afterwards that this behaviour had absolutely convinced her that Alex had seen the attack on his mother. This way of acting out an event is called 'post-traumatic play'. Apparently, it is a common reaction in children who have experienced trauma to want to act out the event again afterwards. Sometimes, they even want to turn the event into a kind of game.

On Saturday, 15 August 1992, a further meeting took place at Andre's mother's home in North London. Present were Dr Jean Harris-Hendrix, Andrew and Monica, Andre and Alex, and the detectives. After about 20 minutes, it became obvious that Alex did not want to talk about the events of 15 July and it was decided to turn the video off.

Shortly afterwards, Alex was drawing and looking at pictures of 'bars' on a window. Earlier, we had tried to explain to Alex what a prison was and, to assist, pictures were drawn to represent a cell.

Whilst Alex was looking at the drawing, Andrew Nickell leant across to Alex and said, 'Alex, who shall we put in the prison?'

Alex said, 'Eric.'

'Who hurt Mummy?'

'Eric.'

'How did he hurt Mummy?'

'With a knife.'

'Did Eric talk to you?'

'No.'

'Did he talk to Mummy?'

'Yes.'

'Did he talk to Mummy for a long time or a short time?'

'Long time.'

'Now, Alex, it's important you tell us if you are talking about Eric who hurt Mummy or a person who looked like Eric. Is it right it was Eric or wrong?'

'Right.'

'Alex, we have, I think, has more question for you and then we will go to the party.'

I said, 'Alex, is Eric the daddy of somebody?'

Alex did not answer, so Mr Nickell repeated the question.

Alex said, 'Dave.'

I began to formulate an idea which would progress this particular line of enquiry, aware that the outcome would be for intelligence rather than evidence, as the methods I was proposing would almost certainly render any information inadmissible. Quite simply, I suggested that electronic listening devices should be installed covertly in Roberts's address, and steps taken to stimulate conversation between Margaret and Roberts on the subject of Roberts's movements on the day of the murder. The authorities required for such steps are not given lightly, however, and the logistics of such an operation are enough to dissuade casual use.

Were we to go ahead with the scheme, it would require us to get the Robertses out of their flat and under our control on at least three occasions – the first to allow the TSU access to the premises in order to carry out a feasibility study; the second, at a later date, to install the required equipment; and the third, obviously, to remove it. Access would be no problem; the professional abilities of the TSU are beyond compare and you would never know that they had paid you a visit. The next step would then be to act as the catalyst to generate the conversation. This, I proposed, would be achieved by bringing both of them in for further questioning and then releasing them.

My report was minuted by all of the 4 Area hierarchy and then taken by hand to the Assistant Commissioner, Specialist Operations, for his consideration. AC Veness was an extremely experienced, intelligent and very practical senior officer and his approach to proactive policing was very supportive. If an operation could be justified within the law, and the circumstances warranted such extreme steps, then Mr Veness would support it. This made him one of that very rare breed, a popular and highly respected senior policeman. If, however, Veness refused authority, then I knew that it would be for a very sound reason.

The plan was well received in principle, but the Assistant Commissioner wanted every other avenue explored before allowing us to progress to using sophisticated technical support. When the report found its way back to my desk, the lengthy and detailed minute added by Dave Veness clearly showed that he had considered the application from every possible angle.

We now reverted to the straightforward OP idea, and got two of the chaps to keep observation on Roberts's house to see if we could establish his routine. My thinking was that if he regularly took the dog for an early morning constitutional, then his apparent failure to do so on 15 July would leave him with a bit of explaining to do.

As it turned out, our covert observations from a school premises opposite over the period of two or three weeks proved one thing and one thing only: Eric Roberts was not one of this world's go-getters. Sure enough, he'd take the dogs out at 8.00pm in the evening, but then wouldn't take them out again until 2.00pm the following afternoon. In addition, none of our house-to-house enquiries in his street, nor our other extensive enquiries on the common, produced any sightings of him or his car anywhere where he or it shouldn't have been.

At the next session with the child psychologist, Paul Miller said, 'Alex, do you know the name of the man who killed your mummy?'

He had been putting the question to Alex time and time again, gently and without pressure – but without response.

The child psychologist said, 'Alex, you know that these big detectives are there to catch the bad man. And you know that anything you tell them helps them with their job. I am certain that little Alex has something he wants to say to these two big detectives. He has got something on his mind that is just between them.'

'It's all right, Alex,' Andre said. 'You can tell everyone what you've told me.' But it didn't make any difference.

Andre said to Sparshatt, 'I think maybe it's that he likes you guys too much. I don't think he's convinced that you're tough enough to deal with this monster.'

They talked to Alex about how there weren't just these two policemen, but lots and lots of them – and they had handcuffs and truncheons and police cars, and cells with big steel doors and locks to put the bad man in so he could never get out.

'Alex, do you know the name of the man who killed your mummy?' Paul Miller asked for what seemed like the hundredth time.

Again, no answer.

Andre said, 'Alex, I'm going to write the name of the person that you told me on a piece of paper. And you, because you are such a big boy, you can read it out to the detective.'

Sparshatt glanced at Andre. He knew Alex couldn't yet read.

Andre wrote a word on a piece of paper, something completely unrelated. He gave the piece of paper to Alex. 'Go and read it out,' he said.

He took it towards Paul Miller, but turned back towards Andre as he 'read' out the name.

'Eric?' Alex said quizzically.

There was so much uncertainty in his voice that Andre said he now felt far from certain.

Once again, we were back to chasing shadows.

Chapter 12

Not only was the problem of Alex's revelations occupying our attention, we were also dealing with an ever-increasing list of potential suspects, as well as trying to make sense of the confusing accounts given by persons on and around the common. Occasionally, however, a suspect would emerge who would justify exceptional activity on our part.

One Tuesday lunchtime towards the end of August, JB came to see me in my office.

'Something Interesting has just come in,' he said. 'I think you and your team will have to go to Liverpool. Grant Johnson had an enquiry concerning a potential suspect ... nothing world shattering, just routine. Then this morning a call came in from Merseyside Police. It seems that the suspect is currently on police bail for a rather nasty aggravated burglary. The suspect broke into a young girl's flat and raped her at knife-point.'

'Bail? What are they waiting for – forensic?'

'Apparently so. It looks like they've probably now got him on DNA but the results are not totally conclusive at the moment.

They're waiting for another probe.'

'So what's the connection with Wimbledon?'

'That's where we've got to be a little careful with this, as the source of the information is a bit sensitive.'

'A snout?'

'Yes, but there's no direct connection between the snout and the suspect – it was an eavesdropped conversation. It would seem that the suspect was talking about his problems with the rape allegation and just out of the blue he said that he was worried that he might get dragged in for the Wimbledon murder.'

'That's a strange thing to say – how good's the source?'

'According to Liverpool, he's totally kosher.'

'Was anything else said?'

'Apparently he then said something about being there at the time. Johnson has found out that this man was indeed living and working in the Wimbledon area in July.'

'It's looking better and better. So what's the plan?'

'A little intelligence gathering on Merseyside to find addresses and associates – usual sort of thing.'

'How long do you want us to give it?'

'A few days, just to get the feel of the man. I'd like you to go today.'

Twenty minutes later, I was back in the office making arrangements for the trip north, including the use of an extra surveillance team from SO11 at Scotland Yard. By 5.00pm the teams were assembled and ready to go, and by 10.00pm we were at Admiral Street police station in Liverpool.

I was given the full background on the suspect, and the following morning, with the aid of local officers, I briefed the teams. Our objective was to be straightforward intelligence gathering, which basically meant just getting behind our subject – referred to in surveillance jargon as an 'India' – and staying there, watching where he went, whom he met and what he did. Twenty-four-hour cover would be a necessity, as we were told that our suspect was prone to nocturnal activities, some of them highly unpleasant and unlawful. The aggravated burglary and rape of which he was suspected had been committed during the small hours of the morning.

The operation was largely uneventful until the early hours of Friday morning when our India emerged from his address and began to wander, apparently aimlessly, through the back streets. The decision was made to let him run because there was a chance he might take us to another address – it was an intelligence-gathering operation and, if he was our killer, we couldn't risk not knowing of any possible alternative addresses where evidence may be hidden.

In view of his strongly suspected nasty habits, it was a brave decision – even more brave when he disappeared around the back of a large house which had been converted into flats. Obviously, we couldn't send a man round the back of the premises without showing out, but we couldn't just sit there in case he was breaking into a flat and was about to attack another young girl. It was an awful dilemma and after five or six minutes the time came when action had to be taken. Just as the order was to be given to go in, he reappeared and continued his wanderings. It had been a nerve-wracking few minutes. A check of the house showed no signs of any attempted break-in.

Later the same day, I took an urgent phone call from Wickerson. 'Keith, the wheel's come off!'

'What's wrong?'

'I can't go into all the details on the phone, but the *Sunday Mirror* have got wind of what you're doing up there and they're going to run the story the day after tomorrow.'

'That's bloody wonderful – how the hell did they got hold of it?'

'Your guess is as good as mine. Bob Chapman got a phone call from one of their reporters. Obviously Chapman didn't confirm or deny, but it's their intention to run the story.'

'This is a highly sensitive investigation, for God's sake! Can't anything be done?'

'Such as what? I suppose we should be grateful they even told us what they're planning.'

Worse was to come as the day unfolded. I could tell that things had gone wrong as I listened to the commentary on the small set.[1] An unknown male had called at the address and our man had left with him. The pick-up from the address had gone smoothly enough, then, as we waited for the 'Contact, Contact, Contact' from the next member of the team and the handover of control, there was a very long, deafening silence.

The team immediately did a bomb burst (dispersed) in the local streets in an attempt to pinpoint the subject again, working on the 'Pace, Time, Distance' principle; i.e. working from the point of the loss, how fast was the India travelling, how much time has elapsed, how far could he have got in that time?

There was a lot of activity on the small set as the surrounding streets were checked. In these situations, the longer the loss is maintained the less the likelihood of picking him up again. The next step is to dispatch units to any other known addresses and wait to see if the India pops up there. But we drew a blank and our India was completely off the radar screens for the next 24 hours.

What we had done was fairly standard; we had 'boxed' the address with units and had control of the front door, so when the India came out the 'eyeball' on the door would give a direction and the unit covering the junction towards which he was heading would pick him up as he passed. Unfortunately on this occasion, the 'eyeball' missed the fact that he had got into a car, obviously some way down the road when he was out of sight. The pick-up man, expecting a pedestrian, was a little slow and didn't notice our subject drive past. A basic mistake, but not totally unforgivable. After all, our man had never been seen in a car and didn't, to our knowledge, possess one.

'Do you think he's sussed us?' I asked the local co-ordinator.

'He's not shown any signs of having been looking. We've not been compromised – we just got complacent.'

[1] The Met Police use two radio systems: the main set, which transmits throughout the MPD, and the small set, which has a more limited range. It is normal for Specialist Operation squads to have vehicles which are fitted with both main and small set radios. Small sets can also be encrypted which prevents the more sophisticated criminals from monitoring our radio transmissions. Body sets which are covert radios with remote radio ear pieces are linked to the small set system. These are used by foot surveillance teams.

'We've got the other address covered, have we?'

'We have, but the area's quite hostile. I don't know how long we can keep a man in.

'If I can get a van, will that help?'

'Depends on how good the van is, the locals seem sensitive to strangers.'

'We'll keep the OP in at this end and best you and I go and see about begging a van or a vehicle with a boot OP for the Toxteth address.'

The local Regional Crime Squad had an office at Admiral Street and very obligingly lent us what we needed. Keith Richardson manned the vehicle.

By 6.00pm we still hadn't made contact and I was beginning to get worried. I didn't fancy the idea of our suspect opening the Sunday papers and finding out that he was the subject of a surveillance operation. I obviously wanted to break the news to him myself.

By 6.30pm Wickerson was on the phone wanting to know what was happening. I hadn't told him about the loss and he wasn't over the moon when I did.

I said, 'The biggest problem is the papers. If they run the story and we haven't nicked him, there'll be more than a few red faces.'

'He'll turn up. He's got to.'

'But it might not be before tomorrow. There's no two ways about it, Mick, you're going to have to get hold of Bob Chapman and he's going to have to put some pressure on that reporter.'

'It doesn't look like there's much option, really. Keep me posted.'

The bottom line was that he turned up late on Sunday afternoon after the boys and I had spent an uncomfortable and miserable continuous 24 hours on duty. The story didn't make the Sundays but they had a field day with it on Monday and Tuesday.

The unwarranted press coverage was a sign of things to come. The local populace had gathered outside the nick like an uneasy lynch mob. To my mind, it was a frightening example of how the media could manipulate the public. I had no doubt that, had they got hold of the suspect, they would have torn him limb from limb.

The suspect was the thirteenth suspect so far to be taken in for questioning. We took him back to London, but in order to avoid the massed ranks of TV and press outside Wimbledon, we went to Rochester Row police station in Victoria. The suspect was interviewed and eventually his alibi proved conclusively that he hadn't killed Rachel. He'd been working for a small family firm of undertakers on the day of the murder and, strangely enough, he had actually been present in the mortuary shortly after Rachel had been brought in.

The postscript to this episode was that it cost the Met £16,000 in overtime for no result other than obtaining some interesting intelligence for the Merseyside inquiry. This came in the form of some notes written by the suspect as he was trying to work out who had grassed him for the rape; he had thrown his scribblings in his dustbin and, whilst we were waiting for him to surface again, the boys pinched the contents. The suspect was a violent sex offender and was subsequently convicted of the Liverpool offence and sentenced to a term of imprisonment.

Chapter 13

We asked Andre if he would agree to take Alex back to the common. We were desperate to discover any detail, no matter how small, which would explain the exact sequence of events that had taken place that morning. Jean Harris-Hendrix had no problems with this. She told of other cases where she had taken children back to the scene of a disaster in which they had been involved; apparently, only good had come of it. For some children, such a visit had even 'unblocked' them, allowing them to recall or express more than they had before.

We all met up at Wimbledon Police Station. The child psychologist and Paul Miller joined Andre and Alex in their car. As agreed, Andre explained to Alex that he was there today to help the police, and that they were just going to walk the way that he had gone with Mummy that morning, and then they would go home.

We followed Andre as he drove to the common and pulled up in the Windmill car park. I watched as he undid Alex from his car-seat in the front. Alex climbed on to his father's lap and appeared very tense.

Andre opened the door to get out but Alex wouldn't let go of the steering wheel. He tugged gently at Alex's arms but he wouldn't budge. Eventually, he agreed to get out and we all set off along the route that he had taken with Rachel that morning.

Paul Miller and Dr Harris-Hendrix walked with the Hanscombes, and the rest of us were spread out either in front or behind. At first, Andre carried Alex in his arms, but before long the toddler wanted to get down. For the rest of the way, he walked cheerfully along beside his dad in the sunshine.

We left the car park behind us and walked along the path. Eventually, there were trees on our left and the tumulus lay ahead.

'Which way did you go next, Alex?' Paul asked.

We carried on and reached the top of the mound. Alex wanted to run down it with Andre. I was sure that this was indeed the general direction they would have gone that morning, judging by the witness sightings. But we still hadn't been able to establish from Alex at what stage of the walk she had been attacked.

'Were you going that way with Mummy that morning, Alex?' Andre asked, pointing down the slope. 'Were you going to the pond?'

Alex didn't answer. He was more interested in the blackberries which were beginning to appear in the brambles.

He set off again and seemed about to follow the path down the mound and under the canopy of trees where Rachel had been murdered, but I didn't really get the impression that he was leading us in any definite direction. He kept stopping and looking round from time to time as if trying to find his way. The undergrowth and brambles had grown since the beginning of the summer, and it was hard to see clearly through the trees for any distance.

'Which way did you go, Alex?' Sparshatt asked.

Alex hesitated between two paths, looking more and more confused. I knew it was hopeless. Then, as Alex jumped a shallow ditch, he slipped and fell, cutting his leg. As he looked down to inspect the damage, he saw blood. His little face crumpled and he let out a long wail. Andre scooped him up in his arms and carried him back to the car.

The next session with the child psychologist, towards the end of August, was again attended by grandparents and other members of the family besides Andre and Alex, Sparshatt and Miller.

They had been going over much of the same ground for weeks now, still seeking the final details to complete the picture.

We had learned a great deal from little Alex. He had described the killer's clothing and hair; the fact that he was white, didn't have a bike or a dog, and that he had acted alone. He had also told us that the bad man had been carrying a black bag, from which he had produced a knife, and it was a hunting knife. The killer, Alex said, had not lowered or taken off his trousers, and had washed himself in the stream afterwards and then walked away in the direction of what we knew to be the cemetery.

Sparshatt and Miller filed a report every time Alex met with Jean Harris-Hendrix. They said that each session had begun with someone, not necessarily the child psychologist, asking Alex something like, 'Do you remember the day that your mummy was killed?' or 'Do you remember getting out of the car?' or 'Do you remember all that happened next?'

Alex faithfully answered the questions, but Andre was beginning to voice concern that the process had hit the law of diminishing returns. In the beginning, everything Alex was able to tell the grown-ups had made him feel better, and the process was therapeutic. But now, with only little gaps left to fill in the scenario, Andre feared that his young son was reaching saturation point.

We still needed all the help we could get, of course, and were keen to continue as long as Jean Harris-Hendrix felt it wasn't being harmful. She said that she believed this was still the best thing for Alex.

This particular session seemed to be going the way of other recent ones, with Alex, whilst not being particularly difficult, just showing little interest in talking.

Out of the blue, however, he suddenly started to talk about how, on 15 July, his trousers had come to be wet from his feet up to his knees. This had always been a mystery to us. The grass had been wet, but the condition of Alex's clothing when he was found suggested that he had been standing in water at some stage. Where could that have happened? Was it before or after Rachel was killed?

Alex explained that Molly had run off, and he had got wet chasing her through the wet grass.

Having returned from a tiring and highly expensive trip to Liverpool, we had to settle down and re-assess the situation. The question was, where do we go from here? I was still loath to accept the stranger attack theory, if for no other reason than the statistical unlikelihood of such attacks.

At this time, I was still sceptical about the psychological profiling aspects of this inquiry. Like most detectives, I felt much more comfortable with logical explanations which featured tangible evidence and readily understandable motives. JB, Mick and I were experienced investigators who understood the value of the 'start from the centre and work out' theory, but all the obvious routes seemed to have drawn a blank. Mr Roberts was still worthy of further attention, but in the light of his alibi, none of us was sure how to progress with that line of enquiry.

Meanwhile, the prospect of a slot on BBC's *Crimewatch* was being offered. The programme is well regarded within the Job and has achieved some excellent results. Whatever it is about TV coverage, it does seem to encourage recalcitrant witnesses to come forward when they otherwise wouldn't have bothered, so the squad were hopeful that a major appeal might turn up something useful.

The problem still remained we had no eye-witnesses and, as such, no definite leads to follow up. There were a number of suspicious sightings on or around the common and quite a few of these still had to be identified. One in particular was of a 6ft skinny white male with long blonde or grey-streaked hair, possibly in a pony-tail. This suspect, who appeared to be wearing blue or grey boxer shorts and trainers, was carrying a bundle under his arms, and had been seen by a witness named Fortescue running up Norstead Place, which is adjacent to the A3. The suspect was therefore dubbed 'the A3 Runner'.

The problem with this particular sighting was the timing. The witness claimed that he saw this runner at between 10.00am and 10.15am. Originally because of this, the suspect was discounted as the sighting was before the murder had occurred; however, a second visit to Mr Fortescue revealed that, at around the same time as the sighting, he remembered seeing the police helicopter overhead. If this was correct, then the timing had to be wrong as the helicopter didn't arrive in the area until 11.15am. The A3 Runner was therefore potentially back in the frame. Certainly his behaviour and mode of dress, if Mr Fortescue was correct in his recollection, was strange, despite the fact that it was a very hot summer day. All efforts to trace this man had so far failed and therefore the A3 Runner was a prime candidate for the *Crimewatch* programme.

Early one Monday evening at the beginning of September, we were in Wicko's office discussing progress – or the apparent lack of it. We had accumulated a large number of E-fits throughout the first six or seven weeks, but which should we broadcast?

'We've got plenty to choose from,' said Wicko. 'I think the A3 Runner has got to be one of our best prospects.'

I said, 'I don't make you wrong there, but one photofit isn't going to make much of an appeal. What else do we go with?'

JB said, 'We've got to get the balance right. I don't want to bombard the public with too much, it'll confuse them. I think one other E-fit and perhaps some publicity for Mr Britton's profile.'

I asked with a raised eyebrow, 'If you're concerned about the public being confused, won't the profile do precisely that?'

'I don't think so, Keith. We're already working within the parameters of Mr Britton's advice. All we'll be doing is asking the viewers to focus their minds along the same lines and hopefully it might jog someone's memory or remind them of something that they hadn't previously considered to be important.'

'Anyway,' Wickerson added, '*Crimewatch* seemed very interested in the profiling aspect and you never know what it'll produce. So what about the other photofit?'

I said, 'I think we need to give it some serious consideration; if we put out the wrong picture we could waste a lot of time chasing red herrings. We don't want to waste an opportunity of having a nationwide appeal – and one that we appear to have control over.'

'There's the man seen by Mrs Corsan, but his shirt is the wrong colour if we're going to take notice of what Alex said – or what about the man with the red face swishing his hands in Queensmere?'

'I think we should go with the Queensmere suspect,' JB said. 'I know the timing's vague but it's the suggestion that he may have been washing his hands. What do you think, Keith?'

'He's as good as any and better than most; even if he's not the man, we may as well identify him to stop the defence throwing him up as a smokescreen when we do get our man.'

'My thoughts exactly,' said Wickerson. 'The same goes for the A3 Runner.'

The conversation continued for some time in the same vein, but the decision had been made. JB took some leave a few days later, and it was whilst he was away that a line of enquiry began that was to end at the Old Bailey and disaster.

One of the unsung heros of the Nickell inquiry was, to my mind, DC Grant Johnson, without doubt one of the most diligent and intuitive officers on the squad. He had spent a lot of time familiarising himself with the common, and could always be found with his nose in the statement binders keeping himself up to date. Indeed, it was whilst reading through the details that he identified the statement of one particular witness as being of importance.

Grant was an extremely big man, 6ft 3in-plus, and built like a brick outhouse, yet remarkably quietly spoken for a man of his stature. People often assume that big people are slow and lumbering, but not so in this case. Grant had the ability to keep senior officers on their toes, not least because of his outstanding knowledge of the criminal law and police procedure. Normally, the first indication that he had come up with something would be when he would sidle up to you and open the conversation with, 'Can I have a quiet word with you please, Guv'nor?'

Wickerson and I were discussing overtime expenditure in my office one morning shortly after JB had gone on holiday.

Mick said, 'Bob Chapman has gone ballistic over these figures; we're going to have to cut back. Just look at this: three-and-a-half grand for the TSG.'

'That was the bill for fingertip searching for the weapon – which we have spectacularly failed to find. I reckon we should extend the search area.'

'You and me both, but everybody wants paying and the AMIP budget won't stand it. Bob Chapman is down to about 80 grand for the rest of the financial year. He's worried, to say the least. We only need to cop a couple of stickers and he'll be skint.'.

'So you tell me how we can cut back and still function properly. My boys are working flat out but we can't do the job in eight hours a day. There's no piss-taking going on. Anyway, we're not the major problem – the Ree-Gee are paying the first 32 hours a month for my boys.'

'I'm not having a pop at your team. I know all about the subsidy from SO9. I'm just telling you what the top man said.'

'So what's the solution? We've just about cracked the back record conversion but *Crimewatch* will hopefully generate a lot of new lines of enquiry. We can't let it slip or we'll be back to square one. Can't we get some dough from the centre? There must be a contingency fund for jobs like this?'

'There's always ACTO's fund but, generally, it's like getting blood out of a stone. I'll have a think about it.'

Before he could continue, Grant Johnson poked his head around the door. 'Good, you're both here. Can I have a quiet word?'

'What's the problem, Grant?'

'It's not a problem, Guv, it's this statement.' He handed the open binder to Wickerson.

Mick looked at the statement and handed the binder to me. 'Jane Harriman – she's made a video of her route and come up with a photofit. Has something come to light?'

'I think it might be important. I know she's just one of a large number of people who reported suspicious-looking males but I went back and had another look at what she had said.'

'Why pick on this particular witness?' Wickerson asked.

'Something rang a bell when Alex came up with the description of the man with the white shirt. But I didn't really think that much about it until I came across the Phelan statement again about the man with the bag washing his hands in the stream.'

'Go on,' Wickerson encouraged.

'I remembered having read a statement somewhere about a man with a white shirt and a black bag, so I went back through the binders and read Mrs Harriman's.'

Like Rachel, solicitor's wife Jane Harriman had been on the common on 15 July for a family outing. With her three youngsters, aged between three and thirteen, she set off from the Windmill car park at 9.45am, heading towards Jerry's Hill in the vague direction of the A3. In the course of their stroll, Mrs Harriman described seeing a suspicious-looking man on no fewer than three occasions.

The first sighting, as she headed down towards the logs close to the vicinity of the Surrey Regiment memorial, was of a man walking towards her wearing dark trousers and a white button-up shirt, with short dark hair, an unusual gait, and carrying a black bag.

Mrs Harriman was instantly apprehensive. She described him as about 5ft 10in tall, with close-cropped, dark brown hair, wearing a white T-shirt and dark trousers and clutching a dark-coloured sports bag. It seemed to her that he was walking with a sense of purpose. She first noticed him as their paths were converging head-on from a distance of about 50–60 yards. It was brightly lit so there was no problem about her getting a good look at him. He was in his late twenties or early thirties, with a thin, babyish sort of face.

It was just about 10.10am when they passed each other, going in opposite directions. Her youngest son was taking an intense interest in some rabbit droppings as the man passed close by and Mrs Harriman's gaze switched between his face and that of the little boy. She thought he might have heard the young boy's observations about the rabbit droppings and, as they passed, she said, 'Good morning,' and he looked away. She thought that was strange and had a good look at him.

The man walked on about 8ft past Mrs Harriman, appeared to falter in his stride momentarily, then walked on again. That was at about 10.10am. She then went on with her family to the Curling Pond and was sitting there on a tree stump with her children when, all of a sudden, she looked up and saw the same man walking back. She thought it was strange, but it was definitely the same man.

Then she noticed an attractive blonde lady, who had later been identified as a police officer's wife called Pauline Fleming, and this chap appeared to be following her. Mrs Harriman watched as he followed her around to the far side of the Curling Pond, and down a bridle path. He had an odd look on his face and walked with a slight but distinctive stoop. 'He was walking briskly, as if in a hurry, but a bit nervously,' Mrs Harriman said. She called the children because she was now feeling nervous about strange men in the woods behind her. She was also very concerned for the safety of this girl and checked her watch. It was 10.17am.

At 10.23am, the man with the odd, loping walk emerged again from the woods on her left-hand side. She watched him walk back around the pond and off back towards the logs, which led him more or less on a collision course with the woods where Rachel was found. The man was wearing what appeared to be a thin belt or strap round his waist, over his T-shirt. Mrs Harriman was sure it hadn't been there earlier. She watched him disappear back through the gap in the trees and vanish from sight.

'At first I couldn't make much sense of the route that Mrs Harriman described,' Grant said, 'so I had a look at the video and the map she made. Then I went up and walked the route – and two things struck me. First, how close the last sighting by Harriman of this man is to the murder scene and then how adjacent the Phelan sighting was to the scene – and it was on the same route as the track taken by the police dog.'

Was the killer heading for the murder scene as Mrs Harriman watched him lope by? It was about 10.23am when she had sighted the sinister stranger for the last time. We already knew from Roger McKern that, at 10.20am, Rachel and Alex were walking from the opposite direction towards Windmill Wood.

Was it the same person, Grant Johnson wondered, that Mrs Amanda Phelan had seen washing his hands in a stream just after

10.30am? She had been suspicious when she saw the man crouch in the water with his hands lowered as if rinsing them. 'I thought it was odd,' she said, 'but I couldn't get a good look at his face because he kept his head down.' The man, wearing what she thought was a cream or white sweater and blue jeans, stood up after a couple of seconds and then headed off in the direction of Putney Cemetery. Mrs Phelan took the same route shortly afterwards and said that her dogs had suddenly started barking furiously at the bushes near the graveyard. 'I thought somebody might be hiding in there,' she said. 'The dogs wouldn't behave like that otherwise.'

Jane Harriman had been anxious to help us in any way she could, and assisted Scotland Yard's Facial Identification Unit in building up an artist's impression of the man she had seen. The final video-enhanced picture shown to her a few days later was, she said, 'a very good likeness'.

Mrs Harriman also went back to the common to retrace the exact route she had walked on the day of the murder. It was clear that she and her children must have been following the same route as Rachel and Alex, just minutes ahead of them, and going at the same pace.

'And what you're saying is you think the Harriman suspect and the Phelan suspect are the same bloke?' Wicko said.

'It's a bit more than that. Jane Harriman saw this bloke three times within a 15-minute period, give or take. Her last sighting was of him heading back towards the logs at 10.22–23am. Chronologically and geographically, 10.23am was about five-and-a-half or six minutes from the time and scene of the murder. Look, it might be better if I showed you on the big map in your office, Guv.'

Wickerson was out of the door like a shot with Johnson and me in his slipstream.

Grant went straight over to the map.

'Right, where am I?' he said half to himself as he studied the large map of the common. 'Yeah, here we are,' he pointed to the map. 'The Curling Pond is here, that's where the Harrimans were when they saw this bloke on the second and third occasions. Now, on the last time he headed in this direction and was last seen about here,' he pointed to the rough area. 'But he was going in the direction of the logs, which are here. The murder scene is here.'

'Which, in all fairness, Grant, is still some considerable way off,' I added, playing devil's advocate.

'It looks a long way on the map, but I've walked it and the map's misleading. It's no more than a few hundred yards. But the point is, when he got to this point in the area of the memorial, he had three options as to which route to take. He could go over the top of the mound, to the right, or left around the mound. If he had doubled back, Harriman would have seen him.'

'That makes sense, and if he had taken the left-hand route, surely he would have been spotted by someone. If my memory serves me right, weren't Brooks and Horne in that area?' I hazarded.

'That sounds about right.'

Johnson continued, 'If the Harriman and Phelan suspect are the same bloke, it would seem that he must have taken one of the other two possible routes because the drainage ditch or stream is here.' He indicated the position. 'So if he took one of these routes he would have been heading more or less directly to the scene and the interesting thing is that, when I walked both of these routes, I did the distance in five-and-a-half to six minutes and that wasn't pushing it.'

Grant looked justifiably pleased with himself as Mick and I digested the potential implications of what he was saying.

Wickerson broke the silence after a minute or so. 'Right, we're happy that the attack took place round about 10.30am and this suspect was last sighted at 10.23am – that means that six minutes would make it 10.29am. If he went over the top, he could have seen Rachel in the open space at the other end of the mound and slipped down here to cut her off.' He pointed to the place where we had found the flattened area of grass. 'Alternatively, if he had taken the right-hand path along the side of the mound, six minutes would still put him in the right place – that's if your timing's right.'

'I've done it two or three times, Guv. If you like, I'll take you up to the common and show you what I mean. It's easier to see what I'm getting at if you actually walk the routes.'

We did exactly that. Grant was right; not only was it surprising how close the various locations were to each other, but walking the routes gave you a real feel for what he was saying. Now, we knew that he could only have gone in two directions. He either had to go back over the mound, or he could have walked around the right-hand side as he faced it from the A3 – and either way would have led him to the spot where Rachel was killed.

We formed the view that what he did was go over the top and, as he approached the summit, he could look down and see the open space of ground where we knew Rachel had been walking.

Having returned from our demonstration, Mick and I were discussing Grant's theory.

'You've got to admit, Keith, it's got possibilities and, having visited the common, it's even more impressive. But even if he's our man, we've still got this bloody great gap of five or six minutes. I think we should scrap the Queensmere suspect and go with the Harriman suspect for the TV.'

'It's still a bit of a quantum leap, but if we go with this one we might be able to fill that missing five or six minutes as well as identifying chummy. I think there might be something to be said for linking the Harriman and Phelan sightings – a search of the box for men with black bags might be useful, don't you think?'

Wickerson nodded. 'I don't suppose the common was crawling with men carrying black bags but it might give us an idea of how safe it is to link the sightings.'

It turned out there were about half-a-dozen sightings which could loosely apply to the black bag criterion. However, only three remained as unidentified, and they were those by Harriman, Phelan and Fleming.

In the week leading up to 17 September, there was a new sense of urgency and anticipation in the incident room. Not specifically because of the emergence of the Harriman suspect, as there were still other lines of enquiry nearer to home, which many believed might pay dividends. It was more the fact that, after two months of exhaustive enquiries and no definite suspect having come to light, there was a sense of frustration and failure, and the *Crimewatch* programme offered the prospect of breaking the deadlock.

We were expecting a good response from the appeal. Rachel's murder was still making front-page news and it was obvious that the public's outrage and concern was still at fever pitch. The team view was, give them some specific requests for assistance and they will give us the missing pieces of the jigsaw puzzle. The A3 Runner and the Harriman suspect were the most pressing of the hundreds of lines of enquiry, and Paul Britton's profile had the potential to provide other valuable lines of investigation. None of the squad really understood the mechanics of 'profiling', but the powers-that-be seemed to be endorsing its use as a means of 'prioritising lines of enquiry and resources'.

Paul Britton had been asked in the past whether details of his work could be referred to publicly, and he had always said 'no'. This time, because of the particularly high risk of the killer striking again, he agreed to let his psychological profile form part of the programme. The day before the broadcast, he spoke to Nick Ross, one of the *Crimewatch* presenters, and explained exactly how the material should be used.

On the night itself, a team of about half-a-dozen officers went to the studio with JB, recently returned from leave, to assist with answering the phones. The rest of us manned the incident room.

The atmosphere in the incident room was electric. People seemed unable to settle, and spent a lot of time milling around in little groups, drinking endless cups of coffee and speculating on what the next eight hours would bring. There was a lot of nervous laughter and banter. As we all crowded into the main incident room to watch JB go through his paces, morale was as high as our expectations.

There was an intense silence from the 30 or so officers as the opening sequence ran. This was broken by an anonymous voice from the back.

'I bet you a tenner that JB forgets Nick Ross's name and calls him "young man"!'

The remark was greeted with raucous laughter, rather too much for the quality of the joke, but to my mind just an indication of the tension that was crying out to be broken.

About 20 minutes into the broadcast, Rachel's face appeared on the screen and the low buzz of mumbled conversation, which had provided the background throughout the programme so far, ceased.

As JB appeared, I could sense people sitting forward anxiously in their seats, and as I looked round the room at the expressions of concentration, it put me in mind of proud but nervous parents hoping against hope that their offspring wouldn't forget their words in the Christmas nativity play.

As soon as our bit had finished, people began to drift away to make last-minute cups of coffee before the first of the calls. The general consensus was that JB had done all right.

Barely had the kettle had time to boil, when the first phone began to ring. Like some highly contagious disease, the ringing spread and, within minutes, the incident room was infected with frantic activity. As soon as a receiver was replaced, it rang again. A crude shuttle system began to operate; as one officer replaced a phone and completed filling out the message form, another would slide into their seat and answer the next call.

The completed messages were passed to the team of receivers. They were then marked with appropriate instructions and given to the indexers to be put on the box and the necessary Actions raised. Mick and I were monitoring the messages as they came in and adding our views to those of the receivers.

This continued unabated until well after midnight. The reports coming back from the studio confirmed that the response they were getting was on a par with ours – overwhelming.

The 800 calls, by and large, fell within three distinct categories: suggestions as to the identities of the A3 Runner, the Harriman suspect, and persons who fitted the profile. The quality of the information varied from the totally ridiculous to the very promising. Despite the apparent craziness of some of these messages, none was ignored, and they all found their way on to the system to be investigated.

Mick and I were in my office ploughing through a pile of forms when Paul Penrose appeared in the doorway.

'This bloke here,' he said, looking down at the sheet of paper he was holding. 'He's been propped up two or three times as being the Harriman suspect. We've had a couple of people nominated more than once, but he sticks out. He's a local and the people phoning in are saying he's a bit of a loner and weirdo. Name of Colin Francis Stagg.'

Wicko said, 'What else do we know about him?'

'We're running the checks at the moment – but he's already on our system. He was stopped by a PC trying to get back on to the common at about midday on the 15th.'

'Back *on to* the common?'

'That's what the box says, but there wasn't a lot of detail. He was given a low priority because he was coming on, or trying to come on, rather than leave.'

'Whereabouts was he stopped?' Wicko asked.

'The cemetery underpass.'

According to the box, when questioned about his movements, Mr Stagg had said, 'Yes, I have been on the common. I was on the common from 8.15am to 8.50am this morning.'

Unfortunately, we didn't know the exact time of this encounter because although the PC wrote down what was said, he didn't record the time. By reference to CAD messages concerning the timings of deployment and withdrawal, however, we would later be able to put it between midday and 1.00pm – an hour-and-ahalf to two-and-a-half hours maximum after the murder had occurred.

The message hadn't been allocated a particularly high priority at the time, since the brief had been to stop people who were leaving the common. Ideally, the PC should have recorded the time, because that could prove crucial with respect to the levels of knowledge that Stagg might have.

'What else?'

'The messages that I've seen say that he's a ringer for the E-fit, spends a lot of his time on the common and is a bit strange – what's more, he lives within spitting distance of the common.' He consulted his bit of paper again. '16 Ibsley Gardens, which is on the Roehampton Estate.'

At that moment, Sean Phillips, one of the research team TIs, came up to Paul and handed him a piece of paper. 'Excuse me, Guv. I've got the result of that CRO.'

Penrose raised an eyebrow. 'Mr Stagg's got form,' he said. 'And it goes back to 1980, according to his CRO number.'

'Right,' Wickerson said to Phillips, 'nip up to the Yard and draw his fiche, will you? And Paul, can you get an urgent registry check done?'

Just over an hour later, we had Colin Stagg's CRO fiche (microfiche) in our hands. He had very limited form – one conviction for the theft of a couple of pieces of steak from a local supermarket. But, more interestingly, one for possession of an offensive weapon – a set of martial arts rice flails. That rang a bell. I picked up the psychologist's report.

'You seen what Paul Britton's written about this?' I said. '"Likely to have unusual hobbies, low-level interest in martial arts." Mr Stagg's worth a look.'

Mick said, 'What do you think we should do?'

'Fools rush in. Let's send someone down and look at the address. We don't want to go crashing in and find he's out, him hear about it and go on the trot. That might be a little bit embarrassing.'

It is a cardinal rule of policing that, if you've identified the suspect, you should 'house' him – i.e. identify where he lives and make sure he's in, without arousing suspicion, because he could be disposing of stuff. The best time to hit somebody is early in the morning, for the simple reason that, if they're not on the premises, then the chances are you're not going to find them there at any time.

We sent along a couple of night-duty CID, Paul Miller and Bill Lyle. They sat outside his address, saw him going out very early in the morning, and thought, That man's the photofit! It turned out he'd been out doing a paper round, which was his only form of employment, and quite unusual for a 30-year-old. At about 8.30am, he came out again and stood on the balcony. Bill Lyle phoned and said, 'Guv'nor, our photofit has just walked out. What do you want us to do?'

Forensic evidence deteriorates with every hour that passes. If this man was the killer, now was not the time to procrastinate.

I said, 'If you're happy you can get hold of him, nick him and we'll come down.'

Bill and Paul approached the row of council houses. As they were about to go up the steps, a woman who was wandering past obviously recognised Bill and Paul for what they were. She went up to Paul, took him to one side, and said, 'I was here to check on what number he lived at because I saw the programme and thought, That looks just like Colin. I wanted to go back and check so I could phone the police.'

She introduced herself as Lillian Avid and said that she knew she'd recognise Mr Stagg's house because it had a very distinctive door. Looking up, the officers saw what she was talking about. Nailed to the front door was a hand-painted sign that read: 'Christians beware: a pagan dwells here.'

Chapter 14

I got to 16 Ibsley Gardens about ten minutes after Bill and Paul had arrested him. I knocked on the door and Paul answered. Mr Stagg was in the hallway.

I said, 'Good morning, Mr Stagg. I am DI Pedder and I am investigating the murder of Rachel Nickell on Wimbledon Common on 15 July 1992. I understand that you have been told that you have been arrested on suspicion of having been involved in that offence?'

'Yeah, but I don't know anything about it he replied in a South London accent. 'I wouldn't hurt anybody, not even an ant. It's against my religion.'

'My officers and I now propose to search your premises.'

'You ain't searching nowhere unless you've got a warrant.'

'Mr Stagg, I am perfectly entitled to search your premises without warrant by virtue of the provisions of the Police and Criminal Evidence Act 1984.'

'You need a warrant and you know it.'

'I'm afraid to say that you're wrong. I propose to search your address as I'm entitled to by section 18 of the Police and Criminal Evidence Act, which states that an officer may enter and search any premises occupied or controlled by a person who is under arrest for an arrestable offence, if he has reasonable grounds for suspecting that there is on the premises evidence relating to the offence for which he is under arrest or to some other offence which is connected to or similar to that offence. Now that is what the law says – do you understand?'

Stagg made no reply, instead just glared at me.

'Mr Stagg, if you want me to explain anything which I have just said, I'm perfectly willing to; however, I assure you that I am acting within the law and that your premises will now be searched. If you are unhappy about your treatment, you are entitled to make a complaint on your arrival at the police station. Do you understand?'

'I ain't got much choice, have I?'

'No.'

After that exchange, he fell into a sulk.

The ridiculous thing was that, although as far as I knew this man might be the most vicious killer that this country had seen in a long time, my thoughts on first seeing him turned to one of my eldest son's toys. Short, reasonably muscular, with close-cut, dark hair, Colin Stagg was dressed in a black T-shirt with capped sleeves, cut-down denim shorts, sports socks and trainers. He looked exactly like Action Man.

I noticed, too, that he was reluctant to hold eye-contact and, after the initial face-to-face confrontation, it was difficult to get him to look at the person who was speaking to him. Again, this reaction put me in mind of my sons, who, like most four- and seven-year-olds, had a tendency to sulk when they didn't get their own way.

There wasn't any active resistance to the police presence but he was clearly angry and seemed to lack the courage to display his annoyance openly. There were a couple of occasions when I turned round suddenly and caught him glaring at me; there was venom in his expression but he immediately looked down as I looked in his direction. It was unusual behaviour and not at all what I was accustomed to. The normal reaction to unwanted or unexpected visits by the police range from the vociferous to the physically violent. Silent sulking was a new one on me.

Mr Stagg toured the house with us. It was a fairly silent affair. He said nothing unless spoken to, and the Police and Criminal Evidence Act prohibits the questioning of suspects under such circumstances. The officer is entitled to ask some questions to 'establish ownership of articles or to establish reasonable suspicion to ascertain whether an offence has been committed and whether the person to whom you are speaking may reasonably be suspected of having committed that or some other offence', but you are not allowed to conduct an interview. The other caveat is that such questioning should be contemporaneously recorded and the person invited to sign the note as being a correct and accurate account of what was said.

The main reason for having the householder accompany the searching officers is to pre-empt subsequent allegations that any incriminating evidence had been 'planted'. Obviously, such questioning under these circumstances would, by virtue of Mr Stagg's sole occupancy of the premises, be totally unnecessary.

It was a major concern of mine to ensure that breaches of PACE did not occur. In view of the importance of the inquiry, I was not about to risk obtaining evidence only to have it ruled inadmissible.

The layout was similar to many such maisonettes on council estates. As I stood in the hall, immediately to my right was the kitchen, a small narrow room with the sink adjacent to the front window. There was a series of cabinets and cupboards, all about 20 years old and veneered with Formica.

Leaving the kitchen, immediately in front of me were the stairs and a small meter cupboard. The stairs ascended towards the right. Also to the right was the door to the living room. The downstairs loo was situated to the left of the front door.

The living room was quite large, about 12ft by 18ft, with a gas fire with a wooden surround at the far right-hand side; the wall behind it was covered in a teak veneer. The main furniture was a dark draylon three-piece suite, brown with white tassels around the bottom.

To the left of the fireplace was a small, dark wood bureau and, to the right, a sofa, a glass cabinet and a set of bookshelves. I went over and looked at the titles; most were books on the occult.

The carpet was light in colour. The ornaments, of which there were dozens, looked mostly like seaside trinkets. There were a large number of pictures on the wall, all of woodland and country scenes and, over the fireplace, a shield and crossed swords. Also fixed to the walls all around the room were a number of other swords and large knives.

However, what attracted my attention most was something on the coffee table in front of the sofa.

Lying open was a copy of that day's *Daily Mirror*, with the full-length picture and E-fit picture of the Harriman suspect.

I looked at the picture and said, 'Looks a bit like you, doesn't it, Colin?'

'It don't look nothing like me!'

'I think it looks extremely like you. Did you watch the TV last night?'

'Yeah.'

'Didn't you think that perhaps it looked a little bit like you, so you can't be too surprised to see us here this morning?'

'No, I didn't think it looked anything like me. Perhaps there's a resemblance, but then they said that he was 5ft 10in and I'm only 5ft 8in and I ain't got a white shirt like that, or a black bag.'

He got quite excited and volatile at this point, but that isn't too unusual. It isn't a pleasant experience having the police search your house.

Upstairs wasn't as tidy as downstairs. To the left at the top of the stairs were two bedrooms, with a third bedroom and bathroom on the right.

The first room on the left was the box room which Stagg slept in. Its walls were emulsioned eggshell blue, and his bed was a small, single divan with off-white, brushed nylon sheets. Affixed to one wall was a small altar, a sort of shelf affair with various pictures and trinkets of the occult.

Paul found a girly mag under the bed and pulled it out. We got a bit of a nasty shock when we opened it and pages were wet and sticky. However, we made no comment and the magazine was returned from whence it came.

Mr Stagg went ballistic. 'Yeah, OK, so fucking what? There's nothing perverted about it. I'm a human being. Don't start making snide remarks.'

'Mr Stagg, no one is making snide remarks.'

We moved on. The next room on the left was the 'black' room. It was quite large, about 10ft by 14ft. All the walls were painted black and were decorated with numerous chalk drawings of horned gods, one of whom he described, when asked, as 'Herne'.

Mr Stagg had done these drawings himself and was obviously quite a talented artist. One of his works was particularly striking, a painting of Odin being tormented whilst tied to a tree.

The carpet had once been of quite good quality but was now adorned with a pentagram within a circle of about 8ft in diameter. The design had been painted directly on to the carpet with white gloss. At strategic places within the circle were positioned various stones, and right in the centre was what looked like a large triangular piece of slate, which a closer look revealed to be a piece of wood that had been painted grey.

By the window on the floor was a pile of pigeon feathers, which caused me some concern.

'There ain't nothing wrong with it!' Mr Stagg exploded. 'Small minds, that's the trouble – stupid, small-minded people. It's my beliefs, all right?'

'Mr Stagg, no one is passing remarks or making judgements.'

'You're all the same, I know what you're thinking. It's my choice and my religion. I don't practise any rites.'

The only furniture in this room was a light, wood-veneered double wardrobe which was locked. We asked Mr Stagg to open it, and inside found a quantity of camping and survival gear. When asked, he described himself as a survivalist. We also found a couple of SAS-type books on how to survive, and some horrendous-looking knives. The last item in the wardrobe was a black-hooded cloak.

We moved on. The bathroom was unexceptional; the suite was pink. The third bedroom was used as a gymnasium. The walls were painted white and the floor was covered with lino tiles. There was a rowing machine, a set of weights and a bench. There was also a punch bag, stuffed with old clothing, which we removed for analysis. All around the room, at picture rail level, was a collection of open-crotch photographs; Mr Stagg obviously went in there and pumped himself up while looking at pictures of naked women.

The tour of the house completed, we seized all items of clothing and a quantity of knives and swords, and Mr Stagg accompanied us back to Wimbledon Police Station.

The clock was now ticking. We had three days in which to interview our suspect before we had either to charge him or set him free.

Chapter 15

There was more than sufficient circumstantial evidence to justify Colin Stagg's arrest, but the process obviously doesn't stop there. The investigator's main responsibility is to establish the truth; if that means eliminating the prime suspect as a result, then so be it.

The fact that this inquiry meant so much to the team, and to me personally as the senior interviewer, meant that I wanted to take advantage of every available facility. Before starting the interviews, I therefore rang Paul Britton at the Towers Hospital in Leicester and asked if he would want to give any specific advice as to how I should approach him.

'How did this person come to your attention?' he asked, his voice very calm and even, his choice of words, as ever, precise and careful.

'As a result of the *Crimewatch* programme. He was named as being one of the persons in the photofit pictures that were broadcast.'

'What else can you tell me about him?'

'He's 28 years old, and unemployed apart from a paper round.

He lives alone in a council maisonette. He's been described as being a loner. He also has an interest in the occult. In fact, his back bedroom has been turned into some sort of pagan shrine; it's all painted black and there was a pentacle painted on the carpet. He also had stones positioned around the pentacle, and there were also chalk drawings of different horned gods on the walls, and some strange letters or symbols.'

'That sounds interesting. Can you tell me – was there any pornography?'

'Only fairly soft porn, nothing that I would describe as extreme.'

It suddenly occurred to me that perhaps Paul would consider Colin Stagg's magazines as hard-core. Policemen tend to become inured to things and very little seems to shock them. There was no doubt that my maiden aunt would have considered them to be disgusting, but her views might not necessarily be shared by the vast majority of people. I had certainly seen much worse as the result of searching different addresses. As these thoughts went through my mind, it suddenly dawned on me that I was only entertaining these ideas because I was talking to a psychologist. What was the psychological definition of soft- or hard-core? Or, for that matter, run-of-the-mill?

'Is he a local man?'

'He lives about a quarter of a mile or so from the common, just on the other side of the A3. In fact, if you compare him against the profile, he is a very good match.'

'That's interesting. You understand that I cannot give you advice about the person you have in custody because I haven't seen or spoken with him? The extent of any assistance would be based upon what I have concluded about the killer, and that is on the basis of what I have observed of the scene and the other witness evidence.'

'I understand that – or at least I think I understand.'

'Then, on that understanding, I would advise you to begin by trying gently to win his confidence and get him to start to talk about himself and his background. Stay away from the specific events of the day in question. Be firm, but reassuring. If this is the man, he may – under the right circumstances, and to the right person – want to talk about it. He may, on the other hand, not be eager to relive the events of the murder, and he may, in the fullness of time, need to be made to realise that there is an inevitability that he will have to face up to what he has done.'

The first part of this advice was what I would have done anyway. But as for the rest, I was not sure I fully understood what Paul was getting at. 'Is there anything that I should specifically not ask him, or for that matter anything that I should?'

'Not at this stage. I would suggest that your priority is just to get him to communicate and then build on that. You can phone me again once you have spoken with him if you think I can be of assistance.'

I thanked him, put down the receiver, picked it up again and called Wickerson for an update. Officers had begun a systematic search of Colin Stagg's home and garden for evidence which might link him with the murder, even though we realised that in the two months that had elapsed he could, if he wanted to, have destroyed any clothing or shoes that he might have been wearing. The forensic lab were able to report that none of the knives in the maisonette bore any traces of blood, and none matched the wounds on Rachel's body. It looked as if we were going to have to rely entirely on Colin's verbal evidence. A quick confession, I hoped, and it would all be over.

The first interview is tactical stuff. You get people to talk about anything innocuous to try to build up a rapport and get them talking, and then you can start getting down to the nitty-gritty.

I sat opposite Colin in the interview room that afternoon and pushed the start button on the tape recorder. I confirmed the names of the police officers present and the fact that Stagg's solicitor, Graeme Woods of Keith Hollis Woods, was attending, together with a social worker as the 'responsible adult' required to be in attendance in certain cases under the terms of the Police and Criminal Evidence Act.

'I do painting,' he said. 'I read a lot, a bit of gardening, I used to do archery down the local club. I gave up because it got too expensive. That's about it.'

'Any outdoor pursuits?' I asked.

'At the moment, just walking the dog, though I have been planning to do some backpacking. I used to do it in the past.'

'When you say backpacking, you mean ...?'

'Yeah, rucksack, tent, everything, you know ...'

'Living rough or wild?'

'Yeah.'

'As nature intended, so to speak?'

'Yeah.'

We chatted about his hobbies for a while, with me breaking off the interview from time to time to initiate Actions to check up on what he was telling us.

We talked about his background. We learned that Colin Francis Stagg had been born on 20 May 1963 at King's Hospital, Chelsea, at a time when the Stagg family was living in Humbolt Road, Hammersmith. Vic Stagg was in regular work as a billposter but, when Colin was five, Vic lost his job due to failing eyesight. The family lost their tied house and were forced to move over the Thames to the Alton Estate in Roehampton. Vic was unable to find other work and the marriage began to crack up.

Colin was always a shy boy, he said, attending first the local Heathmere Primary School, then Elliot Comprehensive. He had been bullied as a boy, apparently over the way he walked.

Hilda Stagg left home when Colin was about 12, and he never forgave her – especially as Vic Stagg suffered his first heart-attack within a week of her leaving. Colin had three brothers and a sister, but he was closest to his father. The two shared each other's company on walks on Wimbledon Common and listening to records. Colin developed an interest in pop music and bought a guitar, teaching himself to play a few chords, and joining a band called The Filth. Their one and only gig had been in a pub in Fulham.

Colin played truant a lot from secondary school and, despite an apparent flair for languages and art, he left with no O-Levels. He became increasingly withdrawn, and shy and awkward with girls. He was happy to be alone with his dog, Brandy, his guitar and his paints. Amazingly, perhaps, at the age of almost 30, he was still a virgin.

In 1986, Vic Stagg suddenly died and Colin found himself alone in a property suitable for an entire family, with no job, no commitments, and all his rent and overheads paid for by dole and welfare payments. The last time he and his mother had met was at Vic's funeral in 1986. They didn't speak.

When Colin took over the tenancy, his brothers moved out.

'Basically I kicked them out,' he said. 'There was a lot of trouble with Lee always fighting and it just got on my nerves.'

In the Stagg family history, we discovered from other sources, brother Anthony had been jailed in 1986 for raping a 19-year-old girl on Putney Heath, and brother Lee was into drugs.

'What sort of person would you describe yourself as?' I asked. 'Are you a sort of friendly, outgoing person, or ...'

'I am a bit introverted, keep to myself.'

'Shy?'

'I used to be painfully shy when I was a teenager.'

'But you've got over that?'

'Yeah.'

'It just strikes me that some of the interests you said seem to be solitary pastimes. You spend quite a lot of time by yourself?'

'Yeah.'

'Like your own company?'

'Yes, and my dog.'

'How would you describe your social life?'

'Well, I'm always indoors, apart from taking the dog out. That's all I do really.'

'You don't visit any clubs or pubs or ...'

'No, I hated pubs when I was a teenager and I couldn't get used to them, so I prefer getting a couple of bottles of drink and staying indoors, put my feet up in front of the telly.'

It was time to probe further. I said, 'That's a little bit about your background. Now, as you were told this morning, you have been arrested on suspicion of the murder of Rachel Nickell which occurred on 15 July. It's a matter of two months ago. Can you remember that day?'

'Yeah.'

'Can you tell me why you remember it?'

'Well, because of what happened, obviously, and the way I felt that day – splitting headache, I hadn't had a headache since I was a teenager. It was that morning I woke up with a painful cramp in my neck. It must have been the way I was sleeping or something, and after I did my normal things during the morning and I had breakfast and did some shopping. Then I took the dog straight over the common.'

'What time was that?'

'It was about half-past eight.'

I asked Colin where he had gone on the common. Using the gridded map he traced a route that took him through the underpass under the A3, up the path past Scio Pond and to the Royal Surrey Regiment memorial.

'There are some ravens there,' Colin said. 'I normally feed them every day and I went round that hill there. I would pass the pond on the right-hand side and came back round the hill again. I went through the same underpass and come home, the same way I came.'

'Did you see anyone else whilst you were out walking that morning?'

'The only people I saw was actually before I got to the underpass on the way there. There's a little sort of path that leads right up to the underpass which I normally take.'

'And who did you see there?'

'Well, first of all I saw a woman with dark hair. She had a little buggy with a kid in it, and she had two little dogs. She was going towards the pond as I was coming away from it. I said, "Good morning," to her, and she said, "Good morning," and behind her was a man walking his little dog. I said, "Good morning," to him but he didn't reply. So I just thought, Miserable git.'

'What did he look like?'

'He was a bit stocky, a bit taller than me, he had dark, short hair and something like mine. He had a white top on and he just seemed, you know, had an arrogant look on his face, you know.'

'About how old?'

'A bit older than me. Late 30s, early 40s.'

'Which way was he heading?'

'He was behind the woman, walking behind her.'

'And they were heading away from, or towards, the pond?'

'Towards the pond. As I was coming up the little path they were going down.'

'Can you tell me what you were wearing on that morning?'

'What I would normally wear every day. It's a pair of jeans and white Dunlop tennis boots, black T-shirt, and I think I wore my black leather jacket on that day because I was just getting over an illness and I felt the slightest bit of cold. It was later that day that I was actually feeling a lot warmer and so I put my shorts on, my sunglasses and everything.'

'You say you had a headache. What's that all about?'

'I think it was the way I was sleeping that night because there was a lot of pain at the back of the neck, and I just felt, you know, drowsy. Because normally if I didn't have the headache I would take him right over the hill, right over to the playing fields, and I just wanted to get home as quickly as possible because I felt drowsy and wanted to sleep.'

'So how long were you on the common for?'

'Must have only been for about 15 minutes.'

'Fifteen minutes, so you would have been back home by what time?'

'Quarter-past nine, something like that.'

'Quarter-past nine. So you say that you went out at about half-past eight?'

'Yes, it takes me a while to get to that road. And to get into the common it must have been getting on to nine by then.'

'So you were back home by quarter-past nine. Did you see anyone on the way back from the common?'

'No. No more than usual, the usual people. People that you see not in the common but on the estate. I went straight home and then just fell asleep on the settee.'

He said that he went straight back to Ibsley Gardens, ate a

couple of Ryvita crispbreads, and fell asleep on the settee in front of some sort of game show on the telly, possibly hosted by Tom O'Connor, he couldn't remember exactly who.

According to Colin, he was later woken by the sound of helicopters at about 10.30–11.00am. He was sure of the time because he thought, I've got to take Brandy out again now, but I didn't really feel like it.

'So what did you do then?'

'Well, I noticed that the weather had brightened up a bit, had got a bit warmer, felt a bit humid.'

'And what were you wearing?'

'Shorts, cut-down jeans.'

I showed him a pair of jeans we'd found at his home, and described them as 'whitish'.

'Faded,' he corrected me. 'And a black T-shirt and the boots I was wearing that morning, white socks, and a pair of sunglasses.'

'The shoes you were wearing on that day – have you still got them?' I asked, mindful of the prints that had been found in the soil around Rachel's body.

'No, I threw them away two days ago.'

'Where did you throw them?'

'In the big dustbin at the end of the building.'

'Why did you get rid of them?'

'Because they fell apart. The heel came off the day that I threw them away.'

I asked him again what he had done after being woken up by the sound of helicopters.

'I just put the lead on the dog and walked towards the common, to the second underpass, past the school and that's where the police stopped me.'

'Was there any reason why you went to the second underpass and not the same route that you went in the morning?'

'I do it every day, you know. Take different routes. It gets boring going the same route …'

'So when you got to the underpass, you say you were stopped by the police?'

'Yeah.'

'And what time do you say that was?'

'I'm not sure, but I reckon the police did take down the time. I asked what had happened and they told me there'd been an incident on the common. I thought it was flashers or perverts or something, then he told me that a woman had been murdered. Well, he actually said a girl had been murdered out there, so that annoyed me at first. Then he said, "Well, you can't take your dog in the common, we are clearing the common of people." I said, "OK, then." Then I came back out the underpass and went straight up to the Bessborough Road shops as I was going to the butchers, and so I told the butcher what had happened.'

'Did you discuss what had happened on the common with the butcher?'

'Yeah. I mean, I felt like I had to tell someone, you know.'

'Yes.'

'It was a bit of a shock locally, you know.'

'What did you say to the butcher?'

'I just said ... you know, "Have you heard what's happened on the common?" He said, "No, what?" I said, "A young girl's been murdered over there ..."'

'What time would this have been?'

'It must have been gone eleven, half-eleven or something.'

'So what did you actually know had happened at that stage – just the fact that a girl had been murdered?'

'Yeah, that's what he said. A girl's body had been found over there, and the officer asked me if I saw anybody suspicious over there or have I heard anything ...'

I asked Colin to go over the timings again, and he reiterated that he had left home at 8.30am, walked through the underpass, and on to the common. He said he was back home by quarter-past nine or thereabouts, and fell asleep. He was woken by the noise of helicopters, tried to get on to the common a second time, and got to the butchers at about 11.40am or 12.00.

'Did you see anyone else on the way home?' I asked.

'Not on the way home. It's later on that I took the dog out for another walk around the buildings. I bumped into another old woman that I know and told her what happened ...'

'When was the last time you've seen that lady?'

'When I got arrested, outside the building – that was the woman, she was coming along my balcony. I think she wanted to look at my door 'cos I had all those signs on my door, she was just curious.'

What about the weird slogan on his front door, I asked? 'Christians don't knock – a pagan lives here' or something like that. What did that mean?

'Oh, it's just to get rid of bible bashers,' he said.

And the black room with its pentagram, stones and symbols?

Colin paused for a second or two. 'It's not anything to do with Satan,' he said. It was, he explained, all part of his belief in the Wicca religion,

which pre-dated Christianity by thousands of years. 'It's basically the old religion, the pagan religions of Britain and Ireland.'

Stagg went on, 'It's our belief that all life is precious, all, like, y'know, like animal life. Everything has a spirit, y'know, trees, even rocks, even a breath of wind has got a spirit.'

I looked at him quizzically. 'So you believe that all life is precious?'

The photographs of Rachel Nickell's mutilated body filled my mind. Stagg said that so deep was his conviction of every creature's right to survive, he still deeply regretted once 'viciously' killing woodlice with a magnifying glass as a ten-year-old.

'I couldn't harm an animal, even if I tried,' he said. 'Although I admit I do take that knife in case I have to skin or kill an animal if I was backpacking, as in a survival situation, but I've never done it ...'

'You do carry knives?'

'Not every day, no ... I was wearing my jacket so I must have had my little Mauser pocket knife at the time. I carry that with the little flint of magnesium block because I believe in always being prepared, you know, if you are caught in a survival situation, at least you've got something to make a fire with.'

'Hardly likely on the common, is it?'

'You never know.'

'We found two rather large knives at your address ...'

The larger one, said Stagg, was for chopping wood, the smaller one for skinning rabbits, if the need ever arose. 'If I wanted to skin an animal in a survival situation, to tell you the truth, I don't think I would. I feel that no matter how civilised we are, if you get caught up in a survival situation you'd have to do such things to survive. To tell you the truth, I would feel guilty about killing even a little animal, but our ancestors have been doing it for thousands of years to survive.'

We talked more about his Wicca beliefs, then I asked him about the *Crimewatch* programme. What had been his reaction to seeing the E-fit?

'When it came out with that description I thought, That could be me,' he said. 'But I thought, Hang on, he's over 6ft tall, white shirt, carrying a bag. I never carry bags over the common.'

'Do you possess a black vinyl bag?'

'No.'

'Did you ever?'

'No.'

I asked if he had seen the home video shown on the programme of Rachel Nickell playing with her young son.

'Yeah.'

'It was quite poignant, wasn't it?'

'Yeah.'

'Did you know Rachel at all?'

'I didn't know her, no.'

Had he ever seen her on the common during his many walks there?

'I saw somebody that looks like her about two years ago,' he said. 'She wore a green striped top, like a T-shirt, and red shorts, and she was pushing a little baby in a buggy. I was actually sitting on Kingsmere when she came round. That was the second time. The first time I saw her she was already there by Kingsmere and I was just getting over the illness the first time, and I was very conscious of my physical appearance because I was very skinny and pale.

'She was lying on the grass with her little kid. She looked up and smiled at me. Then I thought, Nice-looking girl, you know. You can't chat up a girl when you're looking really rotten and that, so I didn't bother.

'I went back the next day. She saw me and she walked over to the grass where she was the day before, and she took her top off and her shorts. She had a bikini on and she was sunbathing. I decided to do the same where I was and took my T-shirt off and just lay back ...'

'And how long ago did you say this was?'

'It was about two years ago.'

Colin said he remembered the incident because at the time he was suffering from an illness brought on by an allergy to wheat flour and wasn't feeling too well. 'I was hoping I would bump into her again ... Well, she smiled at me and I thought, If I could have got chatting to her, you know, find out if she was unmarried or whatever ... If a girl smiles at you, you know, you feel like your luck's in, you know.'

I suddenly wondered, could Rachel, by smiling innocently at a stranger on Wimbledon Common, have become the object of a sexual obsession over the next two years that finally led to her death?

'She was blonde, was she?' I asked.

'Yes, she had blonde hair.'

'It was strikingly blonde?'

'Pretty blonde, you know.'

Colin described this woman as wearing her hair in a ponytail, sort of up at the back. And what about the child, I asked? Was it light-skinned as well?

'I think it was pretty dark-skinned,' said Stagg.

The enquiries to trace the people Colin Stagg described seeing began more or less immediately after the interview had concluded. A search of the box was done and no one even remotely similar was found.

As for the man who he'd thought to be a 'miserable git', it struck me that he was more or less a mirror image description of Colin himself. I didn't immediately think too much about it – I only became suspicious when I ran checks and neither the man nor the woman appeared to be in our system.

Did it mean that Colin was clever enough to know that the Harriman suspect would be linked to the murder? Answer: yes. First, he would know about the link if he had committed the murder; and second, at the stage when this chap was first talked about, Colin did not know the extent of our evidence or information. If, for example, he believed there was a chance that he might have been seen, he may well have considered it a clever move to introduce this other man to try and muddy the waters and to give himself room to manoeuvre. On the other hand, if he wasn't making it up, why couldn't we trace either the man, or the woman with the pushchair? Not being able to trace one I might have been able to accept, but not finding either was stretching my goodwill a bit too far.

Later that day, when Lillian Avid and Susan Gale, who both knew Colin but were unknown to each other, came into the police station within hours of each other, they both gave statements that raised even greater difficulties with regard to our suspect's version of events.

Chapter 16

Lillian Ava Avid had lived on the Alton Estate for 12 years, and had first met Colin Stagg at the Job Centre in Putney two years earlier. They saw each other maybe a couple of times a month as they walked their dogs to and from the Alton Estate to exercise on Wimbledon Common.

'We mostly spoke about the dogs, not much else,' she said to the officer interviewing her. 'He certainly never spoke out of turn.'

On the day of the murder, however, Colin was behaving 'very strangely'.

'What do you mean by that?' she was asked.

'He's normally fairly reclusive and doesn't say much to anybody, keeps himself to himself. The love of his life is his dog Brandy, and all he does is walk on the common and do his paper round.'

Apparently, she and Colin would exchange a few words, mainly about their dogs, or whether or not he'd found a job. 'He never spoke out of his way, we mostly spoke about the dogs. Whenever I saw him, he always wore a navy or black T-shirt and jeans.

'On 15 July, I didn't know the murder had taken place. All

morning I just saw the helicopter flying over and I just wondered what that was about. I learned about the murder when the neighbour opposite me knocked on my door. My neighbour is Mrs Woodward. She knocked on my door I believe between twelve and half-past – it could have been quarter-to-twelve, I'm not quite sure, as she came home a bit earlier that day from work. When Mrs Woodward knocked on the door, I answered it. She said, did I hear about what's happened over the common? I said "No ".

'Then she said, "A lady and a little child's been hurt." How she knew was because she works over that way and she always comes across there, but she had to walk around a different way as it was cordoned off. Mrs Woodward stayed talking to me for about five minutes.

'After she had gone, I took my dog out for a walk, between twelve and half-past. I was heading towards the green, just along the way from where Colin is.

'Colin came rushing towards me. He appeared very agitated and sort of excited. He said, did I hear about the murder on Wimbledon Common? I then said to him, "Was she murdered then?"

'He said, "Yes, the woman with the little child. I often used to stand there on top of the hill and look down where it happened."'

Mrs Avid had thought to herself, How does he know where it happened? She certainly didn't know the exact spot herself – only what her neighbour had told her, that a woman and child had been hurt somewhere on the common, and that the whole area had been sealed off to the public since it happened.

'Then he said to me, "I must have missed it by ten minutes. It was on my normal route."

'I said to him, "You probably could have helped her when it happened, if you'd been there at the time."

'He turned round and said, "Yah, yah, yah," – that's how he speaks. He was so excited that I said to him, "Are you sure you didn't do it?" because of the way he was acting.'

Stagg had just grinned and replied, 'Nah.' Mrs Avid said she felt edgy at the way he was behaving; there was definitely something odd about him that day.

Mrs Avid then said to the officer, 'There's something else ... He looked as if he'd just bathed – he was fairly pink and his hair was wet.'

'What was he wearing?'

'A white T-shirt and white shorts, and trainers, his hair looking neat and newly washed. He made me feel sick with the way he was talking, made me think he'd done it, because he's never been like that before, the way he was talking to me that day.

'His hair always is very tidy, but he looked extra clean, very immaculate. His clothing looked new to me, all fresh. I didn't really look at his face too much, it was his clothes I was looking at. I was shocked as they were so smart.'

So perturbed had Mrs Avid been by Stagg's behaviour, that she went home and telephoned her daughter in Kent for advice. 'I felt sick and ill and worried,' she said. 'I am a naturally nervous person and I was dubious as to whether to get involved or not.'

Her daughter assured her that there was only one course of action. Mrs Avid duly telephoned Wimbledon Police Station, spoke to a woman officer in the incident room, and waited for detectives to visit. Unfortunately, no one ever arrived. Mrs Avid's evidence was probably buried amongst the mountain of messages.

Then, on 17 September, Mrs Avid saw the videofit.

'I was sick in my stomach, gutted,' she said. 'The *Crimewatch* image was a very good image of Colin Stagg, it was just his head, his hair, the style of his hair and his face.'

She had slept on it overnight and decided she must contact the police again. In the morning she went out, intending to walk past Stagg's home to check what number he lived at, and then call Wimbledon police again. She'd just been about to knock on another door in the street to enquire about Stagg when he emerged three doors away. Mrs Avid asked him, 'Oh, where's your dog? Aren't you taking him for a walk?'

'Nah, just to the shops.'

And it was at that moment that a man had stepped between them, took Colin Stagg by the arm, and said, 'I want to talk to you.'

Mrs Avid could not have been more adamant about her evidence.

'The conversations I have mentioned are word perfect,' she said, 'not just the gist of what was said, everything. I have absolutely no doubt about that. On 15 July, the way Colin Stagg was speaking, I was thinking, Did he do it, did he do it? I said to myself, I'm sure he must have changed his clothes. I just had this feeling that he did. I thought to myself he must have changed his clothes if he did do it.' Of course, Mrs Avid's recollection may have been confused about this. She may have put two and two together because Stagg was a bit weird – he may have had nothing to do with it and the white shirt might either not have been changed or she was wrong about the colour.

While I had been interviewing Colin Stagg, various members of the team had been making extensive enquiries about the Wicca religion in which Stagg so openly confessed his interest.

The question had to be asked: could witchcraft have been a factor in the murder? The team obtained the opinion of experts at the British Museum and other leading authorities in ancient cults and religions in an attempt to define the teachings of Wicca.

One of the first questions they were asked by a 'high priestess' of Wicca was whether Stagg was his real name or had he changed it? The stag, she said, was among the most powerful of all the pagan symbols.

Wicca, we learned, is a religion based on the love of nature, the sun, the moon and the seasons, and involves witches and wizards with supernatural powers and magical rites in woodland settings. There was evidence of human sacrifice way back in the cult's history. Centuries ago, in parts of Brittany, huge wicker baskets would be filled with potential victims for sacrificial slaughter. They would be set alight in front of chanting crowds as a token to the nature spirits.

In 1973, the cult was featured in a film starring Edward Woodward and Britt Ekland, called *The Wicker Man*. Woodward played a detective sent to a Scottish island to investigate the disappearance of a schoolgirl. He unearthed a terrifying world of devil worship and pagan rituals, and was eventually burned alive inside a huge figure of a man woven out of wicker.

Today's followers of Wicca, we discovered, could be numbered in thousands, and The Pagan Federation had produced a useful booklet for those interested. Leading practitioners were trying to establish their own recognised church in England, with legal rights of service and protection under the laws of blasphemy.

The foremost authority on Wicca in Britain, Michael York, a PhD from the Academy for Cultural and Education Studies in London, provided an expert view. Though not a practitioner of Wicca himself, his 14-page assessment was based on more than 200 hours' participation and involvement in the religion, talking to leading members and watching rituals.

Dr York wrote:

> *The Wiccan religion takes many forms, but its central features include a focus upon the female metaphor for the Godhead (usually designated the Goddess), a regard for the sacredness of nature and belief in the inherent or potential divinity of every human being. A masculine image of the Godhead is sometimes included (referred to as the God) and is recognised in such configurations as Herne the Hunter or the Green Man of British folklore tradition. But because of the virtual elimination of the feminine element in the Christian expression of Western culture, Wiccans tend to stress their understanding of, and concern with, their female configuration for divinity. This last is seen as comprising all the various forces of nature, the physical embodiment of the world and the spiritual reality to be found behind the phenomenal or natural world. This ubiquity of divinity in all beings leads to the Wiccan assertion that every human being is inherently divine. This, in turn, leads to the Wiccan affirmation that each individual is responsible for his or her own actions.*

This was, of course, precisely what Colin Stagg was saying, in his own words, about his beliefs and assertions.

Dr Yorke quoted the Archdeacon of Durham, Michael Perry, who wrote in his book *Gods Within, a Critical Guide to the New Age*:

> *Wicca is a gentle religion, practised alone, in small groups called covens, or larger groups called groves.*
>
> *The rites and gatherings of Wicca are timed in general to the phases of the moon. The essential Wiccan ceremony consists of invoking the Goddess by magical practice within the confines of a sacred circle created for the occasion. The objective of Goddess invocation and the accompanying ceremony is to bring about inner transformation, the helping of others, or the healing of the earth. To my knowledge, both through first-hand observation and through reports of other academics and clergymen, Wicca never seeks to harm others or to practise so-called 'black magic' ... In my opinion, there is nothing insidious or malevolent in the practice or expression of this particular nature-based religion, which respects the individua1, the interaction of all life, and the healing processes which are seen as nature's balance.*

It was fascinating stuff, but in the light of the religion's clear non-malevolence, in all likelihood a blind alley. In any event, logic dictated that if Colin Stagg sincerely believed in Wicca's principles, he was hardly likely to have daubed unsubtle slogans on his front door. By the same token, if there were sinister overtones, the same would apply.

Chapter 17

We had Lillian Avid saying that Colin Stagg had approached her at about midday in a state of excitement – 'it looked as if he'd just bathed' – and in different clothes from the ones he'd been seen wearing by PC Couch. Mr Stagg had also said that he had 'missed it by ten minutes'.

But as if this lady's evidence wasn't worrying enough, a Mrs Susan Gale had also contacted the incident room on Friday morning. She'd seen the *Crimewatch* programme and had heard that Colin had been arrested. She came in to say that she remembered the morning of the murder particularly well because she had her mother-in-law staying with her and she normally didn't walk on the common that early. What was more, she normally walked longer than she did, but because her mother-in-law had stayed overnight and was beginning to fret about not having collected her pension the day before, she wanted to get home at a certain time in order to get her pension picked up, which is what she did. In other words, the morning was unique, and it stuck in her mind.

She said, 'That's why I know the day, and this is why I'm certain of the time because I know what time I got home, and I know what route I took. As I was coming off the common at 9.25am, I saw Colin wearing a white T-shirt and blue jeans, coming on to the common via the Putney Vale underpass.'

'How do you know it was Colin?'

'I've known Colin since he was a teenager.'

Mrs Gale explained that she lived with her husband and children on the Alton Estate. She'd lived there for 14 years or so.

She had two dogs, which she took for walks on Wimbledon Common quite often. She tended to take them during the week, and with her husband at weekends.

'The estate is very large,' she said, 'but I've come to know some people as friends and some just to say hello to. One of the people I know, and who I'd worked with at some time, had a sandy-coloured mongrel called Brandy, which she gave to Colin Stagg.

'When Brandy went to Colin Stagg, I'd spoken to him very occasionally. I saw Colin wearing T-shirts mainly, jeans, a leather jacket, casual clothing. The T-shirts were white mainly, sometimes black.

'Before Colin Stagg got Brandy, he had another dog, a black mongrel which appeared to be old. I saw them on Wimbledon Common occasionally. After he got Brandy, I continued to see him on Wimbledon Common. I saw more of him once he had the new dog, usually once a day.

'When I go to the common, I use the underpass by Putney Vale Cemetery. On the estate side by the underpass is some grass. I've seen Colin Stagg on occasions while I've been there. He'd be walking his dog, going under the underpass to the common.

'When I saw Colin Stagg, I wouldn't speak to him as my older dog is quite aggressive and I'd try to keep him apart from other dogs. I'd sometimes acknowledge him.

'I had a usual walk when I went on to the common. After going through the underpass, I'd walk along the path to the Curling Pond, and then carry on to the monument, and then go over the large mound, which is sort of three hills, then down to the other side, heading in the direction of the windmill. Before I got to the windmill, I'd do a sharp right back to the underpass. I'd normally go on my own with the two dogs. I would usually go between 8.30 – 9.30 in the morning, sometimes earlier. I would mainly see Colin Stagg when I was coming back, but it would vary.

'Apart from the underpass, I've seen Colin Stagg near the windmill and going through the underpass and coming back. If we approached each other with dogs, I'd be worried that my dog might be aggressive. I'd sometimes go the other way, or Colin would go the other way, as he knew what my dog was like. I carried a dog lead with me on the common. I believe Mr Stagg carried a dog lead with him on the common. Apart from the dog lead, I never saw him carry anything else on the common.

'Apart from his clothing, I saw a bag on him. It was a bum-bag, a waist bag – black, I think.

'On Wednesday, 15 July 1992, I went on to the common. I left my home at roughly about ten-to-nine. My mother-in-law was staying with me at that time. I was going to drive her home to collect her pension that morning. I wanted to be back between half-nine and ten to do that. I was intending to take a shorter walk that morning, as my mother in-law had to get home to cash her pension.

'I went to the usual underpass at Putney Vale. It takes five minutes to get from my home to the underpass. I followed the path going generally to the left, in an area known as Jerry's Hill. Normally, I would turn left and go towards the Curling Pond. I went left on that morning. When I got to the point where the paths divide, I met a lady with another dog. When our dogs came together they had a fight. We separated them. The lady was following the route I normally take.

'After the dogs had fought and been separated, I didn't carry along my normal route. I turned right towards the windmill. I turned back on myself by the side of the three hills towards the windmill. The hills were on my left. I turned left as I passed the three hills, I didn't go towards the windmill, I turned back towards the A3.

'I went towards the memorial and the Curling Pond. I then went through the trees towards the underpass. The path I'd been along cut across me. As I approached where the paths crossed, I saw Colin Stagg with Brandy. He was coming as if from the underpass. The path he was on went towards the windmill. I believe he saw me. He waved as if to say he'd seen me, as he always grabs hold of Brandy and I always grab my dog when we meet, and walked straight ahead.

'When I first saw him, Brandy was not on the lead. He either put him on the lead or held his collar when he saw me. He was wearing a white T-shirt on the top half of his body. I don't think it had any sleeves. I think he'd been wearing a white T-shirt for a few days. From where I was, the shirt looked clean. I believe he was wearing blue jeans. He may have been wearing trainers, I'm not too sure.

'He had a bag around his waist, a black bum-bag. The bag was about 9in long and about 7in deep, I would say. Colin is about 5ft 9in tall, aged about 30, slim build, short mid- to dark-brown hair. He walks very stooping. It is a distinctive walk.

'I met him at about twenty-five-past-nine, half-past nine. I got to my home at twenty-five-to-ten, twenty-to-ten. From where I saw him, it is about a ten-minute walk to my front door. I did not see him again that day.'

'How do you know it was that day?'

'I told you, my mother-in-law was staying with us and that's how I know, because I altered my normal routine for that day.'

'How can you be sure of the time?'

'Because I was at home ten minutes later and that would have been the time that it would have taken me from seeing Colin to getting home.'

'Did Colin see you?'

'Yes, in fact Brandy wasn't on his lead – he saw me, and because our dogs fight, it was from a distance, he waved, put Brandy on a lead, and I went home and Colin was on the common.'

Mrs Gale said that she'd seen Colin after that day, but they didn't speak beyond a passing hello or acknowledgement.

'After I learned of the murder on the common, I didn't continue to walk there each day. When I watched *Crimewatch* on television, I saw an item about the murder of Miss Nickell. A photofit was shown during that item. When I saw it, it brought Colin Stagg to my mind. It was a very good likeness of how Colin appeared in July.'

Mrs Gale also said that on 15 July, when she came across Colin Stagg, he was in her view for about five seconds, and no more than 25 to 50 yards away from her. There was nothing to obstruct her view of him. It was quite a bright, warm day.

'At that stage, I'd known Colin Stagg for about nine years,' she said. 'I'd seen him wearing the bum-bag a couple of times. I can't remember if I saw him wearing it after 15 July.'

On top of Mrs Avid's evidence, all of this began to worry us a little bit, because there was Mr Stagg saying he was at home by 9.15am – or at the latest by 9.30am, according to his other version – and that he had fallen asleep. Also, it was profoundly at variance with what he had said. He had said he came home by the top underpass, and walked around Jerry's Hill, yet here was Susan Gayle saying that at 9.25am he was coming on to the common with his dog Brandy, and he also had his bum-bag on.

Obviously, you do not take things at face value. I checked PC Couch's notes and confirmed that Colin had said, 'I was on the common between 8.00am and 8.50am.'

According to Susan Gayle, that was clearly a lie. And according to Lillian Avid, Colin had, at midday, mentioned the murder of a young girl.

I came out of the interview room and spoke to Mick Wickerson. I asked him, 'What levels of knowledge did you have at around one or two o'clock on the day of the murder, with regard to the time that Rachel had got there – or even who she was?'

Mick said, 'It wasn't until very late on in the afternoon, early evening, that we'd begun to get an idea that Rachel arrived just before ten o'clock.' To all intents and purposes, Rachel could have been there since seven or eight o'clock – she could have been lying in that position for God knows how long.'

So even the senior investigating officers didn't realise at that stage that 10.30am was an important time. I thought, That's strange, how did Colin know it was important to tell lies about timings? He was quite happy to admit being on the common between 8.00am and 8.15am – so how did he know that the murder hadn't occurred at that time? Why was it important for him to lie about not being there, and not being seen by Susan Gayle at 9.25am? (Of course, Stagg may have been mistaken as to the timings, and our own theories wrong.)

Add to this the evidence of Amanda Phelan, who had seen a man fitting Colin's description and carrying a black bag, washing his hands in the stream at about 10.30am, and we were becoming very concerned. Colin appeared to be lying, and appeared to have had knowledge as to the time of the offence when he made this statement to the police officer, that even the SIO didn't know.

We put to him what Lillian Avid had reported he'd said – 'I missed it by ten minutes.'

'Did you have this conversation?'

'Yes.'

'Did you say ten minutes?'

'I may have said 15 minutes.'

'But Colin, that still places you on the common, on your own admission, at a time when you say you were at home asleep on your sofa with a terrible headache.' Colin then went through an entire spectrum of emotions. He became tearful, he became belligerent. 'They're all lying about me,' he said. 'Everyone's trying to fit me up. Why are they telling lies about me? You can't believe what Lillian Avid's saying – she's over 60, did you know that? She's senile.'

DC Martin Long and I continued to question Stagg the following day. It was clear that our suspect knew the common like the back of his hand. He walked there two or three times a day and occasionally visited his father's grave at the adjacent Putney cemetery. He knew the correct names of the hills, ponds, paths, woods and other features. He also knew their history, from the Curling Pond which Queen Victoria had ordered to be dug for one of her favourite winter sports, to the triple mounds of Jerry's Hill, where the highwayman Jerry Abershaw was taken to the gibbet in 1795. Interestingly enough, Jerry used to ride out from the Bald Stag at Kingston Vale.

Stagg stuck to his story that he had risen at 6.30am as usual on 15 July, done his paper round, walked the dog at 8.30am, then gone back home. He maintained that it wasn't until he was woken from a nap by the noise of the police helicopter that he went out, in shorts, T-shirt and sunglasses, for a second walk with Brandy. Trying to get on to the common, he was stopped and told by a policeman at the A3 underpass that a girl had been killed on the common.

'I was shocked,' Stagg said. 'I gave him my name and address and thought that would be it. Everything I have told you is the exact truth. I am not a murderer. I could never hit a woman even if I wanted to. I don't even hit my dog.'

Martin asked him if he was the man seen by some witnesses on the day of the murder, carrying a black bag, with a belt or dog lead round his waist. Impossible, Stagg said. Was he the man one witness had spotted washing his hands in a stream? Emphatically not.

'I don't have a black bag,' he said. 'And I only take a bath on Thursdays and Sundays. It's my routine. I've never washed my hands in the stream. It smells. If I did that, I would smell.'

He denied vehemently that he had seen Rachel on the common that morning. 'I would have noticed someone like her. I had told a neighbour that I thought I had seen her two years ago with her baby in a buggy. I didn't see her, I swear on my dog's life. I couldn't kill her. Even when my dog does something wrong, I can't even hit him.'

Just when we had him on the ropes with some tricky questions, the tape would run out or something else would happen to cause a delay and give him a breathing space. In the three or four minutes it took to take out the tape, label it, seal it so that it could not be tampered with and then place a new, clean tape in the machine, the respite would have been sufficient for him, assuming he felt it necessary, to gather his thoughts and we were back to square one. Stagg visibly pulled himself together during each such break. He seemed to be like a new man, changing even his body language. The obvious answer would have been to use longer-playing tapes but the Met only seems to have 30-minute tapes.

It was also becoming increasingly evident and alarming that if Colin Stagg was the killer – and we couldn't assume he was, and he may well not have been – then he was unlikely ever to confess. Of course, he may well have been telling the truth and had nothing to confess relating to the killing.

Following a long and tiring Saturday of interviews, Martin Long and I were sitting in my office drinking a couple of well-deserved cans of lager.

'Don't know about you, Keith, but I'm knackered.'

'It's been a long day and I'm not sorry it's over,' I said, stifling a yawn. 'It was like banging your head against a brick wall.'

'It's a new one on me. I mean, why bother telling lies when you can just ignore the question you've been asked and spout nonsensical bollocks?'

I laughed at the painful memory of trying to get a straight answer from Stagg.

'I must admit he's either got a skin like a rhino or he's on drugs. He certainly doesn't embarrass easily. I don't know, Mart, perhaps I'm losing my touch.' I should point out that no trace of drugs was found when the house was searched.

'You can't do any more than you've been doing. It's just that it don't seem to matter what you confront him with, he just denies it and claims that they're all out to get him. All that stuff about Mrs Gayle getting it wrong – I mean, for heaven's sake, Guv, she's known him for years and is positive that she's got the day right.'

'Yeah, I know, and Sparshatt's checked and double-checked. No, he's lying – and he knows that if he accepts what she said it blows his alibi right out of the water. He's got to say that she's got the day wrong, but it's just his bad luck that Mrs Gayle had her mother-in-law staying with her and remembers the day because she had to get back to take Mum to get her pension.'

'But how you're going to get him to admit he is lying beats the hell out of me.'

'He should have been an MP. I've never met anyone as good as him for ignoring what you ask him and then rambling on about things that don't drop him in the shit.'

'There's no doubt about it, he's got some very strange ideas. JB will be well pleased when he hears that, according to Colin Stagg, anyone knocking 60 must be senile.'

The time came to get a warrant for further detention so we could hold identification parades the following day, and for further enquiries to be made.

I said to Mr Wood, Colin's solicitor, 'We have the press camped all around the nick, in people's back gardens with ladders up over the walls. We can't afford a picture to be published in the press because we have identification proceedings, that would jeopardise any further identification procedures. So, to keep him out of the way of the cameras, we'll reverse the van up to one of the less accessible doors, vision-wise, to the press. We'll put a blanket over his head, get him in the back of the van, take him into court, and generally make sure that nothing happens to jeopardise the identification proceedings.'

The solicitor agreed to this and said, 'Colin, don't worry about it, because it's in your best interests. There's lots of press outside so the police are going to put a blanket over your head. Just trust them and walk down the road.'

'Why have I got to do that, then?'

'You don't want any unnecessary publicity,' replied his solicitor. 'And of course, you might be innocent.' And, naturally, that could well have been the case.

Chapter 18

On the Sunday, we held an identification parade. The rules and regulations concerning the running of parades and other ID procedures are a minefield. First, the parade has to be organised and conducted by an officer of the rank of inspector, and this officer must be totally independent of the inquiry for which the parade is being done. Then, once the request for a parade has been made, no officer with any connection to the inquiry can have any involvement in the arrangements or running of the parade. Annex A to code D of the Codes of Practice govern the conduct of these procedures.

Because of the aggravation involved in holding parades, a purpose-built Identification Suite had been established at Brixton Police Station. This is staffed by an inspector, a sergeant and half-a-dozen PCs. The centre is equipped with a parade room which has a one-way glass window running its entire length so that witnesses can see the line-up, but the participants on the parade can't see them. There are facilities to video the proceedings, and segregated waiting rooms to keep the witnesses apart from the 'stooges', volunteer members of the public who stand on the parade to make up the numbers.

The major problem in the past had been collecting enough volunteers to stand on the parade who are acceptable to the suspect's solicitor as being sufficiently similar to the suspect in height, age, general appearance and position in life. This can be a time-consuming exercise and the problem was always what to do with the volunteers whilst the arrangements were being made. Inevitably, they would end up being fed cups of tea and sticky buns in the canteen. This was far from a satisfactory solution, for the same problem would occur with the witnesses. Common sense and fairness dictated that these two groups had to be segregated.

Defence lawyers had in the past tried to allege that identifications were unreliable because witnesses may have come into contact with stooges, and the ID was made by a process of elimination. That is to say, that the person on the parade that they picked out must have been the suspect because they hadn't seen him in the canteen or wherever with the others. By and large, this would be an unfair allegation, but they only needed to cast the shadow of a reasonable doubt.

For these reasons, very strict guidelines had been set down. In general terms the rules are these:

(1) The parade shall consist of at least eight persons (in addition to the suspect) who shall so far as possible resemble the suspect in age, height, general appearance and position in life. (Code D annex A para 8)
(2) All unauthorised persons must be excluded from the place where the parade is held. (Code D annex A para 6)
(3) Once the parade has been formed, everything afterwards in respect of the parade shall take place in the presence and hearing of the suspect and of any interpreter, solicitor, friend or appropriate adult who is present. [Unless, as in this case, the parade involves a screen, in which case anything said to, or by, any witness at the place where the parade is held must be said in the hearing and presence of the suspect's solicitor, friend or appropriate adult *or* be recorded on video.] (Code D annex A para 7)

(4) When the suspect is brought to the place where the parade is to be held, he shall be asked by the Identification Officer whether he has any objection to the arrangements for the parade or to any of the participants in it. The suspect may obtain advice from his solicitor or friend, if present, before the parade proceeds. Where practicable, steps shall be taken to remove the grounds for objection. (Code D annex A para 10)
(5) The suspect may select his own position in the line-up. Where there is more than one witness, the Identification Officer must inform the suspect after each witness has left that he may change his position in the line. Each position in the line must be clearly numbered. (Code D annex A para 11)
(6) The Identification Officer is responsible for ensuring that, before they attend the parade, witnesses are not able to:
(i) Communicate with each other about the case or overhear a witness who has already seen the parade.
(ii) See any member of the parade.
(iii) On that occasion see or be reminded of any photograph or description of the suspect or be given any other indication of his identity.
(iv) See the suspect either before or after the parade. (Code D annex A para 12)
(7) The officer conducting a witness to a parade must not discuss with him the composition of the parade, and in particular he must not disclose whether a previous witness has made any identification. (Code D annex A para 13)
(8) Witnesses shall be brought in one at a time. Immediately before the witness inspects the parade, the Identification Officer shall tell him that 'the person you saw may or may not be on the parade and, if you cannot make a positive identification, you should say so.' The officer shall then ask the witness to walk along the parade at least twice, taking as much care and time as he wishes. When he has done so, the officer shall ask him whether the person he saw in person on an earlier relevant occasion is on the parade. (Code D annex A para 14)
(9) The witness should make an identification by indicating the

number of the person concerned. (Code D annex A para 15)
(10) When the last witness has left, the Identification Officer shall ask the suspect whether he wishes to make any comments on the conduct of the parade. (Code D annex A para 18)

In the case of Colin Stagg every one of the above rules was rigorously applied. No one from the squad was allowed anywhere near the parade. Every effort was made to ensure fairness to the suspect and also to guarantee the integrity of the witnesses.

Jane Harriman picked out Colin Stagg without any hesitation whatsoever, which now caused us another problem. For not only did we have Susan Gayle saying, 'He came on to the common at 9.25am,' we also had Jane Harriman saying, 'Yes, this is the man I saw on three occasions on the morning of the murder, at 10.10, 10.17 and 10.23am.'

In other words, the murder happened at 10.30am, and there was Colin Stagg, geographically and chronologically, just five-and-a-half minutes away from the time and the scene.

We knew that the blows could have been inflicted in at least three minutes, and we knew from the time that Mr Murray found the body that the murder couldn't have happened any later than 10.30am, and it certainly couldn't have been too much earlier than 10.30am.

At this stage, having had the positive identification, we were extremely concerned that Colin had got something to hide. It wasn't just my interpretation, he was quite clearly saying various things which were provable as being untrue. And then there was this anomaly with PC Couch's statement. Colin appeared to be telling lies – but why?

We took him back through his entire history.

He had told us he had had a couple of short-term relationships with girls called Ms X and Ms Y. We followed this up. For me to speak with the girls in question would have been in contravention of police procedure. In view of the nature of the murder inquiry and the fact that she was the ex-girlfriend of a man who was suspected of being a sexual killer, it would have been highly questionable for a male officer to undertake the delicate questioning that was required. WDC Bernie Bennett, an experienced detective, was deputed to interview Ms Y. Bernie handled the sensitive enquiry very well; even if it had been proper for me to talk to Ms Y, I very much doubted that she would have been inclined to discuss the sexual nature of her relationship with Colin to a male officer.

Ms Y said she regarded Stagg as brighter than average. She knew he had passed an entry exam for the RAF when he was 19 but had been unable to enlist because of a medical problem.

Ms Y also told us that they had never had a full sexual relationship; she said Colin was a bit strange and appeared to have sexual problems. He had confessed to her that, amazingly, at the age of nearly 30, he was still a virgin. His efforts at intercourse had failed because he 'just couldn't get it up'. Stagg never tried on anything of a sexual nature with Ms Y, but when she packed him up, he got quite angry. Again, that began to worry us a little bit, because Paul Britton had talked about a sexual dysfunction.

There were occasions over the three days that I got the distinct impression that I was interviewing two or three totally different people. That was not to say that Colin Stagg's behaviour gave rise to any suspicion that I was dealing with some sort of multiple personality disorder, but he seemed to us to be trying to manipulate Martin and me in an attempt to engender sympathy, and when that failed his tactics changed and went from weak and weepy to a resolute refusal to except facts that could be proved beyond dispute and from there to aggression. In fact, the more we revealed to him, the more resolute became his denials – in particular, his allegations that people were conspiring against him and telling lies. Throughout the interviews, as and when Mr Stagg's behaviour appeared to be contradictory, and in some cases downright confusing, I would ring Paul Britton; according to him, Stagg's denials were indicative of his cunning and basic intelligence.

Stagg claimed that he was a truthful person and never lied, and even when we proved he had indeed lied, he still refused to accept it. When faced with unpalatable facts, rather than answer the questions he responded by changing the subject and attempting to use nonsensical arguments to support his story. Mr Stagg was a most frustrating man to deal with.

Paul's advice was simple. 'You must remain calm, you must be firm and you must make him understand that it is inevitable that the truth will come out.'

'I understand what you're saying, Paul, but it's like talking to a brick wall. He's telling lies. He's been picked out on an ID parade by one woman, identified as being on the common much later than he's prepared to admit, and that was substantiated by another woman who has known him for over ten years. Quite frankly, I have the feeling that if I told him that Christmas falls on 25 December he'd deny it.'

'Keith, you must understand that if this man is responsible, it may be that he has blocked it from his memory and is refusing to accept, even to himself, that he has done this terrible thing. Again, I can only emphasise that if this man is the killer, you must show him the inevitability that the truth will come out, and that if he is blanking something from his memory that he will have to face up to it eventually.'

'What would you suggest is the best way of achieving that?'

'Patience and a firm approach. I would suggest, for example, that you don't give him the opportunity of a denial. Perhaps if you can show him a photograph of Rachel as she was found, and state that this was as he last saw her. It may make him realise that blanking it from his memory is not going to work. Ask him what it was that suddenly made him do what he did. Was it something that Rachel did that made him lose control? Or something that she or Alex said? Reassure him; tell him that he can tell you. You're not there to judge, but to understand.'

I took Paul's advice. The photo was chosen very carefully in consultation with JB and Wickerson. Obviously, we didn't want to give away any of the confidential information for fear of it becoming public knowledge, and subsequently being inundated with false confessions. The photograph, labelled by us as KP27, and which I signed and dated in front of his solicitor, was a shot of Rachel's body from behind and at a distance of about 15 to 20 feet. Rachel was lying on the ground, but the angle was such that, apart from the top of her head, all you could see of her body was the back of her thighs; her trousers had been pulled down, but all of that area was in shadow. In short, the photograph was sufficient to give an impression of a dead body, but no specific detail of injuries or the position of Rachel's hands or head.

Paul had said, 'It's possible he's trying to convince himself that he hasn't done anything. It might be that if you show him a photograph, it might bring it all back.'

It didn't. It produced very little reaction at all.

Although there were no admissions from Stagg about the murder, he did, however, make one interesting confession during 12 hours of interrogation. He admitted to us that he was a flasher. He agreed that he was the naked man reported by a woman witness as wearing 'nothing but sunglasses and a smile' some time between the day of the murder and 24 July, nine days later.

Colin eventually got quite heated when I was talking to him about the nude sunbathing. This very attractive young lady says he was lying there with no clothes on and he said that he looked up and saw her walking towards him and he thought, Should I cover myself up? – no, sod it, why should I? If she doesn't want to see, she doesn't have to walk past.

He then tried telling us that there was nothing wrong with it because one of the Rangers had seen him nude sunbathing and hadn't said anything to him.

I said, 'Colin, what are the Rangers up there for? What do you think is one of their major problems?'

'Indecency.'

'Yes, that's right. So you're telling us that you're lying there in all your naked glory and this Ranger rides past and says, "All right, Colin, no problems, you've missed a bit with the suntan lotion, you don't want to lie there too long, you'll get burned." You're telling us this?'

He said, 'Yeah.'

'What about this woman that you indecently exposed yourself to?'

'I didn't indecently expose myself to anyone. I was just sitting there and as she walked past I just put my leg up to cover myself.'

The story that she told officers was more a question of Colin opening his legs and there he was, fully erect. 'He opened his legs, which were together, in front of him,' her statement read. 'When he opened his legs, he exposed his penis, which was fully erect.'

'I remember the incident, but my penis wasn't erect,' Colin said. 'It was lying across my leg ... I was sitting up and my penis was lying across my leg, like it normally does.'

So we had a man who was telling lies, who had committed offences of indecency, and who had been expressing a knowledge very early on that he shouldn't really have had, about where the murder had occurred and the fact that he had missed it by ten minutes.

No two ways about it, Colin Stagg was the short-haired suspect; but the problem we had was, did the short-haired suspect kill Rachel Nickell? Colin was obviously on the common, and he appeared to be lying for some reason, but what on earth it could be we couldn't think of. So Colin continued to be a worrying prospect, and we did not have a single shred of concrete evidence with which to charge him.

The question of how much evidence you need to charge someone is rather like saying, 'How long is a piece of string?' In the old days, the police were rather more magisterial and we would actually assess whether there was credible evidence to support the charge and that really would be the sole criterion. Now we tend to consider wider issues such as the probability of obtaining a conviction. We look at the whole picture and take the strengths and weaknesses of the case into consideration. The police are no longer the prosecuting authority; that position has been taken by the CPS. If we do prefer a charge, the CPS have the ultimate responsibility to decide whether it should proceed beyond the first court appearance. In 99 cases out of 100, the decision to charge is not challenged by the CPS. The problems usually occur later in the procedure if additional evidence is requested when a 'not guilty' plea is entered, and this additional evidence is either not forthcoming or fails to come up to standard.

The above really refers to straightforward jobs; anything of a contentious nature would normally be dealt with by bailing the suspect and putting a report up for advice. Even in cases where there is credible evidence, the CPS may still decline to prosecute. The Attorney General's guidelines state that, because of the pressure on the courts and the cost to the public purse, there should be a greater than 51 per cent chance of securing a conviction. Helicopter vision really comes into play in this decision-making process; everything is considered – stated cases both for and against the prosecution case, even the public perception of, and attitude to, the offence in question.

In this particular case, we had a lot of circumstantial evidence that was based largely on what appeared to be lies and inconsistencies during the interviews, and identification which placed him on the common very proximate to the time and scene of the murder. There was enough to be extremely concerned about this man, but insufficient to pass the 51 per cent rule. We probably could have argued that there was credible evidence to support the charge and even got it past committal, but under these circumstances, getting it past the CPS would have been the major hurdle and, applying their criteria, I couldn't disagree with them.

We had no forensic, we had no eye-witness to the offence, but what we did have was a man who looked very much like Jane Harriman's photofit, and had been identified by Jane Harriman as being the man she claimed she saw that morning. More importantly, she saw him following women.

We had Susan Gayle, making a lie of his so-called alibi, and there couldn't be any question as to the fact that she got the right man – even though the defence would probably say that she'd got the wrong day. But she was taxed about that at great length and was quite convinced that it was the day of the murder.

We could have charged him with the murder on circumstantial evidence. However, what would probably have happened was that we'd have got it through committal, only to lose it at a half-time application by the defence that it was unsafe to put to the jury. I think we realised that, at the time, we didn't have a 51 per cent chance of a successful prosecution.

So we had to bail him out – but not before we charged him with indecent exposure. He was bailed in his own recognizance for the murder, but kept in police custody for the indecent exposure because of the media interest.

Detained over a period of three days after we had obtained a court order for further detention, Stagg was duly charged with indecent exposure and taken next morning to Wimbledon Magistrates' Court.

The magistrates listened to evidence that a woman walking her dogs on the common's playing fields had seen Stagg lying completely naked, apart from sunglasses, with his clothes piled up nearby. 'He opened his legs,' the prosecutor said, 'exposing himself – and smiled.'

Stagg did not look particularly concerned as the magistrates fined him £200 with £20 costs. The offence, said Graham Wood, to a packed courtroom, had nothing to do with the murder inquiry, 'but because his name has been released to the press, Mr Stagg's reputation has been sullied.'

After his case had been heard, Stagg was released on bail in respect of the Rachel Nickell inquiry, but we announced that he might still face further questioning.

Trying to make a getaway out of the rear doors of the court, he ran straight into a waiting posse of reporters and photographers, all eager to hear what he had to say about being held for three days as a suspect for one of Britain's most horrific murders.

'I had nothing to be afraid of,' he said. 'I'm an innocent man and want to see the person who killed Rachel caught just as much as everyone else.'

He then knocked over a photographer's tripod, stuck two fingers up at the remaining cameramen, and loped off with his characteristic gait.

In the next few days, we confirmed to the press that we were anxious to trace Colin's brother, Anthony. His rape conviction four years earlier bore enough interesting similarities to the Rachel killing to warrant a closer look. Anthony, who looked very like his brother Colin, had attacked his attractive 19-year-old victim while she was walking her dog. It had happened on open land at Putney Heath, close to Wimbledon Common, much like the Rachel attack. We wished to question him with a view to eliminating him from enquiries. Anthony Stagg was traced to his home in Worcester and was able to provide a watertight alibi for his movements on 15 July.

During the same period, Colin dispensed with the services of Graham Wood as his solicitor, and went to Ian Ryan of Russell-Cooke, Potter & Chapman. He was quoted as saying that he wanted to start suing the Metropolitan Police for wrongful arrest.

Chapter 19

In late September, a woman who had initially contacted Crime Stoppers was given the number of the incident room at Wimbledon and called us with some very disturbing information. She would not give her name, but said she had some information about the Rachel Nickell inquiry; she had been having a relationship with her cousin, which she thought was incest, and was afraid of finding herself arrested if she agreed to an interview. Cliff Davies, a uniformed skipper who had been seconded to the inquiry, and a TI called Sean Phillips, tried to tell her that this wasn't the case, but she would not have it. She hung up.

The next day she called again, this time revealing that her name was Helen. She said that her cousin, a man called Gary Edmondson, had confessed to killing Rachel Nickell. He had allegedly said he didn't mean to murder her but just wanted sex and 'freaked out' when the little boy screamed. Helen said she thought Gary had another man with him at the time.

We were in the formative stages of starting the undercover operation, but still had to keep our minds open to other possibilities. So convincing was her story that we had every reason to believe her call was genuine. The action to TIE Gary Edmondson was given the highest priority.

For another month, Helen made numerous other calls to the incident room, but failed to deliver any concrete information which would lead us to the suspect.

Then, at the end of October, she finally told us that Gary was hiding out at an address in Manchester. We got a rough address and phone number which we traced, and a team of officers immediately drove north to check out the information. Gary Edmondson was not at the house but Helen had given the correct phone number at the address and had correctly identified one of the other occupants. We now had even more reason to take her seriously.

Next time she called, Helen said she had now been threatened by the second man allegedly involved in attacking Rachel because she was asking too many questions. She said she feared for her safety if the two men got to know she was talking to the police.

This was beginning to sound horrendous. In the course of one conversation, we managed to glean from her a rough age for her cousin, and started searching through the National Registration of births, marriages and deaths at St Catherine's House, and poring over hundreds of electoral rolls in south-west London, where he was supposed to live. We couldn't find him.

Two weeks later, we got another call, this time from an American-sounding woman calling herself Josie. She said she was worried about another girl living in the same house, who was somehow linked to the Rachel Nickell inquiry. Josie, who said she was an American student attending an economics course in London, claimed the other woman, whom she named as Helen, had told her she knew who had murdered Rachel. It looked like further confirmation of the Gary Edmondson lead.

Josie phoned several times during the next two weeks, giving more and more detail about Helen and Gary, but she, too, failed to produce any nitty-gritty information that would enable us to move in and make an arrest. 'I don't want to get involved,' she said.

In an attempt to trace Josie, we now checked at universities where Americans might be studying as exchange students, as well as at the US embassy and universities in California, from which Josie said she had transferred to a college in England. Nothing.

Then, by pure chance, Sean Phillips and I happened to be in the incident room on a Sunday afternoon when the phone rang in the researcher's office. I picked it up and started recording the conversation. It was the first woman again.

'Where are you ringing from, Helen?'

'A call box.'

'Where is the call box?'

'In Lewisham.'

She started talking about her American flatmate, and the whole thing dovetailed in very nicely.

We chatted for a minute or two, and meanwhile she was putting money in at a rate of knots.

Afterwards, as I listened to the tape with Sean, I said, 'Do you reckon she was phoning from Lewisham?'

I rang up the telephone exchange and asked, 'What is the minimum length of time that you get for ten pence?' The operator said that on a Sunday it was something like 90 seconds, though it went in bands around the country.

We counted the number of clunks and timed the conversation. In the course of a call lasting just three minutes, she had inserted six or seven coins. The smallest coin a callbox accepts is a 10 pence, so the call had cost a minimum of 70 pence – which ruled out Lewisham. We worked out from the band of charges that she must have been phoning from outside a 50-mile radius of London. In other words, Helen was telling lies.

We put a trace on the line, and the next call from Helen was quickly pinpointed to Cheltenham in Gloucestershire. It was made from a firm called the Cheltenham Induction Heating Company in Saxon Way. We ran checks on all five women employed by the firm, and Cliff and Sean drove down to the West Country on 24 November, nearly two months after the first call had triggered off the enquiry.

They went into the local police station, and as soon as they mentioned the name of this company, a young WDS in the office said, 'Susan Eyles – she has previously made spurious allegations of rape and all sorts ...' The officers confronted Susan Eyles, who admitted she was the bogus Helen. Eventually, during a tape-recorded interview at the local police station, she confessed that she had, in fact, made up the whole thing.

Susan Jacqueline Eyles was charged with wasting police time, put on probation for a year, and recommended to seek psychiatric help. Her wild-goose chase had cost us almost £6,000 and kept murder squad officers from following up genuine lines of enquiry.

Nobody ever found out why she did it. In almost every major police inquiry, there will always be some bitter or twisted individuals who complicate our lives and waste huge amounts of time and money by supplying false leads.

As Wickerson said, however, at least it proved we were not conducting the inquiry in a blinkered fashion once Colin Stagg had been accepted as the prime suspect. If we had excluded all suspects apart from Colin Stagg, we certainly wouldn't have followed up her story so vigorously, and used so many and so varied a range of police resources.

There was another episode that proved that we were being open-minded about Colin Stagg's involvement or otherwise in the killing. Four months after the murder, two of the team flew to Italy to interview a gravedigger who had disappeared on 16 July, 24 hours after Rachel's murder.

Henry Lavelle, aged 28, worked at Putney Vale Cemetery, next to Wimbledon Common. On the day of the murder, a police tracker dog had followed the suspect's scent from the murder scene into the graveyard. A Mrs Marjorie Piper, who had been visiting the cemetery that morning, had told officers how she had heard someone running quickly on the other side of the fence, though she could not see anyone. She thought no more of it until she heard of the murder, then realised it might have been the killer running away. Officers who questioned 20 other graveyard workers were told that Mr Lavelle had travelled to Europe the next day to look for a job in a vineyard. He had just been traced through Interpol, and we decided that, because of his proximity to the murder, he must be interviewed in person. The officers flew to Treviso, 16 miles north of Venice, to speak to him at the offices of the British Consulate, but were able to eliminate him very swiftly from further enquiries.

All of which went to show that we were as much trying to eliminate Colin Stagg as incriminate him. It was just a question of solving the problem – did he or didn't he? – and depending on which answer we came up with, we would adapt our future action accordingly.

Chapter 20

The whole squad had noticed the facial resemblance between Eric Roberts and Colin Stagg, and there was no getting away from the fact that, when asked a closed question, young Alex had said that Eric should be put behind bars. However, whilst Roberts did look like Colin Stagg, he didn't look as much like Colin Stagg as Colin Stagg did, and Colin Stagg looked extremely like the photofit impression of the Jane Harriman suspect. Coupled with that was what Harriman said about the way this man was walking. Colin Stagg, on his own admission, in letters to Julie Pines, had stated quite clearly, 'The women around here laugh at me because I've got this funny way of walking.' Game, set and match for Colin Stagg being the Harriman suspect, as far as everybody was concerned.

However, the worry remained that if Alex picked out Colin Stagg at an identity parade, Stagg's defence would raise the issue of his reliability as a witness.

As a fail-safe, we took possession of Mr Roberts's car, took it to pieces and examined it forensically – a bit pointless, really, because even if we found traces of Rachel Nickell in that car, it wouldn't have proved a great deal either way, by virtue of the fact that they had gone on car trips together. If we found blood, for example, all he had to say was that she'd nicked her finger one day, or had had a nose bleed.

So it was back to square one – apart from some small traces of blood that had been discovered on his training shoes, and the suggestion by other parents from the school that Eric was besotted with Rachel. The blood had been found by the lab during routine forensic examination, but the traces were so minute that we couldn't even group them, let alone DNA them. When I now double-checked the results, someone at the lab said, 'Why don't we try PCR?'

I did not have the vaguest idea what he was talking about. It turned out that PCR stood for Polymerise Chain Reaction, a relatively new development involving a process which grew blood from the original minute trace, and from there the DNA analysis could be carried out. In this particular case, the test failed to work, but despite the fact that we couldn't even group the blood, Eric still had blood on his shoes and he had to be asked how it got there. We turned up at Eric Roberts's clean but chaotic flat and brought him in for questioning.

I perceived Roberts as a woolly-headed individual. He was a thinker and pontificator rather than a doer – the sort who knocks the establishment but is unwilling to do anything about changing it. There was a vagueness to his existence, he and Margaret taking it in turns to lie in bed all morning on alternate days, not working and generally enjoying the life of Riley. Not that this made them bad people.

We put a lot of effort into him, and the cynical policeman's mind suggested: very young, very attractive young lady; Eric Roberts, one of life's victims, infatuated ... I could just picture the scenario – he tries it on, she rebuffs him, he loses his temper.

The interrogation probably breached most of the current thinking on what constitutes oppression. We probed and pushed and picked holes in Eric's answers. He was told about the gossip which had circulated about his relationship with Rachel. He admitted that he found her very attractive, and in a nutshell, fancied her something rotten. But he also said that he accepted he was no oil painting and he realised that Rachel did not reciprocate his feelings. This quite naturally led us on to the 'unrequited love' line of questioning: 'Come on, Eric, take a deep breath and tell me the truth. You tried it on with Rachel, she gave you a knock back and you lost your temper – didn't you?'

'No. It wasn't like that. Rachel was a lovely person. I couldn't hurt anyone, let alone her.'

'You expect us to believe you? You were obsessed with her, weren't you?'

'No, I wasn't obsessed with her – not in that way.'

'Well, in what way were you obsessed with her?' asked Wickerson.

'I wasn't obsessed.'

'You just said you were.'

'No, you're getting me confused, Rachel was a lovely person. I just ...'

'You just what, Eric? You killed her, didn't you?'

'No, no, I didn't. I've told you I couldn't ever have hurt her.'

By this stage, he was becoming tearful and distressed.

'Look, Eric. You say you weren't obsessed.'

'Yes.'

'But you're not a rich man, are you? ... Your business went to the wall, didn't it?'

'Yes, but what's this got to do with Rachel's murder?'

'Alex has named you as being responsible.'

The look of shock on Roberts's face had to be seen to be believed.

'No, that can't be right! I didn't! I wouldn't have hurt ... I couldn't have hurt Rachel or Alex.' He was in tears.

'Then, there's the blood on your trainers and the fact that you phoned us on the evening of the 15th before we had released Rachel's name. You said that you thought you knew the dead woman and you even offered to identify her body. That's strange behaviour by any standard, isn't it?'

Eric Roberts didn't answer immediately; he was in shock.

'What blood?'

'We've found traces of blood on your training shoes. You remember we took possession of some of your clothing?' He nodded. 'Well, Eric, the lab found blood on your shoes. It's Rachel's, isn't it?'

'No. It can't be Rachel's.' He sat looking down at the desk shaking his head. 'No,' he continued, 'you've made a mistake ... it can't be Rachel's.'

Wickerson was just testing the water and gauging his reaction. We hadn't got a clue whose blood was on the shoes.

'Can I see the shoes?'

'Why?'

'If I knew which pair of shoes you were talking about, I might be able to tell you how I got blood on them. But there's no way it could belong to Rachel.'

I produced the shoes from under the desk and opened the brown paper bags in which they were sealed. I put them on the desk and pointed to the areas which had been marked with tiny specks of blood.

'Look. These spots are human blood. How did they get there?'

He sat and stared at the shoes. He was obviously racking his brain for an answer. He rubbed his eyes with both hands then looked at Wickerson.

'I remember. It's my blood. I half-killed myself down at the railway arches where my business used to be.'

'How?'

'I pulled a steel shutter down on my head. I bled like a pig. It must have come from there. It's my blood.'

'Is there anyone who can verify your story?'

'There was no one else there when I did it. Margaret should remember that I hurt myself, though. But it was ages ago.'

'When?'

'Last February or March, I can't really remember.'

'Did you go to hospital?'

He nodded.

'Which one?'

'I think it might have been St Georges.'

'Well, was it or wasn't it?'

'I think it was, but I can't really remember.'

I must admit that my impression that Eric Roberts was a total airhead was being confirmed by the minute.

'Did you call an ambulance?'

'No, I think I must have driven myself, I can't really remember.'

'You know we will obviously check up on what you've told us, don't you?'

'Yes. I'm telling you the truth.'

'OK, if what you've told us checks out it might explain the blood, but what about what little Alex told us? Why should he name you?'

'I don't know. Perhaps he was confused, but I didn't kill Rachel, I was at home. Margaret told you.'

'Yes, that's right, but it wouldn't be the first time a woman has lied to protect her man, would it?

'She's not lying, I was at home.'

'So what about all these people saying that you were besotted with Rachel and that you followed her around like a puppy?'

Again, he was close to tears and he placed his head in his hands and rubbed his eyes.

'Look, I really liked Rachel ...'

'There was more to it than that. *Wasn't there*? Regular walks on the common together – you tried it on and Rachel didn't want to know, that's why you killed her, isn't it?'

'*No! No!* I didn't kill her. I didn't kill her. I couldn't do anything like that.' He had broken down in floods of tears.

'So you expect us to believe this was a platonic relationship? Well, I'm sure it was on Rachel's part, but you misread her friendship and tried to take it further, didn't you?'

'No ... look, I admit I found her attractive, even more than that she was beautiful but she wasn't interested in me in that way. If she had have been I would have jumped at the chance, but she wasn't. I wouldn't have done anything that would have jeopardised our friendship, I ...'

'You what?'

'I loved her ... but not in that way. Everybody loved her.'

The interview continued in this vein until we'd exhausted every possibility, but he was right. Everybody that knew her loved her; she was just one of those special people.

Mick Wickerson and I had given him a severe verbal battering in front of his brief – so much so that the solicitor sat there shocked at some of the tactics. It wasn't rubber hoses, but it was an interrogation rather than a simple question and answer. He didn't slip up once. Eric Roberts was alibied, there was no forensic, the blood on his shoe could be explained.

In the end we said, 'OK, fine, we're satisfied.' We bailed him out and said, 'You understand why we had to do that?'

'I understand perfectly. You had an unpleasant job to do.'

In truth, we'd been satisfied before we even brought him to the station that in all probability he'd had nothing to do with Rachel's death, but because of the problems raised by the disclosure process we had to go through the motions. Had we not bothered, the defence would have had a field day by making allegations of a 'closed-minded and incomplete' approach to the investigation.

The way the questioning of Alex was done by Andre could well have given rise to the suggestion by the defence that Alex's recollections were unreliable because of the delay and the fact that possibly his account may have been tainted by things his family may have said within his hearing. Ideally, an evidential debriefing should have been conducted under controlled conditions which would not have allowed closed questioning. Had the process of questioning Alex been conducted in a more evidential manner, perhaps this information may have been regarded in a more favourable light. As it was, what Alex had said, because of the circumstances, was evidentially worthless.

So whilst we were still not sure about Stagg's involvement or otherwise, we at least felt happy with Eric Roberts.

Chapter 21

The publicity surrounding Stagg's conviction for indecent exposure had had two momentous results for us. One was that Jane Harriman, after seeing Colin on the television news, rang us and said, 'I was 100 per cent certain at the ID parade, but after seeing him walk I'm now 120 per cent certain I've identified the right man.'

Even more significant, however, was that we got a phone call from a girl called Andrea Parker, who thought we should know that Colin Stagg had responded to a lonely hearts ad she had placed in a magazine about 18 months prior to the murder. They'd had a short correspondence, but his letters became so obscene that she never wrote back again. That phone call was to change the whole course of the inquiry.

DS Steve Ward went to see Ms Parker, a factory worker, at her home in South London. He took a statement, and she showed him the letters Stagg had sent her nearly two years before, and which she had kept hidden away. The contents were disturbing, to say the least. Having only exchanged the normal preliminary pen pal niceties with a woman that he didn't know, Stagg had decided to start sending her material describing sexual activities that he would like to carry out on the common, near a fallen tree, and close to a stream. There were, we thought, definite echoes of the Rachel Nickell case here, and it began to cause us severe problems.

The whole incident had started when Andrea Parker placed the following small ad in the personal column of *Loot* magazine:

> *Lonely, shy, overweight, white woman, age 33, not very attractive, separated and waiting divorce, looking for white guy, 28–38, who, like myself is understanding, loving and likes home life. Must be non-smoker and love animals. Is this you, why not write now. Box 6109.*

Soon afterwards, she received a reply from Colin Stagg:

> *Dear 'Overweight, Lonely, Shy'*
>
> *Hello, my name is Colin. I am white, 28 years old, I live on my own with only my dog for company. I am only 5ft 7ins tall, black hair and blue eyes. My interests are keeping my home good, walking in the countryside with my dog, watching television (only if there is something worth watching) or just reading a good book.*

The letter continued in an unexceptional fashion, with Colin explaining that he was keen for Andrea to reply as he had never had a girlfriend nor for that matter ever even kissed a girl. He emphasised that he is a red-blooded male whose thoughts are never far from the subject of women. Colin disclosed that in the summer he likes to sunbathe naked and walk about his house 'starkers', but reassured Andrea that he is not a pervert and will understand if she is not interested.

At this point Colin introduced the subject of sexual fantasy and writes:

But if, due to distance, we cannot meet perhaps we can

'communicate' with each other, by sending letters about our 'fantasies'.

He continued his correspondence with further details of his domestic situation and an apology for his 'static' letter. He told Andrea that if she didn't want any 'thrills' he would still be happy to write to her. He signed off 'Yours Truly C. Stagg'.

Andrea wrote back, but Colin did not reply immediately. When he did, the contents were largely as you would expect in the preliminary stages of a 'Lonely Hearts' correspondence. He opened with an apology for the tardiness of his reply and went on to assure her that he was not concerned that she had described herself in her advert as 'overweight and not very attractive'. He wrote: 'I am not a shallow man that is influenced by "a pretty face". It is true that I have never had a girlfriend, although I have asked many girls out, but like I said in my last letter, "They just don't want to know."'

It was part of the next passage of the letter which, as an investigating officer and in the light of the evidence of Mrs Jane Harriman, interested me most. Colin continued: 'Although I am 5ft 7in tall I look much smaller, in the cold light of day, and I have an odd way of walking, that is why girls do not want to know.'

He explained he was uncomfortable with people and for this reason his only companion was his dog Brandy. He told Andrea that he preferred to stay in with a good book rather than socialise in pubs, but still longed for female company. He also declared his love of nature: 'Although I am no "macho" man, neither am I a wimp. I like to be also in the great outdoors, I love being in "wild" open spaces in all weathers too.'

The rest of the letter catalogued his hobbies as being: gardening, music through the spectrum from classical via Iron Maiden to Clannad, ancient and mediaeval British history and playing the guitar. He also flagged up his interest in reading about the occult and phenomena but explained: 'I am not a "weirdo or a satanist", ghosts and religious experiences fascinate me.'

He finished with a potted history of his family and a brief

description of his home, and as a final thought requested a photograph of Andrea and her telephone number before concluding:

> *I am sorry this reply to your letter is a bit late, but I hope your still interested in me.*
>
> *I would love to know more about you and your 'feelings'. Please reply.*
>
> *Colin XXX*
>
> *PS Send me your address so we can communicate properly.*

Following this communication, Andrea supplied a phone number and Colin called her. Later he wrote:

> *Dear Andrea,*
>
> *I'm sorry I left you so rudely on the phone, I just ran out of money. I didn't want to ring you back, because (I don't know if you noticed), I was a bit nervous, I do not know how to speak to people at the best of times, let alone a woman.*

Colin continued by disclosing that he had had a question which he had wanted to ask Andrea whilst they were talking on the phone but hadn't had the courage. He wanted to know whether it would be all right for them to exchange letters detailing their sexual fantasies. He wrote:

> *I am not a 'weirdo pervert'. It's just that I have never had anyone to confide in about my 'feelings and desires', if you do not want this, then that's OK.*

He explained he was a healthy and red-blooded man and the opportunity to write and receive such correspondence would ease his frustrations. He assured Andrea he would understand if she was not keen on the idea and asked her not to be offended by his suggestion. Colin persisted with the subject and informed her that he had included a fantasy letter in the same envelope but if she was not interested she should rip it up. If this was the case he asked if she would tell him otherwise he might send her another. The letter then moved on to other matters and Colin spent some time assuring Andrea that she was more attractive than she believed herself to be, and expressing the hope that she would write again soon as he was lonely. As a parting shot he again referred to the enclosed fantasy letter and his hope that Andrea would not be offended by its style and contents. He wrote:

I have written it 'bluntly', because I don't know any other way to write it, like I said, I'm just an ordinary 'red-blooded' man with pent-up frustrations.

Please understand.

Hope to hear from you soon.

Colin

The 'other letter' which Stagg referred to read as follows:

MY FANTASY
(ONE OF THEM ANYWAY)

It is a warm mid-summer evening, just getting dark, I'm wearing, like I usually do, at that time of the year, just a T-shirt – pair of shorts (nothing underneath them) and sports socks and pumps, I'm walking on my own, taking a lonely quiet stroll over the local park.

Colin continued to set the scene by explaining that due to having drunk a few beers he is feeling relaxed and looks for a quiet and secluded spot amongst the trees where he can strip off and masturbate. He described this process in graphic detail. Having climaxed he then becomes aware that he is being watched. His observer then appears:

She is a middle-aged woman, mid-thirties, not exceptionally attractive but, not bad, she smiles at me, and says 'It's all-right love, don't panic. I couldn't help spying on you, and what I saw you do, really made my day, to see you wank yourself like that, really turned me on. And I was wondering if you would do it again right in front of me so I can see it close up.'

The narrative continued with Colin describing how he again begins to masturbate and the woman's apparent approval and pleasure at his actions:

Then smiling she says to me 'Undo my skirt and slip it off', which I quickly do, we are both now naked. She sits up and faces me, she then puts her hand around my throbbing cock and slowly starts to pump me.

This leads to a further three lengthy paragraphs of extremely detailed descriptions of rear-entry intercourse, oral sex and mutual masturbation. The fantasy encounter concluded with:

I lay on top of her so our naked bodys are now joined by the sticky mess. Then we start to kiss passionately, then she says 'I've got to go now, it's getting late perhaps I'll see you again, tomorrow night'. And she smiles as she walks off.

THE END

Appalled and disgusted by his outpourings, Andrea Parker had written back giving Stagg a flea in his ear, and ended the relationship. He had not written to her again.

We had a problem. We couldn't eliminate Colin Stagg from our enquiries, and he was definitely telling lies.

I had previously had a somewhat 'open mind' about psychological profiling, bordering on downright scepticism, but this had altered after Colin Stagg's arrest because the similarities between the profile and the suspect were so spot on.

Paul Britton's profile of the killer of Rachel Nickell had stated:

(1) *The offender was a stranger* – over the course of three days of interviews, it became apparent that Rachel and Colin didn't know each other.

(2) *He would be aged between 20 and 30 years* – Colin Stagg was 28.

(3) *He would have poor heterosocial skills* – it had become apparent that Stagg had few friends and had only ever had two girlfriends; one relationship lasted less than a week when he was about 16 or 17, and the other was for a period of about three months with Ms Y. This relationship ended about Christmas time 1991. Stagg took this very badly.

(4) *He would have a powerful deviant sexual fantasy life* – we had our suspicions that he had such a fantasy system, which was confirmed when Andrea Parker came forward. The sending of unsolicited sexual fantasies seemed to support our suspicions.

(5) *He would have a history of failed or unsatisfactory relationships if any* – this linked in with the point about poor heterosocial skills.

(6) *It would be likely that, in addition to sexual deviation, he would suffer from some form of sexual dysfunction* – the interview with Ms Y seemed to confirm that Colin had some sort of sexual dysfunction, and seemed to shy away from full intercourse.

(7) *It was likely that he would be attracted to or use some form of pornography* – the meat slab photographs around his gym and the magazines under his bed, albeit fairly run-of-the-mill, definitely fitted the definition of pornography.

(8) *That there was a 50 per cent chance that he would have a previous history of offending, although this does not necessarily require previous convictions or equivalent seriousness* – possession of an offensive weapon, and the revelation in

interview of indecently exposing himself on the common, both supported this.

(9) *The offence will have been rehearsed in general terms in sexual fantasy, but the precise details and victims will have been chosen on the basis of opportunity and driven by the strength of the offender's impulse on the day* – there was nothing at this stage to indicate that this was the case with Stagg.

(10) *That the offender will have been of not more than average intelligence and education* – certainly, Stagg's educational history supported this, leaving school early with no qualifications, but he was definitely intelligent; or, at least, cunning.

(11) *That if he is employed, he will work in an unskilled or labouring occupation* – Stagg was a paperboy and jobbing gardener.

(12) *He will live in a relatively isolated lifestyle. He will be single, living at home with parents or alone in a flat or bedsitting room* – correct in Stagg's case.

(13) *He will live within easy walking distance of the common and will be thoroughly familiar with the common* – correct in Stagg's case.

(14) *Probably not a current car user* – correct in Stagg's case.

(15) *That the offender, in the few days immediately after the offence, will have been excited or upset, but it will have subsided to its normal level thereafter* – evidence from Mrs Avid and Mr Heanan, the butcher Stagg said he visited on the afternoon of the murder, supported this.

(16) *He will have solitary hobbies or interests, these will be of an unusual nature, this may include a low-level interest in martial arts* – Stagg's interest in the occult, possession of the offensive weapon, rice flails and his books on survivalism all seemed to support this.

(17) *That in Paul Britton's view it was almost inevitable that this person would kill another young woman at some point in the future, as a result of the strong deviant sexual and*

aggressive fantasies and urges – all I could do was hope that this part of the profile was wrong.

Now I was keen to learn more. I decided to present Paul Britton with all the material we had on Stagg, including all the interview tapes and the Andrea Parker letters. We spoke several times over the next few days as he worked his way through it all.

I also asked him the $64,000 question: 'What I need to know is if there is anything in the interviews that would allow you to say, categorically, that in your opinion this man could not be responsible for the murder of Rachel Nickell, based upon the offender profile and deviant sexuality analysis that you gave us.'

The answer was: 'No, I can't say that there is anything there that is indicative that this is not your man; in fact, he could comply with certain criteria that would suggest that he may well be – but you can't say that with any degree of certainty. You can't say that he is, and you most definitely cannot say that he isn't.'

'On what basis could you say, "Yes, he has eliminated himself from the investigation"?'

'Well, for example, if he said he'd been happily married for two years and has a baby, that wouldn't be consistent with the killer. Or if he had a long-term occupation that required a high level of intellect; or if he demonstrated that he had had successful, stable relationships with women. Then I would have thought this to have been inconsistent with the psychological profile, and these things would eliminate him.'

Having explained all this and listened carefully to the tapes, Paul told me that he found none of the factors that would definitely eliminate Colin Stagg from the inquiry. It didn't mean in any sense that he was guilty, only that he should not be disregarded.

So the problem still remained – Colin Stagg couldn't be eliminated and we could place him geographically and chronologically five-and-a-half minutes from the time and scene of the murder.

Where could we go from there? What on earth could we do? If it wasn't him, we needed to know it wasn't him, because he was a compelling suspect; we would be tempted to divert valuable resources away from the rest of the inquiry to try and further the case against Colin Stagg. If it wasn't him, we needed to know so that we could stop wasting our time.

Chapter 22

The Job were making more noises about scaling down the inquiry and time was of the essence. With the justifiable failure of the CPS to back a murder charge against Stagg after the September arrest, we had all been hearing rumblings that senior officers at the Yard were pessimistic about continuing an inquiry which, in their view, had no realistic hope of bringing about a successful conviction, and which was using valuable funds that could be better deployed elsewhere.

We were appalled at the thought of abandoning the investigation at this stage. I could not put a precise time to it, but it began to occur to me that an undercover operation was perhaps a potentially beneficial line of enquiry which might lead to resolving the questions raised by Colin Stagg. In the right circumstances, I reasoned, he might confess his innermost thoughts, fantasies and secrets. If the operation was a success, it could lead to the discovery of material evidence, like the murder knife, or soiled clothing, that would provide incontrovertible evidence for a jury. Who knows, Stagg might even confess his involvement in Rachel's murder? Alternatively, if he was innocent as he claimed, it would give him a chance to clear his name once and for all, and allow us to focus our time and energy in other directions.

I wrote a report which went up to SO10, the Yard's secret operations unit, and DS Peter Holman, a covert ops specialist, informed me one Friday afternoon that, 'yes', in principle, it would be feasible to do it, and that it would be put forward for authority should I submit the request in writing. However, caution ever being the Met's watchword, he decided that some input on the type of officer to be employed should be sought from Paul Britton.

I made a phone call to Paul that Saturday evening from home. As usual at the time, I was restless and found it difficult to relax and put the inquiry out of my mind. I'd be sitting, half-watching TV, when something would occur to me concerning the inquiry and I would have to check it out, either by phoning Mick or by going through the copy bundle of statements.

I recognised the softly spoken tone at the other end of the line.

'Have there been some developments?' Paul asked.

'In a way. It's just something that I've been considering and I'd like some advice.'

'What can I do for you?'

'Paul, I've been kicking something around and I need to ask you a hypothetical question. Based upon your analysis of the murderer's deviant sexuality, do you think it would be possible to design a covert operation that would allow us either to eliminate a person from the inquiry, or in which a person might further implicate themselves?'

'You mean an operation where knowledge of the particular sexual deviancy of the murderer would be used to give someone the space to reveal their involvement in the killing, by letting them build up some sort of relationship with someone who they feel safe with?'

'Yes.'

There was a long pause. 'Yes, it's possible. I can think of several ways to do it, but it would mean that someone would have to get close to the suspect.'

I said, 'An undercover policeman?'

'It could be a policewoman. Whichever, the undercover officer would make contact and allow the suspect to befriend them. This relationship would be designed to create what I would call an escalating pathway of revelation, whereby the suspect might eventually choose to disclose aspects of his sexual functioning. There would be plenty of cut-offs inbuilt along the way – decision points where the suspect could choose to go in several directions. Only if he chose the previously specified and very particular pathway, would there be any basis for the operation continuing. If any other pathway was followed, then the operation would end because the suspect, from my point of view, would have eliminated himself.'

Still no names were mentioned. Paul's analysis of the killer's powerful and violent fantasies had been written before anybody had come under suspicion. Nothing had happened since then to change his opinion.

I said, 'So, more specifically, how would it work?'

Paul outlined two hypothetical covert operations designed to exploit what he called the powerful deviant psychosexual functioning of Rachel's killer.

'Let's assume that communication is established – triggered by a chance meeting, say, or perhaps an exchange of letters. In the right circumstances and with the right confidante – someone with a specific history and personality – the suspect would begin to reveal the fantasies that demonstrate his need for extremely violent non-consensual sexual activity.

'These would include the use of a knife to stimulate, penetrate and control the woman in his fantasy; also the degradation and extreme domination of her to the extent of dehumanisation. At the same time, he would become sexually and aggressively aroused.

'As he revealed more, the fantasies would increasingly come to feature a venue that closely resembles the woodland in which Rachel was murdered. At their highest intensity, they would replay important aspects of the killing itself, and the suspect would derive potent sexual gratification from recounting them. Not for intellectual stimulation, but as his most powerful aid to masturbation.'

I was intrigued by the thought of using a female officer, which hadn't occurred to me.

'And this can be done by letter?' I asked.

'In the initial stages, yes, but the murderer would quickly try to progress the relationship from written correspondence to personal meetings and then intimate encounters. He will want to present himself as a person attractive to the confidante and is likely to fabricate whatever story he thinks is necessary to secure physical intimacy in the early stages of the relationship.'

'He'd invent things?'

'He won't immediately implicate himself in the murder – remember, he has a strong sense of caution and self-preservation. But as his deviant sexual arousal intensifies, this would overwhelm his caution and could lead him to reveal knowledge of the circumstances of Rachel's death that would only be known by the killer.'

Paul warned that the behaviour of the suspect and the course of the relationship could be adversely influenced by external events, such as media coverage of the case.

'The murderer is cautious,' he said. 'As long as he believes the police investigation is getting nowhere and that public attention is shifting away, then he'll be less concerned for his safety – he'll think he got away with it. But if he has reason to suppose that the police have an ongoing, high-level interest in the case, then he's going to be more cautious and suspicious of any relationship.'

'Paul, nothing like this has ever been done before,' I said. 'If it's approved, would you be willing to sketch out a plan for us and act as a consultant?'

'You say it's never been done before – would it be legal? I'm not a lawyer, I don't know very much about the legal aspects of something like this. Would the CPS say, "Yes, it's all very interesting but it's inadmissible; it amounts to an interview not under caution, or even entrapment"?'

'The lawyers are going to go over this one with a fine-tooth comb,' I said. 'There would be no point going ahead if the CPS said it was illegal and wouldn't stand up in court. This has to be the whitest of white operations, Paul.'

Paul said, 'Well, if that's the case, it will have to be run under very strict conditions. I can design an operation along the lines I've explained, but it will require a suspect to actively climb a series of ladders whereby he either eliminates or implicates himself by his own choices. I am not willing to design an operation that is the functional equivalent of putting a person on the edge of a slide and giving him a nudge so he has no choice where he goes.'

I couldn't have agreed more. No one would have relished the prospect of the wrong person being charged and the real killer left out there to murder again.

Paul went on, 'I have your assurance that the object of this exercise is not solely to establish guilt?'

'No, not guilt – the truth.'

'You must understand that any advice I give will be based on what we know about the offender, and not this other man. I wouldn't feel comfortable giving advice on any other basis.

'Let me put it this way – when I gave my profile, I also included my views on the killer's pyschosexual functioning. If you remember, I stated that this man was suffering from a sexually deviant-based personality disturbance, the detailed characteristics of which would be extremely uncommon in the general population and would represent a very small sub-group within those men who suffer from more general sexual deviation.'

'I remember something like that, but I'm not sure that I understand what you're saying.'

'Well, it's the rarity of this specific form of deviance that will make this person stand out. My advice would be based on my knowledge of this and not upon what I know of this other person.'

'So we're looking for a pervert amongst perverts?' I said, pleased with myself at my grasp of the situation. It was a short-lived pleasure as Paul gently corrected me.

'I wouldn't put it quite that way, but in essence we are looking at an extremely rare form of sexual deviance and I would expect to see certain manifestations of this – but only from the right person. So you see, any assistance will be based upon this premise and not tailored to appeal to the subject of your inquiry. Are you comfortable with that?'

'I think I am, but I'm not too sure what those who instruct me will say. Are you saying that if our man fails to respond in the way you expect the killer to react, you would be in a position to say that we're barking up the wrong tree?'

'Providing, as I say, that the person concerned has not had his levels of suspicion raised and expresses his true self, I think he would necessarily eliminate himself from the inquiry.'

'That's an interesting thought. I must admit it's not exactly what we had in mind. My idea was just to get an undercover officer to befriend him and hopefully to win his confidence. In that way, if he starts to talk about the day in question we might resolve some of the mystery that still remains. If he was responsible, we might even discover what he did with the bag and the weapon.

'But, of course, there's always the chance that whoever we use might not win his confidence and we'll be no further forward – that's why we wanted some advice on the type of person we should use. But, obviously, based on what you've said, we shall have to have a rethink.'

'You understand why it wouldn't be right for me to advise you on the type of person that may be, how shall I put it ... acceptable or appealing to this particular man?'

'I can see that it might be open to misinterpretation but, in all honesty, I must emphasise that we're not conducting a witch hunt. It really is an exploratory exercise, solely to answer the question: Did he or didn't he? And if he didn't, why was he telling lies about being on the common? And if he did, what's he done with the items I mentioned earlier?'

'I have no doubt about your good intentions but I must confine my actions to those I have described.'

'As far as I'm concerned, Paul, it's not a problem. In fact, if I've understood correctly, it may even be to our advantage. Now let me get it straight in my own mind. You've said that under the right circumstances, and working on what you know about the offender, it might be possible to either eliminate or implicate the subject of this particular line of enquiry.'

'Correct.'

'And this would be based upon whether or not this person displays the same sort of almost unique sexual deviance as the killer?'

'In simple terms, yes. The detailed configuration of this form of deviance is very specific and extremely unusual and I think it would be possible in the right conditions to achieve that result.'

'Can you give me a brief outline of how you would envision it working? Just so I can report back to the top brass.'

'I shall need to give the matter some more thought, but the killer, as I previously mentioned, was motivated by his sexual fantasies and a desire to enact those fantasies. He had rehearsed the offence many times in his masturbatory fantasies and eventually his levels of caution were overwhelmed by his levels of arousal. I would expect that elements of this specific form of deviance would manifest themselves in the offender's behaviour.'

'Playing devil's advocate, how could we be sure? I mean, the man we're talking about is certainly strange and obviously displays some worrying sexual tendencies but how can we be sure that he's displaying these specific manifestations and isn't just another pervert?'

'Without going into details on the telephone,' Paul continued patiently, 'it would be possible. You must remember that the offender is a very rare creature indeed and it would very soon become apparent whether this man is or is not suffering from the same form of deviance. That is providing, of course, that this person is confident and comfortable enough to make disclosures to whomever is chosen as his confidante. If disclosures are made, it would then be a question of comparing them against the blueprint of the offender's expected behaviour.'

'And what if the two match?'

'Would I be able to say that this person and the killer are one and the same?'

'Yes.'

'The answer to that is no – well, not just based on the comparison of expected and actual behaviour. But it may be that, if this is the right person, he may make disclosures about his involvement. Certainly, I would expect the offender, in the fullness of time and if his levels of suspicion have not been raised, to make such disclosures. In the absence of such disclosures, such a match would merely show that the killer and this person suffer from the same form of very rare sexually deviant-based personality disturbance – and whilst it is extremely rare, it is not unique. However, I would describe the probability of two such persons both being on the common at the relevant time as vanishingly small.'

'And if they don't match?'

'In my view, that would necessarily eliminate him from the investigation.'

'You've certainly given me food for thought. Perhaps you could give some more thought to the subject and I'll give you a call some time on Monday?'

'I'd be delighted to help in any way I can, subject to what I've already said.'

I put the phone down and my mind began racing at the potential impact this might have on the inquiry. It was a radical idea and radical ideas are not always well received by those in authority. But, however unorthodox it was, there was much to recommend it from the viewpoint of resolving the Stagg dilemma.

I sent a report to Bob Chapman, the area DCS. My report found its way to Neil Giles, a DCI; then to Roy Ram, who was an Acting Commander at the time, and from him to Dave Veness, who at that time was Deputy Assistant Commissioner, Specialist Operations. They were all extremely supportive.

Very rarely would a commander get involved on a face-to-face level with such matters. The nittygritty is hammered out by the likes of DCI Giles and the officer concerned, and then Neil Giles reports to Roy Ram for his sanction or recommendations to be complied with prior to authority being given. This was the case with the Nickell inquiry.

The idea of a proactive psychological operation had not figured in the initial report, purely because of the timing of the report and the conversation which started the thing off. The covert operation was begun on the authority granted as a result of the initial report. The psychological analysis of the material or information obtained really didn't affect that authority. The idea was to gain information and that was what was authorised; what was subsequently done with that information in the formative stages had no bearing on that authority. After all, there was no guarantee that the undercover officer would successfully befriend Colin Stagg, and the operation would therefore fail at the first hurdle.

The support from Roy Ram was in the form of the very positive minute placed on the report. He actually went as far as to say that, yes, there was a lot to recommend this suggestion, 'and if we enter into this enterprise we enter it with our eyes wide open'. There were, he noted, a few problems regarding the admissibility, and there was no doubt that we would be pushing back the edges of the envelope, but his view was that, even if we didn't get an evidential result, we may well put in quite a significan't step forward and be able to identify whether Colin Stagg was or wasn't the killer – and, in his view, that would be a major step forward.

And, indeed, it would be, because if we found out that it wasn't Stagg, we'd have achieved what we set out to do; and if we found out that it was him, then by the same token we'd have also achieved what we set out to do.

But what about the problems of entrapment, enticement, acting as an *agent provocateur* – whatever heading it came under, it was sure to be grist to a defence lawyer's mill. There was no point in pursuing the operation if the Crown Prosecution Service was likely to rule it unethical and therefore inadmissible as evidence in a court of law.

The plan therefore then went to Guy Morgan, a police solicitor, to check that we weren't actually committing some sort of civil trespass against Colin Stagg. His view was that we weren't, and provided we didn't damage or interfere with his real or personal property in any way, we were perfectly at liberty to do what we were proposing to do.

Interestingly enough, he also said that he would be rather more optimistic of the admissibility of his evidence than I had suggested in the report, when I had obviously suggested that there may well be legal difficulties. But I wasn't a barrister, and had no legal qualifications other than 20 years' experience of dealing with lawyers and the CPS – though I'd taken the precaution of doing some preliminary research on precedents. A couple of cases, Christou v Wright, and Bryce v Khan, seemed to deal with this particular type of operation.

To my delight, the CPS gave our plan the go-ahead. At last, we had a solid line of enquiry, with at least some hope of a result at the end of it.

The SO10 office at New Scotland Yard is a place shrouded in mystery and visitors are, by virtue of the sensitive work done there, not made overly welcome. Very rarely is access to the office encouraged, reports and reward payments being dealt with at the counter.

My first call at this inner sanctum was at the invitation of Neil Giles. As I waited at the counter for a member of staff to arrive, I read the large forbidding notice on the wall: 'NO UNAUTHORISED PERSONS BEYOND THIS POINT. SO10 PERSONNEL ONLY.'

As I was musing on this, Neil Giles appeared, beaming from ear to ear. Neil is a fairly short man, with dark curly hair and a beard. I very quickly formed the opinion that he was a workaholic, but despite his obvious dedication to his work, I felt there also lurked just beneath the surface a wicked sense of humour. I reckoned Neil Giles and I were going to get on well from the start.

He walked at a brisk pace with me in his wake. We reached his office and he shut the door behind me. 'Take a seat, Keith.'

Giles settled himself down behind his desk, which was piled high with manila folders, all marked 'Secret' or 'Confidential'.

'Right. This report of yours.' He reached forward and opened the document. 'It shouldn't be too much of a problem.'

'That's encouraging.'

'The boss seems quite taken with the idea. It's a bit of a departure from our usual work but we should be able to do something for you.'

'That's what I like to hear. So where do we go from here?'

'There are issues that have to be carefully considered – the selection of the right officer, the legal implications, and the potential evidential value of anything we might discover.'

'I realise that this sort of operation can be a minefield from the admissibility viewpoint, but that's only one of the possible directions that this project might take us. It could be that he'll row himself out [put himself in the clear] and admissibility won't be an issue.'

'I accept that. But there's also the question of whether we might be committing some sort of civil trespass against this Colin Stagg. All these aspects have to be considered, but as I say it shouldn't be too much of a problem.

'It's just the way we do things. We have to make sure that we're acting within the law and also that the ends justify the use of our resources. But, in this case, we seem to have plenty of support from the top.'

'Good. You obviously realise the problems we've had with this particular inquiry and, quite frankly, I can't think of any other way of resolving this particular issue. So any assistance would be more than gratefully received.'

'Mr Ram is more than keen to do what he can to support you. Even if the operation takes us along the line where this bloke puts his hands up and we fall foul of the admissibility question and lose the lot at court, the top man believes that we would still have achieved a considerable amount. On the other hand, if it rows him out again, we've still achieved a lot. Provided that solicitors give the green light from the civil liberties angle, you'll get all the support you need from this department.'

'Once we get the go-ahead, what's the next step?'

'We'll have to play it by ear. This is a far cry from our normal undercover work because we're not dealing with commodities such as drugs, firearms or stolen property. We're all going to be on a steep learning curve. But because of the nature of this job and the higher potential risk to the officer, Roy Ram will want considerable back-up to be available and he'll take some persuading to allow face-to-face contact on the common.'

'The back-up I can understand, but restrictions on the face-to-face contact's going to be a bit of a problem.'

'If those are the rules, you've not got any choice but to stick to them. Let's not worry about that at the moment. I'm sure we can come up with a way round it.'

The conversation continued for half-an-hour or so, just really kicking about a few ideas. The Met is a cautious organisation and even SO10 is subject to the same restrictions as the rest of us. I left the building feeling encouraged.

Paul Britton had by now devised two personality types for the UC operation – one male, one female. He emphasised that they were likely to appeal not to Colin Stagg, because the operation was not designed to Colin Stagg's specification, but to appeal to the killer of Rachel Nickell. We were not trying to entrap Colin Stagg – as much as wanting him to incriminate himself, we were trying to eliminate him.

What Paul had come up with was a series of filters; the idea was not to create a gigantic slippery slope down which any suspect would have to slide to the bottom, if placed at the top and given a push. A truer analogy was of creating a series of step-ladders and platforms up which, and along which, the suspect, Colin Stagg, would have to travel in order to fit the criteria of the design of the operation – i.e. the design being to appeal to the killer of Rachel Nickell. And that was the linchpin of the entire operation – it was not designed to fit Stagg, it was designed to fit what we knew about the killer from what Paul had told us in the sexual fantasy analysis.

The three things we knew about the murder were the witness evidence, the offender profile, which was the general outline, and the sexual fantasy analysis, and that was the thing that had been totally ignored to start with. We didn't realise the importance of it until Paul said, 'This is how this could work – in my view, this is what makes the killer tick, and if this man goes along certain paths and takes certain options, then he fits with the killer.' That wasn't to say that Colin Stagg was the killer, but what it would do was show that Colin Stagg suffered from the same extremely rare form of sexual deviance as the killer.

Paul had said, 'The chances are in the order of millions to one against finding two people suffering from this same form of extreme sexual deviance in the same location.'

So although the operation might be able to identify whether Stagg had the same form of sexual deviance, it would not be sufficient to prove that he was the killer. Paul would never be able to say that because of what had happened, Colin Stagg was the killer. He could only ever make the statement that they both shared the same extremely rare form of sexual deviance. We would then have to look at the other evidence, and our view was that it would be a matter for the jury. The 12 men good and true would have to ask themselves: 'OK, we have the killer of Rachel Nickell and this man Colin Stagg, with this infinitesimally small percentage of the population – and, in fact, an infinitesimally small percentage of the sexually deviant population, which makes it an even smaller percentage – suffering from this identical form of deviance, and then we have to look at how many other of these people were on Wimbledon Common, were quite clearly telling lies, and expressing a knowledge of the offence that they shouldn't really have.' A tough call, but nobody said jury service would be easy.

Paul estimated that the operation should take between two and sixteen weeks to complete, but stressed that the most important aspect of the proceedings was to make sure that Colin Stagg's levels of awareness and suspicion weren't raised, because that could either extend the period, or thwart the operation totally.

It took until January 1993 for us to be in a position to proceed.

It was essential that the operation be run hand in glove with Paul Britton, who had drawn up the detailed profile of the killer soon after the murder and who would be able to identify significant behaviour patterns in Colin Stagg. What was more, his professional standing and expertise in forensic psychology would give the operation the authenticity it would require if it was to stand up in court.

Paul was requested to give a pen picture of the type of officer that may be used, and he came up with two possibilities, one female, one male. He still didn't know that Colin Stagg was to be the subject of the covert operation, although he knew he remained a suspect. He was designing an operation based on the deviant sexuality analysis that he had drawn up of Rachel's killer months before Colin Stagg ever came under suspicion.

The male, he said, had to be white, aged 25 to 30, and of fit appearance. He had to be quite intelligent but should slightly downplay this and be comfortable describing a range of sexual fantasies and actions that were similar to – but obviously fall short of – those attributed to Rachel's murderer.

It was important that the undercover officer's background story included examples of him either having successfully dealt with police in an interview situation or never having been interviewed because the police hadn't been able to get close enough to him. He had to be self-sufficient; cautious in the early stages of the relationship and surprised or impressed as the subject began to disclose his own activities. They would be forming an exclusive club with their personal exploits being the criteria for admission.

As their mutual trust grew, the officer would gradually disclose more of his history, including violent sexual crime. This would help to create an environment where the suspect could feel safe and even boastful in revealing his own background, without any mention of Rachel Nickell or possible shaping of his choices by the officer.

The second confidante, Paul stipulated, should be a white female, aged between 20 and 40, with blonde or fair hair that was at least shoulder-length. She had to be attractive in a traditional or glamorous sense. She should appear to be sexually knowledgeable but not promiscuous, and be attracted to 'interesting' or experienced men who were able to live by their own rules.

She had to be able to respond to any cues given by the suspect and acknowledge being sexually aroused by coercive activity in which she is, preferably, slightly passive but often active. She should be willing to indicate her previous enjoyment of sharing experiences with men who have taken her through sexual fantasy which has progressed from romance into violence and have shared their exploits with her.

An interest in occult religion would be a useful element in her background and she should be impressed by men who indicated they were willing to achieve their desires in action, even when these clearly conflicted with the accepted range of social behaviour.

Chapter 23

DCs 'Ozzie' and 'Lizzie' were both from SO10, one of the most secretive units at Scotland Yard. The squad is involved in all aspects of undercover policing, from infiltrating gangs and protecting juries, to acting as decoys or posing as contract killers. However, apart from a few people manning the office, SO10 have very few permanent staff of their own. They work by running courses and recruiting suitable operatives, who are then posted within the Met to ordinary departments, only being drawn in for specific jobs as and when required.

'Operation Edzell', as it had been named, was going to be an unusual operation for SO10 because we wouldn't be dealing with an illicit product but a relationship.

The officers they sent us were of the highest calibre. According to Neil Giles, Ozzie was a veteran of many operations, and DC Lizzie James was probably one of SO10's most experienced female officers. She had worked in the field of drugs, terrorism, fraud and, most recently, had helped to break a child prostitution ring. Although newly married, Lizzie had apparently shown no hesitation in volunteering for a task which might expose her to extreme sexual deviancy, and a man suspected of committing one of the most horrific murders in years.

At 6.30am one morning at the beginning of January 1993, on a day that was extremely cold but clear with blue skies, Nick Sparshatt, Mick and I drove to a central London address to pick up Ozzie and Lizzie and take them to a meeting with Paul Britton in Leicester. I was impressed with the style of the houses, huge Edwardian mansions now converted into flats.

Nick pulled up outside the address and I got out. I walked briskly to the door, my breath making white vapour clouds in the cold morning air. I pressed a buzzer and Lizzie answered immediately.

'We'll be straight down.'

I waited on the doorstep, and a few seconds later I heard the clatter of two sets of footsteps and the sound of a woman giggling. The door opened and both undercover officers appeared. I introduced myself and ushered them to the waiting car. Lizzie was definitely the extrovert of the pair. Oz was much quieter, but with an air of confidence and calmness about him. He was tall, athletic-looking and in his early thirties.

Even at that time in the morning, Lizzie bubbled with general conversation and trivia. Not in a million years would anyone mark her out as being a police officer.

It was also immediately obvious that she had an agile mind, and from the off she was relaxed and friendly, not in the least uneasy in the company of two senior officers whom, until that morning, she had never set eyes on. This outgoing nature and an ability to assimilate into any company was clearly one of the assets that had made her such a successful undercover officer; that, and a shrewdness that she disguised with giggles and laughter. Even at this early stage, there was no doubt in my mind that she had the ability to perform the potentially dangerous and difficult task which we had in mind for her.

It is worth noting at this stage that in order to protect the identities of the undercover officers, certain details as to their physical and character traits naturally have to be withheld.

In complete contrast to his colleague, Oz sat passively in the rear of the car, probably quietly assessing us. We were well on our way up the M1 before we broached the subject of the inquiry.

Wickerson turned to face Oz and Lizzie and said, 'So, what has Neil Giles told you both about this job?'

Lizzie was the first to speak. 'Not very much really. He told us it was a job to do with a murder, and seeing as both you and Mr Pedder are from Wimbledon, I suppose it has got to be for the Rachel Nickell inquiry.'

'How much do you know about that murder?'

'Only what we've read in the papers.' Lizzie looked at Oz for confirmation. He nodded.

Wickerson continued, 'Before we give you all the details, I want you to know that there is, if we are correct in our suspicions, a great element of risk involved in this. It may well be that he's not the man, but if he is the man, and we're able to find out through your endeavours, you could be placing yourself in personal jeopardy – in particular you, Lizzie. You can pull out now if you don't want to accept the job.'

'Most of our work has an element of risk, Guv,' Oz said.

'We both appreciate that, but this is a little different. If the man we're looking at is the killer, this is what he's capable of ...'

Wickerson opened his briefcase and produced a couple of mortuary photographs of Rachel. We had to demonstrate that the murder was appaling, and give them the opportunity of deciding whether or not they wanted to take on the job. It would have been unfair not to let them know the full extent of what they may be getting involved with. If Colin Stagg was responsible, then they had the right to know what he was capable of doing, especially in Lizzie's case. It wasn't a case of 'Look at these, aren't they awful?' As professional officers, they had to be fully briefed, not only for the sake of the investigation, but also for their own safety.

The pictures didn't show details of all of the injuries and this was a deliberate omission; if the operation was successful and Colin Stagg began to disclose facts, we would then know that the integrity of the facts disclosed could not be questioned, by virtue of the fact that the person to whom they were disclosed had no knowledge of things that only I, John Bassett, Mick Wickerson and perhaps the lab sergeant and the pathologist were aware of. Nor would Oz or Lizzie ever be allowed access to some of the more detailed aspects of Rachel's murder, in particular to the highly specialised reports of Dr Shepherd and Paul Britton. It was felt that they should have only the basic information, such as any member of the public would have gleaned from newspaper and TV reports, in case they inadvertently dropped something of a specialised police nature into conversations, which would alert Stagg and send him scuttling off before the operation was complete.

'Can I say again, if you decide not to take job,' Mick said, 'no one will think any the less of you.'

There was absolutely no hesitation; they both looked at the pictures, and were shocked, and there was a moment's reflection over what they were looking at, but never any reticence on either of their parts to get involved.

I watched as the photographs were passed between Oz and Lizzie. There was a brief silence as the full horror of Rachel's death was taken on board.

Lizzie said, 'I'll do it.'

'I'm in as well,' Oz said.

'You're sure?'

'Quite sure, Guv,' they replied almost in unison.

'Let's be clear about this,' I explained. 'As I said, it might be that the man you're going into didn't kill Rachel. The purpose of this exercise is to try and answer some questions which are giving us cause for concern about this man's movements on the day of the murder. If we're successful in infiltrating this man's life, the result may just as likely eliminate as incriminate. We're entering this with an open mind.'

'Am I right in thinking that the bloke is the one who was in all the papers?' asked Oz.

'That's the one – Colin Stagg.'

'What's the game plan?'

Wickerson said, 'Keith has worked out the details with Paul

Britton and Neil Giles, so perhaps he'd better explain it. Besides, when it comes to the psychological side of things, I haven't got much of a clue what he's on about.'

I said, 'I'll do my best to give you a simplified version, but Paul will give you all the academic stuff, if you want it, when we get to Leicester. Basically, Paul Britton designed this operation. You may or may not know that he also helped with the investigation by preparing an offender profile. It was certainly in the papers.'

'Some American guy came over as well, didn't he?' Lizzie said.

'That was Robert Ressler, an ex-FBI man, but officially he didn't have anything to do with the investigation. Unofficially he did, and he prepared a profile for John Bassett. I don't know what you know about profiling, but Ressler's and Paul's were both very specific – and almost identical. Quite impressive when you consider that they were done independently of each other.'

'It seems a little strange to be dealing with shrinks,' Ozzie said.

'I felt the same way,' I said, 'but give it a chance. I'm sure you'll both be impressed with what Paul has to say. Paul gave us a profile that consisted of two quite distinct parts. The first part gave us general offender characteristics – things like age, race, occupation, hobbies, area of residence. In total, there were 17 points in the first part, the most worrying of which was the last point, which stated that the offender would almost certainly offend again in a manner that would lead to the death of another woman.'

The smiles and grins disappeared.

'This first part was used as it was intended; that is, to help with suspect acquisition.'

'And when Colin Stagg got arrested, how did he match up to this profile?'

'He was more or less a perfect match, but that isn't why we're looking at him. And to be perfectly honest, he didn't get arrested as a result of the profile having narrowed him down as being one of a number of other suspects. He got identified as a result of the E-fit picture that was shown on *Crimewatch*.

'The excellent fit to this profile isn't why we're looking at him. Our problem is, our feeling that he is obviously not telling the truth about his movements on the day of the murder, and he's been identified by an excellent witness who can put him five-and-a-half minutes geographically and chronologically from the time and scene. In addition, there's another witness who's put him on the common at a time when he says he was elsewhere, thereby, if she is correct, blowing his alibi out of the water.

'Mick'll fill you in later on what you need to know. Suffice it to say that there are questions that need to be answered, and hopefully this'll be our way of doing it. Now, it is the second part of the profile that is the basis of our operation. In the opinion of Paul Britton, this offence was committed by a person who is suffering from a sexually deviant-based personality disturbance – well, that's the technical name for it. Whatever you call it doesn't really matter; the bottom line is that it was this condition that was the driving force behind this man committing the murder. According to Paul, this man was acting out his deviant fantasies when he murdered Rachel. I'm reliably informed that what was done to Rachel, how, when and where it was done, amongst other things, has enabled Paul to be very specific as to the precise nature of this man's sexual deviance. Thankfully, this is a very rare creature indeed, and it is that rareness that will hopefully enable us to either eliminate or implicate Mr Stagg.'

'I'm not sure I'm following this,' said Lizzie.

'It'll get clearer – at least I hope it will. Paul has told me that because the killer has this very rare, but quite specific, deviance, he would expect certain things to manifest themselves in this person's behaviour. So if we know the killer's expected behaviour, it is a matter of seeing whether Mr Stagg's behaviour matches that of the killer.'

'And if it matches, does that mean that Mr Stagg is the killer?'

'Not necessarily, Oz, but I'll come on to that in a minute. But what we could say with certainty is that if it didn't match, Colin would necessarily eliminate himself from the inquiry.'

There were still puzzled faces.

'Look, I'm not explaining this very well. The theory is, Paul Britton has designed this operation based upon what he knows about the killer, not about Mr Stagg. If you like, he has a blueprint for the killer's expected behaviour. Under controlled circumstances, this design will be applied to Colin and we'll then compare the blueprint of expected behaviour to the actual behaviour.'

'How do we control these circumstances?'

'Good question, Lizzie. That's why we're going to see Paul. Each of you will assume a persona that has been designed to appeal to the killer. Paul will brief you, don't worry about it. You will then be introduced into Mr Stagg's life. Each of you will be acting independently of one another, but at the same time. This way, we're hoping for feedback from Colin as to how each of you is doing.

'And before you ask; Oz, you'll hopefully introduce yourself to Colin whilst he's out taking one of his frequent trips to the common. He's a dog lover and we can provide you with a suitable mutt. Your paths can accidentally cross on a few occasions until he gets used to seeing you then you can attempt an intro and take it from there.

'You're slightly different, Lizzie. You're going to become his pen pal – to start with, anyway.'

'I know you've got the answer to this, Sir, but won't he think it's a little strange if a woman just starts to write to him out of the blue?'

'I would think he would, which is why it's just as well he's previously had a pen pal. The thing was, she got the hump with him when he started sending her unsolicited sexual fantasies. He doesn't know that we know this, so he shouldn't smell a rat if you write saying that you used to know this woman but you've fallen out with her – and whilst you were staying with her you sort of came across one of his letters and thought he sounded interesting.'

'That could work. So what are the nuts and bolts?'

'You write him letters, the content of which will be decided by Paul Britton, and hopefully he writes back. His replies are analysed by Paul Britton and we send back an appropriate reply.

'Meanwhile, Ozzie befriends him on the common, portrays himself as the type of person that Paul will brief him on, and with a bit of luck the old male bonding will work and we've got a double-pronged UC operation.'

'But how does all this psychology work?' Ozzie asked.

'I can only try to explain what Paul has told me. I'm not sure that I understand how it works, or how he does what he does, but in a nutshell we will be offering Colin the opportunity to express himself freely. Now we know that he has a penchant for sending fantasy letters, or at least he had, and if he reverts to sending Lizzie that sort of material, and if he's the killer, the same very specific and rare elements of sexual fantasy should appear as were found to be present in what the killer did to Rachel. I should stress that it would be conditional upon his levels of suspicion not being raised and his level of arousal overcoming his natural caution. But for it to work, we must maintain a passive role and let him make the running. If sexual fantasy material is received, we mustn't introduce new or more extreme themes. Everything's got to come spontaneously from him. Are you with me?'

'So far.'

'If this is the right man and he feels comfortable with his confidantes, you two, then Paul Britton would expect that he will begin to disclose details of the offence not only in fantasies but also in reality. So in a way, Ozzie, that partly answers your question about matching behaviour. Except that if only the sexual deviance is the same, without the other disclosures, Paul Britton would not be able to say that that means the killer and Colin are one in the same person. Whilst the detailed configuration of this particular condition, if that's the right term, is extremely rare, it isn't unique. But that being said, Paul reckons that the chances of two people with this same condition being on the common at the time of the murder are, in his words, "vanishingly small".'

'And if it doesn't match, he's out of the frame?'

'That's about it. You'll have to get Paul to explain it properly. I've probably got it arse about face but that's the gist of it. Anyway, there's always the more traditional aspects – we might get the knife or some of the clothing back and we can all understand the benefits of that type of evidence.'

'Talking of which, what's the evidential standing of Paul Britton's work?' Lizzie asked.

'That's a bloody good question. The answer is, it's never been tested before, but psychologists are accepted as expert witnesses by the courts. At the end of the day, we're just going to have to suck it and see.'

At 10.00am, we pulled up outside the modern, red-brick reception area of the secure unit and walked to the electronically controlled doors. You could see at a glance that the secure unit was in total contrast to the rest of the Towers Hospital. The main body of the hospital was dark and depressingly Victorian, like the institutions which seemed to feature in every low-budget horror movie I had ever seen. Arnold Lodge was new and comparatively bright, yet I found it a more profoundly depressing place than the old buildings. The attempts of the interior designers had failed to mask the purpose of this place. No amount of sparkle and shine could hide the fact that within these walls were some of the most disturbed and potentially dangerous people in the country – apart, that is, from the one we were hunting.

The security was thorough, although attempts were made to keep it as relaxed and unobtrusive as possible – an almost impossible task as the 16ft-high wire mesh fence which surrounded the lodge was a constant reminder that the priority was to keep the residents in.

The doorman scrutinised my warrant card and pressed the buzzer to release the first of the security doors. We entered the secure foyer area and waited for the door to close behind us. This area was like an airlock; the second interior door to the waiting room couldn't be opened until the first door was secure.

Paul's office was about the size of a broom cupboard, with barely room for a desk and filing cabinet. The desk was piled high with papers and reference books. Behind it was a white board, full of incomprehensible graphs and terminology. It was clear that the six of us couldn't cram in here, so he led us to a conference room. Paul, in his quiet but genial, understated way, immediately put everyone at ease. He exuded an aura of understanding and patience. I had met Paul before so this didn't come as too much of a surprise, but it was interesting to notice how two experienced UC officers, who by necessity had to be sceptical and cautious, opened up in front of him.

Paul said that Colin Stagg's lonely hearts letter to Andrea Parker had automatically suggested a means of introducing an undercover policewoman. If a friendship blossomed and the suspect remained in the picture, this was likely to progress into telephone conversations and then personal contact. Paul described to Oz and Lizzie in clear detail the type of fantasies and deviant behaviour he would expect them to face if they encountered the murderer of Rachel Nickell.

'Rachel's killer isn't going to come across, at first, as a monster,' Paul said. 'You won't be able to see what goes on behind his eyes. He may present himself as a lonely young fellow looking for companionship, but you must understand that the true killer will be exploiting and manipulating you all the way. What is happening inside his mind is something you'll never have come across before.'

Paul then gave advice on what they might expect if this was the right man. A discussion of sexual deviance is not an easy thing for most people to come to terms with; it's particularly unpleasant for females, by virtue of the fact they tend to be on the receiving end, and for a normal heterosexual male it's hardly an everyday thing to do.

'Should this subject matter come up in conversations with Colin Stagg,' Paul said to Oz, 'you will have to work extremely hard not to show signs of revulsion. You might not physically be aware of showing signs of revulsion – and this would apply equally to Lizzie – but what you may well be doing is giving the game away by the expression on your face, in your eyes, or your lack of eye-contact.'

He explained that when the operation went ahead, he would teach them how to avoid letting Colin Stagg subconsciously pick up any reticence on their part.

He said that if Colin Stagg was the killer, he would be suffering from forms of sexual dysfunction. His view was that the killer was probably heterosexual and sexually inexperienced, to the point of being unlikely to differentiate between the female vagina and anus for purposes of sexual gratification. 'But until you talk to these people,' Paul said, 'you can't actually find out for sure what's going on in their mind.'

Wickerson intervened at this point to impress upon them again that the operation was not designed for Colin Stagg, it was designed for the killer of Rachel Nickell. If Colin Stagg was the right man, he would fit the template; if he wasn't, he wouldn't. Either way, our problem would be solved.

Paul stressed again that the success or failure of the whole operation would depend upon Colin Stagg's levels of outside awareness and suspicion not being raised. It was important for him not to think of the inquiry that was going on at Wimbledon as being anything other than an ordinary, run-of-the-mill sausage machine, churning in information at one end and turning out sausages of actions at the other.

If the media, for example, were to start saying that forensic psychology was being used in this case and unusual things started happening in Colin Stagg's life, he might well associate the two; his levels of awareness would shoot up and his suspicions would be raised. We already knew him to be a cunning man, and able to deal adequately with pressure if he was given time.

We drove back down the motorway in sombre mood, everyone lost in their own thoughts. Even Lizzie was uncharacteristically quiet. As we approached the outskirts of London, however, she said, 'Mind if I ask you something, Mr Pedder?'

'Go ahead.'

'It's just that I noticed something when we were driving to Paul's. Something that you said about Rachel. It's odd, but both you and Mr Wickerson refer to Rachel very much in the present tense.'

I looked at Mick. 'It's true,' he said. 'And Monica, her mother, still says "Rachel is ..." as opposed to "Rachel was ...".'

For my own part, I didn't have an answer for Lizzie. All I knew was that Rachel had become almost a part of everyone's family. I couldn't explain why it had happened, but it had. No one would have disputed the fact that Rachel was a very special person, and I would have gone as far as to say that I actually felt that I knew her. If you delve into someone's background as much as you do in the course of a murder inquiry, that's not an unnatural feeling. But when you delve into someone's background the way we did with Rachel, and come up with nothing that puts a blemish on her character, not a single person saying a single bad word about her, you begin to feel that she is the perfect sister or girlfriend that you would have liked to have had. There had been a genuine feeling of loss amongst the squad, and I could only suppose that the reticence to refer to Rachel in the past tense was a reluctance to accept the terrible things that were done to her.

I shrugged. 'She was, let me think – paragon's the wrong word, because she was a 23-year-old, lively, healthy woman – she was kind, she was generous, she would go out of her way to help people; she just did not deserve the horrible death that she suffered.'

There was probably more that I felt, but it was impossible to put into words. There was a sense of loss and grief, but I couldn't understand why. How can you grieve for someone you didn't know? It was, in retrospect, because you got to know her after she was dead. I wouldn't make her out to be a saint, because I didn't think she was a saint. I didn't doubt that she was as capable of having a shout and a rant and a rave like the rest of us, but she was so genuinely warm and loving, a kind and good person.

I shrugged again. 'Lizzie, I think maybe it's just that nobody can come to terms with the thought of so much goodness and loveliness being cut down in its prime.'

Nick Sparshatt, who had spent so much time with Alex and his father, said, 'And then you look at little Alex and the circumstances of him being there and seeing it all happen ... his mother hacked to death so quickly, just three minutes from start to finish, and him lying there, face down in the mud having been chucked through the brambles. I used to find it heart-rending to watch Alex talking to his dad and the child psychologist.'

We received a poignant reminder of those conversations between grieving father and son just a few weeks later.

On 26 February, Andre contacted us and said that he had recently taken Alex for a runaround on a beach. Alex had picked up a stick and wanted his daddy to play sword-fighting with him. Andre had also picked up a stick, when Alex stopped what he was doing and looked thoughtful.

'I was playing sword-fighting when the bad man came!' he suddenly announced. 'He pushed me in the mud! That wasn't nice!'

Andre agreed with him that it wasn't nice, and said, 'Where were you when the bad man was hurting Mummy?'

'I was with Mummy.' Then, out of the blue, he added, 'Why does the bad man like you?'

Andre told us he was stunned. He could only assume that Alex's logic was, Why hadn't the bad man attacked Rachel when the family was all together? Why had Andre been spared?

'He doesn't like me,' Andre told him. 'He's afraid of me ... he would never have attacked Mummy when I was there. He knew what I would have done to him.'

'He had a bag,' said Alex.

'Oh, and what did he have in the bag?'

'A knife ... if Thunderbirds were around they would catch him!'

Andre asked Alex where the man came from.

Alex motioned to his right. 'I saw him. Mummy saw him ... it was black, I think.' His expression changed to one of anger. 'He pushed me over!' he said, his little voice indignant.

Chapter 24

Once the green light had been given for Operation Edzell to commence, the only problem that remained was how to turn the theory into practice. The psychological side was obviously Paul's province, but the nuts and bolts of the day-to-day running were mine.

Yet again, I made the 100-mile journey to Arnold Lodge to consult Paul. I pulled up outside the reception area of the secure unit and battled my way through the wind and rain up to the electronically controlled doors.

The security man scrutinised my warrant card and pressed the buzzer to release the first of the security doors. I entered the secure foyer area and waited for the door to close behind me. The second interior door then opened, allowing me through to the waiting room.

'Take a seat, Inspector, I'll tell Mr Britton that you're here.'

I sat in the waiting room for a few minutes, passing the time by reading the posters on the wall. There were the usual warnings to visitors about not bringing contraband into the unit and advisory notices about the residents' rights under the Mental Health Act.

'Inspector, if you would come this way, Mr Britton's outside waiting for you.'

I walked back through the airlock and out into the rain where Paul was standing.

'We've moved offices since your last visit,' he smiled. 'Not very palatial but it's only temporary.'

Heads bent against the rain, Paul and I hurried along the outside of the fence until we came to a locked gate. He fumbled with his keys to let us through.

'It's just up there, in the Portacabin. You go ahead, I'll lock up.'

The term 'office' was a bit grandiose for the 8ft by 8ft box which had become Paul's working environment.

'Take a seat, if you can find any space.'

I looked around the small room; the place was piled high with files, the desk, the filing cabinet and the two spare chairs were all full to overflowing. I picked up several folders from the first chair and looked around for somewhere to put them.

'Just dump them on the floor. I'm a bit short of space at the moment.'

'It reminds me of my office – I've got a similar filing system.'

'Believe it or not, I do know where everything is. So how can I help you?'

'It's really just to kick about a few ideas as to how to get the undercover operation off the ground. You advised that it would be preferable for the initial contact between Lizzie and our subject to be made by way of a letter.'

'That's right. There are several reasons why I think this would be the best approach. But the remoteness of communicating in this way would allow us time to assess the responses and reply accordingly. I think this is the most compelling reason to adopt this approach. You must remember that I stated at the outset that I would expect certain responses from the killer, but that the levels of his caution and arousal would be a critical factor. Anything that raises his levels of caution would be counter-productive, so a wrong word or reaction from Lizzie in conversation could, if this man is the one we're looking for, do exactly that.'

'I understand that, and until this man feels comfortable, we wouldn't want to do anything to put him on guard.'

'I'm not ruling out conversations and eventually meetings, but in the very delicate early stages we must tread carefully. It would be very difficult to control a conversation by reason of its dynamic nature, so initially I would advise against it.'

'The idea of becoming pen-pals has a lot to recommend it. For a start, it would provide a safe method for Lizzie to communicate with our man. Also it gets round the problem of him wanting to progress the relationship to a more physical one, and we can't allow that to happen.'

'No, and I feel that that side of things would become inevitable fairly soon after face-to-face contact has been made.'

'The top brass are happier with the idea of letters,' I said. 'However, the problem still remains how to introduce Lizzie to Mr Stagg. That's why I've come to see you. I wanted to run an idea by you to see what you think.' The problem as I saw it was how to explain a letter just dropping on his doormat out of the blue. Whichever way I looked at it, an unsolicited letter from a complete stranger would to my mind make him smell a rat. So the solution had to be to find some connection, some common ground which would make the letter seem less unnatural.

'Sounds a pretty tall order.'

'That's what I thought until I remembered Andrea Parker. Colin Stagg doesn't know that we know about his previous letter-writing to Miss Parker. Obviously, because of the way they stopped writing to each other, we couldn't get Lizzie to pretend to be Miss Parker, but it suddenly dawned on me that Andrea Parker was nonetheless our way in. If Lizzie claims to have been a friend of her's but now they have fallen out, perhaps because of Andrea's old-fashioned outlook on life ... the exact details need to be ironed out, but what if Lizzie claims that she had been staying with Andrea prior to their fall-out and had come across some of Colin's letters and thought he sounded like an interesting person? What do you think?'

'Very ingenious. It certainly gets around the problem of going in cold. The major hurdle is winning his confidence; the connection with someone he knows should go some way to achieving that.'

'I thought that, but the way he and Andrea stopped writing could be a problem. But having said that, the fantasy letters to Andrea weren't mentioned when I interviewed him – admittedly because we didn't know about them – and they were written over a year ago. I gave him a thorough series of interviews and covered just about everything we knew about him. He must feel fairly safe that Miss Parker didn't contact the police.'

'That would be a reasonable assumption in view of the fact that you didn't question him about them. I think it's a good device. But I would advise that you emphasise the breakdown in friendly relations between Lizzie and Andrea, and make the letter sound as open and friendly as possible. You know the sort of thing – very chatty, the normal lonely hearts club type of letter. There's no chance that this man and Miss Parker are still in contact?'

'None. Andrea's moved, so he can't contact her, and from what she said there is no way that she'd want to renew contact with him. We wouldn't want to take any chances. We're only going to get one shot at this.'

'Absolutely, so there's no point in rushing our fences. The first objective is to make him feel comfortable and, once that's been achieved, she should begin to divulge, slowly, the various traits of the persona which has been designed for her.'

'Let's not count our chickens. We might fall at the first hurdle – he might not even reply.'

'I would be optimistic, provided his levels of caution are not raised.'

'I took your earlier advice about making him think that the inquiry was just going through the motions – like "a sausage machine just churning out routine lines of enquiry" you said. I cancelled his bail and returned the majority of his property. With a bit of luck he should be feeling quite relaxed.'

'Let's hope so. We don't want him looking too closely at the things going on around him.'

In the days that followed, the part of the operation involving Oz went ahead. One of the major selling points of this operation was the fact that I had pointed out to the powers that be that this was a very cheap alternative to 24-hour surveillance, which was cost-prohibitive. It could take years. As Paul said, another attack could happen at any time; it depended upon external pressures and publicity. That is, it could happen at any time if this was the man who'd done it; if this wasn't the man who'd done it, we'd have wasted 24-hour surveillance – 3 surveillance teams of 12 people each, 36 officers a day – that was £3,600 a day, for just the staffing level. That is a million-and-a-half pounds a year just for wages. So it was a useful way of monitoring moves, and that was what really sold them on the idea.

We immediately hit snags. It proved impossible to engineer a plausibly coincidental meeting on the common between Oz and Stagg. In the end, I said, 'Let's stop trying it this way; let's get hold of a flat near Colin, furnish it properly, have it plumbed up for sound and vision, and stick Ozzie in there. If he's on the estate, it shouldn't take him too long to strike up a relationship or an encounter with Colin and take it from there.'

It took us about two or three weeks to get the requisite authorities, and then to find a suitably sited flat. The plan was all ready to go when Oz fell foul of a debilitating virus which made him lose control of his limbs and have blackouts. We couldn't just slip somebody else in, because Oz had been round there while the place was being decorated, getting the feel of the area, talking to the neighbours, setting the scene, feeding in a few bits of information, making sure he was coming across as the right sort of personality. If somebody else turned up now, the neighbours might think it a bit strange.

The Oz plan went to nothing, but luckily it was not an essential part of the operation; it was just an extra safety net, an alternative way of monitoring what Colin was actually thinking about. We decided to go ahead with just one undercover officer.

At that time, Lizzie was working at a central London police station. We got her released from her normal police duties and seconded to Wimbledon to make sure that during the undercover operation she did her homework properly, and that the evidence that was obtained was properly dealt with. Quite apart from that, it was going to be such a stressful thing for her to be dealing with, it would in my view have been totally unfair for her to have gone back to her station at the end of each day and be expected to deal with everyday mundane matters as well.

Paul concentrated on getting her ready for her task. Once her relationship with Colin progressed from letters to telephone calls, it was going to be impossible to predict the course of conversations. Much was going to depend upon Lizzie being able to make the right decisions quickly. Her courage, intelligence and quickness of mind were beyond reproach, but as Paul said to me, 'She will possibly be dealing face-to-face for a long period of time with someone who might be a sexually deviant killer. Can she be self-effacing and passive, but sexually open to ideas and fantasies?'

Lizzie told me that one morning he put her to the test. Sitting very close to her in the seminar room, he leaned across and whispered something to her. He watched her body language. Would she flinch or move away?

'What did he say to you?' I asked her.

'He said, "You've got lovely blue eyes."'

Lizzie had had no idea what was happening, but she read things quickly, had smiled and given a laugh. It was the first of many tests that she passed with flying colours.

Lizzie needed to memorise her cover story in the finest detail. Her childhood, schooling, family and friendships had to be plotted out so that she could answer any question without hesitation or mistakes.

We emphasised again to Lizzie that the undercover operation was designed to allow Colin Stagg either to eliminate or implicate himself in Rachel's death by showing whether he had the same sexual deviancy as the murderer. If this proved to be the case and he had killed Rachel, then perhaps he would reveal knowledge about the crime that only the guilty man could have. For the operation to work, moreover, Colin Stagg always had to be making the first move; Lizzie couldn't put words into his mouth or ideas into his head. She could only react to the cues as and when he provided them.

Paul said that, to begin with, Lizzie had to demonstrate caution about revealing details of her past, telling him that she feared that exposure might place her in jeopardy. When she did talk to Colin about her cover story, she had to release the details slowly, as if she were becoming more secure in the relationship. 'But something will be holding you back,' he said, 'an obstacle that prevents you from committing yourself fully. You regard yourself to be different from ordinary people in the most profound way, but you find it difficult to explain why. You're looking to find out whether this man feels the same way.'

It was absolutely vital in the early stages of the relationship that Lizzie did not express any interest in, or knowledge of, Rachel's murder. If Colin mentioned it, then Lizzie had to show only passing curiosity and then change the subject. If it happened again, Lizzie should continue pushing it away. Only after three or four references, could she allow herself to be drawn into a conversation about Rachel and say, "All right, tell me about it."

By the same token, it was also important that Lizzie never introduced any of the violently aggressive and sadistic themes that Paul predicted would drive the fantasies of the killer, such as the physical control, verbal abuse, knives and the humiliation of women. She could not lead him in any way whatsoever by revealing new ideas or lines of discussion; she could only reflect back on subjects Colin had already raised. Only then could we prevent the possibility of an innocent man being led into making untrue claims in a bid to win sexual favours from Lizzie.

'He'll be devious,' Paul warned. 'If he is Rachel's killer, he'll try to secure sexual intimacy without putting himself at risk. He'll try to find out all he can about Lizzie James and what she desires so that he can create some scenario which he hopes will satisfy you.'

'Will he make things up?' Lizzie asked.

'Quite possibly,' Paul said, 'but eventually his deviant sexual drive will reach a level where it outweighs his tendency for caution and self-preservation and he may begin to reveal detailed knowledge of Rachel's murder. If this happens, you should agree to listen but indicate that you need proof that he isn't just fabricating the story to impress you and get you into bed.'

Having taken Lizzie through her cover story, Paul had to make sure she was comfortable with her new persona. If she ever came face to face with Stagg, she wouldn't have the luxury of time.

In a real case scenario, when the suspect revealed something of himself and asked for Lizzie to do the same, she had to be able to converse comfortably about having had certain sorts of sex with men, even when the man sitting opposite her might be a sadistic murderer. We even simulated telephone calls where Paul played the suspect. It all took quite a lot of practice, but I watched and listened as Lizzie grew in confidence.

'How long will it take?' I asked on one occasion, my mind ever watchful of the cost and time pressures.

Paul drew me a graph plotting Stagg's likely responsiveness. 'You're looking at a journey of 24 to 26 weeks from start to finish. It should take between two to 16 weeks for Lizzie to establish a relationship which will lead to some sort of rapport. If it hasn't happened by then, you might as well discontinue. Once the fantasy exchange has started, you should have gone the rest of the way within the next two months.'

I asked, 'What if he hasn't revealed any knowledge of the murder by then?'

'Then you stop and regard it as an elimination. He's either got nothing to hide, or he's never going to reveal it.'

On Monday, 18 January, Mick and I were in the office we were now sharing. Accommodation had become scarce and the prolonged murder inquiry was stretching the hospitality of Wimbledon division almost to breaking point. After nine weeks I had been evicted from my original office and offered temporary accommodation in the CLO's (Community Liaison Officer's) office. Then, just after Christmas, the CLO had not unreasonably wanted his office back. The only option was to move another desk

into Wickerson's office and for me to take up residence with him. This wasn't a problem as we both got on well; the only bone of contention was the fact that Mick was a rabid anti-smoker and, by this stage, I was on about 60 a day. Every time he moaned about the smoking, I told him that he was adding to my stress levels and felt it necessary to light up to compensate.

'We're set to start tomorrow then, Keith?'

'Fingers crossed, I'm waiting to hear from Lizzie to confirm she's got the accommodation address. Once that's done, we're ready to go.'

'I suppose there's no alternative to using an accommodation address?'

'Not that I can see. I know it's less than perfect but what other options do we have? The letters have to be delivered somewhere and a kosher address is out of the question. It would be just our luck if he took it into his head to try and visit, or check it out.'

'Point taken, but he could do that with the accommodation address and he might find it a little strange if he discovers it's not a residential address.'

'We've decided to save him the trouble – we're going to tell him. My old mum always told me that honesty was the best policy. Lizzie and I have worked out a cover story.'

We knew that the first letter was all-important, or Stagg's suspicions would be aroused and the operation halted in its tracks. We knew Stagg was an animal lover, and as cover for Lizzie we suggested she was working as a cat minder. The story was also a handy explanation for the different telephone numbers she might have to use in future contact with him, and an excuse for not being able to invite him to visit, because she was in someone else's home.

'Let's face it,' I went on, 'if he swallows the story as to why Lizzie wrote to him in the first place, he should accept the explanation for why we're using the accommodation address. We've got nothing to lose. If he doesn't reply then it's back to the drawing board. My thinking is that we should give him all of the bad news in one go. It would be worse if he replied and then found out that the address was iffy – that'd raise his levels of suspicion just a tad, wouldn't it?'

'You're right – so what's the cover story for the address?'

'Simple to the point of being pathetic. Lizzie, because of some domestic problems, is having to move and until she has got herself properly settled she's using the mailing address to prevent her post going astray while she's between houses. Hardly machiavellian.'

'You mean, it can't be anything to do with the Old Bill, because if it was, they'd have come up with something a bit more impressive.'

'Spot on.'

'Of course, the other scenario is: the Old Bill must be fucking mad if they think I'm falling for something as daft as this.'

'There's always that possibility …'

There was a knock at the office door.

Jim Garlinge and Andy Palmer staggered in. 'We've got that document safe you asked for, Guv – where do you want it?'

'Just over by the door, Jim, thanks,' I replied.

There was a lull in the conversation whilst the two DCs manoeuvred the heavy cabinet into position.

'Expecting a bit of confidential mail, are we?' Wickerson smiled.

'You never know your luck.'

At that moment, the phone on Mick's desk rang. It was Lizzie. We exchanged a few words and I replaced the receiver.

'It's all systems go,' I grinned at Mick. 'She'll be over in the morning and we'll do the first letter.'

Mick and I were both in at the crack of dawn, excited at the prospect of getting started after so many weeks of meetings and report writing. I busied myself assembling the necessary books, forms, property bag, seals and labels that would be needed. Mick was dashing about dealing with his divisional responsibilities, clearing the decks so we could concentrate on the important business of the UC operation.

At about 9.30am, Wickerson returned to the office with a tray of breakfast.

'Right,' he said, mouth full of toast, 'what's the game plan?'

'The first letter should be simple enough. I checked with Paul

Britton last night – all we need is a fairly open, friendly and chatty letter. Once we've done it, I'll give him a ring and run it by him. We then either post it or make any changes that he might think are necessary.'

'What about the actual mechanics of writing it?'

'Subject to what you say, I thought we could all sit down, kick a few ideas round, then do it sentence by sentence.'

'That makes sense. I know you've got it covered, but what system do you intend using for the continuity?'

'Whatever we do, I've no doubt it'll be wrong should it end up in court. But we can only do our best. Once the letter is written, Lizzie will photocopy the original and exhibit the copy. She'll hand it to me and I'll seal the copy in a property bag. The seal number and a description of the exhibit will be recorded on a form 66. A corresponding entry will be made in a property book and I'll then place the exhibit in the safe. In addition, we'll all make and sign notes as to the procedure we've used.'

'What about for his letters, should we get any?'

'Much the same, except Lizzie will collect the letter and bring it back here unopened. She'll open it in our presence and photocopy it, she'll then seal the original in a property bag having protected the letter with card just in case we need to have it ESDAd (examined by Electrostatic Document Analysis, a method of reaching indentations made by overwriting on paper). She'll then hand the original to me and I'll follow the same procedure as for the letters she writes.'

'That sounds fine – so we'll use the photocopies as our working copies?'

'Yes. But as I said, should we ever end up in court, the defence will probably find something to complain about.'

Shortly after 10.00am, Lizzie came bustling into our office, full of energy and enthusiasm.

'Oh, it's cold out there! I've just abandoned my car in the yard, that'll be all right, won't it, Sir? Here we are, I've bought some nice blue note paper especially.'

Lizzie was clearly very keen to get on with the job and, despite the very serious nature of the project, her natural exuberance was bubbling through to the surface. 'So, how do we start?'

'We've got to come up with a letter that's chatty, friendly but not over-confident. Paul Britton suggests that you should come across as being a little unsure and cautious. Any ideas?'

Mick said, 'What about something like, "I hope you don't mind me writing to you"?'

'A little blunt and to the point,' Lizzie said. 'How about – I hope you're not offended by this intrusion?'

'That's good. Perhaps then something about "You don't know me but ...", and then go on to explain the Andrea Parker connection.'

'OK, how about this then, Mr P? "Dear Colin, I hope you're not offended by this intrusion. You don't know me, but I feel that I have known you for years."'

'It's got a nice ring to it. OK, put that down.'

Lizzie started the letter and it was by this method that an hour or so later we felt quite pleased with our first effort. I rang Paul Britton and read him the finished product, dated 19 January 1993:

Dear Colin,

I hope you are not offended by this intrusion as we have never met before, but I feel as if I have known you for years.

You may remember writing to a woman called Andrea, Andrea was an old friend of mine and a little old-fashioned in her outlook if you know what I mean! A while ago when I stayed with her, while she was out I read a letter that you had sent her, I hope you remember. This letter has been on my mind and interests me greatly, I find myself thinking of you a lot, I would be very interested in getting to know you more and writing to you again.

I will tell you a bit about myself. I am divorced (like Andrea) and quite frankly have had my fill of shallow, one-way relationships, as I have had my fingers burnt too many times.

I am 5' 8" blond, aged 30 and I have been called attractive in the past. My interests may sound boring, but I don't socialise much and prefer my own company, I read a lot and have often contemplated writing a book. I have an odd taste in music, my favourite record being 'Walk on the Wild Side' by Lou Reed.

I am a bit cautious but not paranoid, I would appreciate it if you didn't let Andrea know that I've written to you as our friendship has dwindled. I have taken an accommodation address in London so you can contact me there. (I am in the process of moving flats and I don't want any letters going missing.)

I am in Central London about twice a week.

I hope you are not upset by this letter and I look forward to hearing from you soon,

Lizzie
X

P.S. my name is Lizzie James.

We faxed a copy to Paul and he called back to say, 'That sounds fine. The general tone is warm and friendly. There's just the right amount of caution and uncertainty. I don't think there's any need to change or add anything. It'll do very well. Are you going to post it today?'

'We should catch the lunchtime post.'

'Good luck! I'll wait with interest to see if you get a reply.'

There was now nothing to do but wait. The fact that the ball was in Colin Stagg's court and that there was nothing I could do to control the game left me with a feeling of helplessness. I tried not to think about it, but without much success. After all the planning and hard work, I had to accept the very real possibility of not getting a response. Both Mick and I had resigned ourselves to the idea that we had a nerve-wracking few days, perhaps even weeks, ahead of us.

What made the waiting even more painful was the fact that the powers that be on 4 Area werc again making noises about closing down the inquiry. JB had given a speech at our Christmas lunch only a few weeks earlier and had stated that, in all probability, we would all be returning to our divisions in the New Year. The prospect of leaving the case unsolved was something that had caused a great deal of unhappiness amongst the squad. There were a great many outstanding lines of enquiry and a lot of unanswered questions, which obviously included the Stagg issue. All we needed was the time to explore these avenues fully, and we could only cross our fingers that we'd be given the latitude required.

JB, Mick and I were fighting a rearguard action; from the first week in January, hardly a day went by without demands from divisions for the return of their staff.

'Bob Chapman raised the question of closing us down again today at the AMIP management meeting,' JB said with the air of a condemned man.

'What did you say to that, Boss?' asked Wickerson.

'The same as I always say – I told him how many outstanding Actions we had and that I would advise against it at the moment.'

'They've got to be joking, Guv,' I said with more than a hint of impatience. 'How the hell can we put the inquiry to bed when we haven't looked at everything yet?'

'It's not Mr Chapman, Keith, but you've got to understand that he's under constant pressure from division to get their staff back. The financial state of AMIP is another factor. This inquiry has been an incredible drain on money and resources and he's got another six or seven murders to fund.'

'Perhaps I'm being naïve, but I don't see that the Job can justify closing us down purely on financial grounds.'

Wickerson was quick to defend JB. 'It's no use having a pop at the boss, Keith. I know how you feel but don't shoot the messenger, eh?'

JB smiled in his familiar avuncular fashion. 'We're all on the same side, Keith; we've got a little bit of grace yet.'

'I suppose we could always shed some more staff,' Wickerson said. 'We can't cut back on overtime – we haven't had any for weeks.'

I nodded. 'The team haven't been paid for overtime but that hasn't stopped them putting in the hours.'

Everybody working on the inquiry was so dedicated to the task that they didn't want to go back to other duties with the case unsolved. It wasn't because they were having an easy life, because they weren't. They were doing some really ball-breaking, boring stuff and, what was more, they were losing money by being there. If they were back at their own nicks, they would have had an overtime allowance, but our overtime had run out long ago. On their duty sheets, they would often show on duty for eight hours, and then just put, 'Five hours overtime not claimed.' They even came in on their days off. Nothing could shake them from the belief that this job was worth doing. Seldom, if ever, had I experienced such fierce loyalty to the integrity of a squad.

'Both Mr Chapman and Commander Coo understand that,' JB said, 'and they're grateful to the squad for their dedication.'

'With all due respect, Guv, they're not doing it for the gratitude – they're doing it because they want to catch the bastard who killed Rachel.'

'He's right, JB – there'll be a mutiny if the inquiry is closed. Look, we'll try to cut back some of the staff, that might ease the pressure a little. What's our exact strength at the moment, Keith?'

'Twenty-six or thereabouts.'

'We'll have a look at the manning levels and see if we can't trim the squad,' said a resigned Wickerson. 'It's a pity we couldn't have accepted the offer of funding from that group of businessmen,' he added wistfully. He was referring to a very generous offer made by a group of wealthy business people who lived locally. They had offered £500,000 to fund the inquiry, but due to certain government regulations, it was impossible to accept. JB had several meetings with this generous and public-spirited group and submitted the proposal for approval. Apparently, the Met is allocated a set amount of funding from the Treasury and, if they had taken this money, the Treasury would have reduced the Met's funding by the same amount, so there would have been no point in accepting.

With the threat of closure constantly in the background and the enormous workload of other inquiries, both Mick and I were hoping for a reply to Lizzie's letter, preferably sooner rather than later.

'I don't reckon we'll hear anything for at least a week,' Mick said. 'If I were him, I would want to think about it for a few days before putting pen to paper, and that's if he decides to reply. Then he'll probably take a bit of time composing his response. Lizzie mentioned Andrea Parker and he knows he was a naughty boy in relation to those letters.'

'She did give him a flea in his ear. It might put him off replying at all. Maybe it wasn't such a good idea using Andrea as a way in.'

'What was the alternative?'

'There wasn't one.'

The UC operation was being run parallel to the main inquiry and under a cloak of the greatest secrecy. Any leak could jeopardise the operation and, ultimately, the entire investigation. This meant that Mick and I also had to deal with the other aspects of the investigation. We both had to put the UC operation to the back of our minds and give our attention to the more routine activities of the squad. It was difficult but it had to be done. We still had a responsibility to keep an open mind and conduct an investigation which was as thorough as possible. The purpose of Lizzie's role was, after all, a search for the truth – whatever that may be.

Normal routine was followed for the rest of Wednesday and the morning of Thursday, 21 January. Mick had disappeared off to a Divisional senior management team meeting, much to his disgust. He wasn't a great supporter of the 'talking shop' method of policing which had become so prevalent in recent years. Mick was more of a 'Let's get the job done and talk about it later' type of copper.

Whilst I had the office to myself, I was taking the opportunity to draw up the duty rotas for changing the tapes in the video cameras we had installed to keep an eye on the underpasses leading on to the common from the A3 side. I had had video cameras mounted on tops of blocks of flats, watching the underpasses 24 hours a day, because if we had another offence on the common we didn't want to be faced with the ridiculous situation that no one had seen the person leave the common. We didn't want to be faced with a situation of somebody saying, 'I was there at 8 o'clock, I was at home by 8.55 – no, tell a lie, I was there between 8.30 and 9.15.' That way, we could see him going on and off the common but, more importantly, we could see what he was wearing and have a record. It was a ball-aching job, so when the phone rang I wasn't sorry for the interruption.

'It's me!' Lizzie gushed. 'Guess who's had a letter then?'

'Are you serious?'

'Honestly, I couldn't believe it when I rang up the accommodation address.'

'Have you collected it yet?'

'No, I've only just put the phone down. But I thought you'd want to know straight away.'

'I love it when a plan comes together! How long will it take you to pick it up and get down here?'

'I'm at the Yard at the moment. I should be about an hour-and-a-half – might even be sooner.'

I replaced the receiver and sat back in my chair. This was incredible – a reply within two days! I could feel the excitement building up inside me. Yet if I was being objective, it should have been hard to understand exactly why I felt this way. What was I expecting the letter to contain? It was only the first step on a very long journey. But it was an important step. Contact had been established.

The almost indecent haste of the response also made me slightly uneasy. Had he seen through it?

Wickerson returned from his meeting and after what was probably the longest hour-and-a-half of my life there was a knock on the door. Without waiting for an answer, Lizzie effervesced into the office, shutting the door behind her.

'Where is it then?' I asked expectantly.

She produced the letter with a flourish. She opened it. 'One envelope and one letter.'

'Well, what does it say?' Wickerson asked eagerly.

'Shouldn't I photocopy it first?' Lizzie asked. 'So we can preserve the original?'

'Just testing. Off you go then.'

Lizzie returned a few minutes later with the photocopy. She sealed the original and handed it to me.

'OK then, Liz, do you want to read it or shall I?'

'I'll do it, it's my letter and it might be private! Oh, it's all in capitals ...' Again the giggle. She began to read.

DEAR LIZZIE,

THANK YOU SO MUCH FOR YOUR LETTER, WHICH I READ WITH GREAT INTEREST, CAN YOU LET ME KNOW WHAT I PUT IN THAT LETTER TO 'ANDREA', AS I DO NOT RECALL SENDING ANY LETTERS TO SOMEONE OF THAT NAME.

Colin indicated that he would be interested in writing to Lizzie on a regular basis as he felt she and he had things in common, not least his dislike of socialising. He stated he liked his own company and enjoyed a quiet but comfortable life walking with his dog Brandy in the local parks. His taste in music ran from classical through slow sexy jazz to heavy metal, and he also spent much of his time reading about his many varied interests which included archaeology, history, astronomy, wildlife and nature.

He described himself as being 5ft 7in tall with short black hair, stockily built but not fat due to his weight-training regime which he had been following for about a year, but he was keen to add this was just to stay in trim and he was no Arnie Schwarzenegger.

He stated that where he lived was on the whole a quiet place and that despite being on the dole he managed to get by. He liked sunbathing in his garden and took pride in keeping his home 'spic and span'.

He stated that he did not like small-minded people or being dictated to as to how he should live his life. He wrote:

WE MUST EACH FIND OUR OWN PATHS TO TRAVEL ALONG. I DO NOT LIKE PEOPLE WHO ARE CLOSED MINDED. I'LL ADMIT TO YOU THAT, EVERY SUMMER I LIKE TO DO A BIT OF NUDE SUNBATHING OVER MY LOCAL PARK, IN A SECLUDED SPOT OF COURSE. JUST TO GET AN ALL-OVER SUN TAN, BUT PEOPLE THINK THAT IS 'PERVERTED', SMALL MINDS, SMALL INTELLIGENCE.

Colin concluded by saying it would be nice to have someone with whom he could communicate and asked for a photograph. He added that he hoped Lizzie would send an early reply as he wished to get to know her 'intimately'.

He signed off 'Love Colin' with three kisses.

Mick and I sat in stunned silence throughout the recitation. At the conclusion, Lizzie said, 'I think I've clicked.'

'It looks like it. Well done, Lizzie. It's an interesting letter. That bit about not knowing anyone called Andrea for a start.'

Wickerson said, 'But I don't think it's a surprising reaction on his part, bearing in mind what type of material he sent her.'

'But then he followed on with, "Can you let me know what I wrote in that letter?" '

'I think he's just testing the temperature of the water,' put in Lizzie. 'I mean, there were a couple of other sorts of indirect sexual references, the nude sunbathing and that last bit about wanting to get to know me "intimately". It's not so much what he's written, it's more the inference, the between-the-lines bits.'

'It's no use sitting here speculating, we're not the experts – Paul is. I think we should speak to him and see what he makes of it.'

I rang Arnold Lodge at once. Paul wasn't there but I left a message asking for him to ring me back as soon as he could. Lizzie and Mick continued the discussion while we waited for the call.

'You're quiet – what's wrong, Keith?'

'Nothing really, I was just thinking – it's a bit of an anti-climax, isn't it?'

'What were you expecting ... a full and frank confession?'

'I'm not sure what I was expecting. It's brilliant that he's written back. But I don't know, it just seems so ordinary when you look at it in the context of all the theorising and work we've done.'

'You're forgetting that you were the one who kept on reminding us that we could be in for a long haul – and that if Paul Britton's operation worked, it could just as easily row him out as row him in.'

'I know that, Mick, but you have to admit that we were both like cats on hot tin roofs when we found out he'd replied. It's just that now we've read the letter, the sense of excitement and anticipation seems to have fizzled out a little.'

'Well, I think it's a brilliant result!' Lizzie beamed. 'He's answered our letter and he's done it very quickly. All we have to do is write back and see what his next effort produces. And if that's the same as the first, we'll try again. It's just a question of reducing his levels of caution. That's what you're always telling us, Mr Pedder, both you and Mr Britton.'

'Lizzie, you're absolutely right. It's a very encouraging start. If he's our man, of course he's going to be cautious; even if he isn't, he's still going to be a bit circumspect. After all, it can't be every day a letter from a strange woman drops on his doormat. No, you're spot on, Lizzie. We've got our starter for ten, let's just see where it takes us. That's what the operation was designed for.'

The phone rang. I leaned across the desk and answered it.

'Keith, it's Paul Britton.'

'Guess what we had in the post today?' I motioned to Mick to pass me the letter.

'Is it safe to speak on the phone?' Paul asked. He was always very security aware – certainly more so than most police officers.

'I can read it to you, leaving out the names.'

While I read the full text, Paul listened intently without making any interruptions.

When I'd finished, there was a pause, then he said, 'It's an interesting letter from several viewpoints. He seems to be testing the genuineness of the sender. Obviously, I would like to see it for myself, but his request for information about the other lady I would suggest is a device designed to test the bona fides of the sender. There also appear to be preliminary indications of sexual expectation.'

'Do you mean the references to the nude sunbathing and his wish to get to know our girl "intimately", in inverted commas?'

'Yes. But really I would like the opportunity to see the letter before going any further. It might also be beneficial for us to get together before you send the next letter. There are a few things that we should discuss. How about next Tuesday morning?'

'Ten o'clock?'

'I'll look forward to it.'

'Before you go, is there anything else you can tell us about his reply?'

'Well, the underlying theme is caution. Your device for introducing Lizzie appears to have satisfied him initially but he's not totally comfortable. I think we shall have to try to allay his remaining reservations if the designed operation is to be successful.'

'That sounds ominous – and we were just congratulating ourselves on getting a reply.'

Both Mick and Lizzie looked concerned at this turn of the one-sided conversation which was all they could hear.

'No, it's a positive and encouraging start. But we have to remember the basic principle of the operation. It was designed for the killer and in order to assess whether this man matches that blueprint or not it is essential that his levels of caution remain low. As we discussed right at the outset, I would expect the killer to make certain disclosures, but in order for that to happen he must be comfortable with his environment.'

'I remember.'

'And you will also remember the analogy I gave that the operation was, in fact, similar to providing this man with a blackboard on which to write?'

'Yes – which is why we must give him the opportunity to spontaneously express himself without shaping his responses.'

'That's right, and in that way he will either eliminate himself by virtue of his behaviour or he will pass through the series of filters built into the design of the operation.'

'The ladders and platforms we spoke about?'

'Yes, that's right.'

Paul and I said our goodbyes, and as soon as I put the phone down Mick and Lizzie started to bombard me with the obvious questions.

'What sounds ominous?' asked Mick.

Lizzie looked worried. 'Is something wrong?'

'All Paul was saying was that Colin is obviously still a bit wary and doesn't seem to have totally bought the story. He needs to be made to feel more comfortable and confident. He wants to see the actual letter before going further. But he did say there were preliminary indications of sexual expectations.'

'What was the ladders and platforms bit about?'

'It was just an illustration of the safeguards built into the design. You know, the argument that we're not creating a slippery slope down which any man if placed at the top would slide, but a series of ladders and platforms up and along which Colin would have to climb if he is going to match the killer's expected responses. It's all to do with the very specific nature of the killer's sexual deviance in the context of the full spectrum of deviance. Well, at least I think it is. I guess we'll have to wait till Tuesday to find out more.'

Above: Rachel's memorial tree on Wimbledon Common.

Below: Carole Wood, doubling for Rachel during a reconstruction of the murder.

The murder of Rachel was a tragic waste of a young life and its brutality shocked the nation.

Colin Stagg, after his wedding to Diane Beddoes.

Top: Colin Stagg's brother, Lee Stagg, reading a statement to reporters about the *Mail on Sunday* report.

Below: Diane Stagg leaving South Western Magistrates Court in 1997. Diane admitted assaulting two police officers.

Stagg pictured taking his dog for a walk.

In 1996, Stagg burnt this copy of the *Mail on Sunday*, that carried a report highlighting the evidence against him that was never brought to court.

DI Keith Pedder, the author and man who conducted the investigation.

Chapter 25

Lizzie's second letter to Colin, dated 27 January, began:

Dear Colin

Thank you for writing back, at first I was a bit worried about posting my letter to you but when I saw your reply I was pleased and reassured, even though you've only written back once I don't feel as if we're strangers. (Its nice to know that there is a like mind out there, sometimes I also get lonely (like you) and find it difficult to get on with other women, but then I find them so boring and trivial, I don't want to know them!

Paul's advice had been that the letter should be warm in tone and suggest that she was working towards understanding Stagg's views, and did not reject them. Lizzie continued with personal details about her life, and wrote that the letter to Andrea Parker had been revealing in more ways than one.

Stagg's reply arrived just a few days later, on 6 February. He said that he did remember sending a letter to 'an Andrea' some time ago, and admitted it was 'a bit explicit'. However, he said he would like to send Lizzie similar letters that revealed his fantasies about them being together, and that she might like to reciprocate with hers:

I CAN, IF YOU WANT, ENCLOSE A 'PERSONAL' LETTER WITH THIS ONE, ABOUT A 'FANTASY' I HAVE HAD SINCE YOU FIRST WROTE TO ME. YOU HAVE BEEN ON MY MIND EVER SINCE, I HOPE YOU ARE NOT OFFENDED BY MY 'LETTERS', IT'S JUST I HAVE ALWAYS HAD AN OPEN MIND ABOUT SEX, BUT I'VE NEVER REALLY FOUND ANYONE ON THE SAME WAVELENGTH.

He did indeed enclose a sexual fantasy. He had suggested that he could, if Lizzie liked, enclose such a letter, but obviously totally unconcerned as to whether 'she liked' or not, he sent one anyway. He also enclosed a photograph of himself.

The sexual fantasy detailed an unexpected visit by Lizzie to Colin's flat. In a very few lines, Colin deals with the introductions and then embarks on the sexual encounter. Lizzie is led to the back garden, and a graphic description of his imagined activities is given. Colin graphically describes the state of his manhood and his reaction to Lizzie's body. The naked couple make their way to his lawn:

LUCKILY ALL THE NEIGHBOURS ARE IN BED, SO NO-ONE CAN SEE US, BUT THE THOUGHT, THAT SOME-ONE MIGHT, EXCITES US BOTH, YOU LAY ON THE WARM DAMP GRASS HOLDING MY HAND I SIT ASTRIDE YOU, SLOWLY MASTURBATING MYSELF, AS I STROKE YOUR HAIR, YOUR LAYING THERE SMILING ...

The imagined sexual activity continues with Lizzie masturbating Colin to ejaculation 'as you scream in ecstasy'. From the garden, they retreat to the bedroom, where they engage in intercourse in a variety of positions throughout the night.

We did not want to reply until we had seen Paul, and our next meeting with him was not scheduled until 15 February. Lizzie therefore stalled with a non-committal Valentine's card, which depicted two cats and the printed message on the cover: 'It's nice to have a friend ...' And inside: '... as special as you. Happy Valentine's Day.'

She also added her own handwritten message:

Roses are red,
Violets are blue,
There may be a letter
arriving for you!

Guess who
x

Colin also sent Lizzie a card, and I took the whole correspondence up to Paul on 15 February.

'It's happened so quickly,' I said, very pleased with the way things were going. 'His second letter and he's already writing fantasies.'

'An unexceptional fantasy,' Paul remarked, taking a little of the wind out of my sails. 'It's a long way short of implication.'

'But by the same token, it doesn't eliminate him?'

'No.'

Paul said that the letter confirmed that Stagg had been testing Lizzie James, as he had known the sexual content of his letter to Andrea Parker. It also indicated an attempt to elicit sexual fantasies from Lizzie James without prompting, he said. There was a high level of sexual need indicated, but a lack of heterosexual relationships within which to fulfil that need. The fantasy indicated a preference for outdoor sexual activity, Paul said, and excitement at the possibility of being observed. There was also a slight indication of a devious sexual attitude towards the female participant. All in all, however, Paul said that the erotic content was unexceptional. The fantasy was very similar to the sort to be found in any pornographic magazine. Paul advised that her return letter must not significantly raise the intensity of sexual expression, nor must she introduce the sexual themes that he'd predicted of the offender. In other words, as we'd always agreed, she mustn't 'shape' him in any way; Colin had to make the running.

Two days later, Lizzie received another letter from Colin:

DEAR LIZZIE,

THANK YOU FOR THE VALENTINES CARD, IM STLL WAITING FOR YOUR NEXT LETTER, AND I HOPE MY LAST LETTER TO YOU WAS OKAY, AND I HOPE MY PHOTOGRAPH DIDNT FRIGHTEN YOU. I CANT WAIT TO SEE YOUR PHOTOGRAPH, SO THAT I CAN PUT A FACE TO YOUR LETTERS, I BET YOUR A VERY SEXY, GORGEOUS WOMAN.

He then embarked on details of his personal habits, including the fact that he liked to masturbate when reading *Escort* magazine. An invitation was issued to Lizzie to drop in if she got some free time:

I'M ALWAYS IN. IF YOU ARE A BIT WARY ABOUT ME THEN BRING A FRIEND, FOR I KNOW THAT THERE ARE A LOT OF DANGERS FOR WOMEN (AND CHLDREN) THESE DAYS, WITH ALL THESE WEIRDOS AND NUTTERS ABOUT.

He also took pains to explain that he had an open mind about sex, which he considered to be very important. On this occasion, he did not include a separate fantasy letter but embodied one in the main text. It begins:

I CANT WAIT TO SEE YOU LIZZE. EVERY DAY I THINK ABOUT YOU, WONDERING MORE ABOUT

YOU, LONGING TO HOLD YOU NEAR TO ME, FEELING YOUR WARM VIBRANT BODY CLOSE TO MINE, PRESSING MY LIPS CLOSE TO YOURS, TAKING YOUR PASSIONATE HEART FOR MYSELF, ID LAY YOU DOWN GENTLY, AND SLOWLY UNDO YOUR CLOTHING, MAKING YOU PANT WITH EXCITEMENT...

The fantasy progresses to the two of them indulging in oral sex, and then full intercourse. Paul's assessment was that this letter established the explicit sexual nature and expectations of Colin's correspondence, but that the fantasy was, again, unexceptional in content.

Lizzie wrote back on 19 February and, as requested, she enclosed a photograph of herself. She'd spent a fortune on hair extensions to try and disguise her appearance in as natural a way as possible. It was important, both for this and future operations, that she was not readily identifiable in the photograph, just in case it ever fell into the hands of the media. With the hair extensions, it was possible to position her hair in such a way as to partly obscure her features. The picture was taken with Lizzie looking over her shoulder, with a torrent of blonde hair cascading over half of her face. The photograph looked so natural but even her own mother would have had difficulty in identifying her.

Paul had advised that her response should indicate that she wasn't shocked by Colin's writings, and did not reject his sexual expression. She wrote:

Dear Colin,

Thank you for both your letters, I'm glad you liked the Valentines card.

Your letters were certainly enlightening and I did enjoy reading them, the first one was so real, if I closed my eyes I could almost feel you sat astride me and feel your weight pressing me into the grass. Your second letter I viewed as an extra treat. You really write well and I bet this is just the tip of the iceberg when it comes to your thoughts. There's a lot more to you than meets the eye, Colin, I'm sure your fantasies hold no bounds and you are as broad minded and uninhibited as me, I cant wait for your next letter, you have a clever mind and you're a brilliant 'story teller', you'll have to wait for a letter like that from me, (I'm a little slow to start, but I'm working myself up for the big one). (Ha! Ha!)

The rest of Lizzie's letter was very chatty in tone. She explained that she did not smoke, take drugs or drink to excess. She also gave personal details concerning her strained relationship with her family, particularly her mother. She described her nomadic existence over the preceding ten years, having lived all over the country. She concluded:

I'm sorry but I don't know where Roehampton is, Although I could find it in my A to Z, I don't know much about London only the West End, (You know the tourist things).

I'm living just on the outskirts near Slough, but in a couple of weeks I'm moving out. But no doubt we'll get together soon.

Write soon Colin, I can't wait to get your letter in my 'little handies'.

love
Lizzie
x

Colin replied almost by return of post. Again the letter was in two parts, the first clearly designed to build the relationship, and the second consisting of another fantasy, this one written under the heading, *A Special Treat for My Beautiful Lizzie.* He began:

THANK YOU FOR YOUR LETTER, AND THAT BEAUTIFUL PHOTOGRAPH, I COULDNT BELIEVE HOW ATTRACTIVE AND SEXY YOU LOOK, YOUR VERY BEAUTIFUL LIZZIE, WITH THAT LOVELY

LONG HAIR, AND THOSE SEXY EYES, ITS BEEN A LONG TIME SINCE I FELT THIS WAY ABOUT A WOMAN.

Colin proceeded to declare his feelings and desires before continuing with:

IM SO GLAD THAT YOU LIKED MY 'LETTERS', AND THAT YOU TOO ARE AS BROAD-MINDED AND UNINHIBITED AS ME, I CANT WAIT TO READ SOME OF YOUR FANTASIES!

The letter went on to provide more details of Colin's personal history – the break-up of his parents' marriage and his father's subsequent death in 1986 due to a heart-attack. He described his three brothers and sister and reiterated that he liked the quiet life, preferring the countryside to the claustrophobic and polluted city.

The 'special treat' for Lizzie began:

ITS A HOT, SUNNY DAY, WE BOTH DECIDE TO GO OVER TO THE LOCAL PARK AND HAVE A PICNIC, WE PACK SOME LIGHT FOOD, SNACKS AND THINGS, AND A BOTTLE OF CHILLED WINE. WE ENTER THE PARK, JUST WALKING ARM IN ARM, LOOKING FOR A GOOD SPOT TO SETTLE DOWN ...

The fantasy continues for two pages. After Stagg and Lizzie have settled in a small clearing by a fallen tree, the wine is cooled in a stream nearby. Stagg graphically describes them having rear-entry vaginal sex over a fallen tree trunk. This is followed by oral sex on Lizzie, then front-entry vaginal sex. In total contrast to the coarse and crude adjectives and imagery of the majority of the prose, Colin concludes on a romantic note:

I RAISE MYSELF SLIGHTLY OFF YOU AND PRESS MY LIPS TO YOURS, MAKING YOU OPEN YOUR

EYES, A FEW TEAR DROPS, RUN DOWN YOUR CHEEKS AS YOU SAY, 'I LOVE YOU, I LOVE YOU SO MUCH', I REPLY, 'YOU LOOK SO BEAUTIFUL LAYING HERE, LET'S NEVER BE SEPARATED, YOURE THE ONLY WOMAN I WLL EVER WANT, YOUR SO DELICIOUS, SO FULL, SO HOT AND VIBRANT, I LOVE YOU LIZZIE'. BY NOW THE SUN STARTS TO GO DOWN, WE DRESS OURSELVES AND FINISH THE WINE, IT STARTS TO GET DARK, BUT A FULL MOON SLOWLY RISES IN THE SKY. 'SHALL WE GO HOME THEN?' I SAY TO YOU. 'LETS STAY FOR A WHILE AND WATCH THE MOON TOGETHER, BESIDES, IM NOT FINISHED WITH YOU YET!!', YOU SAY, AS YOU LOOK INTO MYEYES...

(CONTINUED IN THE NEXT LETTER)
BUT LIZZIE THAT WILL BE THE NEXT 'TREAT' FOR YOU, I WiLL START WHERE I'VE LEFT OFF, I HOPE YOU'VE ENJOY IT SO FAR!!!

I thought that the contents of this latest letter were highly revealing from the investigative point of view and, when I next met Paul on 25 February, my enthusiasm for what I perceived as a highly probative development was hard to hide.

'Look, he's there!' I said. 'He's in the woods. It's just like it was – the fallen tree, the stream, he's talking about entering her from behind. He's recreating the scene.'

Paul tried to temper my enthusiasm. 'Yes, but that's all he's done. Nothing directly links him to the murder and, from a psychological viewpoint, the fantasy is no different from what you might read in a men's magazine.'

The reference to acting out Stagg's sexual fantasy at a future stage was significant, he said, as the person who murdered Rachel would have a tendency to act out sexual fantasies. The tone and content of the fantasy, he added, indicated a completely dominant male and largely passive female where the woman, Lizzie, is substantially used as the focus for sexual release of the man, Stagg, who is the main engine for female sexual responsiveness. Though consistent with the profile, this did not, of course, link Stagg directly with the murder.

Paul said that it was easy to get carried away by the geographical features and the dominant male behaviour. For the covert operation to be considered to be working, it had to move from being generally consistent with what Paul expected of the killer, to being narrowly and specifically predictive of him. He advised that Lizzie shouldn't reply immediately. 'Give him time to reflect and withdraw from the relationship. It's up to him to determine the direction of the operation.'

'What if he doesn't go on with it?' I asked, already suspecting what the answer would be.

'Then that's very clear-cut – he eliminates himself.'

Chapter 26

When Lizzie failed to reply immediately, Colin appeared to think that perhaps he had offended her. He wrote:

MY DEAREST LIZZIE

FIRSTLY I WANT TO APOLOGIZE TO YOU, IN MY LAST LETTER TO YOU, I WENT ON AND ON, AND MADE MYSELF SEEM LIKE A RIGHT PRAT, IF I'VE TURNED YOU OFF ME, IM SORRY. I'LL UNDERSTAND IF YOU DO NOT WANT TO KNOW ANYMORE, I KNOW I SAID I CAN BE A BIT POSSESSIVE ...

THE REASON I FEEL THIS WAY IS BECAUSE, I'VE NEVER REALLY BEEN ATTRACTIVE TO WOMEN ...

Colin's letter continued full of contrition at the thought of having given offence, but this appeared to be short-lived as his thoughts once again turned to the subject of sexual fantasy:

(CONTINUED FROM LAST LETTER)
AS WE LAY THERE ON THE BLANKET ON THE GROUND, HOLDING EACH OTHER CLOSE, WATCHING THE FULL MOON BEAMING DOWN UPON US, THE WARM, STILL, SUMMER EVENING, CARESSING US BOTH ...

Colin's fantasy had started in much the same way as his others, and the subject matter was unexceptional by his standards, the sexual activity involving first oral sex by Lizzie on Stagg, and then penetrative sex. But as I read on, I noticed that there was a subtle change. For the first time, the instigator was Lizzie, not Colin. My layman's interpretation was that Colin was taking a passive role and following Lizzie's lead, and I wondered whether this was his way of attempting to curry favour. The emphasis, to my untutored eye, was more on romance than the frenzied 'wham, bam, thank you, Ma'am' activities which were the predominant theme of his previous letters. Admittedly, lip service had nearly always been paid to romance, but was quickly disposed of so that the subject of sex could take precedence. Even in this letter, despite the interchange of active and passive roles, Colin still managed to display a degree of domination when he wrote about ejaculating over Lizzie's face, and has her 'yelling in ecstasy', "Please, no more."'

I mentioned these views to Paul. He didn't disagree with me, but neither did he find the subject matter particularly illuminating. His comment delivered, as always, in his quiet and precise manner was simply, 'The sexually explicit material indicates Stagg's clear capacity to be aware of some aspects of female agency within sexual relationships.'

I assumed by his response that this was not a major leap forward, but neither was it inconsistent with his blueprint. Further discussion on the contents of Colin's three-page fantasy would only have wasted time, which I knew to be Paul's scarcest resource. We moved quickly on to the question of our response.

Paul's advice was for Lizzie to tell Stagg that she preferred truthfulness to fantasy, that she found the honesty refreshing, and hopefully genuine. At the same time, he said that she had to indicate her openness to dominant male behaviour, without making any suggestion of extreme violence or any characteristics drawn from the murder of Rachel Nickell. Accordingly, she wrote on 4 March:

> *Dear Colin,*
>
> *Please, please, please, dont worry about anything you've written to me, I understand exactly how you feel, only I am a little bit more wary than you, but you are filling me with more confidence each time you write. At last I'm starting to feel good about myself, your honesty is so refreshing, I hope we will always be honest with each other as feeling betrayed, and let down is so difficult to get over, but with you I am starting to feel re-born.*

The reassuring tone and warmth of her reply continued. She said that her own fantasies held no bounds and that her imagination ran riot, sometimes to the extent that it worried her. She explained further:

> *... but sometimes normal things just aren't enough and my demands are greater, not just straight sex, there is so much more to explore. (God! please dont think Im a weirdo) sexually people do not use their imagination, but I'm sure you do and can ... I need someone like that, someone, strong and powerful, your letters are so direct I know you must be, you know yourself you are a mans' man.*

In what was now his sixth letter, Stagg replied:

> *MY DARLING LIZZIE*
> *THANK YOU FOR PUTTING MY MIND AT REST, THE REASON I FELT I MAY HAVE OFFENDED YOU WAS, THAT, YOUR JUST SO GOOD TO BE TRUE, NOT*

ONLY ARE YOU BEAUTIFUL, BUT LIKE ME YOU TOO HAVE A GREAT, OPEN MIND ABOUT SEX

He expanded on this theme before adding:

... AND DONT WORRY I ASSURE YOU THAT MY FANTASIES I WRITE ARE ESPECIALLY FOR YOU, I DO READ STORYS IN MAGAZINES, BUT COMPARED TO MY FANTASIES, THEY ARE VERY TAME ...

At this point, Colin embarked upon another short sexual outburst before apologising and changing the subject back to more mundane matters. He spent the next two pages describing his home, his DIY activities and his work as an odd-job man on the Alton Estate. He rounded off the first part of his letter with:

IM SO LONGING TO READ ABOUT YOUR FANTASIES AND THOUGHTS ABOUT WHAT YOUD LIKE TO DO, WHEN WE MEET. I BET YOUR AS RANDY AS ME IN THAT DEPARTMENT, I HOPE SO. IVE ENCLOSED ANOTHER PRIVATE STORY ABOUT US ...

And finally:

I WANT TO TAKE YOU LIZZIE, LIKE YOU'VE NEVER BEEN TAKEN BEFORE. BY THE TIME I'VE FINISHED WITH YOU YOUR VAGINA WILL BE SO SORE, AND SWOLLEN AND RED ...

Colin then proceeded with:

ANOTHER STORY FOR MY DARLING LIZZIE:

I'VE INVITED YOU AROUND FOR THE EVENING, IVE COOKED A MEAL FOR US. MY SPECIALITY

RICE BOLOGNISE, FOLLOWED BY MY OWN MADE RASPBERRY MOUSSE. THE ATMOSPHERE IS PREPARED, LOW LIGHTS, SOFT, SEXY MUSIC ON THE STEREO ...

The tried and tested formula of Colin's fantasies again came to the fore; the scene having been set, he quickly progressed to describing activities involving oral sex, masturbation and rear-entry, vaginal sex.

In Paul's analysis, the subject matter of this fantasy proved to be of less psychological interest than the introductory letter. He was of the opinion that Stagg's assertion that his fantasies were more extreme than those in magazines, and his expectation to act them out, was in total keeping with Paul's blueprint, but still a long way short of crossing the finish line.

On 11 March, Stagg wrote and told Lizzie of his loneliness and his history of poor relationships with women. He wrote that he could not believe how lucky he was to have a beautiful woman interested in him who had the same exciting outlook on sex:

DEAR LIZZIE, MY DARLING,

I THOUGHT ID JUST WRITE ANOTHER LETTER TO YOU, ITS ONLY BECAUSE RIGHT NOW IM FEELING A BIT DOWN AND LONELY ...

Colin outlined a list of his concerns and explained that his only friend was his dog, Brandy. He stated that, because he was a loner, people viewed him with suspicion. He continued to talk about his lack of success with women:

WOMEN AROUND HERE, HAVE NEVER SHOWN ANY INTEREST IN ME, THEY ALWAYS LOOK AT ME AS IF THEY'VE JUST WIPED ME OFF THE BOTTOM OF THEIR SHOES. MY EX-GIRLFRIEND WAS ONLY INTERESTED IN ME, BECAUSE SHE WANTED TO

GET MARRIED. AND FOR ME, TO BE A FATHER TO HER SON, SHE NEVER REALLY LOVED ME

He made two requests of Lizzie. He wanted her to send him a 'special' letter giving details of any fetishes, and asked for a phone number he could contact her on.

Although his fantasies were containing phrases such as 'screaming in ecstasy' and 'twitching violently inside you', Paul said that too much could be read into such things. Yet the dominant male behaviour continued in the fantasies, and Paul advised that Lizzie's next letter could respond in similar tone to his descriptions of control and humiliation. However, it was important that no defining example of these concepts be offered; Stagg had to be given total freedom to respond in his own way.

Paul predicted that Stagg would respond in one of three ways. He would either:

1) Withdraw from the relationship because the prospect of a sexual liaison based on domination and degradation would be unacceptable to him;
2) Indicate his enjoyment of such things in a private relationship, but this would be at a level no different from that of many consenting adults whose sex life is spiced up with symbolic exchanges of sexual control and submission, even sometimes involving restraints;
3) Attempt to develop a relationship with Lizzie that increasingly focused on physically and sexually violent fantasies that included her, and would ultimately comprise the most serious kinds of sexual assault.

Paul said that anybody who chose the latter option, if he had been the person responsible for Rachel's murder, would find the sexual excitement and expectation arising from these violent fantasies so great that, in due course, it would override his caution. Ultimately, the killer would be likely to disclose his guilt to someone he believed was a confidante, particularly if he felt that such a disclosure would be part of an even greater sexual gratification.

In other words, if Stagg chose either of the first two options he would eliminate himself. It was only if he chose the final option and indicated that his sexuality was consistent with that predicted of the murderer, that the covert operation would continue.

Lizzie wrote:

Dear Colin,

Thank-you for your letters, I was concerned by the second one, its horrible to think of you being lonely and blue, dont worry you wont be lonely much longer.

She began to hint at a secret, something that had happened to her that had changed her whole outlook on life and altered her urges and responses. Her emotions at these feelings, she explained, were a mixture of guilt and excitement. Lizzie obliquely expanded on this subject by saying that it was something she had to overcome before she could embark on a relationship again. She reassured Colin and stated that her confidence in him was growing 'by the day'. In response to his earlier request for feedback on his letters, she was encouraging.

Also in accordance with Paul Britton's advice, she referred to Colin's themes of control and degradation.

She wrote:

I want to feel you all powerful and overwhelming, so that I am completely in your power defenceless and humiliated.

Lizzie carried on with some trivia about looking for a job and having inherited a little money from her grandmother. In conclusion, she said:

Ive been waiting to meet you, its fate, its all coming together for us Colin, weve only got to overcome one last hurdle, to be complete, I can hardly wait, please write soon and remember nothing you will ever say or do will offend me, I know you are a good man, deep down. I hope this letter has cheered you up.

Take care

Love
Lizzie
x.

Paul continued to advise on the tone and principles behind each outgoing letter and the ways in which each one from Stagg could be interpreted or understood. The precise wording of the correspondence was left to us. Commenting on the content of Lizzie's latest letter, Paul said, 'I wouldn't have chosen the word "humiliated" because it hasn't appeared in any of Stagg's letters.' Nevertheless, he felt it stayed within the guidelines he had set down.

Operation Edzell seemed to be going swimmingly, but we now hit an unforeseen snag. A TV documentary on offender profiling was being planned by the *London Programme*, with the participation of an offender profiler from Surrey University called David Canter. The producers wanted to focus in particular on the Rachel Nickell inquiry, and Canter, who did not know that Paul was involved, had been telling the press that although he believed he could help us with the investigation, he had not been invited to do so. The documentary was potentially disastrous for us because, as Paul had stressed all along, so much of its usefulness depended on Colin Stagg believing that everything had gone quiet and the investigation was getting nowhere.

Paul told them that it was his policy never to issue a statement to the press or make any statement to TV cameras unless it was with the express approval of the officer in the case, and he therefore refused all offers and blandishments from the programme's producer.

I, too, tried to put her off by saying, 'Look, we'd prefer if you didn't.'

'Why is that?'

'It's a question of forensic awareness,' I said. 'Offenders wear gloves now because they know about fingerprints. They wear condoms when committing sexual offences because they've heard of DNA. Offender profiling is extremely useful to us, but we'd like to keep it our secret.

'We don't want people to start becoming too aware of the processes involved in general offender profiling, because then they could start "staging", which is leaving deliberately misleading clues behind at a scene.'

Paul had told me that knowledge of offender profiling was now so widespread in the USA that a serial killer would go out of his way to do things which would mislead the profilers over there. And that was what we didn't want happening here.

That was the excuse I gave to the producer; obviously, I could not come straight out with it and say, 'You can't do this – we are running an undercover operation and we don't really want Colin Stagg to think of the inquiry as being anything other than plodding and run-of-the-mill.'

But the programme-makers were like a dog with a bone and they would not let it go. I now had to do an about-turn and prevail on Paul to co-operate with them. The only alternative was to let them interview Canter, a man who clearly had lots of good intentions, but no direct knowledge of the Wimbledon investigation.

We had to come up with a strategy for damage limitation. Paul would give a brief interview to the cameras explaining in general terms what profiling was about, without going into specifics, and giving the impression that it sometimes worked, but not always, and the Nickell case was probably not one in which it would be suitable. The intention was, I hoped, to deflect comment away from the case and to talk about offender profiling in only the most general of terms. We were deliberately trying to blur and fudge the issue of offender profiling because we didn't want a future serial killer's educational video tape being made at our expense.

I was still furious, however. To lower Stagg's levels of suspicion, we had cancelled his police bail and returned the majority of his property, saying that we'd return the rest as soon as it had come back from various places throughout the country. We had wanted him to think that he was well and truly off the hook and now no longer of interest to us. For this operation to work, we had to keep his levels of awareness and suspicion down, and there was this bloody programme set to send his suspicion levels soaring through the roof.

I needn't have worried. Paul was brilliant. He waffled for England that night, and anyone watching the show must have wondered why on earth the programme had bothered putting him in front of a camera.

Stagg wrote again to Lizzie on 18 March. He made it clear that he was not going to withdraw from the relationship. At the same time, his fantasy went way beyond control and humiliation; for the first time, he introduced pain.

Again, the letter followed his usual pattern and was in two parts. His introduction asked Lizzie to tell him what it was in her past which had given her a 'totally different outlook'. He expressed his intrigue and excitement at the prospect of discovering her secret. From that point on, the remaining six pages of preamble was a litany of sexual thoughts. In the crudest of language, far worse than any previously encountered, he spelled out exactly what he wanted to do to her. Domination was, as expected, a major theme, but it was the extent of that domination that proved to be a pivotal issue. Stagg told Lizzie:

> *I WANT TO DOMINATE YOU, TAKE YOUR BODY AS MY PLAYTHING, THE THINGS IM GOING TO DO TO YOU, WILL LITERALLY MAKE YOUR EYES WATER, YOU'RE RIGHT, I DO HOLD BACK IN MY 'SPECIAL' LETTERS. I WANT TO SAY THINGS TO YOU WHILE ABUSING YOUR BODY ...*

He reassured her that he was not a violent man, but in his fantasy he had called her a few dirty names. Despite this, when they got together there would be a lot of love as well as lust. He wrote by way of explanation:

ITS JUST MY PASSION WILL TAKE OVER, YOU WLL BE LEFT HUMILIATED AND DIRTY, I WANT TO, AND WILL GIVE YOU A FUCKING GOOD SORTING OUT, YOU NEED A DAMM GOOD FUCKING BY A REAL MAN, AND IM THE ONE TO DO IT, BY THE TIME I'VE FINISHED WITH YOU YOUR GOING TO BE LEFT, SORE, EXHAUSTED AND COVERED IN MY SPUNK, IM GOING TO PUMP SPUNK IN EVERY POSSIBLE HOLE IN YOUR BODY, IM GOING TO MAKE YOU WORK HARD FOR ME, YOU WILL BE MY SEX-SLAVE, IM GOING TO FUCK YOU, NOT ONLY IN THE BEDROOM BUT ALSO IN MORE EXCITING, PLACES, I KNOW A FEW PLACES AROUND HERE WHERE IM GOING TO TAKE YOU, YOU'LL FEEL SO APPREHENSIVE, BUT I WILL HAVE YOU.

The text continued in this vein and expanded on the aspects of domination and degradation:

I AM THE ONLY MAN IN THIS WORLD WHOSE GOING TO GIVE IT TO YOU, IM GOING TO MAKE SURE YOUR SCREAMING IN AGONY, WHEN I ABUSE YOU, IM GOING TO DESTROY YOUR SELF-ESTEEM, YOU'LL NEVER LOOK ANYBODY IN THE EYES AGAIN.

Prior to issuing another invitation for Lizzie to visit him, Stagg added:

YOU'RE GOING TO GET IT ALL LIZZIE. YOUR GOING TO BE SO SORE, DARLING, YOU'LL PROBABLY FIND IT HARD TO SIT DOWN AGAIN. I

HOPE YOU ARE NOT OFFENDED BY THE DIRTY NAMES IM CALLING YOU I DO NOT THINK YOU ARE THOSE THINGS BECAUSE, BESIDES OUR 'SESSIONS', WE WILL BE GREAT FRIENDS, FULL OF LOVE FOR EACH OTHER, AND ROMANCE.

Stagg then embarked upon a description of his 'local park' where he had apparently sunbathed nude and masturbated. He detailed an encounter with a woman whom he claimed caught him whilst so engaged and to his amazement joined in. The episode included a promise that they, Stagg and Lizzie, could enjoy sex in the open as '*it must be exciting, knowing someone might see us.*'

Before beginning one of his 'special letters', he repeated his request for Lizzie to send him a fantasy:

I WANT EVERY FANTASY OF YOURS IN MY MIND, EVERY 'KINKY' DETAL EVERY RANDY THOUGHT, ANYTHING YOU WANT YOULL GET, BY GOD YOU WLL GET IT, YOU RANDY DIRTY, BITCH ...

The enclosed special story enlarged on the themes in the introduction: force, physical and verbal abuse. However, we noted a distinct new element: sadism.

The scene was set in Stagg's flat following the drinking of 'a lot of wine'. Lizzie is pulled to the floor and ordered to undress. She is grabbed by the shoulders and forced to engage in oral sex. Stagg verbally abuses her. The themes of humiliation and degradation are prevalent. Intercourse then ensues, in which the roughness of the act forces her to scream in agony. More verbal abuse follows. When Lizzie begs for Stagg to stop, his response is:

'IM NOT FINISHED YET,' I SAY AS I FEEL MY COCK SWELLING INSIDE YOU, 'TAKE MY SPUNK NOW YOU SLAG, TAKE IT ALL' I SAY, AS I PUMP IT HARD INTO YOU MY WHOLE BODY TREMBLES AS THE

ORGASM RIPS THROUGH MY BODY, YOUR BODY IS NOW FLUSHED BRIGHT RED, AS YOU LAY THERE, PANTING, EYES CLOSED, 'YOU NEEDED A GOOD SORTING OUT YOU BITCH, YOUR BODY BELONGS TO ME, WHEN I WANT IT I WLL TAKE IT, EVEN IF YOUR NOT WILLING; YOUR CUNT BELONGS TO ME' ...

This fantasy episode concluded with:

(LIZZIE, PLEASE DONT BE OFFENDED BY MY CALLING YOU NAMES, I RESPECT YOU AS A WHOLE WOMAN, ITS JUST THE MANLY SIDE OF ME GETTING CARRIED AWAY.)

I was particularly puzzled by the inclusion of Stagg's final paragraph. It seemed to me that it made a nonsense of his opening statement in the introductory letter: 'I have now some idea what you want.' I recalled Paul's prediction of the three courses of action which were open to Colin. He had clearly taken the third option. He was not sure what she wanted, but he had expressed his own preference.

Paul said, 'The monitoring, caution and testing are obvious, as if he takes a step forward and then comes back again to make sure everything is all right. At the same time, he has turned up the temperature.'

He also commented on distinct elements of sadism in the letter – phrases like 'inflict pleasure', 'screaming in agony' and his 'manly side' getting out of control, and Lizzie being forced to respond in sexual agony and not pleasure.

Lizzie did not reply immediately, and when Stagg wrote again on 23 March, he appeared to be backtracking. He again revealed his loneliness, referring to the emptiness he felt when seeing young romantic couples arm in arm. He says it would be great if she could spend a few days with him. He seemed concerned that Lizzie shouldn't recoil from the extreme content of his previous letter, and talked about the women on the Roehampton estate. He explained that about 12 months previously he had been ill. He was weak and dehydrated. He claimed that women on and around his estate had conducted a whispering campaign against him. They had, he wrote, made fun of him behind his back:

I WOULD HEAR THEM SAY THINGS LIKE, "ISN'T COLIN UGLY NOW, HE'S SO SCRAWNY AND DISGUSTING."

These women, he claimed, ignored the fact that he was obviously unwell.

... BUT BEING SO SMALL-MINDED, THEY JUST MADE ME FEEL SMALL, AND I THOUGHT THAT NO WOMAN WOULD EVER TOUCH ME ...

His letter then changed tack and reverted to the subject of sex. Colin enquired in graphic terms as to the things which turned Lizzie on and expressed a hope that she was noisy when she made love. He expressed the view that the noisier the better.

I WANT YOU TO GO WILD AS I ABUSE YOUR BODY, I WANT YOU 10 SCREAM AND SHOUT AS ORGASM AFTER ORGASM RIPS THROUGH YOUR BODY.

The tenor of the letter became more frenzied as he described the imagined frantic sexual encounter in vivid, adjectival, pornographic terms. The tension in the writing was palpable but to underline the fact he added:

I'M GETTING CARRIED AWAY AGAIN, I JUST LOOKED AT YOUR PHOTO AND I WENT WILD AGAIN, GOD, I WANT YOU LIZZE. OH WELL, OFF TO THE BATHROOM AGAIN, BEFORE I HAVE ANOTHER ACCIDENT ...

In her reply, Lizzie neither rejected Stagg nor showed offence, but nor did she encourage him to develop more extreme themes. 'You don't offend me in the slightest,' she wrote. 'It's as if we are really starting to communicate at last ...'

With her letter she enclosed 'something special for you', a pendant on a chain. 'To me this is the most valuable thing I own, not in terms of price, but in my memories and dreams ...'

Paul said that it was time for her to reveal details of her own history, while pretending to be ultra- cautious. She had to indicate a dark secret in her past that she wouldn't talk about.

In his next letter, Stagg pleaded with Lizzie to tell him her secret and insisted that he couldn't be shocked by anything she had done in her life: 'Even if you told me you were a mass murderer I'd still want you in my life.' Colin wrote of how he liked to walk around his house in the nude. He claimed it gave him a sense of freedom as did naked sunbathing, but only in secluded places as people didn't understand. He added:

> *I LIKE TO SIT IN MY BEDROOM AT NIGHT, LIGHTING CANDLES, SITTING NAKED AND GIVING MYSELF PLEASURE ... I AM NOW WEARING YOUR GIFT AROUND MY NECK AND I CAN FEEL INNER VIBRATIONS WITH WHICH YOU HAVE INSTILLED IN IT.*

The pseudo-mystical tone of this writing then gave way to sexual fantasy. Colin wrote:

> *GOD, I NEED YOU LIZZIE, I WANT SO MUCH TO FUCK YOU HARD, I WANT TO LICK YOUR CUNT DRY, YOU DESERVE A BLOODY GOOD, HARD FUCKING. MY COCK IS THROBBING HARD WAITING FOR YOU. GASP, OOPS, I GOT CARRIED AWAY AGAIN ...*

He enclosed a gold ring – 'I bought it for you last week. I'm sorry it's a bit out of shape, when I got it home I dropped it on the ground and trod on it by accident ...' – and again he pushed for a meeting. If all went well, he envisaged them living together, 'on a trial basis if you're not sure ... I've got a beautiful garden ... I love to be surrounded by nature, the forces are so strong.'

Stagg went on to say, 'I want to dominate you, make your body mine, you will be sorted out so much.'

In Paul's view, there was no evidence of extreme sexual violence in the letter, but he said that Stagg was displaying a willingness to pursue the relationship at all costs, even if, regardless of society's rules or expectations, Lizzie was a mass murderer.

Chapter 27

Slowly Lizzie began to expand on her own particular history without introducing anything new. On 6 April she thanked him for the gold ring, and said that his beliefs were similar to hers, the difference being that hers have involved other people. She told him:

> *... in the past my beliefs have involved other people. I do not see any of these other people now and have not done so for some time as certain things we did together made me have mixed feelings about them. (Don't worry, I'll tell you the full story some day soon.) ... this has made me feel empty and alone ... I often reflect on those times.*

Lizzie told him that she had a job lined up looking after cats and that Stagg would be able to phone her there. When she had some money, they could meet.

They exchanged Easter cards and, on 8 April, Stagg sent Lizzie a long letter. He said that for a long time he had been searching for someone who held the same beliefs as him.

Am I right in saying you practised sexual rituals? ... if so, don't worry. I've always wanted to practise sex rites ... The thought of you being with a group of other believers being naked together and inflicting sexual pleasure to each other, makes me excited ...

Stagg said that one of his fantasies was performing sex with Lizzie and others in woods. He said he wasn't gay, but the idea of seeing another man with her was exciting. He asked more about Lizzie's past secrets, asked again for a telephone number, and said he was disappointed she did not send him any of her fantasies. 'We have to meet soon, Lizzie,' he urged.

Enclosed with the letter was a gift for Lizzie, a talisman shaped like an eye, 'to protect you from rotten, evil, close minded people and everyday dangers. I made it myself, I've always worn it when I'm wanking ...'

There was also another graphic fantasy letter, involving group sex with another couple in a woodland clearing, with mutual masturbation between two men, rear-entry sex, and oral sex between two women.

Paul said that this letter and fantasy contained examples of clear verbal abuse from male participants towards Lizzie during uninhibited deviant sexual activity. The fantasy focused on a lack of consent by Lizzie to sexual penetration, which is disregarded by the males involved.

When Lizzie replied, she said that she was worried they might not be right for each other, and that she is often disappointed by men:

I have only ever met one man who could make me feel complete.
These were due to the experiences we shared, these experiences have shaped me into the woman I am today ... I believe I will only ever feel fulfilled again if I meet a man who has the same history as me. The things that happened when I was with this man were not what normal people would like, these involved

upsetting and often hurting people and even though these things are bad and I feel guilty I can never forget how exhilarating they made me feel. I am keen to feel the same way but not by hurting others ...

She enclosed a phone number, and asked him to call her on 20 April. Stagg wrote a letter, dated 20 April, writing of 'depressive phases':

I AM SO BLOODY FRUSTRATED, I NEED TO HOLD YOU CLOSE SOON, I HAVE TO FEEL A WOMANS BODY CLOSE TO MINE SOON, OTHERWISE I GOING TO BURST A BLOOD VESSEL, I GET TURNED ON SO EASILY.

Later he added:

I GET SO WORKED UP WHEN I SEE A WOMAN I FANCY, BUT ALL THE TIME THEY LOOK AT ME AS IF I AM DOG DIRT.

He said he would try to ring her from a neighbour's, as he did not have a phone.

Paul said that Stagg's continued reference to his perception that attractive women denigrate him was consistent with the possible nature which drove the murderer of Rachel Nickell. In other words, Colin was still failing to eliminate himself from the inquiry.

Stagg failed to telephone on the appointed day, and Lizzie wrote to register her disappointment. She told him not to worry about what women near him think, that she liked him. She said that she wanted to discuss lots of things with him, and repeated that she has lived with a 'terrible secret' which she needs to work through.

In a letter dated 28 April, Stagg wrote of his past, describing how, at the age of 17, he watched a pornographic movie for the first time, and several days afterwards went nude sunbathing on his local common. Lying naked in the long grass he became aroused and began to masturbate. A man appeared from out of bushes and asked to join him. He explained the encounter:

> *NOW LIZZIE, DONT GET ME WRONG, BUT BEING A VERY HIGHLY SEXUAL PERSON, ALL FORMS OF SEX DOES TURN ME ON . . . I'VE FELT GUILTY ABOUT THIS EVER SINCE AND I SOMETIMES GET SO AROUSED WHEN I THINK ABOUT IT.*

Stagg admitted to the homosexual encounter but insisted he was not gay. All forms of sex turned him on, he said, but right now he was only interested in women. He wanted to 'fuck the arse off' Lizzie and leave her helpless and in pain, and a 'slave to my lusts'. He invited her to stay with him over the summer at Roehampton so they could take long walks on the common 'indulging in carnal lusts every five minutes' ... 'Put me out of my misery,' he concluded, 'before I explode.'

At about 5.00pm that afternoon, Stagg telephoned Lizzie for the very first time. The short call was somewhat cautious and stilted on both sides, and they agreed to speak again the next day.

Lizzie's flat was large with three bedrooms in central London. It was tastefully decorated in pastel shades, and furnished with antique and reproduction furniture. We had spent every evening since the 20th sitting there, waiting for the phone to ring. Stagg's flat did not have a telephone, so once she had given him her number, we had no way of guaranteeing that he wouldn't phone at unexpected times.

It was not Lizzie's real number, of course. We had linked her number into a Cascade system, which enables a London address, for example, to be given a Leeds phone number. When somebody dials in, the call will go up to the Leeds exchange and then cascade all the way down the country through other exchanges, until it rings in London. It comes in quite handy in undercover work – as long as you remembered where you were. On one covert operation, an officer was posing as Scottish and using a Glasgow phone number. A meeting was arranged with a drugs-dealer in London and the undercover officer, without thinking, said, 'OK, I'll be there in 45 minutes.'

As a matter of policy, Lizzie was always to be left to have the conversations on her own. It was considered by Paul Britton to be less distracting for her to be by herself when answering Colin's calls. But before the next conversation, I felt I should be at Lizzie's flat to go over any aspects of Paul Britton's advice that she might want clarifying, and generally provide moral support. On the afternoon of 29 April, I was sitting in Lizzie's living room, drinking coffee as we waited for the special phone line to ring again.

'You know, KP,' Lizzie began, 'I was really surprised at how inarticulate Colin is on the phone. He sounds so flat and monotonous – he can hardly put a sentence together. You wouldn't think he could possibly be the same man that writes those letters.'

Paul had explained that the disparity between his ability to communicate fluently on paper and not so well face-to-face was an example of point 3 of the general characteristics profile – poor heterosocial skills. He was also an extremely cautious person.

'I know what you're saying, but I can't say I'm that surprised. He's got no social graces and very little experience of communicating with women.'

'But he's so fluent on paper – well, apart from the handwriting.'

'But there's that degree of remoteness about letters. He's more confident without the actual pressure of having to communicate directly with a woman on a one-to-one basis.'

'We know all about his particular ideas on communicating with women on a one-to-one basis!'

'Just a tad worrying. It strikes me that he doesn't really like women that much.'

'Not in a social sense, no, but there are bits of us that he seems quite taken with.'

'That's what bothers me! I don't know about you, but I get this horrible feeling that he's like a time-bomb waiting to explode. Even if he's got nothing to do with Rachel's murder, there's something very worrying about his attitude.'

Lizzie was deep in thought for a moment or two. 'That letter last week, when he was going on about being "so frustrated" and getting "so worked up" when he sees a woman he fancies ...'

'Yeah, but it was the next bit – you remember?'

'About women looking at him as though he's dog dirt?'

I nodded. 'And that's the second time he's made reference to that sort of thing.'

'Is it?'

'Yeah, four or five letters ago, he said that women always look at him as if he's something they'd scraped off the bottom of their shoe. Paul picked up on it; he reckons that this perception that attractive women denigrate him is consistent with the characteristics of the murderer.'

'You and your memory!'

'It comes in handy sometimes.'

Lizzie checked her watch. 'He's late. Why do you men never do what you say you're going to do when you say you're going to do it?'

'It's only five minutes.'

'I know, but I just get myself psyched up for a certain time and ...'

'I understand. It can't be easy, or pleasant for that matter. Is there anything I can help with?'

'Not really. We can't plan a conversation because there's so much opportunity for him to go off at a tangent. I think I've got the basic game plan mastered. If he asks about his letters, Paul Britton wants me to be sort of non-committal, yeah?'

'Something like ... you're not offended by them, something neutral. And if you get the chance, play up your past. The caution, your concern about making a mistake ...'

'And perhaps some reference to my particular problems, but only vaguely.'

'Sounds good to me. And if he mentions the murder ...'

'I know – don't show too much interest and tell him that we all have our own problems and I'll tell him a bit about mine.'

'Perfect. Lizzie, I wouldn't worry about the conversation drying up, you could talk the hind legs off a donkey!'

Before she could reply, the phone rang in the other room.

'I'm on!'

Lizzie got up and went to answer the phone. I wandered into the kitchen to make another cup of coffee whilst she was doing her stuff. About ten minutes later, she returned.

'OK?'

'A bit better, he's still not exactly silver-tongued. But it was an improvement on yesterday's call.'

'Anything interesting?'

'He started talking about Rachel, though not by name. If I'd really been Lizzie James, I wouldn't have had a clue who he was on about.'

'So what did you do?'

'I blanked it. He tried to go on about the rumours people were spreading about him, and that because he was suspected of the murder he couldn't trust people.'

'What else?'

'He's asked me to go and stay for the summer.'

'Your hubby'll like that!'

'Not a lot!' she said with a smile. 'He's pushing for a meet.'

'How did you get round it?'

'I said I wasn't able to at the moment, he seemed to accept it. I just tried to keep it chatty and light. Shall I change the tape?'

'Yes, then we can get it exhibited and get the transcript done and a copy off to Paul Britton.'

Lizzie told me that Stagg had referred to people on the Alton Estate spreading rumours about him.

'Oh, why?' asked Lizzie.

'Well, I ... I won't tell you on the phone, but I'll tell you in the next letter.'

'Oh yeah?'

'Mainly something that happened last year.'

'Oh yeah. Oh, all right then.'

'Yeah.'

'People just can't keep themselves to themselves,' Lizzie said. 'I know what it's like, I mean it's ...'

'Yeah.'

'It's even worse up north. You know what people are like up north, they just love to gossip about ya.'

'That's right, yeah. Well, this is more than gossip, you know.'

'Is it?'

'It's all-out character assassination, you know.'

Stagg promised to write and explain what happened but Lizzie, as advised by Paul, showed little, if any, interest in the subject, and concentrated on her own life and history. When he asked what she thought of his letters, Lizzie answered him carefully. 'They don't offend me, I don't mind in the slightest,' she said, avoiding saying that she liked them.

Coming back to it later in the conversation, Stagg said, 'It's just that something terrible happened around here, you know.'

'Mmm.'

'You probably read about it in the news, like.'

'I don't really pay much attention to the papers, I haven't got a TV really.'

'The thing is, I was suspected of it.'

'Uh hm.'

'But I want to tell you like I told everybody, I never done anything, you know.'

Again, Lizzie eased away from the subject. It can't have been easy for her. It's impossible to cater for every contingency that can occur in a conversation. In a letter, you can sit down and make sure that your reply or what you're saying is precise and within certain guidelines. But when you're under pressure in a conversation, it's difficult – she's got one ear on the phone listening to what he's saying, and the rest of her is playing the part as an actress. At the same time, she's struggling to try and remain within the confines of the law, which is very complicated, and trying not to go too far. But it was essential that she maintained that fine balance.

Chapter 28

Paul said that both conversations showed Stagg to be cautious, which Jwas to be expected in the early stages of direct contact. In his next letter, however, Stagg explained how he had been arrested for the murder of a young woman the previous year, but stressed that he wasn't responsible. A number of single men had been pulled in for questioning, he said. His neighbours and other locals had told the police a load of rubbish and the police had believed them:

> *I AM NOT A MURDERER, AS MY BELIEF IS THAT ALL LIFE FROM THE SMALLEST INSECT TO PLANT, ANIMAL AND MAN IS SACRED AND UNIQUE ...*

Stagg also mentioned being charged with indecent exposure, claiming it was the result of being victimised by neighbours who had seen his name in the newspapers. They'd also called him names in the street and children had thrown eggs at him and his kitchen window. The latest rumour on the estate, he said, was that he ran naked round his back garden masturbating at midnight.

Another letter, posted very soon afterwards, featured Lizzie being beaten and having her head yanked back with a belt as Stagg enters her from behind and causes her pain. Amongst other things he wrote:

> *I WILL GRAB YOU BY YOUR HAIR AND DRAG YOU SCREAMING INTO MY BEDROOM ... I WILL TAKE YOUR CLOTHES OFF, ALMOST RIPPING THEM ... I WILL MAKE YOU PAY FOR BEING A DIRTY SLUT I SAY TO YOU AS I FORCE YOU ON YOUR KNEES, I PLACE A STOOL IN FRONT OF YOU, AND FORCE YOU OVER IT ... I TAKE OFF ALL MY CLOTHES, AND TAKE A LEATHER BELT FROM MY DRAWER, 'RIGHT YOU SLAG PREPARE TO BE IN PAIN ... I WANT YOU TO SAY SORRY FOR BEING A DIRTY SLAG ... I CANT HERE [sic] YOU' I SAY AS I SMACK YOUR BUM AND YOUR BACK, LEAVING RED MARKS OVER YOU ... TEARS ARE NOW ROLLING DOWN YOUR CHEEKS, AS I FUCK YOU HARD AND VIOLENTLY, CAUSING YOU PAIN, WITH THE LEATHER BELT, I PLACE IT OVER YOUR MOUTH AND I HOLD EACH END, PULLING YOUR HEAD UPWARDS ... YOU LAY THERE INPAIN ... I GRAB YOUR TITS AND VIOLENTLY SQUEEZE YOUR NIPPLES, MAKING YOU RECOIL IN PAIN ... I PULL YOUR HAIR, HURTING YOU BAD ...*

The letter ends, '*I hope this is what you wanted.*'

Paul told me that the letter reflected sexual deviation which focused on violence which was more extreme than that carried out by people who derive pleasure from 'symbolic enactments of deviant and submissive sexual roles' that sometimes arouse individuals or couples, and that this was a strong positive indication of the deviant sexuality predicted of Rachel's killer.

he clinic of Paul Britton. He was an established and xpert by the courts, and his opinions in assessing risk the public, whether a person is safe to be released from a entence, or a hospital, were taken very seriously.

lained that Paul's system was a series of gates in a maze, filter system, bearing in mind that if this man was eviant, he had the entire spectrum of sexual deviance to om.

tagg would start going down certain paths; if he took a turning and started heading away on a tack that was hat described by Paul right back at the beginning of 92, that would naturally exclude him from the inquiry. peration was conducted very strictly - under no nces were we to suggest or introduce new themes, or give ve in the direction that we were looking for, because that tally destroy our credibility. We must never allow the that we were 'shaping' him to be made against us.

ained that one of the fundamental principles upon which eration was designed was the fact that any material by Colin Stagg had to be spontaneous. Our brief was to m with an opportunity to express himself, if he wanted t expression had to be his and his alone. That is to say, we introduce ideas or themes, these had to come from him gy being that we were providing him with a blackboard n which to write or paint. However, once these ideas or been generated and established by him, it would be o incorporate them in our letters. In layman's terms, it al that he made the running and if the ante was to be d to be raised by him.

ame to questions, there was no difficulty or uncertainty gality of the operation - that was taken for granted by Instead, the senior officers, bound up with the and the operational issues such as viability, and risk to of disengaging too early, were almost exclusively ith 'How much?' and 'How long?'

ton was on hand to answer any specific technical

During the next phone call, on 6 May, Colin spoke about visiting his solicitor to discuss a damages claim against the police for wrongful arrest.

'God, you could get a fortune,' Lizzie said.

'I hope so.'

Lizzie said that she did not want to get involved with someone unless they'd done the same sort of thing as her, as the relationship would turn out to be no good. 'I've different sexual expectations,' she said. 'The things that I've been involved in have made me a bit different ...'

Colin said that he was broad-minded, and said, 'You've got me really intrigued, you know ... I've been trying to guess in my last letters ... Every time I think I've got it right, you give me the impression that I've got it wrong.'

Lizzie finally suggested that they meet face to face, and in another telephone call the next day, suggested a picnic in Hyde Park on 20 May, which Colin had told her was his birthday.

Stagg said that he had sent another fantasy, and started describing it:

'I get one of my leather belts out what I normally wear, and I smack you across the backside ... leaving red marks on your skin ... you're lying on the bed in agony ... I tie your hands and your legs to the corners of my bed ... As I'm fucking you and that, I've got to pull your head right back, you know ...'

'Don't tell me any more,' Lizzie said. 'You'll spoil the rest of the story when I get it.'

Stagg said he was turned on, and asked Lizzie if this was the sort of thing she was into.

This was the first time that Stagg had recounted a sexual fantasy to Lizzie on the phone. Although it was less violent than more recent communication, it included a female being made to suffer agony from beating, hair pulling and her head being pulled back with a belt.

Each letter, as it was received, was being picked up from the accommodation address, brought back to Wimbledon, opened in

During the next phone call, on 6 May, Colin spoke about visiting his solicitor to discuss a damages claim against the police for wrongful arrest.

'God, you could get a fortune,' Lizzie said.

'I hope so.'

Lizzie said that she did not want to get involved with someone unless they'd done the same sort of thing as her, as the relationship would turn out to be no good. 'I've different sexual expectations,' she said. 'The things that I've been involved in have made me a bit different ...'

Colin said that he was broad-minded, and said, 'You've got me really intrigued, you know ... I've been trying to guess in my last letters ... Every time I think I've got it right, you give me the impression that I've got it wrong.'

Lizzie finally suggested that they meet face to face, and in another telephone call the next day, suggested a picnic in Hyde Park on 20 May, which Colin had told her was his birthday.

Stagg said that he had sent another fantasy, and started describing it:

'I get one of my leather belts out what I normally wear, and I smack you across the backside ... leaving red marks on your skin ... you're lying on the bed in agony ... I tie your hands and your legs to the corners of my bed ... As I'm fucking you and that, I've got to pull your head right back, you know ...'

'Don't tell me any more,' Lizzie said. 'You'll spoil the rest of the story when I get it.'

Stagg said he was turned on, and asked Lizzie if this was the sort of thing she was into.

This was the first time that Stagg had recounted a sexual fantasy to Lizzie on the phone. Although it was less violent than more recent communication, it included a female being made to suffer agony from beating, hair pulling and her head being pulled back with a belt.

Each letter, as it was received, was being picked up from the accommodation address, brought back to Wimbledon, opened in my presence, and sealed in protective packaging in case we wanted to have ESDA done to see whether there had been anything else written on the paper above or below.

We then gave each one an exhibit number, signed the envelope, sealed it, and did notes proving the continuity of the receipt of the letters and the transfer to my custody. I would then enter them into a log book which was to record all the property that we received from Colin Stagg, and locked them in my safe.

The entire operation was conducted in total secrecy. Mick and I did all the typing ourselves, since we couldn't risk farming it out to someone else, otherwise the cat would be out of the bag.

Mick had an electric typewriter in our office and it was on this that we laboured to knock out the confidential reports and updates for the various senior officers who needed to be kept informed. With the office door shut, we were hidden away from the prying eyes of the station and could run the operation in relatively secure conditions.

The natural inquisitiveness of police officers means that keeping secrets in a police station is very difficult, if not impossible. Coppers, especially if they're any good at their job, have it in their nature to root around and dig up information. The one thing they hate more than anything is a mystery, so there was a degree of speculation as to why this mysterious and very attractive blonde was spending so much time closeted behind closed doors with their DCI and the DI from the murder squad. The three of us tried holding a couple of our meetings away from Wimbledon, at other stations, but the presence of three strangers wandering around other people's nicks only caused three times the amount of curiosity. In the end, we opted for the lesser of the two evils and reverted to running the operation from Wimbledon.

Just a handful of very senior officers were getting regular updates on progress. These reports were verbal. Occasionally, we would commit our progress to paper but, in the interests of security, these reports were kept to a minimum. The usual method was to attend the Area senior management meetings. These would be attended by DAC Johnston, John Coo (Commander, Operations), Tom Jones

(Commander, Support), Bob Chapman (Detective Chief Superintendent) and various others. JB would supply them with copies of Stagg's letters to read and would then hand over to me to explain the progress in the context of Paul Britton's blueprint. The copy letters would then be returned to me and I would dispose of them at the end of the meeting.

On at least two occasions, however, we were summoned to special meetings of the hierarchy and were asked to give presentations as to the theory and practice of the operation. Those present from the Yard included Commander Grieve from Criminal Intelligence; Neil Giles as a representative of Commander Ramm, 5 Area; Detective Superintendent Rowe Hemming; and Bruce Butler of the CPS. The first of these extraordinary meetings took place at 3.00pm on 7 May 1993 at the 4 Area Headquarters situated at Norbury, South London. By this time, Operation Edzell had entered its fifth month, and with the overall investigation already costing well in excess of £1 million, authority was needed at the highest level to continue with Lizzie's undercover. The covert operation was under review and these men had the power to let it continue or to pull the plug immediately.

Wickerson and I gave a presentation using slides, interviews, letters and transcripts from the operation. We explained that the theory behind what Paul was doing was that if we had got the right man, he would very soon start to show his particular preferences, if indeed he was sexually deviant – and obviously there was an indication that he might have been by his penchant for sending unsolicited soft porn through the post to relative strangers.

We emphasised that what we were doing had nothing to do with offender profiling; at this stage, we were purely into clinical and forensic psychology, based upon Paul's experience of dealing with sexually, and sometimes criminally, deviant people in his position as head of the Trent Regional Health Forensic Psychology Service. Trent is an enormous health region, covering a fifth of the population of Great Britain, and it was fair to say that any known sexually or criminally deviant person who came from the population of 12 million people from that region would have passed through the clinic of Paul Britton. He was an established and accepted expert by the courts, and his opinions in assessing risk factors to the public, whether a person is safe to be released from a custodial sentence, or a hospital, were taken very seriously.

We explained that Paul's system was a series of gates in a maze, a sort of filter system, bearing in mind that if this man was sexually deviant, he had the entire spectrum of sexual deviance to choose from.

Colin Stagg would start going down certain paths; if he took a different turning and started heading away on a tack that was outside that described by Paul right back at the beginning of August 1992, that would naturally exclude him from the inquiry.

The operation was conducted very strictly - under no circumstances were we to suggest or introduce new themes, or give him a shove in the direction that we were looking for, because that would totally destroy our credibility. We must never allow the accusation that we were 'shaping' him to be made against us.

We explained that one of the fundamental principles upon which Paul's operation was designed was the fact that any material produced by Colin Stagg had to be spontaneous. Our brief was to provide him with an opportunity to express himself, if he wanted to, and that expression had to be his and his alone. That is to say, we were not to introduce ideas or themes, these had to come from him - the analogy being that we were providing him with a blackboard or canvas on which to write or paint. However, once these ideas or themes had been generated and established by him, it would be acceptable to incorporate them in our letters. In layman's terms, it was essential that he made the running and if the ante was to be raised, it had to be raised by him.

When it came to questions, there was no difficulty or uncertainty about the legality of the operation - that was taken for granted by everyone. Instead, the senior officers, bound up with the practicalities and the operational issues such as viability, and risk to the public of disengaging too early, were almost exclusively concerned with 'How much?' and 'How long?'

Paul Britton was on hand to answer any specific technical

questions generated from my synopsis, and the assembled dignitaries must have found all our answers satisfactory, because we were given the green light to continue.

There were another couple of short telephone calls. Then, on 13 May, Lizzie, who had up to that time revealed very little of her own history, promised that she was almost ready to reveal her dark secret to him.

By opening up her heart to him, she said, she hoped he would do the same in return.

Lizzie said, 'You know I know you told me in one of the letters that you met this man in the park when you were 17 and ...'

'Yeah.'

'And I know what it must be like to sort of confess to something like that but ...'

'Yeah.'

'... but don't worry about it ... I don't think you're gay or anything like that, I just think ...'

'No, I know.'

'... you're just lonely, that's all it was.'

'Yeah, that's right, yeah.'

'So I wouldn't worry.'

'No, I don't. It happened such a long time ago anyway, you know.'

'Yeah, but I wouldn't worry about it ... and you know what you were saying about that woman, quite frankly, Colin, it wouldn't matter to me if you had murdered her. I'm not bothered, in fact, in certain ways it would make it easier for me because I've got something to tell you. I'll tell you on Thursday that, you know, it just makes me realise that it's fate that has brought us together.'

'Yeah, I think so.'

'I don't want to talk about it now but I'll tell you on Thursday.'

'Right. You know I'm innocent of everything. I haven't done anything, you know.'

'Yeah, well, I don't want to talk about that but I've got something I want to say to you ...'

The next day, Lizzie sent Colin the following invitation:

Miss Elizabeth James
cordially invites
Mr Colin Stagg
to Hyde Park
on 20th May 1993, 2pm
for the occasion
of a
birthday picnic.
Be there or be square.

Enclosed was a hand-drawn map of the proposed meeting place. Lizzie said that she would be wearing a floral dress and carrying a Marks and Spencer's carrier bag. 'I'll be standing right next to the lamp- post outside the Dell cafe, next to the Serpentine lake.'

She added: 'PS – I won't keep you too long, so your dog will be all right.'

Chapter 29

We knew that once we'd had the first face-to-face meeting, the life expectancy of the operation would be very limited; Stagg would begin to expect normal boyfriend/girlfriend activities and, obviously, that was not going to happen. Paul thought that he would probably get fed up fairly quickly when things did not go his way. The relationship would fizzle out, either because his levels of suspicion had gone through the roof, or simply because he was not getting what he wanted. Much more serious than that, however, was our fear that if he did turn out to be the man who killed Rachel Nickell – and at this stage we still had no conclusive proof – then Lizzie would be in a lot of danger.

The subject of the first face-to-face meeting generated much discussion within the ACPO ranks. There was a multitude of issues to consider, the most important, of course, being Lizzie's safety. The subject of a second opinion over and beyond Paul's had been raised by Ian Johnson at the conference at Norbury on 7 May. DAC Veness suggested that we get a second opinion, not of the Offender Profile or Sexual Fantasy Analysis, but to make doubly sure that by implementing the undercover operation we couldn't be accused of escalating the situation. If Colin Stagg was the killer, would our actions make him go out and kill again? And if we could not continue with the operation and we still did not have enough evidence, how would we disengage?

There was never any doubt as to the propriety of what Paul Britton was saying about the profiling and sexual fantasy analysis side of things; the seeking of a second opinion was merely a question of ensuring that we were not priming a time-bomb that would one day explode in the public's face.

We went to see an eminent doctor at the Institute of Psychiatry, called Professor Gunn, and sought his opinion on the effect of cutting off the relationship, and what would be the best way of doing it. We informed him of a plan to be used as a get-out clause, which involved Lizzie taking a job abroad. The professor agreed completely with everything Paul had said; in his view, the scenario would not involve Colin feeling rejection. As far as Stagg was concerned, Lizzie would be upset at leaving him, but the offer had been too good to refuse.

The investigation of suspects was my particular task and, as such, I represented the Area interests at meetings between Tactical Operations and Special Operations, Neil Giles having the corresponding role for SO. Not once did either Neil or I find ourselves at variance over the running of the UC officer. In the weeks preceding the first meeting, Neil Giles and I had spent many hours trying to balance the requirements of the operation against those of the service and the law. These discussions invariably took place in Neil Giles's office on the fifth floor of New Scotland Yard.

'The boss is very concerned about the prospect of Lizzie being put face-to-face with our man,' he said to me.

'I think we all share that concern, Neil, but we either go with it or the momentum we've managed to build up is just going to fizzle out.'

'Don't get me wrong, Keith, there's no way I want to see that happen and neither does the boss. The meeting will go ahead but you and I have got to ensure that it's strictly controlled and that Lizzie is well covered.'

'Easier said than done – the problem is going to be finding the right location which will satisfy both sides of the equation. Colin seems set on taking Lizzie to Wimbledon Common, given half a chance.'

'There's no way that that's on.'

'Too right. Apart from the obvious risk of letting him loose on the common with a pretty blonde there's no way we could cover a meet without sticking out like sore thumbs. The common doesn't exactly lend itself to surveillance.'

'That aside, Keith, even if he's not our man, I've seen enough of his writings to make me think he's a danger to women. What's Paul's view on this meeting?'

'He reckons that meetings are a natural progression, but potentially they carry a high risk to Lizzie's safety – particularly if it was Stagg who killed Rachel. He has emphasised many times that Lizzie could be at risk, and not only at meetings.'

'What do you mean?'

'As I understand it, he means that were Colin to discover our little deception, there's a chance he might come looking for her. Paul said he would expect that sort of reaction from the killer.'

'So what happens if he decides to plot up the accommodation address?'

'That's something I've discussed with Lizzie; she's aware of the potential problem. Her view is that the risk is minimal. And I must say that her logic is good. First, she knows what he looks like and he doesn't know her.'

'But didn't we send him a photo?'

'Yes, but she's almost unrecognisable in it. And don't forget the address is in central London, so there are lots of people about. Lizzie reckons it's easy to be anonymous and she always checks the plot before going in. If she's happy, I'm happy.'

'She knows her business. OK, so what about the location for the meet?'

'I've spoken to Paul and it boils down to this – a meeting on the common could have certain advantages ...'

'The common's a non-starter, Keith.'

'Hold on, don't jump the gun. Paul Britton thinks that a meeting near the scene could act as a catalyst and therefore lead to disclosures, but obviously the risk factor would also be high.'

'Unacceptably high.'

'My view exactly. Mind you, Lizzie's champing at the bit to give it a go. Mick and I have had another look at the common from the surveillance viewpoint and it clearly isn't feasible. But bearing in mind that our suspect is a country boy at heart and we're looking to create a comfort zone, we definitely need somewhere with grass and trees and open space. We'll sort out a location sooner or later but then we'll have to come up with a convincing reason why she can't go to the common.'

'You'll come back to me with a location and the cover story? Now let's get down to the nitty-gritty – the cover. I know the boss will insist on the full monty.'

'I was thinking about a surveillance team to shadow Colin from his HA [home address] to the meet, and another team to be in situ to cover the meet and act as a hit team should it be necessary.'

'Why take him from his HA? Why not just use the two teams to plot up the meet? That way there'd be less chance of him burning any of the first team on the way up.'

'Ordinarily I'd agree with you, because seeing as we know his ultimate destination, the follow would only have to be fairly loose. But it might be a useful intelligence-gathering exercise. If he's got evil intent, he might just take us to where he's pugged up the bag or the weapon. You never know what he might do. I was thinking about covering his Charlie Mike [covert surveillance speak for a home address] from 6.00am on the day of the meet, just to see where he goes and what preparations he makes.'

'Sounds good, but I'm still not totally happy that we can adequately protect Lizzie during the actual meet. The team can't be sitting right on top of them and if he suddenly flips, he could have stabbed her before we're able to stop him.'

'What do you suggest?'

'The boss suggested that we get hold of some stab-proof clothing.'

'I've seen those things – they're not exactly covert!'

'I'm not talking about the stuff that the blokes on the street wear - there must be more discreet versions on the market.'

'I'll look into it.'

'The only other stipulation, Keith, is that either you or Mick have to be in direct charge of the operation.'

'You can take that as read,' I said. 'Wild horses couldn't keep us away.'

Body armour – lots of VIPs must wear it, so you would think that it must be easy to get hold of. We started making some discreet enquiries, and eventually found a company who said they could make a garment up to our specifications; the only problem with Kevlar was that, for it to be knife-proof, they'd need to work with 18 layers.

Lizzie tried it on and said, 'You've got to be joking – I can't wear this, I'll look like the bloody Michelin man.'

'Eighteen layers is impractical,' we said to them. 'Could we borrow a few sheets of the material to see if we can come up with a compromise – something more subtle?'

Back in my office at Wimbledon, we conducted a few experiments with a hunting knife and a leg of pork to see how little we could get away with. It was a total waste of time; we discovered that anything that would have been malleable enough wouldn't have protected Lizzie against a knife blade. She opted to go unprotected.

About a week later, I was back at Scotland Yard. I was becoming such a regular on the fifth floor that my presence in the inner sanctum of SO10 came as no surprise to any of the office staff, many of whom I was now on speaking terms with. I poked my head round Neil Giles's door.

'We've cracked it,' I said with a self-satisfied smile. 'Wickerson's come up with a brainwave – Hyde Park.'

Neil thought about it for a few seconds. 'Trees, open space, and we could hide an army there. Perfect.'

'We've been up and had a look, we reckon the Dell café by the Serpentine's the ideal spot – plenty of deckchairs we can deploy our team on or around without anyone raising an eyebrow.'

'Excellent. How far have we got with the other arrangements?'

'We're only going to need one SO11 team because we've shaped up a team from the Ree-Gee at Surbiton.'

'Why the Ree-Gee?'

'Wickerson and Roy Daisley are old mates and we thought it would be a good idea to keep it in the family. On top of that, the Ree-Gee are 'teccos and well versed when it comes to giving evidence.'

'Good thinking. What else?'

'The TSU have been working overtime with the equipment. We've got a Nagra (miniature reel-to-reel tape recorder) concealed in a handbag and the engineer's sorted out an open transmitter so Mick and I can monitor the conversation. The TSU have also come up with a set of aerial photographs of the entire plot and Paul Britton will brief Lizzie on warning signs to look for in our man.'

'What about the protective clothing?'

'Looks like a no-go. I tried Royalty Protection but they'd got nothing remotely covert. We found a company in Stratford that makes the stuff, but the problem is its thickness and inflexibility. Lizzie looks like the Michelin man in it; he'd only have to brush against her and he'd suss her.'

'If we can't do it, we can't do it, but Mr Ramm is going to want reassuring we can get to Lizzie immediately if the wheels come off.'

The wrinkles were eventually all ironed out and we were set to go. The date was arranged for 2.00pm on 20 May 1993. Lizzie had invited Colin to a picnic to celebrate his birthday. She explained the location by saying that she knew central London well and that it was more convenient for her as she only had a couple of hours before she had to get back to her job in the Bedfordshire area.

The day before, Paul sat down with Lizzie in the annexe at Arnold Lodge to prepare her. To Colin, she must appear to be a damaged and disturbed woman, nursing a dark secret and looking for a man who had shared similar experiences. Lizzie had to know how this woman would feel and act and speak; she was the first to admit that she'd never done anything like this before and could not make assumptions.

'He'll want to get close and touch you,' Paul told her, 'but you have to manage the physical distance and keep him away without rejecting him or showing disdain. If he sees or infers that you're not all that you seem, or interprets rejection, he'll see you as another woman saying no to him. It won't be good for the operation or for you.'

'How do I manage the distance?' she asked.

'Fall back on your own distress. You're telling him about what happened to you as a teenager, and the feelings it engendered. These are upsetting and uncomfortable and you can use this pain and hurt to hold him off. He's going to recognise a lame excuse – he's heard a lot of them from women. What you say has to be absolutely real.'

I was at my desk by just after 4.30am on the morning of the 20th, sitting down in front of the electric typewriter and battling with the keyboard as I prepared a briefing sheet for the impending operation. The standard format for such documents is the IMAC system. We have a mnemonic for just about everything in the Job, and this one stands for Information, Intention, Method, Administration and Communication. This covers every eventuality and nobody is left in any doubt as to what they are doing, how they are supposed to do it, why they are doing it, what channels we'd be using on the small sets and finally what administrative arrangements have been made. These include who is responsible for keeping the log, to which nick any bodies will be taken if arrests are made, and where the debriefing will be held.

While Wickerson went to photocopy the maps and sketch plan, I opened the document safe and removed the series of aerial photographs which I had taped together the previous evening. When unrolled, they covered an area of about 7ft by 18in. The detail was breathtaking and every inch of our potential plot was shown.

By 5.15am, the incident room was crowded with Peter Rowling's SO11 team, DCI Roy Daisley and his Surbiton contingent under the command of DI Gordon Harrison.

Wickerson waited for the buzz of conversation to subside.

'Thank you. OK, for those of you who don't know me, I'm DCI Mick Wickerson and this is DI Keith Pedder. Before I go any further, I must emphasise that whatever you hear this morning is not to be the subject of conversation outside these four walls.'

Mick looked around the assembled faces to reinforce his last statement. 'I know you're all professionals, but I make no apologies for that remark. You have obviously worked out that today's operation is to do with the Rachel Nickell inquiry. And that being said you will understand that any snippet of information would be very quickly picked up by the media and spread all over the front pages.

'As you can see from your briefing sheets, the object of the exercise is to cover a meeting that will take place in Hyde Park this lunchtime. The operation falls into two separate parts. The first is to cover India 1 [Stagg] and to take him from his HA to the meet. Roly, that's down to your team.'

Pete Rowling nodded.

'This is fundamentally an intelligence-gathering exercise. We want India 1 covered from about 6.00am. I know that's early, but if he comes out of his address we want you to go with him.'

'Unless,' I interrupted, 'he goes on to Wimbledon Common.'

'That's right,' Wickerson continued. 'If he goes on to the common, there's no way you can be reasonably expected to stay with him – firstly, because he knows the place like the back of his hand; and secondly, you'll stick out like the balls on a bulldog. We would obviously like you to keep him under control as much as possible. We don't want him spooked, so if you're uncomfortable with the situation, pull back.' Wickerson looked at me for confirmation.

'You'll have to play it by ear,' I said. 'But let's not take any chances with this one. He's not particularly aware, but he might be a bit twitchy today. I would suggest that you pull off and cover the underpasses and his Charlie Mike.'

Wickerson continued, 'All right then, with the proviso of the common, stay with him if he comes out. We're particularly interested in any places he might visit, especially if he comes out with anything that he didn't have when he went in. We're interested in any preparations he might make before he heads off for the meet. When he looks like he's heading for Hyde Park, give him a loose follow.

'The second part of the operation is to cover the meet and that's down to DI Harrison's team. So outside the park is your responsibility, Peter, and once there you hand over control to the Regional boys who will be plotted up waiting. After the meet, Peter, you'll take over again and go with India 1. Everybody clear so far?'

There were no dissenters.

'Right, as per the sheet, India 1 is Colin Stagg: 5ft 8in tall, medium to stocky build, 29 years of age – or rather, 30 today. Have we got the photos, Keith?'

I handed round a pile of pictures.

'He's likely to be wearing jeans, black or white cap-sleeved T-shirt, trainers and possibly a black leather jacket.'

A question came from the back of the room. 'How certain are you of the clothing?'

'I'd say 100 per cent, wouldn't you, Keith?'

'From memory, I don't think he owns anything else.'

Another question from the floor. 'This Stagg, I take it he's the man who was in the papers at the back end of last year?'

'That's right,' Wickerson replied. 'OK then, now for India 2, she's as described ...'

Before he could continue, another question was raised. 'Guv, can we take it that India 2 is a friendly?'

Wickerson said, 'There's no point in denying it, she's a UC. Some of you may even know her. So there it is, cards on the table.'

He looked around the room. There was a slight buzz of conversation as officers absorbed the confirmation of what they had probably already suspected. 'You can now see why security is of the essence. If Mr Stagg is the man we're looking for, then he is extremely dangerous and any leaks could place our UC in serious trouble.'

Roy Daisley added his weight to Wickerson's warning. 'You've heard what DCI Wickerson has said and any breach of security will be dealt with very severely – I don't think I need to say any more.'

Wickerson broke the short silence. 'All right then, that's enough of the heavy hand. Let's get on with the business we came for. The meeting is set for 1.00pm at the Dell café, which is here.' He indicated the restaurant on the aerial photograph. 'If you look at your maps, you'll see the Dell is about a third of the way down Serpentine Road as you come into the park from Hyde Park Corner. It's proposed that our girl will meet India 1 outside the restaurant and will then take him to the deckchair area just to the west of the Dell.

'We want the Regional boys to be plotted up in and around that area. Your responsibility will be to provide protection for India 2. In the event that the wheel comes off, you're to get her out of harm's way pronto ... But no one, and I mean no one, is to make a move unless specifically told to by either myself or DI Pedder. We will be controlling the plot and will be able to see and hear everything that goes on. Gordon ...' He looked round the room to find DI Harrison. 'If you can have your boys and girls in position by midday. I'll leave their deployment to you, and we'll use the stables as a forward rendezvous point. All right?'

'No problem. Just one question, though. The weather doesn't look too promising – what are we going to do if it rains? We're going to look a little out of place lounging about in the open if it's pissing down.'

'Again, we'll have to play it by ear, but if the picnic is out of the question, we'll have to hold the meet in the restaurant. Keith and I will have to make the decision when we get there. The restaurant won't cause you problems, will it?'

'Not from the surveillance viewpoint, but communications might be difficult, and you and Keith won't have vision.'

'Perhaps we'd better have a chat about that after the briefing to sort something out.'

Wickerson looked at the office clock; it was approaching 5.30am. 'Time's getting on and I'd like Peter's team in position by six. I'm sorry, Roly, but we've not been able to come up with an OP for you, the area's not easy from that viewpoint. Right, let's get on with the call signs and communications ...'

The more mundane stuff was quickly dealt with and Wickerson finished the briefing with the usual, 'Anyone got any questions?'

Roly said, 'You've not mentioned how India 2 is going to get off the plot by herself, Guv – I mean, it's quite likely that Mr Stagg might want to go with her.'

'You're right, I forgot to mention it. We're going to send a Job flounder ['flounder and dab', Cockney rhyming slang for 'cab'] along Serpentine Road and our girl can hail it and make her exit. Is the cab available, Gordon?'

'We're picking it up from Molesey later this morning.'

'Good luck, everyone – we'll see you back here for the debrief. And don't forget, I want all the briefing sheets back.'

Wickerson, Daisley, Harrison and I headed for breakfast in the senior officers' canteen. We didn't usually use this canteen as we all preferred to eat with our teams, but on this occasion it meant we were guaranteed privacy. We came up with a contingency plan to deal with the eventuality that the meet had to be held in the restaurant, and devised a series of signals for Lizzie to use in the event that she felt at risk. Gordon would be in the restaurant and would try to communicate with us in the observation van, but if we had a breakdown in comms, he would have to make the decision as to whether or not the back-up should move in.

Lizzie arrived at about 9.30am, breezing in with a couple of parcels and the stuff for the picnic. She was wearing a floral dress that was pretty but not provocative.

'Morning, Sirs – I've been shopping! Do you want to see what I've bought Colin for his birthday? A Walkman, like we discussed, and I had a brainwave and bought him this ...' Lizzie produced a New York Yankees baseball cap.

'Very nice, Lizzie, but why's that a brainwave?' enquired Wickerson.

'Because it's so distinctive – you reckon he's always skulking about up the common and if we get any reports of flashings or stalkings and the suspect's wearing something like this, well, you've got to admit it's a bit of a clue!'

We took Polaroid photos of the gifts and settled down to do the paperwork – notes, exhibits, the usual documentation. Chris Hardy and Eric from TSU turned up about 20 minutes later, just as we were finishing.

'All set then, Guv?' Chris asked.

'About as ready as we'll ever be, Chris,' I said. 'What about from your end?'

'A few teething problems, but it's sorted.'

'So what have you got for us?'

He produced a voluminous handbag from his hold-all. 'We've got the Nagra and an open transmitter in here.' He showed us the false bottom in the bag. 'Eric's managed to conceal the mics in the shoulder strap.'

'What about the receiving equipment?'

'All set up in a nondescript [a covert observation van] and you've got the facility to record as well. Eric'll run you through it, it's quite simple to operate. What time do you want us on the plot?'

'11.30. That'll give us time to run through the equipment. What sort of range has it got?'

'Plenty for what you've got in mind, especially as you're going to be right on top of the plot because you want vision.'

'That's right. Shit! I've just had a nasty thought. Serpentine Road wasn't exactly easy for parking when we had a look-see the other day. It'd be sod's law if we couldn't get a space for the nondie.'

'No sweat! I'll get Gordon to put in a blocking vehicle.'

On plots where you have to use a nondescript, in order to ensure you can position the van where you want it, we usually park a car in the space required well before the time of the operation, and then swap them over. Nondies are uncomfortable at the best of times so we try to keep the time they're actually on the plot to a minimum. The crew are loaded into the back and the driver then parks the vehicle and leaves it. Once inside, you obviously can't get out until you're driven to a safe location. However, nondies are very rarely used, as any good villain will suss them. They have a basic rule of thumb for vans – if you can't see through it, it's Old Bill. But in this case we didn't have any choice and, in my opinion, Colin Stagg wasn't particularly surveillance-aware.

Wickerson pushed the phone across the desk. 'Don't forget that the van needs to be able to cover an outside as well as an inside plot.'

I made the call. Wickerson in the meantime was running through the plan. Lizzie was the first to speak when Mick had finished.

'I'm a bit concerned about one thing,' she said. 'If the worst comes to the worst and I start picking up some of the warning signals that Paul Britton told me about ... it seems a bit of a waste if the cavalry come barging in and give the game away. We've put a lot of effort into this operation.'

'Hang on, Lizzie,' Wicko interrupted with a worried frown. 'If the wheel looks like it's coming off, in go the boys. There's going to be no argument about that.'

I nodded. 'Mick's right, Lizzie, we're not about to take any chances with your safety. Apart from the fact that we've grown to like you, Mick and I will be in deep trouble if we don't send you back to SO10 in the same condition that we got you.'

'I'm not suggesting any heroics – if he starts performing, I want to put as much distance between him and me as possible, and as soon as possible. What I'm asking is, do the back-up have to show out as Old Bill?'

'How would you suggest we get round it then?'

'If I start picking up the wrong vibes, I can use one of the signals that Mr Wickerson told me about – you know, fiddling with my hair. That's the standby signal. If I start getting upset and loud, and remove the band from my hair, then that's the signal for the back-up to come in – but instead of declaring themselves as Old Bill, they should come steaming in as concerned members of the public helping out a damsel in distress.'

'It's as broad as it's long,' I said. 'As long as the cavalry arrive, what difference does it make what they call themselves? It seems OK to me, and it has the advantage of not blowing us out.'

'That's what I thought,' Lizzie beamed. 'If we do it this way, I've still got the chance to make it up with him. I can send him a letter apologising for my outburst. Let's face it, once I've told him about the past that Paul Britton's created for me, he shouldn't be too surprised if I'm a little unstable.'

'That's a masterpiece of understatement. If some girl told me that story on a first date I'd run a bloody mile,' I added with a wince. 'So you'd be prepared to go back into him even if he's played up?'

'I can't see the problem. I've got half the Met within spitting distance – besides, we're only going to get one go at this. It's got to be worth it. Paul Britton did say that once we've got on to the face-to-face meetings, the operation would have a limited life-span, so let's take it as far as we can, while we can.'

Just after 11.00am, we got into Wickerson's car and drove towards Hyde Park. There was little conversation; we all seemed lost in our own thoughts as to what the next couple of hours might bring. I looked round at Lizzie, who was quietly watching the world go by. I could not help but admire her peaceful countenance. I had no doubt that her mind was working overtime, but you would never have guessed it from her demeanour. She would have made a terrific poker player. There was no doubt in my mind that it was this ability to mask her true feelings, supported by enormous courage, that made her such a successful and sought-after UC officer.

Lizzie's courage was not only physical, it was also mental. She was searching for the truth, and if that truth happened to be that Mr Stagg was responsible for Rachel's death, she was going to need every ounce of both. We were sailing uncharted waters in the legal sea and the very nature of the operation was undoubtedly going to cause a storm. She knew it, we all knew it. The cross-examination, should it ever arrive, was not going to be a very pleasant experience.

As we approached Battersea, it started to rain. I searched the horizon for signs of a break in the cloud. There wasn't one.

'Looks like your picnic's out of the window, Lizzie.'

She shook herself out of her reverie. 'Sorry, what did you say?'

I nodded towards the windscreen wipers that were beginning to screech as they efficiently cleared the screen of the fine drizzle that was falling.

'Typical – and I went to all that trouble.' She giggled. 'I must have spent at least three minutes in the food department at Marks.'

We pulled into the enclosed car park of some police-occupied stables and buildings within the confines of Hyde Park. Several Ree-Gee vehicles were already there and the teams were making themselves as comfortable as possible in the sparse accommodation that the buildings provided. Chris, Eric and another TSU officer called Pam arrived shortly after us. Normally, there is no way that any form of covert vehicle is taken anywhere near police premises, as villains have been known to check the yards of nicks for unmarked Job vehicles. But on this occasion the nondescript was pulled into the stable yard. We had to be out of the public gaze in order to get in and out of the van, and also for Eric to give me a crash course in the mysteries of operating the equipment.

Once I had mastered the intricacies of the van's monitoring equipment, Eric and I returned to the building where the team had congregated to get out of the rain. The room was part of a single-storey complex, large and airy with light green, painted brick walls. There was little in the way of furniture and such as there was was old and battered – a couple of tatty armchairs, an ancient table and a few wooden chairs. The place was damp and cold; the skeleton staff who'd manned the place had long since ceased to utilise this part of the complex.

There was the usual pre-operation activity of officers donning their body sets, checking earpieces and carrying out signal checks. There is always an underlying air of tension whilst waiting for the off, but it is a matter of honour to play it down. I smiled to myself at the all-too-familiar scene. Memories of my time on the Flying Squad flitted across my mind. I had been there, seen it, done it.

I went and joined Wickerson, who was deep in conversation with Daisley. Wicko turned to greet me. 'Got the radio gear sussed?'

'Piece of cake, but there ain't a lot of room in the back of the van. It's going to be a bit claustrophobic with three of us in there.'

Our conversation was interrupted by Gordon Harrison. 'We're just starting to pick up the SO11 team on the small set.'

Roly and his team were getting close. The range on the small sets isn't that great so it was time for the final briefing and getting the Ree-Gee deployed.

'Where are they, Gordon?' I asked.

'Our man's on a bus, Knightsbridge area. I reckon, judging by the traffic, that we've got 20 to 25 minutes.'

'Right,' said Wickerson, 'decision time.' He wandered over to the window and looked out at the heavy drizzle. 'No sign of it clearing up – looks like we're going to have to have the meet in the Dell.'

'OK, Gordon, time to get the show on the road.'

Mick and I went to find Lizzie, who was passing the time talking to some old friends on Gordon's team.

'How are you feeling?' Wickerson enquired.

'I'm fine, no problems.'

'Not long now. You'd better switch on the Nagra and open transmitter so we can check the signals. Let's just run through your danger signals again.'

'Oh, I'd better put my hair up,' she said as she delved into the handbag for her hairband.

We carried out a radio check and, much to our relief, everything appeared to be functioning as it should. By this time, the small set commentary was telling us that Colin's bus was approaching Hyde Park Corner.

'Best we get the van in position. OK, Lizzie, we're off. Good luck!' Both Mick and I gave her a hug and a peck on the cheek for luck.

'See you afterwards,' she said as Daisley, Wickerson and I squeezed into the back of the van. I took up position at the little consul and put on my headphones as we were driven into our position by Micky Connor, one of the DSs from the Ree-Gee.

'See you later, chaps,' Micky said as he parked the van and got out.

The vision was quite good. We could clearly see the restaurant exterior. The windows had some sort of reflective coating so we weren't able to see inside; they appeared almost opaque from where we were.

Wickerson called Gordon on the mobile. 'Gordon, it's Mick. We're in position, but we've only got vision on the outside. Control in the restaurant is down to you, OK?'

He rang off.

'All right?' I asked.

'Yeah – we've got four inside, plus Gordon.'

At this point, the small set crackled into life. We strained to listen.

Colin was off the bus and heading for the Hyde Park Corner entrance. Control was handed over to a couple of Ree-Gee footies as they followed him into the park.

'What's the time, Mick?'

'Coming up to 20 to. About time Lizzie started to walk down.'

During this time, I had been holding one earphone to my ear just to monitor the signal from Lizzie's transmitter. 'I hope this bloody thing's still working - I'm getting nothing but interference at the moment.'

'I'll give the stables a ring,' said Mick. He dialled the number. 'It's the DCI. Is Lizzie still there? Ask her to give a signal check.'

A few seconds later, I heard Lizzie's voice in my earphones. 'This is a test transmission. One, two ... one, two.'

'Tell her that's fine, Mick. You might as well ask her to start her walk down.'

'Yeah, tell her that's fine and she can start walking down any time she likes.' He rang off.

The small set burst into life again. 'India 1 walking towards the Dell. Standby, standby. India 1 talking to unknown male, IC 1 [Identity Code 1]. He's off again, same direction. It looked like he was asking the time and for directions. It's a stop, stop. India 1 into male toilets – Central 975.' This was the call sign that Mick and I were using.

'Go ahead.'

'Do you want me to go in after him?'

'No. No.'

'Received.'

Four or five minutes passed.

'All units, no change. No change.'

'Received, Central 975.'

I then began picking up the sounds of footsteps from Lizzie's transmitter. Mick's mobile rang. 'Wickerson. OK. Thanks.' Again he rang off. 'She's on her way.'

'I can hear,' I said, pointing towards the headphones.

'Contact, contact!' The small set came to life again. 'India 1 out, out. Same direction, nearside path towards the RV.'

'Eyeball permission?'

'Go, go.'

'Message for 975.'

'Unit calling, go to 975.'

'Yeah, 975, can you check your facility? Golf Hotel's trying to get through.'

'Received ... 975 out.' Wickerson checked his phone. 'Terrific, the battery's on the blink.'

Daisley produced a spare from his jacket pocket. Wicko changed batteries. Almost immediately it rang.

'Is that you, Gordon? You're kidding? If the worst comes to the worst, you'll have to keep in touch by phone. OK.' He finished the call and double-checked that it was still switched on before putting it down.

'What's happened now?' I asked.

'Gordon's saying that they're having difficulty with the small sets inside the restaurant. He reckons that the way the building's constructed and the reflective windows are interfering with the signals. It's fucking incredible, we can put a man on the moon and talk to him as if he's just down the road, but try and transmit a signal a couple of hundred yards and we get all sorts of problems.'

'Let's hope that the open transmitter works inside, otherwise we're going to be up shit creek.'

'What do you reckon, Keith? We've still got time to call it off.'

'True, but we've come this far. Lizzie'll still be protected and she won't thank you if we cancel at this late stage.'

'Let's just play it by ear.'

I could hear Lizzie's footsteps and the quack of ducks as she walked towards the restaurant. I looked in the direction that she should be coming from. She wasn't yet within sight. 'Touch wood, the open transmitter seems to be working. It's as clear as a bell and she's not even in sight yet.'

'Hang on, there's something coming through on the small set.'

'India 1 approaching restaurant.'

'There he is.' Daisley peered out of the front of the van. 'He's got quite a distinctive walk, hasn't he?'

'He certainly has. Our star witness mentioned that walk – with a bit of luck we can get it on video.'

Colin approached the Dell.

'He's having a good look round,' Wickerson said.

'Natural caution. Paul Britton did tell us to expect that sort of thing. Hold up – where's he's gone now? I've lost him.'

'He's gone round the blind side. Any sign of Lizzie yet, Keith?'

'All units – it's a stop, stop outside the RV. 975, did you receive that?'

'Yes, yes,' Daisley replied.

I checked out of the rear of the van. 'There she is.'

'How far off?' Wickerson asked.

'A couple of hundred yards, perhaps a bit more.'

I watched as she got closer. I could have killed for a cigarette; the tension was building with every step Lizzie took. 'What's our man doing?'

'Eyeball permission 975.'

'Go 975.'

'Update on India 1 please.'

'No change, no change – still blind side of RV. Just seems to be killing time out of the rain.'

'Received, for the benefit of all units, India 2 is approaching RV from the green aspect.'

I watched Lizzie as she walked alongside the Serpentine towards us. Soon she was standing beside a lamp-post outside the Dell café, waiting for her date to arrive.

'Lizzie's on the plot.'

Daisley picked up the small set. 'Eyeball permission 975.'

'Go 975.'

'India 2 now in position.'

'Yes, yes, all received. Relay to all units from 975, India 2 now in position – India 1 as before.'

The next ten minutes were something of a nightmare, Lizzie one side of the restaurant, Colin on the other, and neither showing any signs of moving. 'This is bloody good. Talk about "never the twain shall meet". Poor old Lizzie'll be soaked to the skin.'

'Standby, standby – India 1 is on the move.'

'There he is!' Wickerson said excitedly as Colin came back into view. 'Come on, turn left, turn left!'

We waited with bated breath to see which way he would go.

'Yes!'

He was heading towards us. He came round the outside of the Dell. 'He's stopped. What's he playing at? He must have seen her. Come on, Colin, that's her.'

Stagg stood for what seemed like an eternity. Lizzie had her back to the restaurant and was looking out over the Serpentine. She looked at her watch, giving off the body language of a person waiting to meet someone.

'Come on, Colin!' I muttered half to myself, half to my companions. I could hear the sound of ducks over the open transmitter.

'It looks like he's seen her,' said Daisley. 'Yep, he's making a move.'

At that moment Lizzie turned towards the restaurant. 'She's seen him.' Lizzie's face seemed to light up as she strode confidently towards Colin. 'Lizzie?'

'You must be Colin.'

'Yeah.'

'It's like *Brief Encounter*, Colin,' she smiled from beneath her umbrella.

'I know, yeah.'

'You must be soaked, get under ... God, you're soaked. How are ya?'

'Oh, I got here a bit early actually.'

'Did ya?'

'Yeah, I was waiting round the back there.'

'Oh, I was here a bit early but not too early. Oh, it's such a shame, we was gonna have a lovely picnic.'

'I know. Typical, innit?'

'Oh, happy birthday.'

'Yeah. Thanks.'

I turned on the recording equipment, purely a belt and braces exercise, just in case the Nagra went on the blink. 'Contact made, Mick – they're heading off to the restaurant.'

Wicko rang Gordon. 'They're on their way to you, Gordon, about 30 seconds.'

Stagg would not be suspicious, because Lizzie was taking him into an area, and he wouldn't be looking around to see other people arriving. It's a trick of surveillance that if you know where your target's going and get there first, you are beyond suspicion; even if they think they are being followed, they will be looking at people who came in afterwards, and not pay too much attention to people who were already there. Nonetheless, the conversation was strained; Lizzie was doing her best to keep it going. I listened intently and handed Wickerson a spare set of headphones which he and Daisley shared. Once inside, the signal deteriorated but it was readable.

Lizzie said, 'My treat. I'm buying lunch. I promised. What do you fancy?'

'Things are a bit limited, er, 'cos of my diet.'

'Yeah, it's all pasta or something, isn't it?'

'Yeah.'

'What about ...?'

'Just chips and something.'

The meeting was slowly grinding along. Lizzie and Colin both ordered food and then sat at a table.

'Did you get any birthday cards today?' Lizzie asked.

'Only one.'

'Who was that off?'

'Er, neighbour.'

It was a painfully slow process. Paul Britton's words concerning poor heterosocial skills came back to me.

'What ya gonna do tonight?' Lizzie tried.

'Nothing really.'

'Not celebrating in any way?'

'No, brother might come round with a few cans of beer.'

Lizzie asked him about his family.

'Me mum got remarried,' Colin said. 'She lives at Putney, not far from me, you know. But I haven't seen her since she got married.'

'Why's that then?'

'Well, the bloke she married, you know. I couldn't stand him ... he's one of those of annoying people, you know. You've only just gotta be with him and you just wanna hit him.'

'It's like pulling teeth,' Roy Daisley said.

'Give it time, Roy, things should liven up in a minute,' I replied. I was thinking of the proposed game plan we had discussed with Paul Britton the day before.

As it transpired, he didn't have long to wait before Lizzie went into details of the background which Paul had designed for her. How she had been drawn into a witchcraft or occult group when she was between 12 and 18 years old, and where she was gradually and systematically introduced into ritual sexual abuse. This had culminated in her being both a passive participant and an active accomplice in the sexual murder of a young woman. She was to have withdrawn from the group about ten years ago, feeling a mixture of confusion and ambivalence about what had happened. Most importantly, she was to believe that she could only enter fully into an intimate sexual relationship with a man who had had actual experiences that were very similar to her own, and who consequently could understand and share the extraordinary feelings that followed.

She had tried to form relationships since then, but they had always failed. She knew they couldn't be as potent as those she had experienced with the group. These failures caused her considerable emotional anguish, so it could only be with extreme caution that she contemplated the development of a physically intimate relationship with a man.

Daisley sat with growing incredulity as Lizzie's story of satanic group sex unfolded. Stagg, however, sounded unfazed.

'I'm not putting you off your dinner, am I?' Lizzie said.

'That fish is a bit cold, that's all ... the chips are all right, though. Carry on.'

Lizzie told him the story of the ritual murder of a baby and a young woman, explaining how deeply the experience had affected her. The impact on her had been so great that she felt she could never become truly intimate with a man again unless he possessed a similar background to the head of the coven and could understand her feelings.

'I couldn't get it out of my head, what it was like with this man ... Not because the sex was brilliant, the sex wasn't that good if I try to analyse it. It was the whole knowing thing ...'

As Paul had predicted, Stagg said he didn't have such a background but was desperately keen to be part of her life because they were so alike. He said, 'I've got an open mind about everything ... I mean, everybody's got a secret in their past, ain't they?' but referring to what Lizzie had been saying, he added, 'I couldn't do anything like that ... I have my certain beliefs, it doesn't involve human sacrifices.'

'Dare I ask what's going on?' Roy queried as the import of Lizzie's disclosures began to sink in.

'We haven't gone mad,' I said. 'It's all part of a carefully designed psychological operation. It's been going on since January.'

'I'm not sure I'm ready for this,' he said, pressing the single earpiece closer to the side of his head. 'Are you sure about this?'

'It's all in the script, Roy.'

'It's incredible, he's not batted an eyelid. If some bird started telling me a story like that, I'd be off like a long dog, only stopping to phone the Old Bill on the way. I've got to tell you chaps, this is going to make legal history one way or another.'

At that moment, Mick's phone rang. He listened with a growing look of concern on his face. 'Are you sure? Fucking hell! Thanks for letting me know.' He put down the phone. 'We've got a bit of a problem, Keith.'

'How much of a problem?'

'On a scale of one to ten, about twelve. That open transmitter is being picked up on channel 16.'

'What? I don't believe this. Who told you?'

'That was Chris on the phone. Pam was flicking through the main set channels and found it. They thought it must be to do with our operation.'

'There is limited range on that channel. I know that because we used to use it on my surveillance course. At least we're not broadcasting to half the Met. Let's just hope there aren't any other teams using the channel.'

'How could it have happened?' Mick said impatiently.

'It's just one of those things, a fluke. I'll make sure Eric sorts us out an encrypted system for the next meeting.'

'That's if we haven't been blown out of the water. All we need is a journalist with a scanner and that's us done.'

We continued listening for about another 15 minutes.

'Sounds like they're about to make a move.'

No sooner were the words out of my mouth, than the phone went again. It was Gordon. 'OK,' said Wickerson. 'They're on their way out.'

Daisley picked up the small set. 'All units standby, standby.' He peered out of the front of the van. 'All units, Indias 1 and 2 out, out, towards Hyde Park Corner – 27 from 975.'

'Go 975, 27 over.'

'Start your run down to pick up India 2.'

'Yes, yes, all received.'

We watched anxiously as the unlikely couple made their way through the rain. I listened as Lizzie began to explain her plans for getting home. The flounder made its approach along Serpentine Road.

'Right, short but sweet,' Wicko said.

27 broke into the airwaves. 'India 2's seen me, she's waving me down.'

'Received 27, 975 over.'

Wickerson looked at me. 'Final stretch now, Keith – let's hope he doesn't try to get in the flounder with her.'

I strained to hear the conversation from the open transmitter. For some reason, the signal was fading and I had now lost vision of our subjects. There was an uneasy silence for a minute or so. It seemed much longer.

'What's going on?' This from Wickerson, and directed at no one in particular. The silence over the air was deafening.

'975, 27.'

'Go 27,' Daisley responded eagerly.

'India 2 on board and away.'

'Yes, yes, all received.'

'Thank God that's over, Keith.'

'I'll drink to that.'

We sat waiting to be driven off the plot. The small set commentary told us that Colin Stagg had watched the cab disappear and then made his way out of the park. By the time we returned to the stables, he was at the bus stop.

It was with a tremendous sense of relief that we left the claustrophobic atmosphere of the van. The rain had eased off and the first thing I did was light a cigarette as I walked towards the buildings.

Lizzie came to the door to greet us and was brandishing something in her hand. 'Look what I've got!'

'Where did that come from?' I asked with a degree of surprise at seeing the letter.

'It was a parting gift, as I got into the cab he leaned in and gave it to me.'

'That's a bonus. How are you feeling?'

'I'm fine.'

'You did brilliantly, Lizzie. It can't have been easy; I'm really proud of you.'

Wickerson placed a protective arm around her shoulders. 'Come on, let's get you back to Wimbledon and get the debrief done.'

It was a real temptation to open the letter in the car on the way back, but we resisted it. Once in the office, Lizzie opened the letter and photocopied it. We couldn't believe our eyes when we read its contents.

The theme, once again, was the urge in his life to dominate and humiliate the opposite sex. The fantasy detailed Stagg and Lizzie lying down in 'a spot I know over my local common. It is a bit secluded, but rarely someone walks by. It's a hot, sunny afternoon …'

They strip off, and soon become aware of a man watching. They decide to have sex, and Lizzie performs fellatio on Stagg while he leans against a tree. Stagg tells the man to join them. Stagg bends Lizzie over a tree trunk and has rear-entry sex with her. He invites the man to do the same, while Stagg forces himself into her mouth. The fantasy continues with Lizzie being abused by hair pulling, knife threats and verbal assault, culminating in violent sex.

'It's unbelievable,' Wickerson said. 'He must have thought all his birthdays had come at once when he heard your story, knowing that he had this tucked away in his pocket. Just look at this bit, dripping blood on to nipples and holding the knife to my throat …'

'What about this?' I said. 'Cutting flesh, the mysterious stranger producing the knife, the tying up, the verbal abuse – for Christ's sake! And this bit about making you lick the knife. I'll have to give Paul a call – so many of the things he was talking about are in this letter.'

Lizzie said, 'It's not just the letter, but the way he behaved during our meeting. He was just weird. I mean, when I got on to the satanic ritual and the killing of the child, all he could say was his fish was cold.'

'Lizzie, I'll say it again – you did incredibly well. It must have been awful for you.'

I phoned Paul, scarcely able to contain my excitement. 'He's mentioned the knife,' I said. 'He's only gone and mentioned the fucking knife!'

'At the meeting?' Paul asked.

'In a letter. He wrote a letter to Lizzie and gave it to her as she was leaving.'

'What did it say?'

'Stand by your machine, I'll fax it to you.'

Stagg described taking Lizzie to a secluded spot that he knew on Wimbledon Common, where they strip off and lie on a towel in the hot sunshine.

They spot someone watching them from behind a tree and Stagg encourages Lizzie to put on a show. 'Suck me off,' he says, loud enough for the man to hear, and Lizzie drops to her knees and obeys. Then he bends her over the tree trunk and penetrates her from behind, holding her down. Secretly motioning the stranger to come closer, Stagg withdraws his penis and offers Lizzie up to him. Then he grabs her hair, forces her head back and thrusts his penis into her mouth.

Suddenly the stranger suggests they do something dangerous and Lizzie agrees. He goes to his clothing and produces some rope and a knife. The two men grab Lizzie's arms and tie her spread-eagled on the ground face up. The stranger then sits astride Lizzie and draws his knife in a line from her breasts to her genitalia 'Not cutting you just teasing you.'

Colin then describes taking the knife from the stranger and squeezing semen on to the blade before handing the knife back to the other man who: 'places it to your mouth and makes you lick it clean, which you do, you are now so hot and red you are panting so excitedly. Then the man cuts himself on his arm, just enough to draw blood and he drips it on to your nipples.'

The fantasy went on to describe both men penetrating Lizzie and the knife teasing her nipples and being held against her cheek. It ended with Stagg saying that he hoped Lizzie found it satisfying, and reassuring her that no harm would come to her.

Stagg wrote that the story was written along the line of what he feels Lizzie is 'into', yet at no stage had she ever mentioned knives, pain, verbal abuse, dripping blood, fallen trees, streams or woodland. And this letter couldn't have been influenced by anything that happened in Hyde Park, because Stagg brought it with him, already written.

I asked Paul, 'Any particular points of interest?'

'The rarity of the combined elements of deviance. You would only find that present in a very small number of the general male population.'

'What do you make of the last part, the bit about him having written the fantasy along the lines of what he feels Lizzie was into?'

'I fail to see how he could have drawn that inference from anything we had communicated to him prior to the writing of this particular letter.'

'What about the letter we sent him back in March? EJ14 – when we used the expression "defenceless and humiliated"?'

'You really do have an extraordinary memory. Do you recall the reasons why we included that expression?'

'Roughly – I can't pretend to remember it all.'

'Let me remind you. The letter was designed to bring out aspects of possible sexual intimacy.'

'But based upon themes previously introduced by him?'

'Yes, absolutely. If you remember, the subject of our attention was pressing for Lizzie to indicate which sexual activity she was likely to find exciting. You will recall that, at that stage, it is most important to respond, but also most important not to lead him towards the extreme sexual and physical violence which characterised the offence.'

'I remember.'

'And continuing from that, it was decided that when and if in the relationship or correspondence this emerged ...'

'... that we would respond,' I pre-empted him, 'by drawing out and highlighting only those aspects which in one form or another had been previously introduced by him.'

'That's right. And the use of that expression was appropriate in this regard. Also, you will recall that I advised that in order to allow this man freedom of response, no defining examples of these concepts would be offered. That letter was expected to produce one of three responses. First, the prospect of sexual relations characterised by these themes would be unacceptable and he would withdraw from the relationship. Second, he would indicate enjoyment of such activity within a private relationship but in a form widely practised by consenting adults. And it would consist of the symbolic exchange of sexual control and submission sometimes with restraint.'

'And the third, Paul?'

'The last option was that he would attempt to develop a relationship which focused upon sexual fantasy of increasing sexual and physical violence to women and this disclosure would lead to increasing and prolonged sexual arousal of Lizzie in fantasies which ultimately lead to the most serious sexual assault.'

'OK, and based upon that, had he chosen options one or two he would have eliminated himself from the investigation and we could stop the operation.'

'That's correct. And following on from that, I advised that it was expected that a person embarking upon the last option, if responsible for the murder, would find the sexual excitement and expectations arising from these themes sufficiently powerful as to overwhelm caution concerning self-disclosure of his responsibility for the offence – if he believed this disclosure to a confidante would lead to even greater sexual gratification.'

'And our man opted for the third option.'

'Yes he did, and that was why we felt it necessary to continue with the operation. But I've digressed – going back to your question about the use of the expression "defenceless and humiliated". We gave no examples and allowed him freedom of expression. So the themes in this last letter are far too extreme to have been prompted by EJ14. No, these themes have been spontaneously generated.'

'You seem to know so much about Stagg,' I said.

'Not at all,' Paul corrected me. 'I know things about sexual deviancy.'

'So where does this fantasy put Stagg?'

'It's consistent with what I would expect to find in the masturbatory repertoire of the killer. It also has the various elements known to be relevant to the murder of Rachel Nickell ...'

'Give me the bottom line.'

'You're looking at someone with a highly deviant sexuality that's present in a very small number of men in the general population.'

'How small?'

'Well, the chances of there being two such men on Wimbledon Common when Rachel was murdered are vanishingly small.'

The following day, in a follow-up call, Paul said that Colin Stagg had clearly shown himself to be a very lonely young man who was desperate to lose his virginity. Paul knew that he'd say anything to get his end away, but this didn't explain why he chose to reveal such violent fantasies. There were endless other sexual liaisons and escapades he could have imagined and written about, yet he had chosen this narrow, specific pathway of his own accord.

Paul went on to say that quite a large number of people in the general population had sex lives that include elements of symbolic coercion, bondage or sadism. If this was all that Stagg had revealed, then he would have eliminated himself from the investigation. Instead, he had gone far beyond this and shown his arousal at a minute and specific strand of fantasy that featured extreme violence, rape and sexual pain. This had been predicted of the killer months before Stagg ever became a suspect.

Of course, having the same rare sexual deviancy wasn't proof of murder, and the only evidence likely to satisfy a court was if the suspect disclosed details of the murder that only the killer could possibly know. I only hoped that time was on our side.

Chapter 30

In admitting to Colin the part she had played in the ritual murder of a woman and young child, Lizzie had revealed her most intimate secret. Now we could only wait to see how he would respond.

On 21 May, the day after the meeting, Stagg telephoned Lizzie and said that he had written to her explaining his thoughts, and that he wouldn't know how to fulfil her in the way she indicated at their meeting. He said that he had never done anything like the acts described in the letter he'd handed her after the meeting. He assured Lizzie that he wasn't shocked by her revelation, but said he thought she was 'aiming a bit high' in expecting to find someone who'd been involved in deadly rituals. He raised the subject again of the murder he had been accused of; he didn't commit it, he said, and if he had done it, 'I would have told you that I'd done it, 'cos I know I could have trusted you.'

The conversation ended with Stagg asking Lizzie what she wanted to do, and they agreed to 'think about things'.

The letter reflected the conversation; Stagg promised not to reveal her secret and stated that he still wanted a long-term relationship with her.

In a further letter on 22 May, Colin described how his life had fallen into darkness again:

> *I COULD HAVE LIED TO YOU ABOUT THE MURDER, AND SAY I DID IT, JUST TO BE WITH YOU ... I WISH YOU FELT THE SAME WAY ABOUT ME, TOO.*

He goes on to say that he now realises that Lizzie does not return his feelings and that she does not want him to write any more 'special' letters. He signs off with:

> *PLEASE KEEP THE RING AND THE TALISMAN AND MY PHOTOGRAPH. I WILL RETURN YOUR PENDANT IN MY NEXT LETTER AND YOUR PHOTOGRAPH ...*

Paul described the letters and telephone conversations as being cautious. There were two options to explain these reactions: one, that Colin was explicitly stating that he did not possess the personal background or experience that Lizzie James had indicated was possessed by the other man from her past – the same qualities also being possessed by the murderer of Rachel Nickell. Or two, it would be consistent with a negotiating position put forward by the murderer of Rachel Nickell who would be wanting to resist disclosing his involvement in the murder while still achieving his objective of securing sexual intimacy with Lizzie James.

Paul then explained that if the first option was true, no further significant communication could be expected from Colin Stagg. However, should the second option be true, Paul predicted that he might soon either reveal a connection with the Rachel murder or, alternatively, invent a story to match that of Lizzie and the secret she harboured in her past.

Sure enough, during a phone call on 25 May, Stagg began to

relate to Lizzie how, as a 12-year-old boy, he and a cousin had murdered a child and concealed her body while on a family caravanning holiday in the New Forest in Hampshire:

WE NOTICED THIS LITTLE BOY AND A LITTLE GIRL SITTING AT THE EDGE OF THE FOREST AND THAT ... AND THE LITTLE BOY RAN OFF PLAYING ... AND WE TOOK THE LITTLE GIRL INTO THE FOREST AND WE ENDED UP ... IT WASN'T NOTHING REALLY THAT PERVERTED IT WAS JUST, YOU KNOW, WE ENDED UP KLLING HER, YOU KNOW, STRANGLING HER ... THE REASON WHY WE NEVER GOT DONE FOR IT WAS 'COS WE WERE LEAVING THAT SAME EVENING ...

BUT THE THING WAS, WHEN WE WAS ACTUALLY STRANGLING HER, WE FELT EXACTLY THE SAME FEELINGS THAT YOU DESCRIBED TO ME, YOU KNOW ... EVERYTHING WAS BUZZING YOU KNOW, WE WERE JUST FLOATING ... THE WHOLE EXPERIENCE WAS JUST FLOATING ...

He explained that he had not told Lizzie before because he was hoping that they could have a relationship without him having to disclose this information. He told her that he wasn't sure that he could trust her as he was worried about the police finding out because of the other murder.

I rang Paul straight away and we arranged a meeting at Arnold Lodge to talk about this new twist, and to brief Lizzie for the next meeting, which they'd arranged for 4 June, again at Hyde Park.

'You have to minimise any apparent interest in the Nickell murder,' Paul told Lizzie. 'You have to emphasise how vulnerable you feel at having revealed your own past. You've given him a secret that is very precious and fragile.'

Paul turned to me. 'What about this story of killing a girl in the New Forest?'

'We've checked it out,' I said. 'It's a load of codswallop.'

One phone call to the head of Hampshire CID had sorted that one. The officer had no unsolved murders on his books. What was more, he had been in the force for donkey's years and there hadn't been any murders such as that described. The murder rate in Hampshire is very low, and such an event would have stuck out like a sore thumb.

Paul's interpretation was that Stagg might have interwoven details of the Rachel Nickell murder into his fictional account of the New Forest killing, but he warned Lizzie that she had to treat it with scepticism. 'Don't accuse him of lying, Lizzie. Even if it were true, the incident he describes doesn't equate in scale with what happened to you. It doesn't mean he's automatically the man you want to give yourself to, or who could fulfil all the needs you spoke to him about.

'At the same time, you should ask him questions about the murder. Ask him how he felt when it happened. Make him see how you need to know if his experience really does parallel yours. Get him into the habit of talking about the details.'

I was puzzled by this and Paul picked up on it.

He said, 'In that way, you see, he will get used to Lizzie's questions. If he eventually reveals himself to be Rachel's killer, he's not going to be surprised when Lizzie asks him lots of detailed questions, looking for the proof.'

In a phone call two days later, Lizzie teased out details from Colin of the New Forest 'murder'. Stagg said that he'd talk about it, but 'when we start going steady and that, I don't really want to keep bringing it up, you know.'

'How did it make you feel when it happened?' Lizzie asked.

'That's what makes me feel guilty about it, because I enjoyed it, you know ... your whole body felt like really buzzing, everything kind of high ...'

Colin called Lizzie again on 30 May. After some general chit-chat, he described a sexual dream he'd had.

'Was it a real dream or are you just titillating me?' Lizzie said.

'No, it was a real dream ... well, put it this way, when I woke up this morning I had to rush to the bathroom.'

In Stagg's dream, he had had oral sex with Lizzie, followed by penetration from the rear, and then intercourse that caused Lizzie to 'scream in agony ... I withdrew from you and I wanked my spunk all over your backside and your back ... massaged it in with my hands ... when I woke up I had a raging hard-on, you know, and I nearly actually came ...'

After some more general conversation, Stagg said that when Lizzie started visiting him, he would take her over to the common and 'show you spots and that, places.'

Paul's view was that although the fantasy was not remarkable, Stagg was still failing to eliminate himself.

In a short call to Lizzie on Wednesday, 2 June, Colin said that he had drawn a map to show her how to get to Roehampton, which he'd hand her when they met on Friday. He also reiterated that he didn't tell her straight away about the murder he'd committed because it had been dangerous.

Lizzie and Stagg met again on 4 June. Colin presented her with two sealed envelopes, one containing a letter, the other a map showing her exactly how to get to his maisonette at Roehampton. Lizzie opened the letter and they sat on deckchairs as she read it.

It involved Lizzie as a schoolgirl and Stagg as a teacher. Lizzie keeps crossing her legs 'sexily, riding your skirt higher ...' Stagg remonstrates with her, makes her bend over a desk, and he canes her naked behind. Then, pulling her hair backwards, he has rear-entry vaginal sex with her, after which he forces her to perform oral sex on him. At this point, her face is 'bright red and twisted in orgasmic pain ...' Finally, he reciprocates the oral sex, and 'you scream in ecstasy ...'

Lizzie told Colin she felt vulnerable after disclosing her secret to him. Colin said he'd also felt cautious when Lizzie had first started writing to him.

'I was being tricked by the journalists last year, you know, knocking on my door, pretending to be different people.'

He said he had trusted people before but had been badly let down and that was why he was facing problems over the Rachel Nickell murder. 'Cos, it was dangerous for me to admit anything 'cos of last year … 'Cos of the police and that, you know. Do you understand that? 'Cos, I mean, the police are so sure I did that last year, you remember last year? You know, they're just waiting for anything to come up on me.'

His behaviour certainly seemed an indication that he was displaying caution; he had arrived very early and checked the Dell restaurant. Then, having had a good look around, he had taken up a position some 200 yards away and kept observation on the restaurant.

Lizzie had arrived in good time and was kept waiting for some ten to fifteen minutes after the time appointed for the rendezvous – very strange behaviour for a man who is at ease with his surroundings, but not uncommon for someone who is not entirely comfortable with a situation. The surveillance team were in a position to watch him watching her.

In addition, he now made numerous references to the activities of the local police, who, according to him, were constantly stopping him and making their presence felt.

'On the common the other day, you know, the police pulled up and three officers got out and searched me. I was only over there walking me dog, you know. I think they were just bored and that, just saw me over there, you know. See, that's why I still think it's, you know, dangerous to tell you.'

Whether this was true or not, his constant references to the police and also to his arrest for the Rachel Nickell murder were destroying the 'comfort zone' which we were endeavouring to create.

Paul had said right at the beginning that he would anticipate that the operation, provided that no external factors or pressures were brought to bear, could be brought to a conclusion within between two and 16 weeks. I had no idea how he came up with his projected time scale, but I did know that it was dependent on no external factors raising his levels of caution. As we approached the first anniversary of the offence, I worried that the press might start pestering Colin.

Lizzie's annual leave was coming up, and to provide a rationale for two weeks' absence, and lay the foundations for subsequent disclosure of her opinion of established churches, she told Stagg of the sudden death of a friend up north. She said she was going to stay with her friend's parents until the funeral.

On 13 June, Stagg sent Lizzie a letter of sympathy, and enclosed another fantasy. This time, Stagg and Lizzie walk into a clump of trees, and engage in mutual masturbation against a tree:

> *THEN I RIP DOWN YOUR KNICKERS AND THRUST MY DRIPPING COCK STRAIGHT UP YOU WITH ALL MY STRENGTH AND FUCK YOU HARD, MAKING YOU SCREAM IN PAIN AS EACH THRUST PUSHES YOU BACK AGAINST THE TREE ...*

Stagg concluded by writing:

> I HOPE IT CHEERED YOU UP. I'M OFF FOR A WANK NOW ... I CAN'T WAIT TO GET HOLD OF THOSE BLOODY SEXY LEGS, LIZZIE!!!

A couple of days later, Colin telephoned Lizzie. He commiserated again about her friend, and amongst other general conversation said that next time they met, perhaps she'd like to come to his place; he could cook her a meal and she could try some of his home-made wine. Lizzie said that would be difficult, because of work. They spoke some more about the death of Lizzie's friend, then Stagg said, 'I couldn't get your legs out of my mind that Friday ... I really wanted to grab hold of those legs, you know ...'

They spoke again on the telephone three days later, and Stagg reiterated his invitation to Roehampton. Again, Lizzie side-stepped the issue.

From as early as 5 February, Stagg had been asking Lizzie to communicate her own fantasies to him. She had avoided this so far, leaving it to him to make the running, but now, because of Stagg's suspicions about her true identity, it was decided that Lizzie should send him a tape of her own fantasies to convince him that she was someone of a like mind.

We had been putting this off for some considerable time, though Paul Britton had told us that the sending of such material was unavoidable. Stagg's constant requests and rising levels of suspicion made this inevitable, especially as his demands were growing stronger. Stagg had been upping the ante by emphasising his expectation of physical contact with comments like, 'I can't wait to get hold of those bloody sexy legs ...'

At a meeting in Leicester on 23 June, Paul advised that it would now be appropriate for Lizzie to provide a fantasy, but its contents had to be based entirely on elements that Stagg himself had already introduced. It was imperative that Lizzie shouldn't escalate the levels of depravity or physical and sexual violence already introduced. What she wrote could reflect the language and descriptions employed by Stagg and, where possible, mirror one of the actual fantasies that he had already sent to her, but no more.

Having been given Paul's approval for the draft which we had already prepared based on his advice over the telephone, we returned to London and made arrangements with the TSU at Lambeth to record the approved script.

Having read the draft, Paul considered the contents for a moment and, in his now familiar measured tones, said, 'Yes, I think that will serve the purpose. The tone and the circumstances reflect the language and descriptions which he has already employed.'

'There's no way we should tone it down a little?' I asked.

'I think it responds to your needs very well. There is no escalation of physical or sexual violence and it reflects fantasies already prepared by Mr Stagg.' He paused and placed his two forefingers to his mouth. 'In view of the purpose of this tape, I would advise you don't dilute the contents ... your objective is to reassure him of Lizzie's bona fides.'

The tape was duly produced on 24 June, six months after the start of the operation. Lizzie detailed a fantasy involving another female and submissive sex but deliberately did not inject more violence or depravity than that already explored by Stagg himself in the increasingly violent and deviant material he had been sending since 2 February.

We followed the same process as for the other letters, though in this case, the subject matter was close to unpalatable. All the themes mentioned in this unpleasant document had been previously introduced by Colin and were, by now, well established in his writings. We concocted the script line by painful line, discussing the now familiar aspects of deviance as we went.

Lizzie described walking with Colin through woodland on a summer's day, hand in hand. They become excited and kiss.

She goes on to describe how their sex session is interrupted by a young woman with short blonde hair who becomes aroused and accepts Stagg's invitation to join them. Stagg then pulls a knife from the back of his jeans:

> *I get a shock. You are holding a knife. To see your hands on two powerful different swords really makes me pant. You must have noticed by the look of surprise ...*
>
> *You hold the knife near her bright stiff nipples and gently circle one of them with it. A thin scratch appears in a crescent shape around her nipple. It slowly darkens and a small trail of blood begins to dribble down.*

Stagg then takes Lizzie from behind whilst she grasps the girl and feels blood. Both Stagg and Lizzie fall asleep; when they awake, the young girl is gone, but the knife and blood are still there.

None of the elements – the woodland setting, the knife, the third party, the dripping blood – was anything that Stagg hadn't introduced himself.

Another meeting was arranged in Hyde Park on 29 June.

Sitting in deckchairs near to the Serpentine, Lizzie started to read the contents of the latest letter Colin had handed her, while he opened a bottle of wine with a Swiss Army knife and poured some into two used Slush Puppy cups that he'd also brought.

Stagg's fantasy enacted the kidnap and sexual abuse of the daughter of a wealthy businessman, with Lizzie in the starring role. She would be held at knife-point and raped from the rear, while Stagg is pulling her hair and forcing her head back.

The conversation moved on, and Colin asked Lizzie to spend the weekend with him, suggesting they could go to 'some places where I sunbathe'.

Lizzie said, 'I've been to Richmond a long time ago, and it was a bit sort of barren, I thought.'

'Yeah, Richmond Park is. But I mean Wimbledon Common; it's more interesting 'cos there's so many places to hide.' He went on to say, 'Before that happened last year ... I used to go over the common late at night, when it was dark and that, and just strip off and walk around ... at night there's nobody there, but there's a chance that there might be someone there ... I just stand there, stark naked, and I lean back against the tree and just wank myself silly ...'

'So you don't do that any more?' Lizzie asked.

'Er, it's a bit dodgy at the moment 'cos there's still police hanging around over there, you know, to see if that murderer come back again, you know, try again.'

'I wonder if he does?'

'I suppose, in a way, that is a bit of turn-on, you know.'

He told Lizzie that if she went to spend a weekend with him, they could go to the common at night. 'And the thing is, I could take you to the place where it actually happened ...' They could have sex against the tree where Rachel was killed, he said, but 'The only problem is that there are video cameras hidden there.' He knew that because about a month after the murder, some people were caught by the police practising devil worship. They had been detected by the cameras.

Stagg told Lizzie that he had, in fact, been on the common at the time and was still sexually aroused at the thought of what had happened to Rachel.

Lizzie pretended that the penny had finally dropped. 'So that's the thing you were talking about ... you said you'd been arrested for that thing on the common? It was that thing on Wimbledon

Common, isn't it?'

'Yeah. It happened last year.'

'Oh, I didn't know that you were talking about it in your letters. I was thinking, what, I haven't heard anything about that.'

''Cos it was all in the papers, weren't it?'

'Oh, I know, I remember now when, you know, it rings a bell. But, ah …'

'Yeah.'

'Oh, so you're not far from there?'

'No.'

'Oh, did you know her?'

'No, I've never seen her, you know. She was supposed to have been a regular over there but I've never seen her.'

'It's all very interesting, isn't it?'

'I saw someone who was, who was like her once. She was sunbathing over by the big pond over there.'

'Oh yeah.'

'There's like a big lake over there, you know, and … ah … that was a couple of years ago.'

'Yeah.'

'I told the police about it. That could have been her. But wasn't too sure, you know, 'cos she was tall, a bit thin, blonde, she had a little kid with her.'

'Oh, that is interesting. Do you know who's done it? Have you got any ideas?

'No, don't know.'

'Come on, you must know. If you were over there all the time.'

'So do a lot of people.'

'I'd like to meet him. I'd like to see what he's got to say, wouldn't you? He's home high and dry now, isn't he, I suppose. He's laughing.'

'Mmm.'

'What sort of things did they ask you?'

'What, the police?'

'Yeah.'

'Oh, a lot of things. It started off they were being nice to you,

you know, asking me about my lifestyle and things like that and … ah … it got a bit nasty, you know, started asking me things like, you know, why did I murder her and that like, and I was saying, "I didn't murder her," you know, "I've never even seen her over there." I described the woman like I described to you and said that it could have been her but I'm not too sure, you know.

'And you know, to tell you the truth, they think I did it even now. I got pulled over by the police … ah … Bank Holiday Monday, May the 31st.'

'I wish you had done it – knowing you got away with it, I'd think that's brilliant. I wish you had. Screw 'em!'

'Thing was, I was over there at the time it was happening.'

'Were ya?'

'Yeah. The thing was, last year I was getting over that illness, you know I managed to put on a bit of weight and that …'

'Yeah. Did you see anything like that when you were there, if you were there at the time.'

'No, that's the thing, you know, 'cos like there's these like large hills …'

'Yeah.'

'And it happened on that side of the hill and I was over on this side of the hill, you know, it was very …'

'What, at the same time?'

'Yeah.'

'My God.'

'The thing was I had all these splitting headaches and that, I couldn't take my dog too far otherwise we would have gone that way, you know.'

'Yeah.'

'I just wanted to get back home again and doze off.'

'God, you could have seen it, couldn't you?'

'Yeah. I would see him doing it and running away …'

Later Lizzie asked him, 'I wonder if you could have seen him, or seen him doing it?'

'That's right. Yeah.'

'Say, say he raped her and everything, didn't he?'

'Yeah, he done everything, yeah.'

'Dirty sod.'

'He almost decapitated her as well.'

'Did he?'

'Yeah, he stabbed her forty-nine times, they said.'

'Oh, my God.'

''Cos when I was being interviewed by the police, they actually showed me a photograph.'

'Did you see her?'

'Yeah, you know, it was, you know, she was naked and that, you know, and ... ah ... on the ground there was blood everywhere, you know, all over the grass and that.'

'God, you'd have had to be careful, too, not to give anything away.'

''Cos they thought, like, if they showed me the photograph, like, I'd suddenly snap and say, all right I did it, you know.'

'They didn't realise what a mind you've got. I think about things like that all the time, Mister.'

'Yeah, 'cos, I mean, when they arrested me, they searched my place and that because I've got three bedrooms and that, you know.'

'Oh yeah.'

'And in one of the main bedrooms I did paint it black and I had all these witchcraft motifs done in chalk all over the walls and that, you know, and as soon as they saw that, that was it, you know, I was the one who did it, you know, they were so convinced, you know.'

'When you saw these photographs of her, what did she look like?'

'Well, the photograph that they showed me, she was lying down on the grass sort of, you know, when you're a baby and sort of curled up.'

'Oh yeah, yeah.'

'She was like that, but the photograph was taken from sort of her backside upwards and her head was sort of like round, and there was blood all over the grass and that. She was completely naked and ... from that viewpoint I could see her cunt and that, you know, and she was very wide open, you know, so he must have really forced her open, you know. At that time, he was obviously killing her at the time, and I don't know the muscles or whatever, you know, in her body and that made her stay open, you know. The thing was, you know, as he's shown me the photograph, I got a hard-on ...'

'Did ya? Oh God, I hope they didn't see it.'

'No, no, 'cos there was like a table there and that, you know. 'Cos they were taping it all as well, you know, like the police do and everything I was saying they were taking into, you know, seeing double meanings into 'em, you know ...' He went on to say, 'When they asked me if I go over to the common to meet gay men, I said I didn't, you know, about the time I did now and again ... We just had a wank together, and that was it ...

The meeting had been a revelation. Paul said, 'Stagg's description of Rachel Nickell's injuries and positioning of the body are correct. His description of her genitalia and anus are precise, graphic and correct. From examination of the photograph alone, it would not be possible for Stagg to know that "he had really forced her open". Stagg's reaction is consistent with the predictions of the covert operation, i.e. that if the murderer of Rachel Nickell became sufficiently sexually aroused, his pursuit of his objective would outweigh caution and self-preservation and disclose evidence of involvement in murder. Stagg's account of his sexual arousal from the murder is consistent with serious sexual deviation which is only present in a very small proportion of the male general population. However, this feature would be prominent in the sexuality of the murderer of Rachel Nickell.'

At last, we had the first 'guilty knowledge' that we felt could possibly constitute concrete evidence. Stagg had, indeed, been shown a photograph, KP27, during his earlier interviews – a single image carefully chosen to show something of Rachel's body but with little detail of her injuries.

The photograph was a scene-establishing shot that showed Rachel naked and curled up on the grass, with her lower half nearest the camera. It didn't show her neck, hands, face or genitals, yet Stagg had described injuries and other details that he couldn't possibly have gathered from the image he was shown.

Stagg had also described how Rachel had been almost decapitated, even though he couldn't see her neck in the photograph. She lay 'curled up like a baby', he said, and he could see her 'cunt' which was 'very wide open, you know, so he must have forced her open'.

This was a precise description of the condition of Rachel's anus, yet from examination of the single photograph labelled KP27, Stagg couldn't have known such a detail. Only the photographs taken in the mortuary exposed that particular injury. Equally, he described Rachel as being 'very wide open', an interesting observation because not many people would realise that muscles don't contract after death, which is why Rachel's anus was still dilated.

Any doubts we had that Colin Stagg was just a man with sick fantasies and nothing more were evaporating by the minute. He simply knew too much.

I asked Paul about the fact that he'd referred to her vagina rather than her anus.

'Sexually inexperienced men often confuse the two and merge them in their thoughts,' he said. Paul added that Stagg's account of becoming sexually aroused at seeing the picture of the body was entirely consistent with the extremely rare and serious sexual deviation that Stagg had already shown.

Stagg, we believed, had now thrown caution to the wind, and was ready to confess all to Lizzie James.

I felt a mixture of elation and relief. I had wanted an operation in which the suspect either eliminated himself early, therefore saving time and money, or went on to confess. I had staked a great deal on convincing the powers that be to consider the operation, and the decision to start and continue had been taken at the highest level. Now there was no question of Operation Edzell stopping. Having made our first breakthrough, I hoped that Stagg would now either disclose further knowledge to Lizzie, or at least divulge information that would lead us to the murder weapon.

Colin phoned Lizzie the next day, but couldn't talk for long because there were people outside the phone box. He called again on 1 July, and they discussed the murder. Colin said again that he'd found the photograph of Rachel's body a big turn on, and promised to take Lizzie to the common.

It was quieter on weekdays, he said. 'They're good days, really, 'cos you can go behind the bush or something if you feel like having a wank and that.' Later in the conversation he mentioned, 'In the evening go over there and just strip off and that, go to a tree and pretend I'm fucking the tree ... spunking all over the tree ... We could pretend like we were just sunbathing ... it'd be in the evening but you could be lying there naked and that, then I'd sort of creep up on you and just act weird, you know.'

'Oh yeah.'

'And then while I'm talking to you I'd just drop my trousers and start wanking over you ... and I'd get the knife out and that.'

'Uh hm.'

'Pretend to attack you and that.'

'Oh.'

'While I have sex with you ... forcing, forcing myself right into you and that ... I've had a few fantasies where I pretend during the evenings or the full moon and that ... I've changed into a wolf or something and go on the rampage. We could re enact that over the common, or something similar ... I'll show you where I actually was at the time ... it's amazing really.'

Chapter 31

On 5 July, Lizzie, Mick and I were driving up to see Paul Britton, who was at Nottingham Crown Court sitting in on the Michael Sams case. We were going up for a final briefing because Lizzie had another impending meeting with Stagg and we were of the opinion that as a result of the last meeting we were very close to either getting a positive result or reaching the end of the operation without a complete disclosure, so it was important that we dealt with it properly.

We pulled in at Mae's services on the M1. We had some breakfast, then I went to buy some cigarettes while the others returned to the car. As I got back into the front seat, I could see Wickerson in the mirror, just sitting there and holding up a copy of the *Daily Star*.

I did a double-take, turned around and, sure enough, there was a great big picture of Colin Stagg on the front page and the headline: I DIDN'T KILL RACHEL NICKELL. For a moment, it didn't register.

Then I said, 'For fuck's sake, what's going on?'

'Have a read of this,' Wicko fumed.

I couldn't believe my eyes. Across the front and two inside pages was a full interview with the man we had been investigating for nearly ten months, saying he was innocent, and that the police were trying to fit him up for a murder he had not committed.

'Cops hound me because I'm into witchcraft,' read the subhead. 'They think I did it because I believe in witchcraft,' Colin said. 'Just because I've got my bedroom painted black.

'They found some pigeon feathers on my windowsill and reckoned I'd been involved in some sort of ritual sacrifice. In fact, pigeons just sat there and shed a few feathers. I've heard of rituals taking place on the common but I've never got involved. I follow my religion in my own home, my own way.

'The police would play silly games with me,' he said. 'The first night I was in the cell, they kept calling out my name to wake me up or offering me a drink of water when I'd never asked for one. It didn't bother me. I couldn't sleep so I was up reading a book. During the interviews, they kept saying to me, "Why did you do it? Why did you murder her?" I kept telling them I hadn't even seen her. But I knew I was sure to be questioned as soon as I heard about it, but I'd got nothing to hide. I'm always up on the common with my dog Brandy. I never go anywhere without him. But I was there at 9.15am and then went home with a headache and slept. It wasn't the fact that I was questioned about the murder that bothered me. I knew the police were only doing their duty. What really annoyed me was the fact that people in the nearby flats were spreading lies about me. They said that I would pester and annoy women and that I was a pervert.'

'This is fucking tremendous, isn't it?' I said. 'Talk about raising suspicion levels right through the roof – there he is, in total denial, being pictured on the front page of a tabloid newspaper.'

As far as I was concerned, it was a complete disaster. Right from the outset, Paul had warned us that external publicity would influence the disclosures of the suspect, if he was the murderer. Not only would exposure increase his caution regarding self-disclosure, he could also be the recipient of sexual interest from other women, which would obviously dilute the effectiveness of the covert operation.

Then it was time for another double-take, because on the inside they had very nicely juxtaposed Colin's picture against the photofit. The comparison was frightening. It was just like another picture of him. Then we looked closer and there, in the background, on the mantelpiece, was the picture of Lizzie she had sent him. We were quite concerned; we thought, That's all we bloody need, for some enterprising journalist to find out about that and try and blow it up and they might have an idea of what she looked like.

We arrived at the Crown Court at about 10.45am. The original purpose for the visit had been to consult Paul concerning another meeting between Lizzie and Colin, but that was now overshadowed by the *Star* article. We found a counsels' conference room and settled down for the meeting.

'Thanks for seeing us, Paul, we really appreciate it – we know you're a bit a tied up at the moment.'

'Always a pleasure to see you,' he smiled in his avuncular way. 'And how are you coping, Lizzie?'

'I'm fine, thanks. They're looking after me.'

'Good. But if you feel you would like to talk to someone else, you know where I am.'

'That's very kind of you. But I'm fine, honestly.'

'So what can I do for you? You have another meeting coming up, don't you?'

'We did have, but this might change things,' I said as I produced the offending article and handed it to him. 'What do you think of this?'

Paul took the paper and quickly read the three-page article.

'Oh dear, this isn't particularly helpful to our purpose, is it?'

'That isn't quite the way we described it, Paul, no. The question is, has it blown us out of the water?'

I looked round the table to see both Mick and Lizzie nodding in agreement with my question.

Paul Britton assumed his, by now familiar, thinking position; palms of his hands together with both forefingers resting against his mouth, almost as if he were praying. He rested his elbows on the table and looked down. I had seen him do this so many times over the preceding nine or ten months. I looked at him hopefully as he invariably came out with strokes of pure genius shortly after adopting this particular pose.

'This is exactly the type of external influence that I warned you about at the design stage of the operation,' he said. 'But it may be possible to minimise the damage.'

'And still carry on?' Mick asked.

Paul Britton adopted his pose again. 'Yes, I don't see why not.'

'But, Paul, this must have sent his levels of caution through the roof?' I said.

'I think that would be an accurate assessment; but with the anniversary of the murder approaching, it would be reasonable to expect his levels of caution to be raised anyway.'

'I suppose we should have expected the papers to do something like this,' Lizzie mused.

'And how could we have stopped them?' I said. 'Even if they'd told us what they were planning, we couldn't have said, "Don't do it," because the first and not unreasonable question they would ask is, "Why not?" '

'So the situation was beyond our control,' Paul Britton added. 'But now, we have to turn our minds to diverting his attention away from all of this ... Lizzie, you should get straight on the phone to him. Show him you're upset at the story. He's been careless. You've opened your heart to him and told him your darkest secrets and now he's put you in jeopardy by talking to the media. Get him to reassure you that everything is still OK between you.'

'You mean I should play down his problems and build mine up – have a go at him about the position he's put me in by speaking to the press?'

'That's exactly what I mean, but we can take it further. You should place the onus upon him to reassure you that his actions haven't placed you in jeopardy.'

'I should be able to manage that.' Lizzie laughed. 'I'm good at making people feel guilty – just ask my husband!'

'It's not so much making him feel guilty,' Paul said. 'It's more a question of emphasising your fears in relation to your position and concentrating his mind on that. Sort of, "You know my position with regard to what I was involved in before; now there's a picture of me in that paper!"'

Lizzie nodded thoughtfully. 'Yes, I know what you're saying.'

There was a knock at the door, an officer looking for Paul. 'I'm sorry, but it looks like I'm needed in court.'

'Paul, thanks for your help, we'll let you know how we get on.'

'When's your next contact with him?'

'He's supposed to be phoning this afternoon. But in light of this, he may not.'

'If he doesn't, give me a ring this evening and we'll work out a strategy.'

In an attempt to minimise the damage, Lizzie laid into him when he phoned for getting involved with the press, saying she was very upset at the damage it would do their relationship.

'I'm absolutely stunned,' she said. 'I'm absolutely shocked.'

'There's nothing to worry about, you know.'

'Well I don't know ... I mean, I didn't think you were the kind of person that goes to the press.'

Stagg seemed unabashed by the new blaze of publicity he'd brought upon himself. 'You've gotta stand up to these people, 'cos nobody'll say anything to my face 'cos they know I'd smack 'em in the teeth ... I'm just trying to clear my name, you know.'

Just a day or two later, as we were still wondering exactly what our next move should be, Stagg wrote Lizzie another fantasy to 'cheer you up', this time unnervingly linked to the circumstances of Rachel's murder. He set the story on a warm summer's evening on the common where he sits on the grass beside a tree and relaxes. He notices a tall, sexy blonde woman – Lizzie – about 100 yards away, walking towards him. She walks over to a nearby tree, leans back on it and sighs. Stagg hides behind his tree and kneels on the grass. He watches her take off her clothes and masturbate; he then walks over to her and masturbates over her, which startles her:

'YOU FUCKING SLAG,' I SAY TO YOU, 'I'M GOING TO GIVE YOU A BLOODY GOOD FUCKING.'

She turns over to enable him to have sex with her from the rear; he then goes to his clothes to fetch a knife, and during his absence another man appears. This unknown man forces his penis into Lizzie's mouth. Meanwhile, Stagg says:

> *I GET BETWEEN YOUR LEGS AND FUCK YOU HARD AGAIN. YOUARE NOW IMPALED AT BOTH ENDS BY TWO SWOLLEN COCKS. AS I FUCK YOU I DRAW THE KNIFE AROUND YOUR NECK. DROPS OF BLOOD SPLATTER THE MAN'S NAKED LEGS. YOU'RE NOW SCREAMING IN ECSTASY. HIS COCK SPRINGS FROM YOUR MOUTH AND YOU LAP UP THE BLOOD, AT THE SAME TIME HE IS WANKING SPUNK INTO YOUR HAIR AND FACE.*

This fantasy concludes with Stagg performing oral sex on her, then Lizzie's vagina being penetrated with the knife, causing her to orgasm.

Paul's analysis of the fantasy was: 'The description of the female participant of this fantasy, described by Stagg as Lizzie James, is accurate of Rachel Nickell. The sexual fantasy focuses significantly on aggressive, rear-entry sexual intercourse with the involvement of an additional male participant by Colin Stagg who is unnamed. Mr Stagg describes himself as taking and using a knife on the "tall, sexy, blonde woman" during penile intercourse, during which he draws the knife around her neck which, in turn, draws sufficient blood from the female participant to splash over the legs of the unnamed man. He describes the mixture of male semen and the blood from the woman's throat as being sexually exciting, as is his contact of the woman's genitalia with the blade of the knife.

'In this fantasy, Mr Stagg depicts himself as receiving equivalent sexual pleasure from penile intercourse and the use of the knife in a physically and sexually aggressive manner. I regard this material as further evidence of serious sexual deviance, but regard it as being a more potent indication of actual sexual aggression than much of the material previously referred to and would expect it to be entirely consistent with the major elements in the sexual fantasy themes of the person who murdered Rachel Nickell.'

Stagg followed up with a phone call to Lizzie on 9 July. He told Lizzie about another fantasy he'd had about her.

The scene is set on Wimbledon Common. He strips off Lizzie's clothes, 'Almost ripping your clothes off and that ... I force you over the tree trunk and I start to fuck you like mad from behind ... And you're just screaming in agony and that, you know, in ecstasy.'

He then described getting out a small knife and scraping it around her throat: '... I'm fucking you harder and harder ... and as I feel I'm just about to explode inside you and that, I leave a little nick on your neck ... makes a little cut on your neck ... Not anything serious or anything.' He then says, 'I withdraw from you and I force you on the ground ... and I'm brushing the knife against your face and that, 'cos it's got a bit of your blood on it ... Oh God, I've gotta have a wank when I get home ...'

Paul assessed this fantasy as evidence of 'serious sexual deviance'. He continued by adding: 'I note the close resemblance of Mr Stagg's account to various elements present in the murder of Rachel Nickell.'

Personally, the thing that struck me about these extreme fantasies was that the female participant having been subjected to these appaling acts would have been seriously injured at best, and in all probability, dead.

In another call on 12 July, Stagg told Lizzie that he wanted to take her over to the common, strip off, and have sex with her ... 'You've gotta have a bit of spice and everything, you've gotta do adventurous things, ain't you ... the danger ... the danger is that somebody was gonna see us and that ... get you right out there in the open and have a good hard fucking ... it turns you on with the thought of somebody might be watching you, you know ...'

On 20 July, Lizzie and I sat down with Paul for what was to turn out to be one of the last times. Lizzie and Stagg were due to meet at Hyde Park again the next day and we needed to discuss the game plan. Having reestablished a rapport following the article in the

Star, Paul said that Lizzie would now have to use a combination of positive attraction and appropriate reserve.

As ever, Lizzie was so incredibly brave, and always dealt with it really confidently, giving the impression that it was all water off a duck's back, but I knew she was under an awful lot of pressure. The analogy was that she had been raped on paper, and it couldn't have been a very pleasant experience. We had even used her flat for the phone calls, so it wasn't a case of going home that night and shutting the door on it; she was living with it 24 hours a day – not only her, but also her husband, himself a young detective. I felt it was right that he should be told what was going on, and he was so professional about it, displaying a maturity beyond his years.

This meeting was going to be particularly hard on her. We all knew that she would find it much more difficult to keep Stagg at a distance, particularly when his sexual arousal would have increased.

Chapter 32

The next morning, at 11.35am, Lizzie turned on the concealed tape recorder and sat down with Stagg on a patch of grass not far from the Dell café.

Mick and I were observing from the back of a nondescript. After the first meet, it had been only Mick and me in the van because space was so limited; what was more, the weather had improved considerably, which made the van like a sauna.

Lizzie had been briefed as to where she should take Colin. Again, the back-up team were already in position, so it was she and Colin Stagg who were joining their environment, not vice versa. This made for an ideal surveillance scenario, and the van was positioned in such a way as to afford Mick and me a perfect view of the proceedings. We were no more than 50 yards away, watching in sweltering silence as the meeting began.

'Look at that, Keith ...' Wickerson whispered. 'He's brought a copy of the newspaper with him.'

I saw Lizzie look at the paper, and heard her say, 'What's these circles?' It appeared that Stagg had circled several paragraphs in biro.

Colin replied, 'That's where it's all wrong.'

Lizzie read on, then asked, ''Cos they said in the paper here, that you said you weren't there at the time, but you told me you had been.'

Colin said, 'Yeah I was ... I had to say that to them ... I told the police, you know, I wasn't there at the time and that.'

'I mean, you couldn't tell them the truth, that you were there, 'cos ...'

'Yeah.'

I grinned as I listened to the conversation unfold. 'That's handy, Mick, he's marked all the bits where he lied to the press.'

Stagg now briefly described a fantasy in which he and Lizzie have sex in a male public toilet. Stagg said he wanted to act out the fantasies he describes.

'I mean, I wouldn't be writing these things if I didn't want to do them.'

Meanwhile, he started trying to stroke Lizzie's leg and put his hand up her skirt. She slightly shifted position to avoid it.

'Now what's he saying?'

I shut up and concentrated on the dialogue. Mick and I listened with growing anticipation as Colin Stagg got on to the subject of his movements on the day of the murder.

'See, the main evidence was, er ... two women actually saw me there at the time ... one of the women I knew just by sight.'

'I bloody knew it,' I said. 'Did you get all of that?'

'He said that he was on the common at the time of the murder!'

'Not only that – he said that our main evidence was that two women *actually* saw him there at the time. It's the *actually*. He didn't say, "Two women say they saw," or even, "The police said that two women saw me." He said, "Two women actually saw me." I knew Jane Harriman was right when she picked him out of that line-up. He even mentioned that he was picked out and that the other woman knew him.'

Colin put his hand on Lizzie's leg again and pushed it up inside her skirt until he touched her thigh. I listened with increasing interest as I heard him tell Lizzie that he wanted to act out his fantasies. My mind went back to Paul's earlier assertion that the killer would have rehearsed the murder in fantasy many times before his levels of arousal caused him to turn fantasy into fact.

They were now back on to the murder.

'I want someone like the man who did this thing,' Lizzie said.

'That was a bit direct, Lizzie,' Wickerson winced as he heard her statement. 'We might have a bit of trouble over that last bit.'

'Let's worry about it later – she's playing a blinder out there.'

As Colin spoke, he tried again to run his hand up Lizzie's thighs. She shifted position and encouraged him to talk more, but soon felt his hands again and had to move.

Lizzie told him that the murderer fascinated her.

'I think about it. I try and imagine it and the thought of him is so exciting.'

'I wish it was me who done it, you know,' Colin said. 'Cos, I mean, I feel guilty about the thought, you know, it does turn me on a lot, it did right from the beginning, you know.'

'But what bits turned you on? What was the bits that really, you know, turned you on? Seeing the dead body or imagining it, what was it?'

'Things that he did, that he was actually having sex with her at the same time, forcing himself into her and that.'

'Is that what he did?'

'That's what he must have done. Yeah. But I mean he must. He probably went just crazy while he was, you know, while he was fucking her, you know, 'cos she was stabbed about 49 times, something like that ...'

'That's a strange thing to say,' Wickerson said. He was referring to Colin's statement that the murderer was actually having sex with Rachel as he was stabbing her.

'Worrying, isn't it?' I said.

Colin said, 'If you think about it, if he just suddenly attacked her, right, it was a knife that stabbed her, and he gets a big hard-on like, you know, he's getting really aroused and that, then obviously he's gonna force himself into her, ain't he, while he's doing it? I mean, she'd be struggling and the more that she struggles, you know, the more it's all a turn-on, you know.'

'Yeah, but if he stabbed her she might have been dead anyway.'

'Depends where he stabbed her first, you know.'

Lizzie said, 'Didn't they tell you where he'd stabbed her first?'

'No, no, all I know is that he stabbed her 49 times, you know. Her head was decapitated.'

'Was it?'

'Yeah.'

'Why's that, what did he try and do?'

'Probably just trying to cut her head off.'

I had shown him only one specially chosen photograph, and this was on the advice of Paul Britton. It was a distance shot which only showed Rachel from the back; you certainly couldn't see the position of her hands or head. What's more, I had only given him a fleeting look when I asked him whether this was how Rachel had looked when he last saw her.

Yet here was Colin telling Lizzie that Rachel had been decapitated.

'Well, that's not right ...' Wickerson muttered.

'No it isn't – but if you think about those two horrendous neck wounds ... especially as Rachel would have been drenched in blood. If you had inflicted those and had trouble getting the knife out of her throat as we know the killer did ... in the heat of the moment you might be forgiven for thinking that you had severed her head.

'Whatever, he couldn't possibly have seen Rachel's head from the photograph.'

Mick said, 'What's he doing now?'

I listened intently as the open transmitter answered my question. 'Fucking hell, Mick! He's demonstrating how Rachel was left.'

We both leaned forward, trying to get closer to the action. We watched in astounded silence as Colin lay on the floor and adopted an almost foetal position, with his head back and his hands up in front of his face.

Colin was lying on the ground on his left side with his knees pulled up, his head tilted back and his arms to the side, clasped together as if in prayer. 'She was like that,' he said.

'What, lying on her side?' Lizzie asked.

'Yeah, and her head was sort of over like that ...' he tilted his head right back. 'So you know, it must have been sort of half-off, and the photograph was taken from that end you know,' he added, pointing to the direction of his backside.

'Look at his hands, Keith!' There was real urgency in Wickerson's voice. Colin's hands were crossed at the wrists. 'Where have you seen that before? And the head.'

His question was unnecessary; we both knew the import of what was being acted out in front of us.

'And he reckons he got all of this from the photo?' I said.

We watched as Colin Stagg sat up and continued his conversation about the murder. He began to describe to Lizzie the condition of Rachel's genitalia. Lizzie said, 'You say she was like, gaping wide open.'

'Yeah, what, her genitals, yeah.'

'Yeah.'

'Yeah she was, that's the way it ... 'cos, the photograph was like ...'

'So that you could see right up her?'

'Yeah.'

'Could you see that?'

'Yeah.'

'What did it look like, Colin?'

'She was, she was just open, you know, she was just like that.'

We watched as Stagg made a circle with the forefinger and thumb of his right hand.

Wickerson and I looked at each other. The demonstration mirrored almost exactly one of the injuries which we had kept secret. Yet again, Stagg appeared to be giving detailed knowledge of Rachel's body which couldn't be explained by the single photograph he'd been shown.

We listened as Lizzie again pushed her legal luck to clarify what Colin was talking about. She was under tremendous pressure, thinking on her feet all the time, trying to stay in character, fend off groping hands, and still stay within the realms of legal niceties. It was very difficult for her.

'Hang on, Keith – he's saying it was her vagina!'

'Yeah, and remember what Paul said about that?'

'What?'

'He said that he would expect the killer to "assign a unitary aspect to anus and vagina".'

'That he wouldn't differentiate between the two?'

'Something like that.'

'But he knows the difference, look at all those meat slab pictures he had round the walls of his gym.'

'I'm not saying that he doesn't know the difference, I'm saying that he wouldn't necessarily consider the difference important.'

We returned to silence as we watched and waited.

Lizzie said, 'Didn't you see the killer run off or anything like that? Didn't you hear a thing?'

'I didn't see anything or hear anything.'

'I mean, how far a distance is it, how far away is it from where you were to where she was at the time?'

'I'll show you on the map. Right,' he pointed to a place in the newspaper article, 'just round about here.'

As Lizzie chatted on about the ritual murders she had taken part in, Stagg said, 'See the thing is, I can't compete with that ...' and denied that he was the murderer of Rachel Nickell.

Lizzie said that she wanted the man who had committed the murder. Stagg asked her if she wanted to call everything off, and they discussed a bit further the sort of man that Lizzie wanted.

I said to Mick, 'There's no way he's going to put his hands up. He's happy to talk about it, but he's not going to go the extra mile.'

'I think you're right, Keith. I think Lizzie's beginning to get that impression, too.'

He tapped his headphones to draw my attention back to the conversation. Lizzie began to wind up the meet.

'I'm going to have to go,' she said. 'I'm gonna get too upset if I stay here any longer ... I don't want you to see me cry.'

'This could be dodgy,' Wickerson warned. 'I'll ring Mick Connor and tell him to make sure his chaps are on their toes; keep your eyes and ears open.'

As Colin got up to leave, he left Lizzie the newspaper as a souvenir.

'Do you want me to ring you?' he asked.

'It's up to you. It's up to you. I'm gonna have to go. Bye.'

Lizzie started walking away from him, towards Mick and me in the van. She didn't turn around and look back, and Stagg made no attempt to follow her.

And that, I knew, was the end of the undercover operation.

I gave Lizzie James a right bollocking when she got back. 'You should have asked him for his autograph,' I said. 'And if you could have got him to sign and date it that would have been even better!'

When we got back to Wimbledon, we showed Lizzie some of the scene of crime photos. It was the first time she had seen them.

I handed her exhibit KP27, the photo that I had shown Colin Stagg. 'You'll understand why Mick and I were so excited when you see this,' I said. 'He reckons that he got all the details he told and showed you from this.'

Lizzie studied the picture. 'But that's ridiculous - he couldn't see any of what he showed me from this.'

'That's right. Now have a look at these.'

I handed her a set of the scene and post mortem photographs. She looked through them with growing concern.

'But he was spot on.'

'He was, wasn't he?'

'And especially with this one.' She pointed to a post mortem shot which clearly showed the damage and dilation to Rachel's anus. 'Poor Rachel,' she said, a look of intense sadness on her face. 'He couldn't have known about that, unless he was there when it was done.'

'That's what we think. That last injury would not be apparent unless you'd actually pulled her buttocks apart.'

Lizzie handed back the photograph and said, 'What a terrible way to die.'

Chapter 33

As usual, Paul was consulted and asked for his interpretation of the copy tape of the meeting; it was his opinion that mattered, not our gut feelings.

'What do you make of it, Paul?' I enquired.

'I think that the external pressure created by the newspaper coverage has raised his levels of caution with regard to self-disclosure.'

'So have we reached the end of the road?'

'I would say that the contents of this,' he picked up the cassette, 'are indicative of that. He has displayed a knowledge of Rachel's injuries, the disposition of her body and has confirmed that he was on the common at the time of the murder, but specifically denied being the murderer. This behaviour is entirely consistent with the expected behaviour of the killer in the event of external intervention.'

'So that's that, then!'

'If you remember, I said that the newspaper article was likely to have two effects.'

'Raise caution and ...?'

'The second consequence was that he would be likely to be the recipient of sexual interest from a certain type of female correspondent.'

'And as a result, Lizzie's efforts are likely to be diluted in their effectiveness?'

'Fatally diluted, in my view.'

'Do you honestly think that women are likely to be turned on by his notoriety and will want to start a correspondence with him?'

'There's a very strong possibility. You only have to look at the "fan mail" convicted killers receive. The highly explicit nature of some of this type of correspondence would appeal very much to Mr Stagg and, as a result, the effectiveness of the operation would be finished.'

'What sort of woman? No, don't tell me, I don't want to know.'

Paul looked reflective. 'There it is, Keith. I would say that his behaviour is entirely consistent with such a development and, in light of this, I would suggest that there is nothing further to be gained.'

I considered Paul's words for a couple of minutes. 'It's not been a total failure,' I said. 'I think his disclosures concerning his knowledge are highly incriminating.'

'It's by no means been a failure. From the psychological side it's been most enlightening and highly probative.'

'From a detective's viewpoint, too, his explanation as to how he came by his knowledge doesn't hold water.'

'You're obviously the best judge of that aspect of things, but I must say this last meeting has served to confirm my views that Mr Stagg and the killer share the same specific extreme and violent sexual deviation.'

I silently weighed up the import of Paul Britton's words. 'I appreciate that you can't state that the killer and Colin are one in the same person, but what exactly is the extent of what you can say?'

'It is my opinion that Mr Stagg suffers from a sexual deviation featuring sexual pleasure and gratification derived from physical and sexual violence towards women.'

I was scribbling notes as he spoke. 'Go on.'

'The indications are from the nature of his fantasies and his own direct statements to Lizzie that he has strong urges to act out these fantasies in reality. Am I going too fast?'

'No, I'm fine.'

Paul adopted his characteristic prayer-like thinking pose. 'Yes, I would expect that the man who murdered Rachel would also exhibit this form of sexual deviation and, following on from there, I can say that the proportion of men in the general population suffering from such a specific extreme and violent deviation is extremely small.'

'Can you give me an idea of numbers?'

Paul smiled. 'I wouldn't feel comfortable committing myself to a definite number, but if you remember the bar graph I drew on the white board in my office, you'll perhaps understand how very rare this is.'

'And there is a direct and detailed correlation between the two?'

'Keith, if the content of the original Psychological Offender Profile – and I'm using that expression in the wider sense – and the subsequent predictions concerning the behaviour of the murderer during the covert operation were depicted graphically, and then the characteristics and actual behaviour of Mr Stagg during the covert operation were also depicted graphically, then these two representations would sit one directly on top of the other.'

'Impressive – but it's the rarity that I really need to establish.'

'Let me put it this way – I've told you that this is an extremely rare form of sexual deviance, and the probability of two people suffering from this form of deviance being on Wimbledon Common on 15 July at the time of the murder I can only describe as being vanishingly small.'

The upper time limit for the operation that Paul had specified at the outset had now been reached, and it was obvious that Colin Stagg wasn't going to put his hands up.

However, we still hadn't had a decision from the CPS as to whether we had enough new evidence to justify a re-arrest and the potential for charging, which was a problem. One of the major considerations before we started the inquiry, when we had sought a second opinion, was: is there any likelihood as a result of carrying out this undercover operation that we could be escalating a situation and making him do something that he wouldn't otherwise do? The point was that we suspected him of having done one murder; now, by introducing this female into his life and then removing her, if we are in a position where we haven't gained enough evidence to charge him, have we set the wheels in motion for something that can't be stopped and might have dire consequences?

Paul's view was that, no, we hadn't and, no, we wouldn't. His opinion was that it was inevitable that the killer would offend again; the only thing that we might change was the time-scale.

'And by changing the time-scale, obviously we might well have an effect on who the victim is?' I said.

Paul said, 'It's quite possible that it could be someone that he knows, or someone that he's going to stalk.'

We were on tenterhooks, wondering if we'd set something terrible in motion.

On 22 July, the day after the Hyde Park meeting, Stagg phoned Lizzie and asked her to reconsider seeing him. Lizzie refused, saying that he was not the right man for her. She asked him to return her letters, and he agreed.

The same day, Colin wrote to say goodbye. He told her how lonely he was, and how he knows she is, too:

> *OH LIZZIE, I WISH, I WISH SO MUCH THAT I WAS THAT MURDERER, I WISH I WAS THE MAN FOR YOU ...*

The letter ended:

> *JUST A LAST LINGERING THOUGHT FOR YOU MY DARLING, I HOPE YOU ENJOY THEM.*

The lingering thought referred to was a page of drawings, depicting a dagger dripping blood on to a man and woman having rear-entry sex, a naked woman lying down and displaying her genitals, and a large, erect, ejaculating penis.

On 27 July Lizzie received another letter from Colin, returning her tape.

At a conference between the CPS, Paul and us a few days later, it was agreed that Stagg was now unlikely ever to confess to Lizzie, even if he was the murderer. At the same time, in the light of the article in the *Star*, he would probably find that a number of women were willing to correspond with him, thus greatly diminishing the evidential value of the material so painstakingly gathered by Lizzie in the six months of Operation Edzell. It was finally decided that the undercover operation should come to an end.

Lizzie James had to be sent into retirement, and this had to be done carefully. With us now increasingly believing that Stagg was a killer, it was vital that Lizzie break off contact in such a way as to minimise the risk of him becoming angry and being propelled into harming someone else.

Lizzie wrote back to Stagg, thanking him and saying how upset she was that Stagg was not the right man for her. She apologised for having hurt him, and talked about maybe going to America. She said that she'd like to see him one more time before she left.

Colin wrote back on 10 August and said he thought it would be unwise to meet. He admitted making up the story about the New Forest murder, but:

> *I JUST DIDN'T WANT TO LOSE YOU . . . I WILL ALWAYS MISS YOU, DARLING. I HAVEN'T FELT RANDY SINCE WE BROKE UP ...*

Lizzie James went back to normal duties, having helped gather evidence that amounted to 1,700 pages in the file. Now it was time for the Crown Prosecution Service to decide if Colin Stagg had a case to answer, or whether we had all worked so hard in vain.

On 15 August, I phoned Paul and told him that a decision had been made to arrest and charge Colin Stagg. Senior lawyers from the CPS had reviewed all the material and agreed there was enough to make a case. Their only stipulation was that they would not take the case to trial unless Andre signed an undertaking to bring Alex back to the UK to give evidence. It went without saying that nobody wanted to put any pressure on the boy, or cause him any more distress. We were able to assure Andre that his son would not be required in the courtroom itself. Indeed, Alex could be far away from the courtroom, and could testify from any part of British territory via a video link. The CPS also promised that he would not be cross-examined.

During the first week in August, an officer flew out to meet Andre at a French airport, where he signed the undertaking.

Paul had originally said that the operation might take up to 16 weeks. As it happened, we were talking about more than twice that length of time before we actually decided that we had gone as far as we could with it, and that we weren't going to achieve the ultimate goal, as predicted – but that was because of the external pressures of the press, public opinion, and probably the fact that Colin had convinced himself that the story he told the police was the truth – but it wasn't, and we could say that unequivocally.

But what we couldn't say definitely was that Colin Stagg had killed Rachel, because that was something that only a jury could decide. They had to be given the benefit of all the evidence and then decide whether there was a reasonable doubt; there were questions that couldn't be answered, there were some very worrying inferences to the things that had been discovered, and really it was a question for twelve good persons and true to sit down and decide whether this man was safe to go back on the streets, or whether the police were, in fact, talking a lot of psychological mumbo-jumbo.

Chapter 34

Out of the blue, Andre contacted us to let us know that Alex was still talking. He said that he had a video camera, and we asked him to film their conversations and pass us the tape.

In August 1993, he sent us his latest effort. I sat in the little enquiries office, adjacent to the main incident room, to watch it with Wickerson, Nick Sparshatt and Paul Miller. We sat in silence as father and son spoke about the day that had shattered both their lives. It was heart-rending stuff.

Andre had set up the camera in a corner of the room and then joined Alex at his little Early Learning Centre red plastic table. The content of the conversation was very poignant. Even case-hardened coppers like myself had to admit that it brought a lump to our throats and a tear to the eye, for the dignity displayed by Andre during this very difficult and upsetting encounter was only outdone by his shiningly obvious love for his son.

'The bad man was sticking things in her,' Alex said as he drew a picture.

'What was he sticking in her?'

'A knife, that's his knife.'

'Did you see it?'

'Yes, I saw the knife.'

'Did you see it all the time?'

'Yeah, I saw it. I saw it all ... Oh, Dad, look, look, Dad, look, did you see that?' Alex, doe-eyed and angelic, spoke quietly and matter-of-factly, whilst Andre visibly fought to control his emotions as he listened.

'Yes, now you can rub it all off, can't you?'

'I can rub it all off again.'

'So, Alex, was it sunny or raining?'

'It was warm. I couldn't feel any rain.'

'What were you doing with Mummy when you saw him?'

'I was looking for blackberries.'

'Did Mummy see him?'

'I don't think she did.'

'No, did you see him first?'

'Yeah, I saw him first.'

'Did he have a bag?'

'Yes.'

'Did he have a bag like Daddy has, a bum bag that I wear around my waist, or was it a big bag?'

'A big bag. Shall I put, shall I put Mummy on it?'

'You could do, you could draw it. So it was a big bag ... did he have it under his arm or ...'

'No, he had it on his arm.' Alex moved his right arm over to his left shoulder to indicate.

'And did he open it or was it already open?'

'It was open.'

'And what did he get out of it?'

'A knife.'

'Did Mummy see it when it came out?'

'Can't remember.'

'And then what happened?'

'Then he went ...' Alex said, starting to move his right hand around in circles.

'Did he touch you? Last time you told me something happened just before he stabbed Mummy ... Did he hit you?'

'He knocked me over.'

'Did you land on your face or did you go on to your back?'

'I landed on the back of my Thunderbird's head.'

Andre leaned backwards, arms outstretched. 'You landed on your back like that, did you?'

Andre put his outstretched right arm to Alex's chest. 'Pushed you like that, did he, from the front?'

'Yes.'

Andre put his hand up to cover his face. 'Did he push you in the face?'

Alex put his hand over his face. 'Yes.'

'And where were you when the bad man was hurting Mummy?'

'He was already putting the knife in, back when his bag was getting bigger and bigger.'

'Did it?'

'Yes.'

'Did he open it up?'

'Yes, then it started to get bigger and bigger and bigger.'

'Is that him hurting Mummy there?' Andre said, pointing to Alex's drawing.

'No. No, that's when the bag gets bigger.'

'Where were you when he was hurting Mummy? Did you run away to the pond, or did you run up the hill when he was hurting Mummy?'

'I did there.'

'Did you stay there?'

'Yeah, afterwards run away, I run away.'

'Did you say anything to Mummy when you went? Did you tell her anything, did you try to get her to do anything?'

'She's dead.'

'She's dead?'

'Yeah.'

'How do you know she was dead? Was she talking to you?'

'No, she was dead.'

'She couldn't talk any more? Show me the way you were looking when the man was hurting Mummy.'

Alex made no reply, but carried on drawing. Suddenly, he started stabbing the point of his pencil hard repeatedly on the table.

'Do you remember how long his hair was, Alex?' Andre said quietly. 'Did you have a good look?'

'I didn't.'

'Didn't really, did you see his face or not?'

'Yes.'

'Did you see his hair? Did he have a hat on like Daddy's hat?'

'Yeah, he did have a hat.'

'Did have a hat, did he have really little hair like Daddy, or really long hair like Gordon?'

'Your hair.'

'Or was it like Steve's hair – he's got more hair than me. Was it like Steve's hair?'

'Steve's hair.'

'More like Steve's hair, was it quite long then?'

'Yes.'

'Did he have any dogs, sweetheart?'

'Didn't.'

'No dogs there. Was there anyone else there, was there any other men there?'

'When?'

'When Mummy was being ... when he was hurting Mummy.'

'No.'

'Nobody else?'

'No.'

'Who was the first person you saw afterwards, do you remember? Somebody come and help you?'

'Yes, people found me.'

'Was it a man who found you or was it a lady?'

'A man and he gave me to a lady.'

'He gave you to a lady.'

'Yes. I can tell you because you weren't there.'

'No, I wasn't there, was I?'

'No. Dad, there's a pen.'

'Do you want these pens as well? Do you know if he took anything from Mummy, did he go through her pockets or anything? Did he look in her pockets?'

'No he didn't. I've got to rub this out.'

'Yes, rub that out. So what did he do to her clothing?'

'I'm going to write it down, I'm going to write his name down, he said his name.'

'What's his name, do you remember?'

'Escargot.'

'Escargot?'

'Yes.'

'A snail.'

'Yes, he's a snail. Yes, he's a snail.'

'Did he say anything else, sweetheart? Did you hear anything else he said?'

Alex didn't reply.

'Can you help me draw Mummy on this piece of paper?' Andre said, helping Alex to draw. 'That's Mummy, that's Mummy's legs. Mummy is lying down. That's the bad man, he's got a knife. Where were you?'

Alex pointed to Andre's drawing.

'By her feet or by her head?'

'By her head, by a bit of paper.'

'You found a bit of paper by her head?'

'Yes.'

'What did you do with the piece of paper?'

'Put it there.'

'Yeah. Where did you get the piece of paper from?'

'From the floor.'

'And you put it on Mummy, did you?'

'Yes.'

'Shall I draw another one on a big piece of paper?'

'I rubbed it out.'

'I know you did. I'll do it on a big piece of paper that doesn't rub out.'

'I want to rub it out.'

'Yes, well, that's your one to rub out. Alex, when you saw the bad man, was he in front like I am or was he on this side?' Andre pointed to his right. 'Or was he on that side?' he said, pointing to his left.

'He was in front.'

'He was right in front of you, was he?'

'Yeah.'

'Where was Mummy, was she behind you?'

'She was coming from that side,' he pointed from the right, 'or that side, I can't remember. Can't remember which side she was on. Well, we were walking from that side,' he said, indicating from his right, 'and he was just ...'

'Was he in front of you or behind?'

'He was behind.'

'Was he, and where was Mummy, was Mummy behind you or was Mummy walking down in front of you, down the hill?'

'Beside me.'

'Beside you, was she?'

'Holding my hand.'

'You draw the bad man.'

'OK, I'll draw Mummy on the ground. Like that one we did before. There's Mummy's head and there's Mummy's feet, there's Mummy's hands. Here's the bad man. Was the bad man. I'll put the bad man here, look '

'That's very good. That's a very good drawing. That's very good, two legs and two arms and a nose. Alex, where were you, there's the bad man with the knife in his hand. Were you at Mummy's head or at her feet?'

Alex pointed.

Andre said, 'That's her hand.'

'Near her hand.'

'Between her hands and her head.'

'No, there.' He pointed again, but Andre didn't comment.

'Did you see everything, sweetheart?'

'Yeah, I saw everything.'

'Did you look away?'

'Yeah, I looked that way,' he said, turning his head to his right. 'I looked to see if anything else was happening.'

'Did you?'

'Yes.'

'Was it really horrible?'

'Yes, it was horrible.'

'It was a horrible, horrible thing.'

'I'm going to draw the man now.'

'Did he run away, sweetheart, do you remember that? When he was finished.'

'Yeah.'

'Did he run away or did he walk away?'

'Run away. There's Mummy, there's the bad man '

'Where's the knife?'

Alex continued drawing and showed the picture to Andre.

'That's very good. Mummy was standing up then, was that in the beginning?'

'Yes. Now I'm going to draw me. There's the head.'

'Is that you?'

Alex finished his drawing, which Andre showed to the camera.

'What's that? That looks like a knife, a knife in his hand.'

'Yes.'

'Did he take it and put it in the bag then?'

'He didn't have a hat. There's another bag.'

'A different bag then?'

'Yes, a different bag.'

'Alex, afterwards did he put the knife back in his bag or did he throw it away? Did he throw it on the ground?'

'He put it back in his bag.'

'Did he put the bag back over his shoulder or did he carry it in his hand?'

'Put it back over his shoulder.'

'Did he?'

'Look at that,' Alex said, holding up his drawing.

'Is that like him?'

'That's him.'

'That's him, is it? Didn't have a hat on? He had a knife in his hand?'

'Yes. Pull that face off.'

'And where did he go? Did he go down the hill or did he go up the hill?'

'He go back where it was dark?'

'Down the hill.'

'Go back down that way,' he pointed to his right.

'Is that down, because I can't remember now. Is that towards the stream and the pond?'

'That way. I don't know which way it went.'

'Did he go down to the stream, did he look in the stream at all?'

'I don't remember.'

'You don't remember?'

'I don't, Daddy. He's getting dressed back because the pirates' He held up a toy figure. 'He got a pirate '

'Would you like to make the bad man jump off into the crocodiles?'

'Yes.'

'Then he will get eaten, won't he?'

Alex left the room, and returned with a toy crocodile.

Andre said, 'It's good to talk about it sometimes. You don't have to think about it all on your own, do you?'

Alex continued to play.

'Sweetheart, can you just tell me one more time, Alex. Did you see what happened, all of it, or did you look the other way?'

'I saw all of it.'

'All of it.'

'Yes.'

'You saw him stabbing Mummy and everything, yes?'

'Yes. Can I have my rubbing out thing? I rub it out, we are not going to do it again.'

'OK, we're done now anyway. Do you want to do some talking?'

'Yes.'

'What do you want to talk about – what happened, or what you felt? You want to talk about what you felt?'

'Fire engines and firemen.'

'Yeah, let's finish now.'

At the end of the tape conversation, talk did not come easily. We all sat silent, seemingly lost in our thoughts.

It had been a shocking murder in any event, but what had compounded the unthinkable horror of it for us was the fact that, as the latest video proved, Alex had probably witnessed every detail. Yet again, we could only imagine the nightmare the little chap must have suffered, and wonder what permanent scars it would leave on his mind.

The mystery of the scrap of paper, the PIN notification, had been solved at last. But more than that, Alex's revelation proved once again the accuracy of all his evidence so far. We had been so confused as to the significance of the piece of paper that we had kept it a secret even from Andre. It was a piece of information that Andre could not have primed Alex to produce, as he had never had any knowledge of its existence.

Sparshatt broke into our reverie. 'Well, what do you think of that, then?'

'To my mind, it shows that Alex has a vivid and accurate recollection of what happened. His explanation about the piece of paper leaves me in no doubt.'

'Nor me, Keith,' Wickerson said, 'but I can't see us ever being allowed to use the tape, it's far too emotionally charged. Show it to a jury and they'd convict anyone on the strength of it!'

Wickerson was absolutely right. There was no way on earth any defence brief would be happy to let the tape be shown. It was a powerful document, but without doubt evidentially its probative value would be far outweighed by its prejudicial value.

Chapter 35

On the morning of 17 August 1993, at just after 5.30am, Mick Wickerson and I were in the incident room at Wimbledon Police Station, mugs of coffee in hand as we waited for the team to begin arriving. This was the day that we had worked for since the beginning of the inquiry some 13 months earlier. The false starts and red herrings were behind us now. We had put together a case that had been accepted by the most eminent criminal lawyers in the Crown Prosecution Service, and we were now ready to arrest Colin Stagg for the second time.

There was a mood of underlying tension in the team as they assembled for what was to be their final briefing. Clearly, the prospect of resolving Rachel's murder was something to be celebrated, but there was little in the way of banter passing around the room. By this time, our numbers had been much reduced by the constant demands of Area who had relentlessly been clawing back their officers since the end of January, and our once overcrowded accommodation now afforded more than enough room for my depleted staff. I looked at the seven officers engaged in quiet conversation. This was a serious business. Many of them had invested more than a year of their lives in this case and felt that their efforts were at last about to be rewarded.

Mick and I were accompanied by Martin Long, who had been one of the most recent to leave the Wimbledon squad as the numbers were wound down. He had returned to the Regional Crime Squad office in Surbiton, but the moment I'd got the green light for the re-arrest I phoned him and said, 'I want you back here, Mart. This could be it.'

The briefing was extremely short. They all knew the score; it only remained to ensure that we had the requisite exhibits bags and books, and the warrant. Technically we didn't need one, since the provisions of Section 18 of the Police and Criminal Evidence Act allowed us to search the premises of a person who has been arrested, and Colin would have fallen into this category. However, it was belt and braces time.

We drove in convoy to the edge of the Alton Estate and parked up well away from Colin's address. We wanted to conduct the arrest and early stages of the search as quietly as possible, and knew that as soon as the word got out, the press would be descending in droves. There was no way that we could keep it quiet once the uniformed search teams arrived to start digging up his garden, but we wanted to buy as much time as possible. The last thing we wanted was for the media to film Colin being led from his address. The press had already plastered his picture all over the papers and TV, so the damage was done, but our main concern was to keep things as low-key as possible. We didn't want allegations that we were trying to prejudice the case against him, neither did we want to give the media too much opportunity to speculate and invent.

We wandered towards 16 Ibsley Gardens in groups of two and three. The plan was that Mick and I would gain access to the address, then we would call in the rest of the team. I sent a couple of the chaps around the back in case he tried to do a runner.

'DI Pedder, receiving?' My hand-held small set crackled.

'Go, go.'

'We're in position, boss.'

'Yes, yes.'

I knocked on the door and waited for sounds of movement. Thirty seconds or so passed. It seemed like an eternity.

I knocked again, a little harder this time. Both Mick and I strained to hear.

'Signs of life,' Wickerson said as the sound of heavy footsteps on the stairs came from inside. I knocked again.

'All right – who is it?' I heard Colin's familiar voice.

'Open up, Colin, it's the police.'

There was silence for a few moments, then the sound of locks being undone, and the door opened. Colin peered around the part-opened door. Almost subconsciously I took a small step forward and put my foot in the door.

'Good morning, Colin, you remember me – I'm Detective Inspector Keith Pedder from Wimbledon Police Station.' I showed him my warrant card.

'Yeah?'

'I have to tell you that, as a result of further enquiries, new evidence has come to light and I'm arresting you for the murder of Rachel Nickell.'

I moved forward into the doorway, encountering no resistance. I placed my hand on his arm and manoeuvred him back into the hallway. 'You're not obliged to say anything unless you wish to do so, but anything you do say will be put into writing and may be given in evidence. Do you understand?'

'What new evidence?' he asked, suddenly waking up from his bleary-eyed state.

As I led him into the living room, Mick was calling in the rest of the team. 'I have a warrant to search these premises,' I began to explain, 'and that's what we propose to do now. As for the new evidence, I'll explain all that to you when we interview you at Wimbledon later.'

'Who's been causing trouble?' There were tears beginning to form in his eyes.

'There's no point in getting upset, Colin,' I soothed.

'Is it someone round here?' he demanded, the first signs of anger beginning to show through his watery eyes.

'Calm down, Colin.' This time my tone was firmer.

'I didn't do it. Someone's causing trouble.' His tone was now downright aggressive. 'You're gonna fit me up ... you can't find anyone else for this, you're gonna fit me up ...'

'That's absolute nonsense, Colin ... calm down.'

'Come on, let's start talking about what I did that day.'

'Colin, don't speak now because we'll wait until we get you a social worker or a solicitor and we'll go through it at the station.'

I tried to placate him as the team began their search. I told him that he would get the opportunity to give his side of things back at the nick, and that he could call his solicitor as soon as we got there. He seemed to be reassured by this and told Martin and me that he would answer all our questions. 'I've got nothing to hide,' he said.

We took Colin upstairs so he could get dressed. On our return to the living room and just before our departure, Cliff, our exhibits officer, brought to my attention a pile of letters that had been found in Colin's desk. A quick glimpse of their contents was enough to increase the enormous respect that I already had for Paul Britton; the correspondence was from a woman in Wales, and even with just a quick glimpse, I could see that the contents were of a sexually explicit nature. I spotted the words *Daily Star* and wondered if, exactly as Paul had predicted, the relationship had started as a direct result of the article.

'OK, thanks, Cliff,' I said as dismissively as I could manage, and handed them back. 'Log them and seal them.' I didn't want to give Colin any hint of what I had in store for him in the interviews to come.

Curtains twitched and faces appeared in windows as we drove Colin Stagg away from the estate for the second time in 12 months. 'I'm bloody innocent,' he said to us. 'I've been stitched up with this. Now I'm going to lose my home and my dog. The man who did this is laughing at you.'

I said, 'Colin, don't talk now. You'll have plenty of chance to answer our questions. You'll have a solicitor who will give you advice. You can answer the questions or you don't have to answer the questions, as is your right.'

'I answered all your questions last time,' he said. 'Anyone who doesn't answer questions has got something to hide.'

The rest of the team were staying behind to co-ordinate the search. Inside the maisonette, they examined every nook and crevice. Most of Stagg's clothing and any other interesting items were taken away in brown sacks to be examined forensically. This had already been done once before, of course, but a considerable time had elapsed and he could well have felt secure enough to return items or souvenirs of the crime to his home. Outside, blue-overalled investigators had arrived with spades, forks, trowels and a metal detector, and were beginning a systematic sweep of Stagg's back garden. A compost bin was emptied and searched, even pots containing patio plants were checked. Then they dug the garden to a depth of two feet, looking for knives or any other buried items, or for traces of ash which might indicate burned items like shoes or clothing. DAC Johnston had said that he wanted it left in the same condition as it was found, so every plant was carefully exhumed and even more carefully replanted and watered.

The media interest, as predicted, was intense, and the scene of these excavations was a big draw for the TV cameras. However, the garden was to yield no clues.

Once Colin had been booked in, I spent the rest of the morning going over the arrangements and the equipment for the videoing of the interview. This left Mick and JB free to field the flood of press enquiries.

The first interview started at 1.15pm.

'Colin, we're in an interview room at Wimbledon Police Station. The interview I'm about to conduct with you is going to be recorded on an audio tape and also on video tape. If you look up there you can see the camera.'

'Yeah.'

The interview was being videoed simply because it was a resource that was available to me. It was felt that for an interview of such importance, the ability to see the interviewee and his reactions or body language might be useful for a jury. Videoing is the most comprehensive and accurate way of recording an interview and has an advantage over audio recording. With taped interviews you often get noises off – scraping of chairs, coughing, long periods of silence, all of which can be the basis of allegations of impropriety by the defence.

'OK, it's exactly the same as the previous chats that we had, but that was some time ago so I'll explain it all to you again. You don't actually have to answer any of my questions unless you want to. You've got your legal representative here, Mr Ryan, and he can advise you. OK, so you're happy with what's going on?'

'Yeah.'

'All right, so I'll formally caution you. The time according to my watch is 1.15, it's 17 August and, as I've already said, we're in an interview room at Wimbledon Police Station. Can you tell me your full name, please?'

'Colin Francis Stagg.'

'The other police officer present is ...'

Martin introduced himself. 'Martin Long, Detective Constable attached to the South-East Regional Crime Squad.'

'And your legal adviser's name?'

Ian Ryan said, 'Ian Ryan, Russell Cooke & Co.'

'I'm going to caution you, Colin. Do you understand what a caution is? You don't have to answer my questions unless you want to. And anything you do say may be given in evidence. Do you understand that?'

'Yeah.'

'So any answers you give are purely voluntary, yes? OK, we know each other reasonably well, don't we – we had quite a few chats and got to know each other. Can you tell me, Colin – you're here because of the events of 15 July 1992. That's just over a year ago. Can you remember what you were doing on that day?'

'No comment.'

'Colin, we've been through various events of that day,' I said. 'Would it be correct for you to tell me that you went to Wimbledon

Common on one occasion on the 15th before nine o'clock in the morning and got home about 0915 when you fell asleep?'

'No comment.'

'Colin, do you propose to answer any questions that I'm going to put to you?'

'No comment.'

You could have knocked me down with a feather. Colin was within his rights to remain silent, but after all his protestations in the car about being willing to answer our questions, I had really expected him to play ball.

Any interview is made more difficult if only one of the people present actually participates, but in this case I had the added pressure of knowing that my efforts were being recorded for posterity on video, and in addition, I knew there was a closed circuit TV link to the next room where Paul Britton, JB *et al* were also monitoring the proceedings. This unusual step hadn't been taken out of some weird voyeuristic interest. It served a specific purpose: because of the extremely unusual nature of the investigation and its complex psychological foundations it was felt that Paul should be present to monitor and advise the interviewing officers.

To avoid potential legal arguments it was decided that Paul Britton shouldn't be present in the interview room, hence the installing of the TV link. In addition, I was wearing a body set radio and covert earpiece which allowed me to hear Paul Britton's advice.

I pressed on, summarising his version of events for 15 July, as told to us in previous interviews.

'I will put it to you that what in fact happened on that day is that you didn't go home and fall asleep at 0925, but in fact you were seen entering the common by a woman called Susan Gayle.'

'No comment.'

'Well, this woman knows you by name.'

'No comment.'

'I'll put it to you that later, between 10.10am and 10.23am you were seen by a woman who was out with her children in the area of the Curling Pond and heading down towards the Windmill path by the Royal Surrey Regiment monument.'

'No comment.'

'I put it to you that that woman identified you without any hesitation whatsoever on an identification parade.'

'No comment.'

'Do you deny that you were on the common between 10 and 11 o'clock on 15 July 1992?'

'No comment.'

'Colin, do you know a girl called Andrea Parker?'

'No comment.'

'Is it true, Colin, that you wrote to this woman an unsolicited story concerning sexual activity on the common?'

'No comment.'

'Is it also true that you told her that the women locally didn't find you attractive but found you to be almost repulsive, and they laughed at you because you had got a funny way of walking?'

'No comment.'

'Colin, do you intend answering any of the questions I'm going to ask you?'

'No comment.'

'Do you know a girl called Lizzie James?'

'No comment.'

I mentioned the fact that they had exchanged some 30 or 40 letters, and asked him about his professed desire to have sexual intercourse on Wimbledon Common and in open woodland involving the use of knives.

'No comment.'

I talked about the phone calls and meetings, and the fact that he had described to her details of injuries to Rachel that he couldn't possibly have seen.

'No comment.'

I asked him about the newspaper that he had left with Lizzie James at Hyde Park, where he had circled parts of the article and told Lizzie that he had lied to the police about.

'No comment.'

It was like talking to a brick wall. I changed tack again, taking him back to the events of 15 July. I asked him about the gaping discrepancies between his testimony and that of Mrs Avid, Susan Gayle and Mrs Harriman.

'No comment.'

'Within an hour-and-a-half of the offence having happened, you are telling police officers who stopped you lies about the time you were present on the common. How would you have known it was safe to admit being on the common between 0815 and 0915 but unsafe to admit being the person that Mrs Harriman saw, unless you'd seen something or done something?'

'No comment.'

'Colin, it doesn't make sense. You knew far too much, too soon. Are the police officers lying?'

'No comment.'

'Are the police officers mistaken?'

'No comment.'

'Have you any explanation?'

'No comment.'

'The reason you can't admit to being the Harriman suspect is because the Harriman suspect was carrying a bag.'

'No comment.'

'And we know you had a black bag, Colin.'

'No comment.'

'(A friend of yours) describes this bag in great detail. She even draws it. Mrs Harriman describes the bag and do you know what's most important ... the little boy who witnessed his mother being stabbed – he describes the bag that the man that killed his mummy had.'

'No comment.'

'If you were on the common and it wasn't you, give me the explanation.'

'No comment.'

'Why were you so excited and wanted to run around and tell everybody there had been a murder on the common?'

'No comment.'

'You went up to the butcher's, you spoke to Mr Heanan, you spoke to Pat's son in the newsagents. You spoke to a Peter Witt, you spoke to Rita Nagy, you spoke to everybody that you knew.'

'No comment.'

'Colin, we've had all these answers before. I'm pointing out to you that you have since said things and done things which tend to contradict the first version of events that you gave. You have perhaps displayed a knowledge that you shouldn't have.'

'No comment.'

'It's very strange. Everyone seems to be in a major conspiracy against you, Colin. Everyone is lying. Susan Gayle is lying. Mrs Harriman and her children are telling lies. Lillian Avid is telling lies. PC Couch is telling lies. You said to me that PC Couch told you what time the offence had happened. He couldn't possibly have done that.'

'No comment.'

'It was late into the afternoon when we discovered the time the murder had occurred. And as far as the PC on the periphery of the common would have been concerned, it could have happened the night before – but all of a sudden you are telling lies within an hour to an hour-and-a-half after the offence, displaying a knowledge as to when it was safe to have been on the common and when it was safe not to admit being on the common.'

'No comment.'

I noticed that the tape was coming to an end and, at three minutes to two, I switched it off and called a break.

Martin and I took refuge in the incident room for a well-earned rest. I had found the session mentally exhausting. Colin was by this stage aware that we had got to know about his relationship with Lizzie James, but we hadn't yet disclosed to him how. I was saving that for later.

The first thing I wanted was a cup of coffee and the chance to remove my jacket, which I'd had to keep on to hide the body set. I was sweating.

'You're doing a brilliant job, KP,' Lizzie said as she handed me a coffee.

'It's like pushing water uphill.'

'He's definitely wobbly – every time you get a bit near the mark he looks at Ryan,' Lizzie added. 'It's like he's reaching for a security blanket.'

'So much for his promise to answer all our questions, eh, Mart?'

'Yeah, mister, I've got nothing to hide!'

The interview resumed at 3.12pm. I went over the same ground again – his relationships with Andrea Parker, Lizzie James and the woman from Wales and the anomalies in his evidence. I read him quotes from his letters to them, showing his proclivity for forceful sex from behind in woodland settings, and using knives.

'Colin, if we accept what the witnesses say, and I can't think of any reason why they would deliberately lie, because they've got no axe to grind with you, and nor have I. If there is a simple explanation for the anomalies that we've found, I would love to hear it, because I don't want to see a miscarriage of justice. You said to me this morning you were terrified that a miscarriage of justice was going to be done, and I said to you,'if you've not done it you've got nothing to worry about.'

'No comment.'

'Can you see the problem that I've got? These are your letters, these are your sexual feelings; they're displaying violence, degradation and the use of knives, and we have this anomaly where you're clearly, for some reason, not telling the truth about the time that you were on the common.'

'No comment.'

After just 30 minutes or so of this, Colin asked Ian Ryan if he could have another 'personal word'. I stopped the tape at 3.48pm and again the interview was adjourned.

When we resumed at 5.05pm, Ian Ryan had something to say.

'Inspector Pedder, I do feel that there was a great deal of comment in both interviews so far, not much in the way of direct questioning. I think particularly with regard to the last interview that there was a lot of speechmaking, if I might put it like that ...'

'Of course, I understand that, Mr Ryan,' I said, 'but unfortunately a one-sided conversation can sometimes be mistaken for oratory. But, of course, your client is perfectly entitled to say nothing.'

I went back to talking about the letters, quoting long extracts that the psychologist had said pointed to sexual dysfunction. I was trying everything I knew to get a response. Paul Britton's advice was sparse and consisted mainly of a commentary as to his reading of Colin's reactions to my questions. 'He's extremely uncomfortable with this line of questioning ... raise the tempo. I would suggest that you should read another extract from such and such a letter ... He's looking to his solicitor for reassurance.'

There was a look of total hatred on Stagg's face and I could see his muscles tensing at the questions that he didn't like. I could hear the venom in his voice when he articulated the words, 'No comment.'

The subject matter from which I was working was unpalatable to say the least, and this was an added strain whilst struggling to keep up this one-sided interview.

I also quoted the telephone calls, letters and meetings with Lizzie James that appeared to demonstrate that, on his own admission, he had lied to the police, and that he knew things about the murder that only the murderer could have known.

'Where did you get the knowledge of those injuries?'

'No comment.'

'How did you know she was gaping open like that?'

'No comment.'

'How did you know that she nearly had her head cut off?'

'No comment.'

'How did you know that her hands were in that position? Colin, you couldn't have seen that, you were shown one photograph ... How could you have known those things unless you'd been there and seen it? You describe muscles relaxing.'

'No comment.'

'He must have been forcing himself into her as he was doing it.'

'No comment.'

'Colin, you look at what happened to Rachel and you look at the fantasies that you described in your letters. They are so, so close.'

'No comment.'

'Have you any explanation of how you have that knowledge of those injuries? Do you dispute that that conversation took place?'

'No comment.'

'Do you dispute that you said those things?'

'No comment.'

'Do you dispute that you made those actions?'

'No comment.'

'Colin, the problem we have is that you've told lies about your movements on the day. You have displayed the knowledge of injuries that only someone who was there at the time would know about.'

'No comment.'

'How can we explain that?'

'No comment.'

Martin said, 'Colin, you expressed your innocence at great depth to us when we first arrested you. You reiterated that this morning. Now, you were told that we had new evidence and new witnesses had come to light. We've got approximately 12 or 13 people that take a totally contradictory stance to you, to your version of events, that don't know each other. And that ranges from neighbours through to ex-girlfriends, through to police officers, and all you can say is that they've lied. Now you've had a very clear, concise picture of events, that we believe to be taking shape in your mind as this interview's gone on. Are you sure that you still don't wish to offer any explanation for the things that we've put to you today?'

'No comment.'

'You realise the enormity of this inquiry?'

'No comment.'

'That girl was savagely killed on the common and we've been looking for the man for 13 months.'

I said, 'Can you see the problem that you have posed us? We've got to look at it all. My colleague has just said we have all these people saying one thing which contradicts your version of events. We then have to look at the fantasies as they've progressed as you've written to Lizzie James.'

'No comment.'

'The increasing deviance, the increasing domination, the increasing violence, the need to humiliate and dominate,' I said.

'The use of the knife, the blood. You add that to the conversations you've had where you are displaying a knowledge of injuries the victim received that nobody else could have known about, that weren't released to the press ...

'You have the description of her anus. It was wide open. How could you have known that? You couldn't have seen that from the photograph you were shown. How did you know that her head was nearly decapitated?'

'No comment.'

'You said there was blood all over the grass. How did you know that?'

'No comment.'

We were coming to the end of another tape and Colin expressed a wish to break for further advice. I stopped the tape at 5.44pm.

'It's a bit different from last September, isn't it?' Martin said to me with a rueful grin. 'Admittedly, we couldn't get him to answer the questions we were asking, but at least he was talking – total bollocks, I grant you, but he was talking.'

'Yeah, best-laid plans. Where's Paul?' I asked Lizzie.

'Next door. JB was talking to him.'

'Shall we go and join them? Perhaps Paul has some ideas on how to get him to talk.'

We went into the small office, where Mick, Paul and JB were deep in conversation.

JB was the first to speak. 'Well done, Keith, it's not easy.'

'That's an understatement, Guv. Paul, any suggestions?'

'He seems totally unreceptive; he definitely seems to be drawing strength from the presence of his solicitor.'

'What about some shock tactics? How do you think he'll react if we confront him with Lizzie?'

'That could get him over the hurdle of saying nothing or it could just strengthen his resolve.'

'What have we got to lose? OK with you, Lizzie?'

'I've got no problems with confronting him.'

'Right, when we go back in, I'll try again, but if I'm getting nowhere I'll scratch my ear like this,' I demonstrated. 'That'll be your signal to make your way down to the door of the interview room. When you get there, knock on the door and wait until I call you in.'

'How do you want me to handle it after that?'

'I think we want to make it as dramatic as possible – what do you think, Paul?'

'Perhaps if, as Lizzie enters, Martin could vacate his chair so she can sit down. But this should be done in silence. If Lizzie then makes herself comfortable, taking her time before introducing herself. That will give Mr Stagg the opportunity to reflect on the situation.'

'That seems straightforward enough I said. 'You both OK with that?'

I looked at Lizzie and Mart for confirmation. 'Great!'

'I'll give it the "Hello, Colin, remember me?" bit, then I'll go on to tell him I'm a serving police officer and for the purpose of an undercover operation I was known as Lizzie James. I'll let that sink in for a moment or two then I'll go on to put to him the disclosures he made during the last meeting.'

'We should get a reaction of one sort or another!' I said wryly. 'But I wouldn't like to bet on what it's going to be.'

'Don't be so pessimistic, KP!' Lizzie said with confidence. 'It'll be fine.'

'Fingers crossed! C'mon, Longy, back to the grind. Good luck, Lizzie,' I said over my shoulder as we left the room.

'We're not going to need it,' she replied with a smile.

As we walked along the corridor, Longy said, 'She's one in a million.'

'Make that two million.'

We booked Colin back out of the cells and allowed him a consultation with Mr Ryan before I resumed.

The fourth interview started at 6.30pm. I said, 'I must remind you that you are again under caution.'

'Yeah.'

'That you don't have to say anything unless you wish to do so.'

'I just want to say one thing. I'm totally innocent of the murder of Rachel Nickell, and all those correspondences with Lizzie James, either by letter or by conversation, are totally from fantasy and imagination, because she told me that's the point when I turned her on. The idea of using knives during sex doesn't do anything for me at all, because what she described in the past, about what she done, I thought turned her on. I thought I could tell her those stories just to turn her on.'

'Colin, is that your explanation?'

It was the only answer he gave throughout the long process of interviewing. I wasn't unhappy at his response because the carefully documented record of everything that had passed between him and Lizzie would show it to be a lie.

'Yeah, and other than that I'm not gonna answer any more questions.'

'Can I tell you that the first mention of a knife came in a letter that you gave to Lizzie James, and prior to that stage no mention had been made by her about knives?'

'No comment.'

Martin said, 'Why don't you feel that we can explore that? Let's just explore that, the knife aspect of things?'

'No comment.'

'Do you not agree with what the Inspector's just told you? The first mention of the knife came from you?'

'No comment.'

'You told her that you always carried knives?'

'No comment.'

'Did you tell her that?'

'No comment.'

In growing frustration, I resisted the urge to scratch my ear for as long as possible. But in the end, I bowed to the inevitable and set the wheels in motion for the confrontation.

I heard the door close in the next office and the sound of Lizzie's footsteps as she walked at a very deliberate pace along the corridor. I exchanged a knowing glance with Martin and continued with my questioning. It was difficult to concentrate with half my mind racing ahead to what was about to occur.

I heard the *click, click, click, click* of Lizzie's high heels as she rounded the corner from the corridor and came to a halt outside the interview room door. The sharp knock seemed an age in coming.

Rat, tat, tat. It made me jump.

I looked at Martin, then pulled myself to my feet and walked to the door.

'Would you like to come in?' I said. 'Would you like to introduce yourself formally? I've just been talking to Mr Stagg. I would like you to explain to him the conversations you've had concerning his presence and whereabouts on the common, and details of injuries that he has discussed with you.'

I returned to my chair; Lizzie entered and sat down in the seat which Martin had just vacated.

I watched the faces of Ryan and Colin as she settled herself down and, as cool as a cucumber, began her introduction. Mr Ryan appeared more surprised than Colin. Colin just remained passive and stared ahead with a frightening look in his eyes.

'Yes, I am a serving police officer. For the purpose of this interview I am known as Lizzie James. Lizzie James is not my real name, it's a name I use to protect my identity when dealing with matters of this nature. Colin, we've met four times before in Hyde Park. On the last occasion, you described to me injuries that you said the police had shown you in a photograph of Rachel Nickell's body. Do you remember that?'

Ian Ryan said, 'Colin, can I say at this stage that, obviously, neither of us were aware that this police officer would be brought into the interview. It does obviously change the position somewhat; if you feel that you need to break the interview again, given the very serious nature of the allegations against you, then certainly we can ask the officer to do that and I can give you further advice before we proceed any further.'

'Yeah.'

'Yes what?'

'Yeah, I wanna see you.'

I said, 'I would like to say that you are entitled to a break, but I would like you to listen further to what Lizzie James has got to say, so perhaps you can seek full legal advice.'

Stagg elected to carry on. Lizzie went through her evidence about the various descriptions Colin had given her of the condition of Rachel's body and that he'd said that he had lied to the police.

She referred to the fact that Colin had been the first to introduce the subject of knives.

'No comment.'

She read him the letter he'd given her as she got into the taxi after the first meeting in Hyde Park.

'No comment.'

She confronted him with the business about when he was lying on the grass in Hyde Park, demonstrating the position of the body. 'Do you remember, Colin,' she said, making a circle with her thumb and forefinger, 'when you said she was gaping wide open, looking like this?'

At every twist and turn, he said, 'No comment.'

I said, 'Colin, I was listening to what Lizzie James has just said. I shall ask you, why do you feel that way about women? The similarities between what you have described there, and what happened to Rachel Nickell, are quite striking. I must put it to you ...'

'No comment.'

'... that on 15 July 1992, on Wimbledon Common, you murdered Rachel Nickell, causing her death by multiple stab wounds.'

'No comment.'

'Right, unless you've got anything further to say?'

Lizzie said, 'Isn't there anything you want to say to me, Colin? It'll be your last opportunity.'

'No comment.'

The interview terminated at 6.49pm.

Much later that night, when I finally left the station and started driving home, I listened on the radio to Andrew Nickell's dignified and reasoned response to the news of Stagg's arrest.

From the family home in Buckinghamshire Mr Nickell said, 'We have always been optimistic that someone would be found for Rachel's death. The only thing that we would want is that this time the police will have clear evidence that someone was guilty. My wife and I believe in the English system of justice and we hope the person who is arrested has a fair trial. And if he is found guilty, we hope the judge will make an appropriate sentence which, as far as we are concerned, is that he should stay in prison for the rest of his life.'

Stagg's arrest, the culmination of 13 months' hard work, was cause for more than a few champagne corks popping in the incident room that night, but the mood of celebration only lasted until the national papers arrived next morning.

The *Sun* and the *Daily Mirror* had both revealed details of the UC operation involving Lizzie James. Other nationals picked up the line and it was in almost every tabloid on the morning of 19 August.

By and large, the copy was wildly inaccurate, but then, as a tabloid journalist once said to me, why let the facts or the law interfere with a good story? It did, however, contain the basics; it was very simplistic and was run largely on the 'WPC dates Rachel man to secure evidence' line. Fortunately, no mention was made of the vital psychological basis for the operation. The one thing that they did get right was the fact that, without exception, the 'WPC' was lauded for her courage. Lizzie was a detective constable, not a police constable, but there was and still is no doubt about her courage or her dedication to duty.

The printing of this material was irresponsible journalism of the worst order. The case was *sub judice* and the only details which may be published in those circumstances are the defendant's name, address, date of birth, and the offence with which he has been charged. The press should not publish any details of evidence, as if this is read by a future juror it could prejudice a fair trial.

More importantly, we all knew that the UC operation was certain to be objected to by Stagg's lawyers very early in the legal proceedings, and might even be ruled as inadmissible at the committal proceedings, when a magistrate would be asked to decide whether or not there was a *prima facie* case to answer. We didn't want potential Old Bailey jurors to be aware of Lizzie's involvement in case it was never presented as part of the prosecution evidence. They might read about it now, and when the case came up for trial, say, 'Where is it? What's happened to such an important slice of prosecution evidence?' The jury might end up making their decision based not upon the legally sanitised evidence presented in court, but upon the full evidence that was reported in the newspapers.

Mick and I were furious at this turn of events. So were Stagg's solicitors. Mr Ryan complained that we were behind the leak, but it was ridiculous to suggest that anyone on the inquiry would have done anything to jeopardise the prosecution. These boys and girls were dedicated and had worked many hundreds of hours' unpaid overtime.

Over the next day or two, the animosity between press and police over the Nickell inquiry reached a new intensity. The Attorney General issued writs against four daily newspapers, alleging contempt, and Scotland Yard's Complaints Investigation Branch were instructed to launch an inquiry to find out who had leaked the Lizzie story to the press. Every officer on the inquiry with knowledge of the covert operation was questioned by the CIB in an attempt to identify the source of the leak.

The information must have come from somewhere, but my view was that it couldn't have come from a source too close to home because of the inaccuracies. For one fleeting, dark moment I even considered that Colin's solicitors might have leaked it in an attempt to sabotage our case, though I didn't seriously harbour these thoughts for long.

Mick and I were speculating on the possible source when we remembered that Roy Ramm and Neil Giles had visited us about midway through the operation and had given us some disturbing news. Mr Ramm told us that he had a friend and close neighbour who was a reporter for one of the nationals. One Sunday morning, this reporter turned up at Roy Ramm's house to borrow some tools, and in the general course of conversation he brought up the subject of the Nickell inquiry. Almost as an aside, he asked how the UC operation was progressing. Roy Ramm blanked him but it was a worrying event. We discussed the implications at the time, coming to the conclusion that either we had a leak somewhere within the organisation, or this experienced reporter was on a fishing expedition. Our thinking ended up somewhere between the two; obviously this man had heard a whisper, but judging from the inaccuracies in the eventual stories, the source had not been in a position to give chapter and verse on the situation. Nevertheless, it left a nasty taste in our mouths.

A few days later, Mick and I popped into a pub near the Old Bailey for a spot of lunch before heading back to Wimbledon. As we settled down by the bar, Wickerson pointed to one of our fellow customers.

'That's Mike Sullivan from the *Sun*, the bloke who broke the UC story – I'm going to have a few words in his ear ...'

I could see that Mick was angry. 'Don't do anything silly, Mick,' I cautioned.

'I'm only going to tell him what I think of him.'

Mick was off round the bar like a long dog. Judging by the glint in his eyes, I decided that I had better go after him to prevent things getting out of hand. I put down my pint and followed in his wake through the crowded bar.

'Oi – I want a word with you!' I heard him shout.

The subject of his attention, looking somewhat alarmed, turned to face him.

'Sorry?'

'Yeah, you will be!' Wickerson growled.

I winced. I could see this turning ugly.

'What the hell did you think you were playing at, printing that story about the undercover operation in the Stagg case?' Wickerson lambasted the man. 'You could have buggered up the whole job!'

'I didn't the man stammered as Wickerson glowered at him.

'Don't give me that – you're Mike Sullivan!'

'No, I'm not. I work for the *Sun* but you've got the wrong reporter. However, I can see your point.'

The entire matter was resolved over a couple of pints and the incident forgotten about. Until, that is, a few weeks later when Mick took a call from Carol Benewell, our press officer. He was informed that there was a story circulating Fleet Street that he had grabbed Mike Sullivan by the lapels and threatened him with physical violence.

Chapter 36

Colin Stagg appeared at Wimbledon Magistrates' Court on 18 August, looking unshaven and wearing a scruffy black T-shirt and blue jeans. Flanked by two police officers, he bit his lip nervously as he listened to the charge being read:

'... that you did, on July 15 1992, murder Rachel Nickell on Wimbledon Common.'

The accused is not invited to tender a plea at this early stage and, after the briefest of hearings, the magistrate remanded him in custody for 28 days.

Outside the court, an angry crowd had gathered to see Stagg leave, but he was kept in the court cells for several hours and most people had drifted away by the time he eventually emerged in a prison van to be driven to Wandsworth Prison.

Ten days later, Mick Wickerson and I were asked to attend Tolworth Towers to meet Bruce Butler, a CPS special casework lawyer. Such was the complexity of this case, we'd been told, that the CPS felt that the services of the special casework section would be essential.

I was looking forward to meeting the former policeman turned barrister, feeling that here was a man who could look at our problems with the benefit of both legal and investigative expertise.

We were ushered into a large airy room on the 17th floor, with plush blue carpet and photographs of yachts on the walls – pictures, we were later to discover, of Bruce Butler's own vessel. The huge window which covered the entire back wall afforded a panoramic view of the A3 and the surrounding Surrey countryside. The most impressive feature, however, was a leather-topped desk that would have been large enough to play football on, had it not been piled high with statements and correspondence pertaining to our job.

Bruce Butler came into his office. He was of indeterminate age, somewhere between 35 and 45. He had shoulder-length, straight, black swept-back hair and a neatly trimmed beard. The suit he was wearing was clearly hand-made and expensive.

After an encouragingly enthusiastic greeting, we soon got down to business. 'Perhaps you can clear up a couple of points for me?' he said, settling into his chair. 'I have found it very difficult to get a sense of distance and location from the statements.'

'I must admit we had similar problems at the start of the inquiry,' Wickerson replied. 'The gridded maps helped but a visit to the common is really the only way to get things in perspective.'

'Yes, I think we ought to try and arrange a site visit as a matter of urgency. Now, before I actually get on to the statements, I think I should mention the other, more pressing, needs. First, I would like to arrange a conference with Paul Britton; that needs to be done as a priority. I'll travel to Leicester if necessary.'

Bruce Butler explained that he'd need to show the probity of the covert operation and to explain how it was designed to lead towards the implication or the elimination of the suspect. He explained that the sensitivity and precedent-making nature of the case meant the paperwork had to be perfect and every point covered.

'I'll speak to him later today and get back to you,' I said. 'What did you think of his statement?'

'Absolutely fascinating. I was very taken with the hallmarking concept of the undercover operation.'

'I took the view that the material gained as a result of the covert operation fell into the catagory of similar fact evidence,' I probed hopefully.

'I think that's a distinct possibility, but I need to clarify various points with Mr Britton.'

'I think you'll be extremely impressed by him as a witness. As for any immediate questions you may have concerning the statement, I may be able to shed some light on them.'

'If I've read it correctly, what he's saying is that the killer of Rachel Nickell suffers from a very rare form of sexual deviance, and that as a result of the operation he has hallmarked Colin Stagg as suffering from the same almost unique form of deviance?'

'That's correct.'

'And it was as a result of this condition, if I can call it that, that the killer was motivated to do what he did to Rachel?'

'Again, in simple terms, that's right, but you really do need to hear Paul explain it in order to understand the full picture.'

'You may or may not be able to answer this, but exactly how rare is this condition and can he refer me to any database on which he has drawn?'

'It's not simple. Paul tells me that this specific form of deviance is extremely rare. He won't assign a figure to how many men are likely to suffer from it, but he has demonstrated its rarity by way of bar graph and that's impressive. As for a database, there isn't one in existence at the moment. There's the Catchem database, but that's specifically for child murders and abductions, and there's the sexual assault index, but neither of these was relevant in this case. But Paul is a clinician, and has responsibility as the head of the Trent Regional Psychology Service.'

'Yes, I am anxious to establish fully his credentials as an expert witness.'

'He has responsibility for an area that's the second-largest health area in the country, and has within its boundaries a population of about five million. Paul is the head of that area's psychology service, and in the ten years or so that he has held that position, he cannot recall a single case where he has encountered this very specific form of sexually-deviant, personality-based disturbance.'

'Would Mr Britton necessarily be made aware of any person being treated for, or coming to notice with, this condition?'

'He says that he would be aware. He is a consultant psychologist and as the head of the regional service he has responsibility to supervise such cases.'

'So in approximate terms, his area serves about a twelfth of the UK population?'

'I don't know what conclusions a statistician would come up with, but to my untrained eye it shows that we're not dealing with an everyday condition. The other thing he said to demonstrate the rarity was that he would describe the probability of two men suffering from this condition being on the common at the time of the murder as "vanishingly small".'

Bruce Butler's ear pricked up at my last statement. 'Vanishingly small – I like the sound of that.' He made a note on his jotter.

The meeting went on for a couple more hours, with Mick and I explaining points that Bruce wanted clarifying. His energy was as boundless as his enthusiasm and very, very welcome; this man was totally enthralled about the whole operation.

'It goes without saying that this case will go to the Treasury team,' he said at length. 'I was thinking that we should brief Nigel Sweeney to lead, and Bill Boyce as junior, but we've got some homework to do before we get to counsel. I want a Rolls-Royce presentation on this one.'

The first counsels' conference was held at the Old Bailey several weeks later, one Friday afternoon in late November.

I was very buoyed up at the prospect of the first conference. Bruce Butler's reaction to the case had been incredibly enthusiastic and supportive. The evidential potential of the UC operation had really taken his imagination. His view was that the material gained as a result of Lizzie's efforts amounted to 'similar fact' evidence, not because it went to show propensity, but because it was pivotal to the issue of identity. In other words, the correspondence hallmarked Colin Stagg and the killer as having the same, almost unique, form of sexually-deviant-based personality disturbance. Colin Stagg was saying, 'I am not the Harriman suspect'; we were saying, 'Yes, you are the Harriman suspect and, yes, the Harriman suspect did kill Rachel Nickell, based upon intelligence that we've gathered; and what's more, what you've been writing is similar fact evidence and goes to prove that you're the Harriman suspect.'

I was delighted, since that was the argument that I had put forward in earlier meetings with the CPS.

Originally, the emphasis of the thrust of the prosecution case was more towards the evidence that Alex might be able to give, but Bruce Butler had taken the view that the material generated, in addition to serving the investigative 'search for the truth' purpose for which the operation had been instigated, also had evidential value. It was accepted that this view was ground-breaking, and the qualified opinion of a CPS solicitor and the unqualified view of a Detective Inspector might not count for much in the great scheme of things.

Against this background, it was with a certain amount of trepidation that I waited outside the Treasury Counsel office at the Central Criminal Court. Bruce, Mick and Roger Lane were also present. Bruce Butler and Wickerson were passing the time by talking about their shared interest in sailing, whilst Roger and I were busily checking that we had brought the relevant schedules and documentation.

Shortly after 4.30pm, the familiar, black-gowned, rather portly, figure of Bill Boyce strode along the corridor. Mr Boyce had, over the years, been involved in a number of my cases, both on the prosecution and defence sides. I knew him to be an eloquent and effective advocate. His mild-mannered demeanour had lulled many an opposition witness, me included, into a false sense of security, before going on to deliver the *coup de grace*. He was quietly spoken, always courteous, and had a mind like a steel trap.

'Apologies for lateness, gentlemen. Mr Pedder, delighted to see you.' He shook my hand and then did the same to the rest. 'If you will bear with me for a little longer whilst I get rid of this,' he indicated his wig and gown, 'Mr Sweeney and I will be with you shortly.' He then disappeared into his office.

Treasury Counsel are very senior and experienced barristers who specialise in prosecuting. They have responsibility for high-profile and difficult cases. There is a rank structure within the Treasury Counsel office. Bill Boyce was going to be our junior and was to be led by Mr Nigel Sweeney.

We were ushered into a conference room. Mr Sweeney greeted us with the words, 'Gentlemen, come in, come in. This is a fascinating case. I shall enjoy this.'

Nigel Sweeney was widely regarded as being the number two senior Treasury Counsel, Mr John Nutting being the number one. Mr Sweeney appeared relatively young to hold such a senior position; it was difficult to put an age to him, but he appeared to be somewhere in the late thirties to early forties bracket. He was tall and of medium build, with red hair, a beard and, like Mr Boyce, he wore glasses.

The meeting was largely concerned with answering Mr Sweeney's questions concerning queries which had arisen during his examination of the case papers – nothing of a particularly unusual or radical nature. Mr Sweeney was anxious to have a conference with Paul Britton; he also wanted to speak to the pathologist, Dr Shepherd. He wanted to see them separately, his view being that the evidence of both of these experts was capable of providing corroboration for each other. 'I believe that, as a matter of urgency, we should arrange a conference with Mr Britton. I appreciate that he is an extremely busy man and it may be difficult for him to come to London, in which case Mr Boyce and I would be prepared to go to him in Leicester.'

This, in itself, was a memorable statement. Yes, Paul Britton was a very busy man, but the same also had to be said of our two eminent counsel. In my 20 years' experience, I had never encountered such a willingness by counsel to make things more convenient for a witness. Within our legal system, counsels' convenience has always seemed to be of paramount importance. I had seen judges stand cases out of the list because to have proceeded would have inconvenienced counsel. On the other hand, I had seen police officers dragged back from their holidays abroad simply because a case has been unexpectedly listed or a development had occurred which required the unforeseen attendance of the officer. I had even heard one particular judge from the Inner London Crown Court say that a police officer's leave could not be allowed to interfere with the smooth running of his court.

So I well remembered the consideration shown by Mr Sweeney. In fact, throughout the time that Mr Sweeney and Mr Boyce had responsibility for the case, I was to be impressed many times by their consideration as well as their expertise.

Wickerson and I came out on cloud nine. We had presented the evidence to two of the country's most eminent lawyers and they'd not laughed us off the stage. They actually liked what we'd done and thought it was a viable prosecution.

'I thought the conference was a major success,' Bruce Butler said. 'I was extremely pleased with the reaction of Nigel Sweeney. Even the reaction to the occasions when Lizzie James overstepped the mark was encouraging.'

'What was it Mr Boyce was saying about possibly having admissibility problems after a certain point?' Wickerson asked.

'He didn't give any precise cut-off point, but to my mind we shouldn't have any problems up to and including EJ35 and possibly not until much later,' Bruce said. 'But even if we lost everything after EJ35 we'd still be in a position to prove our case.'

Chapter 37

When Colin Stagg was arrested, the job was really only just starting. Committal proceedings were due to begin on 18 January 1994, which gave us just 12 weeks in which to make sure that our case was properly and well presented. For example, it was still a problem getting people to understand that when witness so-and-so said something, it was particularly relevant because of the precise location that he was speaking from, and how that fitted in with what other people saw. The answer was to get a helicopter to take aerial photographs and videos, which were spectacularly successful in clearly showing the proximity of the pivotal locations and sightings.

An aggravating factor was the sheer size of the investigation, which meant that the Senior Investigating Officer could not possibly have all the minutiae of every line of enquiry at his fingertips. During the course of the Nickell case, I was obviously aware of every development as and when it occurred, but with the passing of time, the full reasons why certain decisions were taken, or even what those decisions were, tend to fade. Now, if it can be demonstrated by the defence that the SIO is unable to recall details of certain lines of investigation, it gives an impression that the SIO is incompetent, and by implication, that if the SIO is unreliable, then so is the investigation.

I had faced barristers in court who'd say, 'Come, come, Inspector – this was an important line of enquiry and yet you seem unable to recall any of the decision-making processes. Perhaps if I jog your memory?' If this is done in front of a jury, it tends to call into question your ability as an investigator. You can try to explain that in a massive investigation with over 5,000 lines of enquiry, 1,200 statements, 7,000 nominals, and 4,000 messages, it is well nigh impossible to recall every one in precise detail. However, the risks of trying to fight fire with fire are tremendous. If you go too far, the judge invariably censures you; if you are not robust enough, the defence walk all over you. Whatever you do, the barristers always seem to get the last word. My explanation and examples of the sheer enormity of the inquiry would in all likelihood be greeted with the reply, 'Yes, yes, Inspector, and dare we even contemplate what else you've forgotten? Or perhaps never knew in the first place ...'

With any impending trial, however simple or complicated, I had learned that the best way to approach it is to put yourself in the position of the defence. I ask myself two questions: If I were defending this case, what tack would I take? What are the strengths and weaknesses of the prosecution case?

Using this method, I try to anticipate the lines of attack which the defence may use. Having completed this process and identified likely avenues of defence, research can then be put in hand to make sure that I'm up to speed with all the relevant lines of enquiry. However, with a vast database such as was in existence with the Nickell investigation, we were up against it.

The major problem we faced concerned disclosure, the term used to describe the process by which the prosecution have to reveal their entire case and details of the investigation to the defence. Just about every document ever created as a result of a police investigation, with very few exceptions, falls within the parameters of disclosure, and the aim is to ensure that the prosecution are not concealing, whether by design or oversight, information or evidence which may be useful or relevant to an issue which the defence may wish to raise on behalf of the defendant.

In the past, problems had arisen because certain information was not considered relevant by the prosecution and was not made public. But when it subsequently came to the surface, the defence claimed that if only they been made aware of its existence, it would have had a serious bearing on the conduct of the defence case.

Both the Judith Ward terrorist case and the Guinness fraud trial had a far-reaching effect on the procedures which we subsequently had to follow – the argument being that it wasn't for the prosecution to decide what fell into the category of 'relevant'. The trial judge is the final arbiter in cases of dispute as to whether or not the defence are entitled to see a certain document or genre of documents or information.

There are, however, certain categories of information that the police will always resist disclosing. We rely on Public Interest Immunity to protect the identity of informants, reports between police and the CPS, the source of information on which search warrants are obtained, the location of police observation points, and anything that is likely to disclose an unusual or confidential method of surveillance.

The category 'informants' is not limited to paid informers; we will also protect the identity of casual callers who provide us with information. We rely on the support of the public, and their assistance might well cease if, every time they give us information, their details are provided to the defence, and through them to the defendant.

Schedules of every document, piece of information, evidence and anything else generated through the investigation have to be prepared and the judge has to decide what must be disclosed to the defence. In complicated or protracted cases, this can be a vast undertaking, so in order to save a lot of hard work for the judge, what can happen is that documents which contain sensitive information – within the Attorney General's guidelines – are edited so that the sensitive material is removed and the rest of the document is disclosed to the defence. This was the procedure which we adopted in the Nickell case.

For us, disclosure started in about October 1993, and the sheer volume of information and paper work generated made the process a daunting, very complex and prolonged business – first to do the editing, then the actual disclosure process. It was important to ensure that we could prove exactly what had been disclosed to the defence; we didn't want allegations that they hadn't seen a particular document when they had. Binders were therefore prepared, shown to the defence, and then sealed against their signature and stored securely.

We still had arguments as to what was sensitive and what wasn't, and the judge ended up making an order which allowed them access to just about everything apart from a handful of highly confidential reports and dockets.

We were required to reveal the existence of the video cameras trained on the common, for instance and, as a result, I had to beg, borrow and steal four crime squad PCs and give them the unenviable job of wading through and listing movements and times. We had installed the cameras in January, and they ran though to August, producing two tapes per day on each of two cameras. The PCs had to go through and itemise everything because of disclosure, even though the film was in no way part of our evidence. My view was that there was no need to have disclosed that we had the tapes, because it was an unusual form of surveillance and not something that everyone realises that we can do from over half-a-mile away.

Worse than this, we were also forced to hand over the names and address of over 1,000 people who had made statements, which was in breach of normal procedure, whereby only the names are provided.

The majority of calls and information had been from well-intentioned people, some with valuable information. However, there were a small number of persons who for reasons best known to themselves gave false, misleading or downright nonsensical tip-offs. We even had the odd person wanting to confess to the murder. One in particular was most persistent. He was a mental patient and was always telling the various doctors who treated him that he was responsible. He quite clearly wasn't, being over 6ft 5in tall with a shock of bright red hair, and we had no sightings of any such person on our system. Apart from his distinctive appearance, his very odd behaviour would also have made him stand out like a sore thumb. Putting that to one side, when questioned, he was unable to give the right answers to the some of the very probing questions that were asked relating to the pieces of information which had been kept back. He was obviously a very disturbed man but he didn't kill Rachel.

Things like this could cause potential problems were the defence to raise them in court. Questions such as: 'Officer, is it not right that Mr So-and-so admitted to this offence?'

The only answer would have to be, 'Yes.' If they then followed up with, 'And where was Mr So-and-so at the time of the murder?' we would have to say that we didn't know – because in this particular case we were unable to find anyone who could tell us where he was at the relevant time. He wasn't an in-patient at the time, and had no friends or family who could vouch for him. In effect, there was nobody whom we could trace who could shed any light on his whereabouts. The way questions are asked by defence barristers tend not to give officers the opportunity of expanding upon the short, direct answers which the questions require. If you do try to explain, they will attempt to shut you up.

The problem is exaggerated by the fact that the defence have time to plan these ambushes and have no end of raw material to work with, because they have had the advantage of seeing the whole inquiry. Bearing in mind that we work within a system that requires the prosecution to prove their case beyond reasonable doubt, it can sometimes take not too many of these red herrings to blur matters sufficiently to create that small vestige of doubt in the mind of the jurors.

Our usual reason for withholding witnesses' addresses is to

prevent the possibility of them being interfered with. There is, of course, no property in a witness, and provided they are willing, the defence may speak to them. If the defence indicate that they wish to interview a prosecution witness, we would normally arrange a mutually convenient time and place for this to occur, but in this case the defence said that they must have the 1,000-plus names and addresses because they didn't wish to indicate to the prosecution which witnesses they wanted to speak with. They claimed if they did this, it might assist the prosecution in anticipating certain lines of their defence.

This caused considerable anger amongst many of the witnesses, and we were inundated with phone calls from people who had received letters from Stagg's solicitors.

'I understand that you might be reluctant to assist the defence in this particular case,' said one letter from Mr Ryan, 'but I have to say that if you are not prepared to see me voluntarily, then I will have to issue a witness summons to compel your attendance at the Old Bailey on 5 September 1994, to give evidence on behalf of the defence.'

It was a major blow to police public relations, and I found it acutely embarrassing. All these people had done was try to assist the police. As more than one of them said to me, 'That's the last bloody time I help you lot!'

All we could say to placate them was, 'We're terribly sorry, but we had no choice. The judge ordered it. The fact that you've made a statement to the police doesn't exclude the defence from also having the right to speak to you. However, that's only if you agree. If you don't wish to be seen by the defence, you don't have to be.'

It is open for them to get a witness summons, but that is most unlikely because no solicitor would ever call a witness blind – there's a cardinal rule of the courtroom, and that is never ask a question to which you don't already know the answer.

It is a fact that Britain is policed by consent and with the support of the population. There are approximately 100,000 police officers in the UK and they serve a population in excess of 60 million. The simple mathematics support the claim that we are reliant on goodwill. It has become increasingly common, however, that ordinary, law-abiding citizens are progressively reticent to come forward as witnesses. This has nothing to do with failing police popularity, but is simply a case of once-bitten, twice shy. They are quite naturally not keen to repeat the unpleasant experience of attending court, and who can blame them?

The treatment they receive is disgraceful. Once a case is listed, we have to warn them to attend. They duly do as they are asked, causing great inconvenience to their personal and working lives. They are kept waiting for hours whilst the wheels of justice slowly grind into motion and the legal profession go through their machinations. It is a very common occurrence for the defence to find a reason for the case to be adjourned. The witnesses are then sent away until the date of the next hearing. They turn up again and very often the case is again adjourned at the defence's request. It is hard not to wonder whether they're hoping that an important prosecution witness will get fed up and fail to attend.

If a witness has shown determination and public-spiritedness by attending throughout all the defence's delaying tactics, he or she will then have the ordeal of actually getting into the witness box. Once there, they are at the mercy of the defending barrister, who will claim he is only acting on the instructions of his client. The witnesses are very often brow-beaten, belittled, accused of impropriety, perjury and God knows what else. By the time they come out of court, they have really been through it, and wild horses wouldn't drag them back into another court of law. I have seen rape victims reduced to hysterics by the tactics of defence counsel – their lives, conduct, pre-, peri- and post-offence being held up for very public, intimate and disparaging scrutiny. A comment that I'd heard all too frequently from witnesses was: 'I thought it was *me* on trial in there.' You can only apologise and hope that these unpleasant events will not prevent them from doing their public duty or reporting offences in the future. The truth is that it does and, again, who can blame them?

A third counsel, Simon Dennison, had to be appointed with the specific brief of dealing with the issues of disclosure. The case was extremely important and high-profile, and we had defence solicitors and barristers with free and open access to the police station, and there needed to be some sort of liaison and co-ordination.

Simon, son of a very famous judge, Neil Dennison, understood the full legal requirements far better than any police officer and could argue on equal terms with the defence. He was very robust in his attitude and stood for no nonsense. That wasn't to say he was closed-minded; he was always prepared to listen to reason and, without fail, consulted either me or Mick before making his recommendations.

Simon was somewhere in his early thirties, with a ready wit and an easy manner. Well liked and respected by us all, he very quickly fitted in to the daily routine of the incident room and was accepted almost as an honorary detective. Convention dictates, however, that there exists a degree of formality in the way that police officers and the legal profession address each other. Despite the first name terms that we were on in the confines of the office, the team always reverted to the more formal 'Mr Dennison' or 'Sir' whenever the situation called for it.

Over the following weeks, Mick, Simon and I started having more and more conferences with Bruce Butler and Treasury Counsel. Many of these meetings were also attended by Paul, travelling down from Leicester entirely unpaid and at his own expense.

As the date of the committal got nearer, I would be on the phone to Bruce first thing in the morning; during the day we would exchange two or three more phone calls; and every other day we would be in conference. I would come away from each conference with a briefing note that listed about 40 things that needed doing. I would go away and do those, come back and have another conference, and there would be another 40 things that needed doing as a result of requests that the defence had made, and queries that counsel had made. It was all a matter of dotting 'I's and crossing 'T's, and making sure that we were up to speed and match-fit for the onslaught we fully expected.

Chapter 38

The committal hearing for Colin Stagg was due to begin on 18 January. The CPS lawyers, based on counsels' advice, had by now made the decision to rely not only on Lizzie James's evidence, but also on the probative value of Paul's evidence in relation to the extremely rare sexual deviation that he expected to find in the killer of Rachel Nickell.

Neither offender profiling nor forensic psychology had been used in evidence in a British courtroom before. Enquiries of the Dutch CRI (their equivalent of our Crime Faculty or the FBI) had revealed that offender profiling was used extensively in the Netherlands, but purely as an investigative tool for the purposes of suspect acquisition and the linking of serial offences. Enquiries with the FBI at Quantico, Virginia, however, had revealed a rich source of cases where offender-profiling evidence had been given before American courts. The CPS were keen to have first-hand views on what obstacles they had faced, and whether any of the cases were comparable.

At a counsels' conference on 14 December, Nigel Sweeney and

Bruce Butler requested that Paul and I fly to the United States to ensure that Paul was aware of the latest developments in the field of offender profiling, and also for me to research the legal precedents for the admissibility of psychological evidence. Bruce Butler also asked us to look at the differences between offender-profiling techniques in the USA and Britain. He wanted us to be sure that we were up to date with the American methodology and would be able to compare it with work done in Britain, should the need arise.

A research trip to the FBI Academy at Quantico, Virginia, was arranged very quickly. I called the legal attache at the American embassy in London and was given the direct line phone number for John Douglas, the head of the FBI's Behavioural Science Unit. Nothing appeared to be too much trouble for this man. Despite the fact that the academy would be closed over the Christmas period, he made arrangements for our accommodation and shaped up meetings with the people we hoped to speak with, all senior or supervisory special agents. One of them, Roy Hazlewood, had been a founding father of the BSU along with John Douglas and Robert Ressler, but as bad luck would have it, he was due to retire before Christmas. When he heard we were coming, however, he immediately made himself available.

On 26 December 1993, Paul and I flew out to Washington. It was the first time I had seen him since the counsels' conference, and we spent the first part of the flight discussing Bruce Butler's lengthy brief:

1. *To ensure that we were aware of the latest developments in the field of offender profiling.*
2. *To discuss specific aspects of offender-profiling and its application as formal evidence in prosecution cases, with particular reference to identifying areas of the subject which may be the focus of defence attacks and the manner in which such attacks may be rebutted.*
3. *To collate details of investigations which have successfully employed psychological offender profiling as an investigative*

tool for suspect acquisition and also as evidence of identity in subsequent legal proceedings.

4. *To identify those cases of relevance to the Nickell inquiry and to obtain case reports and transcripts of judgments.*
5. *To identify the relevant prosecutions and psychologists and liaise with same.*
6. *To obtain legal journals, available software and other relevant source material for counsels' information.*
7. *To visit the Delaware State Prosecutions Officer to discuss and obtain details of the investigation and prosecution of the case Delaware v Steven Pennell 1989, a case already identified as being of particular relevance.*
8. *To establish a central point of reference within the FBI to facilitate further contact for the purposes of pre-trial counsels' conferences with those potential witnesses identified as a result of this research visit.*

Once we had allocated responsibilities between ourselves, the conversation drifted over various aspects of offender profiling. I told Paul how, from my sceptical beginnings, I had become a staunch proponent after seeing the nearness of the fit between his original profile of Rachel's killer and that of Colin Stagg. I asked him if he could assign a probability value to the fact that the killer would re-offend in a manner that would lead to the death of another woman. 'Eighty-five to ninety per cent,' he said. However, he was unable to attach a time-scale to this assessment.

I wanted to know as much as Paul was able to tell me about his field of work.

Modern offender profiling, he said, had its beginnings in America in the 1950s. A man dubbed the 'Mad Bomber' had been terrorising New York City for more than a decade, sending threatening letters to newspapers, then following up by planting bombs.

The FBI invited psychiatrist James Brussel to study the evidence, including crime scenes, messages from the bomber and other information. As a result of his study, Brussel was able to tell them to look for a middle-aged, unmarried, Roman Catholic immigrant from Eastern Europe, who lived with his mother in a city in Connecticut. Brussel predicted that the target would be fastidiously neat, would hate his father, and would wear a double-breasted suit.

When arrested, so went the folklore, George Metsky had been an almost perfect fit with his profile, even down to the suit. The only item that did not tally was the fact that he lived, not with his mother, but with his unmarried sisters.

When the FBI asked how he had managed to be so accurate, Brussel explained that in his work he normally examined people and tried to predict how they would react in the future. All he had done was reverse the process, and by looking at the reactions, tried to work backwards to what sort of person would have behaved in that way.

Paul said that psychological profiling had not been widely used in the States during the rest of the 1950s and '60s, but had picked up again when murder rates soared in the '70s and a growing number of killings were found to have been committed by strangers. When the FBI opened its new academy at Quantico, Virginia in the 1970s, it included the Behavioural Sciences Unit. Its officers, mainly involved with teaching, occasionally analysed violent crimes and 'profiled' likely suspects.

None of the FBI personnel were trained psychologists, relying instead on their detective expertise and knowledge of past cases. Within a decade, however, this behavioural approach to crime had led to the establishment of NCAVC, the FBI's National Centre for the Analysis of Violent Crime, and VICAP, the Violent Criminal Apprehension Program, a reporting system in which crimes are summarised in a 16- page questionnaire filled out by homicide detectives. The initial aim of the scheme had been to link unsolved murders right across the country, but it soon became a vital tool in offender profiling as well. It was found that details gathered by local police officers could be used to classify crimes into broad categories, and draw up offender profiles. Much of this work had now been computerised, Paul said, but profiling still relied heavily on a 'brainstorming' approach by experienced FBI agents, underpinned by psychological research. Their success rates compared favourably with those found anywhere in the world.

We hired a car and drove through heavy snow to Quantico. Pulling up outside the entrance, we looked in awe at the enormous glass frontage. The reception area was massive and high-ceilinged, like the interior of a grand hotel. A moving LCD notice board above the desk welcomed us by name, as did the very helpful young lady behind the desk. I could just imagine the reciprocal scene were a group of Americans to turn up at the Police College at Hendon: 'You're who? Sorry, don't know anything about it, mate.'

It snowed heavily the next day, and we were told that the Academy was set to remain closed until it cleared. I expected this to be a major setback to our research, but an hour later a snow-covered Judson Ray appeared. Paul had met him once before, when the American spent a six-month fellowship in the UK at the Bramshill Police Training College. Paul had told me Jud was a fascinating man. Apparently, he had spent 11 years working for a New York homicide division and had once been the victim of a contract hit. He'd survived with three bullets inside him. Before that, as a member of special forces during the Vietnam war, he spent many months behind enemy lines monitoring Viet Cong activity, and was the only one of his platoon to survive. A very brave man indeed – even braver considering that Jud was an African-American and would have stuck out like a sore thumb.

Jud led us to the Behavioural Science Unit, three storeys underground in what was originally designed as a fall-out shelter in less stable political times. We were introduced to Roy Hazelwood, Greg Cooper and Janna Monroe, the latter having the distinction of being the only female profiler at Quantico. Over the years, a number of female agents had joined, but it seemed that only Janna had stayed.

Paul and I felt this conference was going to be of crucial importance, for it would be the first time that Paul's analysis of the murder and conception of the principles behind the covert operation were critically examined by an independent group of experts. On a more personal level, the prospect of having the opportunity to discuss 'my' investigation with the people who had pioneered profiling was exciting to say the least.

The FBI agents obviously knew that we were part of a team investigating a murder in the UK, but up until that morning they hadn't been fully aware of the exact details or the precise purpose of our visit. General offender profiling is used for suspect acquisition in the States, and they thought we were merely after some assistance with a particularly difficult investigation.

Paul and I had decided to give a presentation of the offence and the subsequent investigation. I spoke for two hours, detailing the police action at the scene, the investigative processes which followed and the salient forensic and witness evidence which resulted. I then chronicled the sequence of events which led up to the first arrest of our suspect and what we had found at his address, and the dilemma which our suspect had posed us.

At this stage, Paul Britton took over and outlined his profile, the offender's sexual fantasy analysis and the basis upon which we had begun the covert operation. He itemised the correspondence, the meetings and conversations.

At one point, Roy Hazelwood interrupted, 'Oh, this is a disorganised killer.'

This is one of the categories the FBI uses to differentiate offenders – 'disorganised' referring to crime scenes that show evidence of impulsive, violent acts with little evidence of forward planning or attempts to avoid discovery or detection. In fact, you very rarely find a totally disorganised or totally organised killing; you find them somewhere on a sliding scale between the two. Based upon where they are on that scale, you then make certain assumptions based upon your knowledge and your expertise as to what sort of personality you are looking for.

Paul picked up on Roy's comment and went over how Rachel had been acquired and controlled, the manner in which her body had been displayed and how quickly and effectively her killer had disappeared from the scene, leaving few clues behind. 'These aren't the classic signs of what you refer to as a "disorganised" offender,' he said, and Roy demurred.

The reaction of our American colleagues was enthusiastic to say the least. The idea of a proactive psychological operation as an exculpatory or inculpatory investigative solution really seized their imaginations. Roy Hazlewood seemed particularly impressed and prepared his own profile as a result. Interestingly, it was more or less identical to Paul Britton's.

In the end, we spent the best part of a day going over the case, with the meeting becoming more of a forum for swapping knowledge. Paul Britton's record spoke for itself. His successes were numerous and included some very high-profile investigations – Michael Samms, Jamie Bulger and Abbie Humphries, amongst others. His reputation had preceded him and the FBI were keen to share information. We tapped into the enormous experience of these investigators and detectives, while they were fascinated by the psychological principles that underpinned his work.

We discovered that the Americans were developing two separate strands of profiling. The first was computer-based, and effectively a number-crunching exercise. Under this system, the details of hundreds of previous crimes are carefully catalogued and categorised within the computer database, and can then be compared with the features of any new crime. This can indicate whether the new offence is linked to any other cases in the database, and could help keep track of serial offenders.

The second strand dealt with the development of individual profiles that are rooted more in the psychology of the criminal and his crime. FBI agents studied particular cases and drew up profiles using not only their own personal, sharp-end experience as investigators, but also theoretical knowledge gained from lectures and courses run by psychologists and law enforcement professionals acknowledged to have a special expertise in this area.

The work being done by Greg Cooper *et al* on VICAP was of particular interest to me. VICAP is a national data information centre, whose origins can be traced back to an idea of an LAPD officer named Pierce R Brooks in 1958. The system is designed to collect, collate and analyse specific crimes of violence.

There are three main criteria for offences to be accepted by VICAP:

(1) Solved or unsolved homicides or attempts, especially those

that involve an abduction; are apparently random, motiveless, or sexually orientated; or are known or suspected to be part of a series.

(2) Missing persons, where the circumstances indicate a strong possibility of foul play and the victim is still missing.

(3) Unidentified dead bodies where the manner of death is known or suspected to be homicide.

Rape, child sexual abuse and arson are also included. In a nutshell, this system enables the VICAP staff to determine whether similar pattern characteristics exist among the individual cases. This is achieved by analysing MO, victimology, physical evidence, suspect description and suspect behaviour exhibited before, during and after the crime. The VICAP form is a lengthy document which contains 179 questions to be completed by the investigating officer. The goal of VICAP is to provide all law enforcement agencies reporting similar pattern violent crimes with the information necessary to initiate a co-ordinated, multi-agency investigation which will lead to the expeditious identification and apprehension of the offender responsible for the crimes. We had similar parochial facilities in Britain, but nothing quite as sophisticated as VICAP on a national basis.

Paul said that, in Britain, some schools of offender and psychological profiling used the number-crunching approach developed by the FBI for linking crimes, essentially relying upon an arithmetical series of results.

These percentages, based on convictions in earlier cases, are then used to support conclusions about a wanted sex killer's most likely age, education, criminal history and so on.

However, Paul said, if this is all that an offender profile is based upon, then what about the percentage of serial sexual murderers who don't fit into the criteria? Paul stressed that as a psychologist, he viewed each case as being unique. There was no theoretical reason why a crime must fit into clear-cut boundaries, any more than the criminal who committed it. Unless there is something else at the crime scene to support such findings, Paul thought it could be very dangerous to make judgements based solely on conviction rates and past crimes that have no specific connection with what you are investigating.

The FBI approach to generating individual profiles is well tailored for a huge country with a high level of diverse and violent crime. However, it has proved difficult to transfer it to Europe without adaptation, as the Dutch discovered when they chose the FBI system of categorising sexual crimes and then found that 90 per cent of their rapes, when profiled, fitted into just one FBI category. This clearly made offender differentiation – the point of the entire exercise – extremely difficult.

In the days that followed, we spent several hours in discussion with John Douglas, the head of the Investigative Support Unit, in an office that was filled with souvenirs and memorabilia. Apart from photographs of him with the incumbent and former presidents of the USA, there was a framed and signed cinema poster for the film *Silence of the Lambs*, shot partly on location at Quantico. It was on Douglas that the supervisory special agent in the film had been based.

We were allowed access to FBI homicide files and were given presentations by the various arms of the National Centre for the Analysis of Violent Crime. Their entire system was opened to us and we spent many fascinating but extremely long days researching the invaluable work being done by these dedicated men.

In addition to the case studies, we were allowed access to the magnificent facilities of the Quantico law library. I found many cases where offender profiling had been used to achieve good results. There was a case of Franklin where they actually used the offender profiler's analysis of the crime scene to prove that the offender and the victim were known to each other and that it was a first-time offence – and also to prove that it was an organised and planned crime, and to rebut any allegation that it was a robbery that went wrong. I wasn't quite sure what lawyers would make of it in Britain, but it seemed to me a very valuable tool.

Some of the assessments made by the FBI agents with regard to suspects that they had dealt with have been absolutely astounding. There was one particular occasion where they turned around and said, 'The person that was responsible for this crime will drive a Ford Bronco and it will be black.' I couldn't imagine how they knew that, and even Paul raised an eyebrow. But sure enough, when they got the suspect, he was driving a black Ford Bronco.

Sometimes, they appeared to make quantum leaps of judgement, and they did it in very absolute terms. They had a tendency to use words such as 'always' and 'never', and that was something that I didn't feel very comfortable with. But having said that, there was no denying that they enjoyed enormous success with their methods.

I learned that 'signature' is the term used to describe behaviour of an offender which is unique to him. It has been used to establish the identity of an offender and to link crimes. It differs from an MO, which is defined as being behaviour that is necessary to commit the primary intent offence, to protect the offender's anonymity and to enable him to escape. This is a dynamic thing, it is learned behaviour, and the MO will be refined as the offender becomes more experienced in the commission of his crimes.

The signature, however, is a static thing. It can be best described as what the perpetrator has to do to fulfil himself. The signature is behaviour that is over and above that which is required for a succesful MO. John Douglas, in his book *MindHunter*, wrote:

> *The difference between MO and Signature can be subtle. Take the case of a bank robber in Texas who made all his captives undress, posed them in sexual positions, and took photographs of them. That was his signature. It was not necessary or helpful to the commission of the bank robbery. In fact, it kept him there longer and therefore placed him in greater jeopardy of being caught. Yet it was something he clearly felt a need to do.*
>
> *Then there was the bank robber in Grand Rapids, Michigan. I flew out to provide an on-site consultation. This guy also made everyone in the bank undress, but he didn't take pictures. He did it so the witnesses would be so preoccupied and embarrassed that they wouldn't be looking at him and so couldn't make a positive ID later on. This was a means toward successfully robbing the bank. This was MO.*

I was pointed to some 17 occasions in the United States when criminal courts of first instance had admitted similar evidence to ours at the behest of the prosecutor in proof of identity. Prominent amongst the 17 cases was that of the State of Delaware v Stephen B. Pennell. Pennell, known as the 'I-40 Killer' (Interstate 40), was arrested, charged with and tried for the torture and killing of a number of women whom he had picked up in his specially equipped van.

John Douglas noted:

> *At Pennell's trial, I was called in to testify about the signature aspects of the case. The defense was trying to show that it was unlikely these crimes were all committed by the same individual because so many details of the modus operandi varied. I made it clear that, regardless of the MO, the common denominator in each of the murders was physical, sexual and emotional torture. In some cases, the murderer had used pliers to squeeze his victims' breasts and cut their nipples. He had bound others at the wrists and ankles, cut them on the legs, whipped or beaten their buttocks, or hit them with a hammer. So, though the methods of torture varied – the MO, if you will – the signature was the pleasure he received out of inflicting pain and hearing his victims' anguished screams. This wasn't necessary to accomplish the murder. It was necessary for him to get what he wanted out of the crime.*
>
> *Even if Steven Pennell were still alive and reading this, he would not be able to change his behaviour in future crime. He might be able to devise different or more ingenious methods of torturing women. But he would not be able to refrain from the torture itself. Fortunately for all of us, as I mentioned, the State of Delaware had the good judgment and decency to execute Pennell by lethal injection on the 14th of March 1992.*

The parallels between the signature analysis in the Pennell case and that evidence which was going to be proffered by the prosecution to establish identity in the Stagg case were there to be drawn. Paul Britton's analysis of the killer's sexual dysfunction and the importance that the killer attached to certain acts committed on that fateful July morning seemed to take the behaviour of Rachel's murderer into the category of what the Americans called signature. In fairness, it had to be said that when criminal courts of first instance had admitted evidence of this kind, their decisions had sometimes been overturned on appeal. The case of Pennell, however, was an extreme example that the US appeal system had not overturned all of the 17 cases.

The visit to Quantico had been an unqualified success and we were returning with documentation on cases where offender profiling and forensic psychology had been successful in American courts. Our mission had been to pick the FBI's brains, but the Americans, in their turn, recognised that Paul Britton was the leading exponent in the field of British profiling and he had knowledge and experience which they would find invaluable. Clearly, there was a great deal we could learn from each other and we had ended up discussing how we might work together in the future, perhaps on an exchange basis. John Douglas had discussed with Paul the possibility of setting up a two-centre exchange programme, one half being at Quantico and the other at Leicester.

Shortly after my return to the UK, I received an invitation. The first ever VICAP crime analysis training course was due to be held at Quantico between 28 February and 18 March 1994. The FBI invited me to attend the course, and offered to pay all expenses involving travel and accommodation. As if that was not enough, they also asked that I should give presentations to the course on the role of the crime analyst in British law enforcement and also on the Nickell case. It was a tremendous honour, but one which I was unfortunately unable to accept, since the Nickell case would be *sub judice* until after the trial.

As we flew back to the UK on 6 January, we felt assured that the FBI profilers had independently agreed with Paul's conclusions about the case, and Paul believed we had ample evidence of the

American legal experience with using offender profiling in a courtroom setting. However, it had to be said that it had never been used alone as proof of identity, but rather as a piece of evidence in the chain.

Chapter 39

Within the criminal law, there are three categories of offences – Summary, Indictable and Either Way – depending on the mode of trial.

Summary offences may only be tried in a magistrates' court, either by a stipendary magistrate or a bench of Justices of the Peace – the former being a qualified legal practitioner; the latter, lay-persons who are guided on points of law by a qualified clerk of the court.

Indictable offences can only be tried in the Crown Court by a judge and jury.

Either Way offences may be heard at either court. The defendant has to agree to be tried summarily if the magistrate decides that the case is suitable for summary trial. Amongst the deciding factors are the degree of seriousness of the offence and the limitations on the penalties that the lower court may impose. If, after a summary trial, it is discovered that the defendant has a bad antecedent record, the magistrate may commit him to the Crown Court for sentencing if it is believed that the lower court has insufficient powers to impose a suitable sentence.

Murder is an offence at Common Law and is clearly an indictable offence. Once a person is charged with murder, he or she will appear before a magistrates' court. The purpose of this initial appearance is for the defendant to be remanded in custody whilst preparations are made for committal proceedings. Committal is one of the processes for moving a case from the lower court to the Crown court. There are other ways of achieving this, such as Voluntary Bills of Indictment or a Notice of Transfer, but committal is the usual method. The role of the magistrates is not to decide whether the defendant is guilty beyond reasonable doubt; the test is whether there is *prima facie* evidence that there is a case to answer – or to put it another way, whether a jury might on reasonable grounds find the accused guilty.

The most common method of committal is the new-style Section 6(2) of the 1980 Magistrates' Court Act. This involves the service of statements on the defence who have accepted that there is a *prima facie* case. This is a committal by consent of the defence and the evidence is not examined or tested until the Crown court hearing.

The other method is known as an old-style committal or a section 6(1) committal. This can take the form of solely verbal evidence being given live or a mixture of live evidence and some statements being read. At an Old-Style, the evidence is tested and legal arguments may be presented.

It is open for the defence to present arguments that there is no case to answer and, if the magistrate agrees, the case can be dismissed there and then.

Colin Stagg's lawyers had opted to put their case to the test by asking for a full old-style committal hearing at which the prosecution evidence could be fully exposed and challenged before a magistrate was asked to make a decision on whether Stagg should face trial at the Central Criminal Court. We presumed they wanted the prosecution witnesses in court so that they could face cross-examination, particularly key ones like Paul Britton and Lizzie James. We guessed that defence barrister Jim Sturman intended to submit that their evidence was inadmissible and that there was no case to answer.

Stagg, wearing a grey sweatshirt with a black collar, was escorted into the dock of Wimbledon's brand-new Magistrates' Court by a prison officer on the morning of 17 February 1994. The proceedings were to be heard by stipendary magistrate Terry English, a trained lawyer and a full-time magistrate who adjudicated hundreds of cases a year. It was his job to decide if the Crown had established a *prima facie* case for murder against Colin Stagg and, if so, to commit the defendant for trial by jury.

I hadn't seen Colin for a long time and was struck by the dramatic change in his appearance. The closely-cropped hairstyle had given way to a cut that made him look almost like a schoolboy, and he'd also lost the muscle bulk built up in his home-made gym. I remembered him as stocky and burly, but he looked tiny as he stood in the dock.

The press seats were overflowing. Stagg's mother and stepfather nodded at him from the equally packed public gallery, as did several residents from the Alton Estate. Amongst them sat Colin's new girlfriend, Diane Rooney, who had apparently befriended Stagg after his arrest and visited him regularly in his remand cell at Wandsworth Prison.

Mr English began the committal by ruling that the proceedings should not be reported by the press, other than the basic details permitted by law – name, age, address and the charge faced. He also said that no photographs of Colin Stagg should appear in newspapers or on television during the hearing or prior to any trial that might result.

Bill Boyce stood up and, supported by seven manuals of evidence containing the statements of two dozen witnesses, he began to outline Rachel's final movements on the morning of 15 July 1992.

Boyce said that Rachel had left her flat in Balham at about 9.15am, driven to Wimbledon Common for one of her regular walks with Alex and Molly, and parked her car by the windmill. They then strolled through the park, enjoying the summer sunshine. It was, he said, the 'playful, slow walk' of a mother and son 'at peace with the world'.

The early witnesses for the Crown were people who had been on Wimbledon Common at the time of the murder. One woman and her husband remarked how 'stunning' she looked, with her hair pinned up, holding the hand of a little boy they said was 'dark-haired and cute'. Mr Adrian Lister, himself a regular visitor to the common, said, 'She looked so happy, tossing her hair and laughing. I smiled at her and she smiled back.' He leaned on his car as he turned to watch them disappearing across the grass.

Rachel was last seen alive at 10.20am, Boyce said, as clearly remembered by a reliable witness, Mr Roger McKern. Her body was found exactly 15 minutes later, at 10.35am.

Stagg, said Mr Boyce in his calm, unemotional voice, had been arrested on suspicion of murdering Rachel once before but had denied any involvement, saying that he had left the common before the murder and had gone home to sleep. The Crown, he said, was in a position to discredit this alibi. He would also call evidence from the psychologist, Paul Britton, and undercover policewoman, Lizzie James, which suggested that Stagg had a sexually-deviant personality disorder exactly matching those characteristics shown by the killer of Rachel Nickell.

Stagg's claim that he was back home by 8.30am and safely asleep on his sofa on the morning of the murder was refuted by Susan Gale, the first witness to be called. As she had told us in her statement, she said she clearly remembered seeing him, with his dog Brandy, at around 9.00am that day. She'd left home herself at about 8.50am for a shorter than usual walk on the common with her two dogs.

'My mother-in-law was staying with me at that time,' she said. 'I was going to drive her home to collect her pension that morning. I wanted to be back between half-nine and ten to do that.'

Mrs Gale had spotted Stagg near the A3 underpass, on Jerry's Hill, as she returned home. 'He was coming as if from the underpass. The path he was on went towards the windmill. I believe he waved as if to say he'd seen me.' They always grabbed their dogs, she said, in case a fight started. She had known Stagg for nine years and recognised his distinctive walk. He was wearing some sort of bag around his waist – a black 'bum bag' she thought, about 9in long and about 7in deep. He was also wearing 'a white T-shirt on the top half of his body. I don't think it had any sleeves. I think he'd been wearing a white T-shirt for a few days ... I believe he was wearing blue jeans.' Describing Stagg's unusual gait, she said, 'He walks very straight-backed, it is a distinctive walk.'

She said, 'When I came across Colin Stagg, he was in my view for about five seconds. He was 25 to 50 yards away from me. There was nothing to obstruct my view of him. It was quite a bright, warm day.'

Susan Gale said that she had met Stagg at about 9.25am or 9.30am. 'I got to my home at twenty-five-to-ten, twenty-to-ten. From where I saw him it is about a ten-minute walk to my front door. I did not see him again that day.'

She had thought nothing more about her casual meeting with Colin Stagg, until she saw the *Crimewatch* videofit two months later, showing a suspect the police were anxious to find. 'It reminded me at once of Colin Stagg,' she said. 'It was a very close likeness.' She called the police.

Pauline Fleming said she had seen a man, aged about 29 or 30, walking 'briskly' on the common near the scene of the murder at 9.30am. 'I thought he was someone going off to work,' she said. 'He was walking with a purpose ... as if he was late for something. He was carrying a dark bag in his right hand.'

Another witness, Mrs Amanda Phelan, also gave a description of a man she saw washing his hands in a stream just after 10.30am. She described him as acting suspiciously and thought he might have been wearing a cream or white sweater and blue jeans. Mrs Phelan did not pick out Stagg in an identity parade and neither did Pauline Fleming who told the court that she had seen a man walking near Curling Pond at about 9.30am carrying a dark bag in his right hand.

Jane Harriman said she had been walking on the common that morning with her four children and family dogs. She walked the same route as Rachel only a few minutes earlier. Near a small wood, she noticed a man walking towards her who she described as being 'white, about 5ft 10in tall. He had very close-cropped hair, darkish brown. On the top half of his body he was wearing a white shirt. It was long- sleeved with a collar. He was wearing dark-coloured trousers. I cannot remember what colour they were or the material they were made of. His shirt was tucked into his trousers. He was carrying a dark- coloured bag. At that point, apart from his shirt and trousers there was nothing else on his body. He appeared to be in his late twenties or early thirties. The bag he had was a dark colour. I couldn't be sure what material it was made of, but some sort of vinyl I think. He was holding it by the handles. From a distance, I thought it was a briefcase, but close up it seemed more a sports bag.'

They passed each other going in opposite directions and the man appeared to turn his head sharply, hiding his face. Mrs Harriman continued walking with her children until they reached Curling Pond where they sat for a while. On the far side of the pond, she noticed a woman walking a dog into the trees and, a few minutes later, the man who had passed her earlier took the same path, almost as if following the woman.

Something about his behaviour made Mrs Harriman feel 'a bit worried and nervous'. After several minutes, the man appeared again, re-tracing his route. Now he appeared to have a thin belt around his waist, over his T-shirt.

As she led her children back towards the Windmill car park, Mrs Harriman said she probably passed within 25 yards of where Rachel Nickell already lay dead in the grass. She was able to provide police with a very clear description of the man she had seen by Curling Pond and had helped compile the artist's impression shown on *Crimewatch UK*.

Mrs Harriman did not look at Stagg from the witness stand as she told how she went to the specialist identification suite at Brixton Police Station to take part in an identification parade after the *Crimewatch* programme. Her E-fit picture had resulted in Colin Stagg's first arrest.

'I picked out one of the ten men in the line-up as being the man I had seen on the common,' she said. It was Colin Stagg. The next day, she saw a TV news bulletin showing Stagg rushing from Wimbledon Magistrates' Court after being fined for indecent exposure. 'There was no doubt in my mind that the man I picked out was the man on the common,' she said. Then she saw a report and photo in the *Daily Mail* which left her in no doubt whatsoever that her memory of 15 July was accurate. There was, she said, absolutely no doubt in her mind. The man she had seen on Wimbledon Common, the man who had made her feel 'a bit worried and nervous', was unquestionably Colin Stagg.

'Have you ever made a mistake in identifying anyone?' asked Mr Sturman.

'Not that I can think,' replied Mrs Harriman.

'Never, for instance, seen someone you thought was a friend and it wasn't?' enquired the defence lawyer.

'Possibly, yes.'

'Did you have difficulty picking out the man at the identification parade?'

'I didn't have any difficulty after I had calmed down.' The trauma of the identification parade had clearly upset her at the time, strong as her character appeared to be, but no one was surprised by that.

'Were you ever told Mr Stagg was a strong suspect for the murder?' asked Mr Sturman.

'No, not that I can remember,' said Mrs Harriman.

Was she, asked Mr Sturman, someone who likes to be exact?

'I like to be accurate,' replied Mrs Harriman. She wasn't particularly studying the man on the common, she said, but always liked to keep an eye open for possible danger, especially when she was with the children, and this had made her concerned. There was no doubt, she asserted, that she had seen him at one stage with a belt, or something similar, tied loosely round his waist, an inch or two above his trouser band.

'I would like you,' said the defence barrister, 'to look at Mr Stagg in the dock and describe his nose.'

She hesitated for a moment or two as she looked carefully at Stagg, then said, 'Long and thin, straight.'

'Thank you,' said Mr Sturman, without further comment.

On the third day of the hearing, Mr Boyce began giving a picture of Colin Stagg's lifestyle with evidence from witnesses who had known him before, on and after the day of Rachel's murder.

Various local traders including a butcher and a newsagent recalled seeing Stagg that day and described him as being quite excited as he talked about the discovery of a body on the common. Having known him for years, they described Colin as a loner who seemed more comfortable in the company of animals than people.

Butcher Patrick Heanan had a shop in Petersfield Rise on the Alton Estate, and served Stagg a couple of times a week. 'He is a creature of habit,' he said. 'He's never without his dog. Dogs love him. He seems to attract them. He's very much a loner and never talks to anyone in the street. On the day of the murder he came in at about 11.15am. The helicopter was overhead and I thought at first they were looking for a lost child. Colin came in and said a body had been found on the common. His behaviour seemed normal, although he had never just come in for a chat before.'

Unfortunately, what the court did not hear was what Mr Heanan had said to officers when they first interviewed him. He'd commented that he was so alarmed about Stagg's behaviour, he had thought to himself, Oh my God, Colin, what have you done? It was disappointing to say the least, that the butcher was not prepared to repeat this in his written statement, to be used in the prosecution evidence.

Newsagent Yagnesh Patel, whose shop was also in Petersfield Rise, said he employed Stagg on an early morning newspaper round. 'He's a real loner,' he said. 'He never opens conversations and just replies with a single word. He told me he had been at university.'

Mr Patel said that Stagg had bought a bar of chocolate from him at about 12.45pm on the day of the murder. Stagg had told him that the police were stopping people from going on the common and he couldn't walk his dog. 'He seemed quite excited ... more excited than I had ever seen him,' the newsagent said.

When Lillian Avid gave her evidence, she said, 'By his actions, I was thinking, Did he do it? Did he do it?'

'Did you think he was so clean because he had just washed the blood off?' asked Mr Sturman.

'I had a feeling he had just changed his clothes, he was so clean. I felt he must have changed his clothes, if he had done it,' replied Mrs Avid.

He asked, had she heard a profile of the Rachel killer read out on *Crimewatch* by either a detective or by presenter Nick Ross – characteristics such as the killer being a loner?

'Yes, I did.'

Did the photofit which was shown match anyone else on the Alton Estate?

'No one that I know.'

Mr Sturman asked her to describe Stagg's nose.

'I've never looked,' she said, clearly a bit put out.

What about his eyes?

'Sort of smiley, sparkly eyes,' she said. 'But I don't know the colour.'

I could only assume that the reason for this line of questioning was to try and establish that there was a man on the estate who resembled Colin but had a different-shaped nose. However, when cross-examined by the prosecution, none of the witnesses accepted that there was anyone else who looked like Colin.

Christine Perrior said she gave gave Stagg the odd hour of employment as a part-time gardener at her home on the Alton Estate. 'I didn't speak to Colin very much,' she said. 'I used to let him in the back gate, plug in the extension lead for the lawn mower and let him get on with the work.' She would pay Stagg £10 for 45 minutes' work. He turned up the day after the murder, as arranged, and started the mowing after accepting the offer of a cold drink.

'As I handed it to him, I said, "It's terrible, that murder on the common." He said he usually walked his dog there every morning but for some reason he hadn't that day. I said to him, "Whoever could do a thing like that, especially in front of a child? He must be sick." I said they needed stringing up or shooting. He said he hadn't seen anything ... but didn't really finish the conversation. It just fizzled out.'

Stagg had then nipped home for some ant powder to kill a swarm of the insects invading Mrs Perrior's garden.

Cheryl Lewis, a friend and neighbour from 12 Ibsley Gardens, recalled a conversation she had had with Stagg after his first arrest.

He had described being shown photographs of Rachel which made it look as if her head had been removed from her body and then placed back on her shoulders and that she was Iying in a foetal position. He also admitted to having seen Rachel before on the common, sunbathing by a pond.

That being said, she was charitable towards Stagg after he had been arrested and released for the first time.

'I believed that, because he had been freed, he must be innocent. The way I looked at it, he didn't need me slamming the door in his face. I made him welcome in my home. He was getting a lot of people calling him names and shouting abuse at him. I used to see him more or less every day and he came most weekends for a cup of tea, always with his dog Brandy. He would sometimes stay until 12 o'clock or l.00am, no particular time. Sometimes I would be on my own with him, sometimes there would be other people there, friends of mine. He told me a few things about his time in police custody. He said that every time he tried to go to sleep, someone would wake him up and ask him if he wanted anything. He told me he had been shown photos of Rachel and described them to me. He said it looked as if her head had been removed from her body that she had been decapitated – and then placed on her shoulders and that she was Iying in a foetal position.

'He insisted he didn't do the murder. He said the police had told him he had been seen stabbing a tree on the common, which he denied. He said the police had told him he had seen Rachel on the common, which he also refuted. But he told me that he had seen her over there. He said he had seen Rachel sunbathing by a pond, but I'm not sure which one. Apparently, she used to go to the common quite a lot. I got the impression he had seen her more than once. She used to have a dog with her. I asked him why he kept going back. He said, "If someone accused me of doing something like that ..." then seemed to become upset and stopped.'

In his cross-examination, Mr Sturman hit Cheryl with the 'nose question' straight away. Asked to describe it, she looked embarrassed as she answered, 'I don't really know.' And his eyes? 'They are fixed. He looks straight into you.'

She said she had made a statement to the police about Stagg after discussing the *Cnmewatch* programme with a neighbour. She had never said '100 per cent' that the photofit was Colin, but it did resemble him.

Another of the Ibsley Gardens residents, Tina Woodsell, regularly saw Stagg taking his dog for a walk, sometimes with a lead hanging over his shoulders. She said she had also seen him with a black bag his dad had left when he died.

'Was it a shiny PVC bag?' Mr Sturman asked, referring to the description by some witnesses of the bag allegedly being carried by the suspected killer.

'No, it wasn't.' It was old, she said, battered and with a pattern on the front, and made of hard cloth material.

Asked about the full-length *Crimewatch* videofit, she said it did not give sufficient details to suggest it was Colin Stagg – it was the characteristics of the likely killer, as defined by the psychologist, which had prompted her to contact the police. The second E-fit, just of the suspect's face, was like him, she said.

Mr Sturman asked her to describe Stagg's nose. Another bemused pause and she said, 'Well, basically straight. Nothing unusual about it.'

'And the photofit,' said Mr Sturman. 'Does it look at all like a Mr Martin Butler?'

'No, it doesn't.'

'And do you know Martin Butler?'

'Yes.'

He was, in fact, another neighbour of Stagg's, and was said to bear more than a passing resemblance to him. He had already been eliminated from police enquiries.

Mrs Karina Leonard testified to seeing Stagg with a PVC, leather-type bag on about three different occasions prior to the murder. 'It was a dark bag, about 18–20in long and about 12in deep ... It was made of a sort of PVC, leather-look material.' She recounted one specific occasion on which she could distinctly remember Stagg with the dark bag, in about March of 1992. But afterwards, she said, she never saw him with it again. And, she said, she had also on occasions seen him out walking without Brandy the dog, something he claimed he never did. A small, but significant point, Bill Boyce submitted, in the context of events on the common on 15 July 1992.

A one-time family friend, Tina Molloy, knew Stagg better than most. She was asked by Mr Sturman. 'Knowing him as you do, and forgetting that he is here in this courtroom, do you think he is capable of murder?'

'No, I don't,' she replied. Then she added, 'But are we sure of anybody?'

'Indeed,' said Mr Sturman. 'Did you get the impression that Stagg was "absolutely desperate" to lose his virginity?'

'Yes,' she said, he had made no secret of the fact.

Mr Sturman was clearly out to prove that Stagg, embarrassed and frustrated by being a virgin, was so anxious to have sex with a woman that he had invented the obscene fantasies sent to Lizzie James simply in the hope that it would persuade her to go to bed with him.

Called as the first of the Crown's key expert witnesses on the fourth day of the committal hearing, Doc Shepherd related that he had taken swabs from the vaginal and anal areas for forensic examination. The police had hoped these would reveal body samples – semen, blood, hair or saliva – from which a DNA 'genetic fingerprint' of the killer could be produced. Unfortunately, in the case of Rachel Nickell, the killer had left no traces from which a DNA reading could be made, despite the fact that it was clearly a sex attack of the most frenzied nature. If Rachel had been raped, as it was initially believed, the attacker had not ejaculated to leave behind tell-tale samples of semen. Nor were there any traces of skin or hair caught under her fingernails when she may have tried to fight him off.

Dr Shepherd noted that the anus was widely dilated but there was no evidence of bleeding from either the anal or vaginal areas. There was, he told the magistrate, a mass of stab wounds visible on the body, which was lying between separate pools of blood. There was little more he could do at the scene and he deferred further examination until Rachel's body had been taken to St George's Hospital mortuary. There, in the presence of Superintendent Bassett, Chief Inspector Wickerson and the coroner, Dr Dole, he began the post mortem.

There were, he said, a total of 49 stab wounds – 19 back injuries, 2–6 to the chest and abdomen, 3 to the neck which had virtually severed her head, and one defensive wound to her left hand where she had fought briefly but vainly to fend off the killer. There were two bruises on her forehead and one on her chin. Many of the stab wounds had pierced her heart, lungs and liver. The murder weapon was probably a single-edged sheath knife with a brass hilt, he had deduced.

An album of photos of Rachel's injuries, along with the police videos of the body and murder scene, had already been shown to the magistrate on a TV screen specially set up in court.

Dr Shepherd noted that there were several areas of heavy blood-staining at the murder scene, indicating that Rachel's body had been moved by the killer into the place where she was found, under the silver birch tree, her naked buttocks exposed. He prepared a sketch plan showing the main area of blood-staining under the body, another at an area a few yards away, and separate rings in between. He explained that the amount of blood-staining at the murder scene would be affected by a number of factors – the nature of the injuries which were bleeding, the heart rate, the blood pressure, and the time the victim was in one particular area. Rachel's jeans, he said, were coated in blood almost exclusively in the upper front area. There was significant spotting of blood on the back of the lower leg area and there were fresh mud-stains on the lower front of the jeans. The pattern of blood-staining, on the clothes and at the murder site, showed that the attack had happened in four phases, after the killer had forced Rachel from the footpath into the wood, goading her with painful prods of his knife.

In Phase 1, the killer struck the first fatal blows to the neck at the spot where the largest area of blood-staining was found, some yards away from the body. The relative absence of blood-staining on the lower portions of Rachel's jeans indicated that she had been forced to her knees at this stage. Dr Shepherd said that the savage injuries to the neck were of a type and depth that would have resulted in 'severe pain and shock'. Damage to the muscles of the neck and to the cartilages of the larynx were likely to have prevented her from crying out or screaming for help. From the kneeling position, she would have tumbled forward on to her face, with the haemorrhage from the neck wounds causing the first pool of blood on the ground. The most likely position of the assailant was behind Rachel, with the knife in his right hand. Rachel's jeans and pants were still in position at this stage.

In Phase 2, Rachel was moved, or she staggered, towards the base of the silver birch. The presence of leaf mould on the back of her body and the back of her T-shirt was consistent with her lying on her back at this stage, facing the base of the tree, with the killer lunging at her body with his knife.

Phase 3 began when the killer tried to remove Rachel's jeans and pants. The leaf mould on her buttocks indicated that she was still on her back at this point. The pathologist said, 'Either during, or after, the partial removal of the clothing, Rachel's body was turned and pulled away to the approximate position where she was discovered.' The killer had clearly continued to rain frantic blows on her body.

In Phase 4, the killer sexually violated Rachel's body after pulling her jeans and pants down to her lower calves. 'Anal penetration would have taken place when she was either dead, or at a point so close to death that she would not have responded to penetration,' said Dr Shepherd. Other blows were probably inflicted with the killer's knife after the sexual assault. 'In my opinion,' he said, 'the minimum length of time needed to inflict all the injuries on Rachel's body would be in the region of three minutes.'

Dr Shepherd went on to say that at least 13 wounds had definitely been inflicted after death on the right side of the chest and abdomen with another 9 to the left side of the chest possibly caused after death. There were five deep penetrative wounds to the lungs and three to the heart, any one of which would have killed Rachel. The lack of significant defence wounds suggested that Rachel had been given no chance to defend herself. He said that abrasions to the right side of her chin were difficult to determine. They might have been caused by the rough application of a hand or material, or by her collapsing on to the ground.

Dr Shepherd explained how the killer could have fled from the scene with virtually no blood-stains on him or his clothing, a fact which would have been considered impossible when the extent of Rachel's injuries was initially revealed. He said that only the neck injuries had bled externally, sending blood pumping on to her clothes and on to the ground. As Rachel's heart stopped beating, other wounds had bled internally. Dr Shepherd said that with the assailant standing behind Rachel and with no significant close contact between them, it was 'extremely possible' that the only easily visible blood-staining on the assailant would be on his hands. Any other pinprick blood-stains on the killer could be detected only by forensic examination and would not have been visible to the naked eye.

Had the killer carried out the anal assault with bloodied hands, said Dr Shepherd, there would have been blood deposits left in that area. The dilation of the anus, he said, had been caused by the fact that the muscles had ceased to work after death to perform a normal retraction after penetration.

Mr Sturman wanted to know whether there had been any collusion between Dr Shepherd and Paul Britton in coming to their respective conclusions; whether they might somehow have got together to manufacture evidence against Stagg.

'I have never met Paul Britton at any time,' said Dr Shepherd, 'and I have not discussed any aspect of this case with him. I have seen no reports prepared by him.'

He had, he said, seen only a handwritten report by Robert Ressler, which touched on the subject of offender profiling.

'I am aware Mr Britton is involved in this case,' said the pathologist, 'but it has been made clear to me that I must form my own conclusions. The reports of Mr Britton and his conclusions were, and still are, unknown to me.'

Asked about the object which had been inserted into Rachel's anus, he said that it could have been an animate or inanimate object. 'Within this group, I would include a penis,' he said.

Dr Shepherd confirmed his belief that if the assailant had been standing in front of Rachel when he slashed her throat, he would have been soaked in blood. 'But the angle of the throat wounds is such that I think it is more likely that the assailant was standing behind Rachel at the time,' he said.

Doc Shepherd was asked a specific question concerning the direction of certain of the blows; it was an important question because his evidence actually tended to support what Paul Britton was saying about control, domination and fear-based compliance. It all fitted in very neatly.

Dick Shepherd gave an answer concerning the direction of two of these blows, then added, 'That has always been my opinion.'

It sounded an innocuous enough statement to me, but it rang warning bells in Bill Boyce's head. Later that night, he checked his documents and found that, sure enough, we'd had a conference in chambers where Dick Shepherd had been asked a question concerning these same wounds, and had said that he "had no opinion about it". This reply was minuted on Bill Boyce's conference notes.

Dick Shepherd was now saying that that had *always* been his opinion, and Bill Boyce was concerned because there appeared to be a discrepancy. Now, because it was a conference note between counsel and expert witness, protected by privilege, he was under no obligation whatsoever to disclose it to the defence, but it was a mark of the integrity of the man that he did.

The defence re-called Dick Shepherd the following day. In answer to a question from Jim Sturman, he said, 'Yes, I remember that conference, and I remember saying, "I have no opinion about the direction of that particular blow or sequence of blows." But, until that time, that hadn't been a question that I'd been asked to consider, so obviously I would have had no opinion, by virtue of the fact that it wasn't something that was important to me.'

Jim Sturman said, 'Of course you would say that, now that the police have told you what it's all about, and you've had time to think of an excuse overnight.'

He was calling into question the integrity of probably one of the best Home Office pathologists that we've got, in front of a very experienced stipendary magistrate who wasn't going to be in the slightest bit impressed with this sort of rhetoric.

Dick Shepherd wasn't used to being spoken to like that. When I saw him afterwards, sitting in his car, smoking like a chimney, he had a haunted look in his face as much as to say, 'What the hell was all that about? All I was doing was my job.' He had no axe to grind; he was an independent Home Office pathologist and had no points to make with the police.

Bill Boyce said to us that the defence would have every right to say, 'Well, this was what was said in conference, this is what he subsequently said in court, and we're saying that the two do not sit well together. Because Mr Boyce and Mr Sweeney were present at this conference, we're going to call them as defence witnesses.'

I didn't immediately realise the far-reaching implications.

Meanwhile, it was Paul's turn, and Jim Sturman played his hand early. He aimed to discredit Paul and therefore, he hoped, the entire covert operation. If he couldn't cast doubt on Paul's professional qualifications, he would attack offender profiling and, if necessary, the entire field of psychology and psychologists.

Psychology, Paul Britton told the court, was a well-established discipline, based on medical principles, which had been practised in the UK since the end of the Second World War, and granted a royal charter in 1965. It was on this psychological knowledge, he said, that the art of offender profiling was built.

From his experience, he said, there could be no doubt that the killer of Rachel Nickell was one of a tiny number of perverts in Britain whose sexual satisfaction was gained by acts of sadism, domination and fear, culminating in sexual frenzy and death. He said that the covert operation involving Lizzie James was devised by him with the specific provision that Stagg would automatically eliminate himself if he failed to react in a manner expected of the Rachel Nickell killer.

At the end of the six months of Operation Edzell, he said, Stagg's sexuality was indistinguishable from the offender profile of the murderer, which he had drafted from information available a few weeks after the killing and prior to Stagg becoming a suspect. The fantasies contained in Stagg's letters to Lizzie and his taped conversations with her indicated a man obsessed with gratuitous violence and deviant sex. Of Stagg's fantasies, Paul Britton's opinion was, 'The imagery, contained and predicted, is intense, very clearly described, quite specific, and the intensity and clarity are both consistent with fantasies that are enacted rather than masturbated to.' This was based, he said, on his knowledge of serious sexual offenders and the relevant literature in clinical and forensic psychology available to him.

Not surprisingly, Mr Sturman took a more cynical view of psychology, offender profiling and Paul's findings, calling them 'speculative and unsupported' by anything other than Paul's instincts. Paul disagreed.

'Is Colin Stagg mentally ill?' asked Mr Sturman.

'I don't know, I've never examined him,' said Paul.

Exactly the point, Mr Sturman said. 'If you've never examined him, how can you draw any positive conclusions?' he asked. 'Does he suffer from an abnormality within the terms of the Mental Health Act of 1974?'

'I can't tell you that.'

Aged in his late thirties, early forties, Sturman was astute and articulate. His eyes were piercing and dark, and always put me in mind of a cobra's eyes just before it strikes. He was trying to draw Paul into giving clinical opinions that he knew the psychologist could only properly give if he had examined Stagg.

'How many murders of young women in broad daylight with a young child have you analysed in your career, Mr Britton?'

'None,' Paul said.

It struck me as a ridiculous question. Paul might just as usefully have asked Sturman how many people he had defended who were alleged to have stabbed a woman 49 times. Paul's conclusions were based on his knowledge of human behaviour, and his experience of working with psychological dysfunction of all different sorts.

Because he had been unable to examine any individual in connection with his analysis of the deviant sexual fantasy life characterising the murder of Rachel Nickell, said Paul, he had used the term 'personality disturbance' as a general term rather than a specific psychological conclusion. 'To safely recognise a particular personality disorder it is important to know, among other things, the length of time the individual has experienced, or been subject to, the phenomena.'

One of the more curious facts to emerge about the particular deviancy suffered by Rachel's killer was that it tends first to affect young men in their early teens, arouses intense and violent fantasies for many years, then finally manifests itself in a murderous attack at the age of 28 or thereabouts. Those affected – thankfully, just a tiny sub-group of the deviant population – are walking time-bombs. These, said Paul, were concrete facts which had emerged from studies of many case histories of such abnormalities.

Paul told the court he was aware of the code of conduct governing the questioning by police of a vulnerable person, when a responsible adult must be present. 'I don't know if Mr Stagg is such a person,' he said. 'What I can tell you is that the operation I designed was specifically constructed so as to present whoever was to be the subject of the operation with a series of ladders they would have to climb in a conceptual sense, rather than a slippery slope that any person, especially a vulnerable person, would inexorably slide down should they be pushed.'

Sturman asked was he satisfied that Stagg was telling the truth in his letters to Lizzie, not simply saying anything in the hope of bedding her and losing his virginity?

Paul said, 'I saw nothing, in either the correspondence or transcripts, or indeed anything else concerned with Mr Stagg, which indicated otherwise than the fantasies were genuinely held and, in addition, I would say the fantasies he described are entirely consistent with genuine fantasies reported by people who have sexual deviations. The fantasies are entirely consistent with being quite genuine and entirely inconsistent with being a mere pretence in order to entice someone into bed with him.'

'But a lot of quite normal people have sexual fantasies, don't they?' argued Sturman.

'They do,' Paul agreed. 'Large sections of the population fantasise, but don't put it into effect. I would estimate a significant proportion fantasise about making love in the open air – not less than 25 per cent.'

And how many get their sexual thrills through rear-entry vaginal intercourse? 'That,' said Paul, 'would be an element in the repertoire of a reasonable proportion of married or cohabiting couples.' For instance, he said, part of his everyday work was a special clinic held, with colleagues, for non-deviant couples who experienced some form of sexual difficulty. The work of the clinic required that each partner separately gave a full sexual history which involved their sexual practices and performances. Rear-entry vaginal penetration or intercourse was reported by about 30 per cent of those people. The proportion might be higher in the general population. 'And, may I say to you, it would be precisely for this sort of reason that a close and detailed specification of the offender's sexual deviant fantasies had to be considered rather than aspects which were much more generally evident in the general population,' he said.

Sturman asked if Paul had made written predictions from time to time about how Stagg might react if he was the killer.

'I don't think so,' he said. 'I might have, but it was mostly graphs which would depict the expected path of both the deviant sexual behaviour and sexual violence, together with their intensities against the murderer's level of self-preservation and caution.'

Did he make notes of any such predictions in such an important case, which he might like to produce in court?

'No. I made any observations direct to police officers present at the time. It is my usual practice, when advising police forces, to consult in this way unless I am specifically asked to do otherwise.'

Would Mr Britton agree that there was a lot of academic concern about the discipline of offender profiling?

'There are one or two dissenting voices. Offender profiling, as it is developing in the UK today, is based on three main strands –

detective expertise, the development of databases, and professional psychological expertise. It relies on all three elements to different extents in different cases.' It was certainly the case, he said, that databases – the storing of case histories on computers – was still at an early stage. But it promised to be, eventually, the most important stride forward. Preliminary stages were being undertaken in Surrey – at the university and at police headquarters – in London with the Metropolitan Police sexual assault unit, and in Derbyshire where police now hold the largest such system in the country, which deals solely with abducted, missing or murdered children. 'As a consequence of work in these areas,' said Paul, 'work is being undertaken on behalf of the Home Office and the Association of Chief Police Officers towards the development of more powerful analytical tools.'

Occasionally, in my view, Mr Sturman tried a bit too hard. During one exchange, perhaps hoping that Paul had never heard of the term, or would agree with him, he asked, 'Mr Britton, was this an "overkill" murder?'

Paul said, 'When you say "overkill", do you mean that in the sense used by the FBI?'

'Yes.'

'That's where they say that when a certain number of stab wounds are inflicted, 20 I think, then the assailant must have known the victim?'

Sturman said, 'That is correct, when there are 20 or more stab wounds the victim knew their assailant.'

Paul replied, 'The notion that when someone has 20 stab wounds then they knew their murderer, but if they only have 19 then they didn't, is not a view that we think is particularly helpful here in the United Kingdom.'

But an overkill murder – like the term or not – was strongly suggestive of a personal relationship between killer and victim? enquired Sturman.

'No,' said Paul, 'I wouldn't agree. I am saying exactly the opposite. The FBI now recognise that they might have got it wrong in that area, and are in the course of rectifying it by using professional psychologists in their analysis, rather than just FBI operatives.'

Not surprisingly, Sturman dropped the line of questioning.

Paul said he had analysed hundreds of sexual fantasies and been involved in 60 to 70 investigations with police in which a significant proportion required sexual analysis. Of these, ten to twenty were sexually-motivated murders. 'As far as I know, I haven't ever got a profile completely wrong,' he said.

He denied that the use of the occult and the cover of Lizzie as a catsitter had been deliberately introduced into the covert operation to 'strike a chord' with Stagg.

'In my original profile, there was no specific mention of the occult but I said the murderer would have unusual and solitary hobbies. In designing the cover story of the confidante, I wanted to be sure that it was plausible and based upon cases from which I could provide a detailed background.'

Paul said Stagg's letters had clearly indicated excitement at the prospect of violent death. 'From Mr Stagg's correspondence,' he said, 'I would expect elements of sexual frenzy which could result in the death of the other participant. It is also the case that Mr Stagg reported sexual excitement at the contemplation of just such an attack on Rachel Nickell. The Lizzie James cover story was designed to produce a response to such stimulus from a sexually-deviant personality. It was devised that way precisely because it was such an unusual sexual-deviant persona.'

The chances of two men with the same sexual deviancy being together in the same place at the same time was utterly remote, he said, unless that place was a special hospital or a prison.

Had he been asked to prepare profiles or give detailed consideration to any of the other 30 or so men questioned in connection with the murder and subsequently released?

'No.'

How many people were likely to have responded to Lizzie James in the same way as Colin Stagg?

'I would say the proportion that would produce the fantasies, the detail, the intensity, the aggression and who could give precise knowledge of the disposition of the body of Rachel Nickell, would be vanishingly small,' said the psychologist.

'Vanishingly small,' repeated Jim Sturman, as if he didn't quite understand what it meant.

In his profiling, said Mr Sturman, Paul had listed eight characteristics he would expect to find in the killer of Rachel Nickell – including an attraction to young adult women. What proportion of normal healthy young men are likely to fantasise about normal healthy young women? asked Mr Sturman.

'Most of them, I would expect,' Paul conceded.

Another characteristic listed by Paul was men masturbating over the thought of using a woman as a 'sexual object'. How unusual was that?

'Not unusual at all – about 40 to 50 per cent of males would do it.'

And was it common for people who fantasise to build up an imaginary relationship with the person they were thinking about?

'Yes, it is.'

The number of men displaying sadistic tendencies?

'Small.'

Using a knife in fantasies?

'Extremely rare.'

Physical control?

'Not common.'

Verbal abuse?

'Not common.'

As an expert in fantasies, asked Mr Sturman, had Paul read *My Secret Garden* by Nancy Friday?

'No, I haven't.'

Sturman feigned surprise. 'Were you even aware of its existence?' he asked.

'Yes, I was.'

As an expert in the field of fantasy, did he not feel it was his professional duty to read this?

'No.'

What about fantasies involving anal assault, asked Mr Sturman, how unusual were they?

'Extremely uncommon.'

Female fear?

'Not often.'

And was there anything in Stagg's letters which indicated killing?

'The signs of sexual frenzy were evident and such activity could end in the death of the female participant.'

But doesn't Stagg approach the relationship with Lizzie with an almost teenage naïveté, hoping for the chance of a long-lasting relationship?

'I don't think that is restricted to teenagers,' said Paul.

'But they don't normally fall in love,' replied Sturman.

'But I think a lot of people fall in lust that way,' said Paul, heavily stressing the word 'lust'.

What if Paul Britton was entirely wrong about Stagg and he was just someone who was excited by pornography?

'His behaviour is consistent with fantasies I see in serious sexual offenders,' Paul maintained. 'If he had not responded to this operation it would have had no value. As a clinical psychologist, it would have been my duty to say that he had not exhibited or demonstrated the behaviour I would have expected from the killer of Rachel Nickell.'

Suppose for one minute, Mr Sturman said, that Rachel Nickell knew her killer. Would the whole basis of his analysis collapse?

'From my knowledge of the scene, and the evidence so far, I believe the sexual life of her killer remains the same, irrespective of the degree of knowledge of the person who killed her.'

After two days of evidence and questioning, Paul Britton finally stepped down from the witness box. No wonder he looked exhausted.

Lizzie James had slipped into court during the lunch break, having arrived at the magistrate's entrance in the back of a police van with a blanket over her head. The press were milling around in force, desperate to find out what she looked like. A wooden screen protected her from everyone in the courtroom but Mr English, the lawyers and Colin Stagg, who squirmed uncomfortably on his seat. All the courtroom windows were covered with paper and Lizzie was told to remain seated at all times. The doors were locked and police officers were positioned inside and out as Bill Boyce began to take her through the evidence that was pivotal to the Crown's case.

She was, she said, an undercover officer who had used the pseudonym Lizzie James specifically for the Stagg operation because her true identity needed to remain secret. She would expect to be used in other covert operations in the future and, for that reason, wished for anonymity. There was no objection from Jim Sturman.

Lizzie, with everyone in the court staring at the wooden screen and no doubt trying to imagine what she looked like, told how she had become involved with Colin Stagg through a series of letters, phone calls and meetings. As a result, she had made 31 different witness statements, running into thousands of words, throughout the first six months of 1993.

'And those statements are true?' asked Bill Boyce.

'Yes they are, Your Worship,' she replied, her police training making her address the magistrate directly.

And that was it from Bill Boyce. No further questions.

Jim Sturman stood up and asked, 'In the course of your normal life, forgetting you are a police officer, has any man ever lied to impress you?'

'Yes, he has,' she admitted.

'During all your meetings and conversations, you were acting as a serving police officer?'

'I *was* a serving police officer,' Lizzie replied emphatically.

'You were trying to see whether Mr Stagg would incriminate himself in the murder of Rachel Nickell?'

'No,' she said firmly. 'I was trying to find out if he was implicated or not.'

Citing the fantasy tape she had sent to Stagg as part of the operation, Mr Sturman asked whose imagination had been at work.

'It was a joint effort between myself, Mr Wickerson and Mr Pedder, working within the guidelines set by Mr Britton.'

And what was her reaction when details of Scotland Yard's most secret undercover operation, and her involvement in it, were splashed all over the daily papers after Stagg's arrest?

'Horrified, Your Worship.'

Then that was all from Jim Sturman, too. We could only assume he'd decided to keep his powder dry for the trial and an Old Bailey jury. Just 30 minutes in the witness box and Lizzie was gone.

Magistrate Terry English had, in fact, already read the mass of transcripts detailing her evidence in order to satisfy himself that it was admissible in court. He had formed the conclusion that the material was relevant and should go forward to the trial as part of the prosecution case.

Earlier in the committal proceedings, Mr Sturman had also submitted that Paul Britton's evidence, with which Lizzie's was so closely linked, should also be booted out of court. Mr Britton's testimony, said Sturman, boiled down to the simple assertion, 'I am Britton, therefore I am right.' But, Sturman maintained, there was no scientific analysis to explain his conclusions. 'Psychology is a discipline of the mind – there are no facts to back it up,' he argued. It was evidence that was speculative and unsupported by anything other than Britton's own intuition. 'When asked how it could be checked, Mr Britton simply said, "By other psychologists." This type of witness,' Sturman said, could be a 'dangerous type of animal ... and I don't mean that in a derogatory sense to Mr Britton.'

He asserted that a lot of the letters to Stagg were clearly 'come-ons' from Lizzie James, wholly contrived to get Stagg to commit his wildest fantasies to paper. Sturman said she had written saying that she wanted Colin to take charge, to show her who was boss. 'You would need to be a moron not to know this was a woman who wanted to be dominated,' he said. No wonder Stagg had replied the way he did. Nothing of a violent sado-masochistic nature had been found at his home to back up Paul's analysis, just a copy each of soft-porn girlie magazines *Escort* and *Razzle*.

Sturman further argues that Stagg had complained to Lizzie James that he was sad and lonely and fed up with people sneering at him in the street. 'They were the letters of a man writing to someone he, sadly, believed to be his friend,' Sturman said.

Paul Britton, he said, was a partisan witness, and as such his evidence should not be tolerated. Indeed, the whole offender-profiling package should be thrown out. 'The Crown cannot call this man to give evidence. He has no medical qualifications and he is simply trying to guess Stagg's sexual behaviour. We simply do not know what lunatic was there on the common that day. Mr Britton is trying to prove possible guilt by giving an opinion. Not one single case can the prosecution quote in which a psychologist has pronounced guilt. You are being asked to create legal history.'

That statement annoyed me. Paul hadn't pronounced 'guilt' on Colin Stagg. He had simply said that his behaviour patterns and fantasies were indistinguishable from those Paul predicted of the killer.

Paul Britton, he went on, was simply not competent to give evidence in a case which was set to make legal history if it was sent to the Old Bailey. His interpretation of Stagg's letters, one of the central parts of the Crown case, 'means that, heads, Stagg loses; tails, Britton wins.'

In an impassioned plea, Mr Sturman said to the magistrate, 'The Crown seek to make legal history by calling a psychologist's evidence as proof positive of murder. On the basis that Mr Britton's evidence is tentative at best, and this is a clear case where the evidence offends against all principles of fairness and common law, I ask you to exclude it.'

Bill Boyce got to his feet. Slightly overweight, with dark hair and glasses, he gave the impression of being a very mild man – until, that is, you got on the receiving end of his cross-examination, and then you'd begin to wish you'd never been born.

As far as the prosecution was concerned, he stated, Paul was an eminent and well-respected psychologist of many years' experience and his evidence should be fairly placed alongside any other for a jury to consider. Only then would they have the full picture of the extremely unusual case laid out before them. Only then, with all the evidence fully available, would they be able to make that vital decision as to whether Colin Stagg was a merciless killer or a sick victim of his own harmless fantasies.

Calling the proceedings to an end for the day, Mr English said that he would consider the arguments overnight.

Undeterred by his two failed attempts to have evidence excluded, Jim Sturman bounced back on to the attack when I was called to the witness box.

'Did you consult an expert on the pagan religion during enquiries into Stagg's background?' he asked me.

'No,' I said, 'I didn't personally make enquiries but it was done on behalf of the squad.'

'Did the expert say that, essentially, paganism is a non-violent religion?'

'That is my understanding,' I said.

'And is one of the main themes that any harm you do to another person comes back to you multiplied by three?'

'That is my understanding, but I'm not sure about the multiplication.'

'Did you seek Mr Britton's assistance in interviewing any of the 32 or 33 other suspects who had been questioned?'

'No.'

'When was Mr Britton consulted about Colin Stagg?'

'It would have been about three days after Mr Stagg was first in custody.'

And who was it, he asked, who tipped off the press that Stagg would be appearing at Wimbledon court on an indecent exposure charge after his first arrest, resulting in his picture being reproduced all over the papers?

'I assume a statement would have been issued by the Metropolitan Police Press Bureau,' I said.

He questioned me on what other lines of enquiry had been followed up, suggesting that Stagg had been targeted from an early stage and police had stopped looking for other suspects. I explained how all potential avenues had been followed up, including a visit to Italy to visit a gravedigger who had worked at nearby Putney Cemetery at the time of the murder.

What about other lines of enquiry, demanded Mr Sturman, were they all followed up thoroughly? Jabbing at a bundle of notes in his hands, itemising many thousands of lines of police enquiries, he asked about an enquiry listed as Action 2337 – the sighting of Rachel and Alex talking to a man on a bike on Wimbledon Common in June 1992.

'There were over 5,000 lines of enquiry. I cannot remember them all.'

'About this man that looks like the short-haired E-fit, being stopped in a car on Wimbledon Common. What did you do about that?'

'What does the Action say I did?'

He was asking questions that he already knew the answers to, and I didn't have a bloody clue. He told me the answer.

'Then that's what we did.'

'Why?'

'I don't know, I'll have to think about that.'

We were talking about a vast inquiry, over 5,000 actions, over 1,000 statements, 7,000 names on a computer, and I would defy anyone to carry all of that information in their memory banks. Yet it is a well-worn defence tactic to pick up on some of these, however irrelevant and unmemorable they are, and attempt to expose your apparent lack of memory as a chink in your evidence. They will then gouge away at it until they've got a gaping great big hole – not present in fact or reality, but in the minds of the magistrate or jurors.

How many names altogether were offered by the public as fitting the videofit following the *Crimewatch* programme? asked Mr Sturman.

'Quite a lot.'

'Would the officer agree that Wimbledon Common has more than its fair share of sex pests?'

'I would agree with that,' I said.

'Including a substantial number of those with sexual peculiarities, those who masturbate, flash and have sex in the woods?'

'I don't know about their mental state but, yes, there are,' I agreed.

And were there over 100 people living within a mile of the common who are convicted sex offenders?

'I wouldn't disagree with that,' I said.

Was the officer aware that a man called Curtis was the first to be arrested in connection with the murder?

'I am aware, although I was not involved at the time.'

He fitted the description of the assailant?

'I wouldn't dispute that.'

Was the coroner's assistant's boyfriend warned about revealing Rachel's injuries because it could hinder enquiries?

'He was certainly spoken to.'

Was a decision taken after Stagg's first arrest not to check out any other suspects?

'No, it wasn't,' I said. 'Other lines of enquiry, including some persons who fitted the videofit, were continued for some months.'

Did I remember about a man seen by police at the Windmill car park on 23 December 1992, who would pass as a twin of Colin Stagg?

'I have no recollection but I have no doubt that I was informed. I don't know what action was taken.'

Who put out a press release saying identification was not an issue in the Stagg case?

'Again, that was an issue for the Metropolitan Police Press Bureau. Having seen the Press Bureau log, it reads "ID is not an issue." It is the view of the senior investigating officers that the use of the abbreviation ID led to the terms "identification" and "identity" being confused. The Metropolitan Police view was that identification was not an issue as no further identity parades could be held because Mr Stagg's picture had been published after he left court on 21 September 1992. Any identification parade would have been evidentially worthless.'

Were bike tracks found at the scene of the murder ever identified?

'They were, as a type widely used on various types of cycles.'

Despite Dr Shepherd being able to do a remarkable reconstruction of the murder weapon, using a liver scan, we had never found the knife?

'That's correct.'

Did the police ever consider showing little Alex a video picture of Stagg? 'No, I don't think that was ever discussed. I do recall that discussions were held to consider some form of identification procedure in which Alex would be involved.'

Was that abandoned because the little boy named somebody?

'No it wasn't. He did name somebody but it wasn't Stagg.'

He named a man some people thought was obsessed with Rachel?

'Yes, that's correct.'

Was Mr Britton asked to profile that man?

'No, Mr Britton was not asked to profile any suspect, he was asked to profile the killer.'

Mr Sturman submitted to the magistrate that, on the evidence presented so far, it was surely a dangerous case in which to send a man for trial on a charge of murder. He urged Mr English to throw it out, there and then, and let Colin Stagg have his freedom. He said there was no forensic evidence to link Stagg with the murder, three eye-witnesses on the common had failed to pick him out, Paul Britton's evidence was contradictory and, in the Lizzie James operation, it was 'blindingly obvious' that the ante had been deliberately raised by the undercover policewoman in an attempt to get Stagg to confess. 'I ask you to pause very carefully before you decide whether or not to commit him for trial,' said Mr Sturman.

Mr Boyce, on the other hand, was insistent that there was a strong case to answer. Stagg's alibi of being asleep at the time of the murder had been blown apart, Mrs Harriman's three positive identifications of Stagg were rock solid and Paul, a respected clinical and forensic psychologist with many years' experience, had found his behaviour patterns indistinguishable from those of the killer.

Bill Boyce argued that a jury should be given the opportunity to hear all of the evidence and then make up their minds if Colin Stagg was a murderer or a victim of his own fantasies.

The final day of the proceedings began with Mr English, who had been weighing up the evidence as it went along, ready to pronounce. 'I don't intend to retire for purely cosmetic reasons,' he said. 'I've had 11 days to consider both arguments, which I had anticipated – and it is my decision this case should be committed for trial at the Central Criminal Court.'

He said he was satisfied the evidence was wholly admissible and what the jury should be concerned with was the weight of it and that they should attach what importance they felt it merited in the overall context of the case. He said it was a legal decision based, of course, on the strength of the evidence he had heard.

Ever the optimist, Mr Sturman immediately made a new application for bail, arguing that the prosecution case had just 'limped through'.

Mr English admonished him for implying that the prosecution was playing a weak hand and that they were somewhat lucky the decision had gone their way. 'Mr Sturman,' he said, 'this may not be the strongest case I have ever heard, but it far exceeds the standard you are suggesting.'

I said that the police objections to bail were a belief that Stagg might commit further offences, that he would interfere with witnesses, he might abscond before the trial and should certainly be kept in custody for his own safety.

The magistrate interjected, 'He is innocent in law. We should not be talking about re-offending.'

I continued that it was Paul Britton's conclusion that re-offending was almost inevitable if, indeed, his analysis of the situation proved correct. Stagg, I said, was still writing to various prosecution witnesses claiming that they were telling lies. These letters were causing concern and we had had to move at least one witness from her home. Requests for protection had been made by others. One witness had received a phone threat not to give evidence. Because of Stagg's reclusive lifestyle, he had no community ties which would keep him in the area and he could easily abscond before the trial. Not least of all, the outrage caused by the murder was a threat to his personal safety. 'The estate is divided into two camps – those for Mr Stagg and those vehemently against him,' I said.

Mr Sturman said Stagg had made no direct threats but was 'making contact with various people on the estate to say, in effect, "I thought you were my friends. Why are you saying these things about me?" These are cries from the heart from a man who has protested his innocence all along and will continue to protest his innocence until the day he dies.' He said Stagg was a man who lived simply with his dog, did not feel threatened, and would be happy to stay with a relative outside London until the time came for him to face trial.

Mr English did not hesitate. He said he was turning down the bail application because of the gravity of the offence leading to substantial fears that he would not attend his trial. Stagg was duly taken back to Wandsworth Prison.

For the prosecution team, however, the toughest part was yet to come. The Old Bailey trial, counsel predicted, could last anything up to eight weeks. Nevertheless, we felt there was cause to celebrate. We were confident that we had conducted as thorough and impartial an investigation as possible, and had ended up charging the right man with Rachel's murder. None of us could have slept if we'd thought for one minute that her killer was still at large.

The celebrations, as ever on this inquiry, were short-lived. Bill Boyce and Nigel Sweeney, having sought advice from other eminent lawyers, announced that, with the greatest reluctance, they would have to withdraw from the case and hand over to other Treasury Counsel. Jim Sturman had clearly indicated that he would raise the matter of the Doc Shepherd 'discrepancy' at the trial, and the potential embarrassment and damage to the prosecution case would have been incalculable.

We were forced to change horses midstream.

And then, unbelievably, came another bombshell. Only three weeks later, we heard news that threw into doubt whether Colin Stagg would ever face a murder trial jury.

Chapter 40

In Leeds, mobile grocer Keith Hall had walked from court after the judge's ruling led to a jury acquitting him of killing his wife, Patricia. The evidence of an undercover policewoman, acting in a role uncannily like that of Lizzie James, was, said the judge, inadmissible – thus creating a legal precedent which Stagg's defence team would almost certainly cite at the Old Bailey before the start of his murder trial. There were too many worrying parallels with our own investigation. Lose the evidence of Lizzie James, we feared, and we could lose the case.

Hall's wife had disappeared in the spring of 1992 after neighbours had heard a blazing row coming from their home in Moorland Drive, Pudsey. Hall claimed that she had simply walked out on him in a huff, taking the family Ford Sierra Estate. The car was later found abandoned, with the driving seat positioned to suit Mrs Hall's size. However, a local milkman recalled seeing someone he thought was a man sitting in the driving seat. A short while later, another witness saw what he thought was a man climbing over a fence into a field and running away.

There was lots of circumstantial evidence. Then it was discovered they were going to go through divorce proceedings. Keith had built his business up from practically nothing and his wife was going to have the house, keep custody of the children, and he would lose his business as the result of the divorce. What was more, Patricia Hall hadn't taken any clothes, none of the relatives that she was always in touch with had heard from her, and no money appeared to be moving out of the bank account.

Police suspected Hall of murder and dug in the garden of the couple's semi, looking for a body. They even excavated under concrete at a newly-laid roundabout nearby. Hall was questioned but, on legal advice, said nothing. The police could find nothing to implicate her husband directly.

Then, early in October 1992, a local woman, known only as Eliza, put an ad in the lonely hearts column of the *Wharf Valley Times*. She was amazed to receive a reply from Keith Hall, whose name she recognised, having read about the case. She knew that his wife had only been missing for six months, yet here was Hall looking for a new partner. Eliza phoned Pudsey Police Station and talked to Detective Inspector Jim Bancroft in the incident room. He asked her to write back to Hall to see where it led. Hall replied and told her, 'I want to put some meaning back into my life.'

As the correspondence continued, the police decided to replace Eliza with an undercover policewoman from the West Yorkshire Regional Crime Squad. 'Liz' was picked because she was slightly shorter than Hall, was pretty, knew Pudsey well enough to pose as a local, and was able to switch into the local Yorkshire dialect.

The relationship progressed over the next four months from letters to phone calls, and finally, to a meeting in the car park of a pub. They met several more times over the next five months, mostly for a quiet drink at the same pub. Eventually, Hall produced an engagement ring and asked her to move in with him. Liz said it was impossible because his missing wife might come back to him at any time.

The following evening, 26 February 1993, as they sat in the car park, Liz said, 'I can't marry you – I can't come to live with you because your kids would get to like me, and what happens if your wife comes back?'

Hall said, 'I have these dreams – I know that she's not going to come back.'

The Crown Prosecution Service, which up to that point had said there was insufficient evidence to bring a case against Hall, now agreed that the WPC's evidence gave them enough to proceed. Three days later Hall was arrested, charged and remanded in jail for a year to await his trial. At Leeds Crown Court on 12 March 1994, however, after days of legal argument, the judge Mr Justice Waterhouse, ruled that the evidence of the undercover officer was inadmissible – including the tape-recorded confession. Keith Hall was found not guilty without any of the evidence being put before a jury, and walked from the court a free man.

We had been totally unaware of the Yorkshire operation and were astonished at the number of worrying parallels with our own investigation. We were deeply concerned that Lizzie James's undercover evidence was now in danger, for the Hall judgment created a legal precedent which Stagg's defence team would almost certainly cite at the Old Bailey before the start of his trial.

As Bruce Butler explained, however, the CPS believed that the covert operation in the Rachel inquiry had been designed and run along very different lines and could not be considered in the same light. It had been 'whiter than white', with no hint of entrapment. Our operation wasn't intended to manipulate a suspect into making a confession. It was intended to allow him either to eliminate himself entirely, or to further implicate himself entirely by his own choices. It was only after we had found out what we had found out and had it interpreted by Paul, that we and the CPS decided that this was a matter for a jury.

John Nutting QC was first leading Treasury counsel and an imposing, formidable man; you were aware all the time you were talking to him that you were in the presence of somebody quite exceptional.

With a change of horses, Mick and I were a bit concerned that he might take an opposing view to the enthusiasm for the case shown by Bill Boyce and Nigel Sweeney, but he didn't. Just like Nigel Sweeney, he read through the papers very quickly and picked up the salient points with a speed and acuity that astounded. He then played devil's advocate and asked some very probing questions.

We walked him around the common and his attitude became even more positive when he realised how close the various locations were to each other, and how, when you looked at the witness statements, there could only have been two possible routes that the man with the black bag could have taken. He had to have gone around the right-hand side of the mound or over the top, he couldn't have gone to the left because he would have been seen by Penny Hall and Emma Brooks, who were round that side. We also walked him through the underpass and then through the Alton Estate to see how close Colin Stagg's address was.

We built up towards the trial with very careful preparation, including several visits to Leicester. I took it as a sign that Paul Britton was recognised as an eminent member of his profession that great men such as John Nutting and David Waters, Nigel Sweeney and Bill Boyce, all extremely busy and at the top of their profession, took the trouble to travel halfway up the country to see a witness.

We all gathered for a final case conference in John Nutting's chambers on Friday, 2 September, with the trial due to begin the following Monday at the Central Criminal Court.

Nutting explained that the defence was likely to launch a pre-emptive strike to have the Lizzie James material declared inadmissible and the case thrown out. He advised Paul that he might be required to be in court on Monday, and said, 'If the evidence relating to Stagg's guilty knowledge were excluded, Mr Britton, is your evidence sufficient basis to convict? Be careful before you answer, because you have to see a man walking down the steps for the rest of his life. That's what hangs on the answer.'

Without hesitation Paul said, 'Of course it's not sufficient. I cannot say that Colin Stagg killed Rachel Nickell. I can only say that the probability of there being two people on Wimbledon

Common that morning who suffered from the same extreme and violence-orientated sexual deviation is incredibly small.'

'I'm pleased to hear you say that,' said Nutting, 'because that's exactly what my view is.'

He began to ask Paul questions about the statements that he had given, pressing him harder and harder on the detail and interpretation. Paul began to look embarrassed at what must have felt like a cross- examination in front of the rest of us. Then I realised that Nutting was playing devil's advocate again. He was testing to see how Paul would bear up when faced by defending counsel in Court.

As the meeting ended, the way ahead was clear – if the undercover evidence was deemed inadmissible, then the Crown would drop its case against Colin Stagg. Paul said to John Nutting, 'I get the impression that you' re somewhat pessimistic about the case.'

'Well, let's just say I'm not optimistic,' the lawyer said.

'Do you have a view on the likelihood of the Crown being successful?'

There was a long pause. 'I think it's very finely balanced,' came the reply.

The morning of 5 September was dull and overcast as I travelled to the Old Bailey with Roger Lane, my office manager. Most of the journey was completed in total silence as we both contemplated the investigation of the previous 27 months, and the weeks of trial ahead.

As we walked towards the entrance of the court, I could see a handful of photographers and TV cameramen loitering outside. The Stagg case was being talked about by the media as the murder trial of the year, and the press pack had been digging for background stories. Had Andre Hanscombe really got a new girlfriend in France? Was the rumour true that he had fallen out with Andrew and Monica Nickell over it? Was he back in London for the case? How was little Alex bearing up? And what about Lizzie James? Would she be permitted by Scotland Yard to tell the real inside story of her extraordinary role?

That last 20 or 30 yards' walk from the time of being recognised by the press to reaching the sanctuary of the court was a disconcerting jostle of cameras and microphones. It is difficult to ignore the clicking of shutters and not trip over as a TV cameraman gets right in your face.

'The circus has begun again,' I muttered.

We made our way to the Met Police room to book on. Normally, an attendance at court is a good opportunity to renew old acquaintances as officers from all over the Met gather to give evidence in the many different cases which are tried at the Old Bailey. The police room and the City Police canteen are the central meeting points for officers, and you always see people from your past. The tensions of the forthcoming legal proceedings are temporarily forgotten as you take a trip down 'Felony Lane' with your old cronies. The fifth of September 1994 was an exception, however; the old faces were there in abundance, but neither Roger nor I was in the mood for banter. The lead-up to this day had been a frenzy of activity and we knew that we were in for a fight.

We settled down at a table in the corner to await Wickerson's arrival. I smoked the umpteenth cigarette already that morning and contemplated the large mug of black coffee in front of me. Not for me the 'big boys" breakfast for which the City canteen was famous.

I broke the silence. 'Well, Rog – make or break time.'

Lane puffed on his pipe. 'For you more than most, Guv.'

I smiled ruefully as I recalled Roger's warning to me 12 months earlier when he discovered the nature of the undercover operation.

'You know that if this works, Guv,' he'd said, 'you'll be a long way down the pecking order for a pat on the back – but if it goes wrong, they'll hang you out to dry.'

We lapsed back into silence and Wickerson arrived, looking at his watch. 'Just after ten, we'd better get downstairs and see if Andrew and Monica have arrived.'

Arrangements had been made for a small ante-room to be made available where the Nickells could have some privacy as they waited for the case to begin. Andrew and Monica were already there when we arrived, accompanied by three of my indexers, Sheri

Roberts, Fiona Fisher and Linda Titchner, who had volunteered to look after the family during what was going to be a traumatic and painful time.

Andrew greeted us as we entered. His manner was as I would always expect of him, calm and dignified, no sign of the inner turmoil that he must have been feeling.

Monica looked strained but she was putting on a magnificent show in an attempt to hide her pain.

Without further small talk, Andrew cut straight to the chase. 'What can we expect this morning?'

'As I mentioned the other day, the jury will be sworn in and then sent away whilst the trial within a trial takes place,' Mick answered.

'Yes, I understand that. But what do you think the main thrust of the defence argument will be?'

I said, 'Their main objection will almost certainly be that we've breached the codes of practice and used the undercover operation to get round the rules governing interviews. In a nutshell, they'll be saying that everything discovered by the undercover operation is inadmissible because it's unreliable and prejudicial.'

'Will they win the argument?'

Mick and I exchanged glances. Wickerson grimaced. 'We've got some useful precedent on our side, but who knows?'

I nodded. 'It certainly isn't going to be easy, but we've got John Nutting on our side and he's one of the best. I'm not going to pretend that we haven't got a battle on our hands, because we have – but we won't be giving up without a fight. The bottom line, Andrew, is this – the CPS decided we had a viable case and that view was shared by four Treasury counsel. The magistrate, too, said that there was a case to answer. We've got a fighting chance.'

Andrew reflected for a few seconds. 'This case in Leeds, the Hall case – that was decided after the committal. That must surely be a major hurdle?'

'It hasn't helped.'

No matter how many times I give evidence in the Number One court at the Old Bailey, I never fail to get a surge of nervous excitement as I enter. The panelled walls, metal-spiked dock, and canopied witness box are redolent with the drama that has been acted out within these walls over many decades. It was in this room that Crippen learned of his appointment with the hangman.

The story goes that, as the jury returned, the strains of the Eton boating song were heard from a barrel organ and street singer outside. The refrain of 'Swing, swing together ...' must have been a chilling accompaniment and prophesy as the verdict was announced.

Such is the atmosphere of this cathedral of justice, even seasoned policemen feel compelled to speak in hushed tones. There is a timeless quality to the courtroom, the ritual proceedings, the archaic robes and wigs a reminder of the days when justice was dispensed with a clinical and often lethal regularity.

It must be a terrifying experience for any defendant to emerge from the cells via the stairs at the rear of the dock, the same stairs that many a condemned man has descended to his fate. The aura of this room immediately tells you that matters of great import are decided within its confines. It was a fitting stage to act out the drama of Regina v Stagg.

At just after 10.30am, Mick and I took up our position in the well of the court, seated at the large table below the judge's bench and directly in front of Mr Nutting and David Waters. Facing us were the defence team of William Clegg QC and Jim Sturman. The press benches to the right of the defence were full to overflowing. Like us, they knew that this was a case certain to provoke widespread repercussions whatever the eventual outcome.

At 10.38am, all eyes turned to watch Colin Stagg as he emerged from the bowels of the court and took his seat in the dock, flanked by two prison officers. I studied the man who had been the subject of one of the most controversial police investigations of all time. I noted that he was a lot thinner than at the committal hearing. He had also changed his hairstyle; it was now longer and swept back from his face. He bore little or no resemblance to the E-fit picture that had been responsible for him coming to our notice back in September 1992.

Colin, not surprisingly after so long on remand, looked pale, and this was accentuated by the chunky-knit green sweater he was wearing. He looked up at the packed public gallery as if searching for faces he knew. Just a few feet away, to his right, sat Andrew and Monica Nickell, preparing themselves for the harrowing ordeal ahead. Stagg would have been unaware of their presence amongst the mass of journalists, lawyers and courtroom staff. He returned his gaze to the front and stared impassively as Mr Justice Ognall opened the proceedings.

The judge told the court short-hand writer that if she felt she needed a break at any stage then she only had to ask. He then imposed a reporting ban on the proceedings under section 4(2) of the Contempt Act 1981, designed to prevent the risk of prejudice – in this case the chance of jurors hearing controversial evidence which would not later be used in the event of a full trial.

I felt a surge of relief as Mr Justice Ognall uttered his first words. All the months of hard work and issues that had caused so many sleepless nights were about to be resolved, one way or the other.

Mr Clegg was soon on his feet, outlining the defence objections to the evidence gained from the UC operation. One of the main planks of that argument was, as expected, the judgment in the Leeds case. His next application came as more of a surprise. Mr Clegg asked that a jury should not be sworn in until the legal arguments had been completed. It would, he suggested, create an air of mystery in the minds of the jurors if they were sworn and then dismissed for a week or more before being called back to hear the evidence. Surely, they would wonder, he said, what had gone on in their absence? It would be better for them not to be concerned with mysterious legal procedures and certainly not to speculate on such matters.

The judge ruled that the jury should not take their seats until the legal arguments had been concluded, and his judgment on the crucial matter of Lizzie James's evidence had been delivered. That, Mr Justice Ognall said, meant that he would need to familiarise himself with all the hundreds of pages of evidence which had been gathered during Lizzie James's undercover operation. He set himself three days to plough through the transcripts of the bundles of letters, the tape-recorded meetings and the many phone calls that had passed between Stagg and Lizzie. Only then, he said, would he be sufficiently well briefed to hear the prosecution and defence arguments for and against the admissibility of this essential section of the Crown case.

Both Wickerson and I raised eyebrows at this revelation. I scribbled him a note: 'I don't believe this ... he's had the bloody stuff since July!'

Mick shrugged his shoulders in reply.

So there it was – less than 40 minutes after the start of proceedings, the case was adjourned for three days. It was a tremendous anti-climax. My heart went out to Andrew and Monica. What they needed was a conclusion to the nightmare that had haunted them since that terrible day in July 1992, the knowledge of who and why that is so vital to help victims' families come to terms with tragedy – they did not need a false start.

As we left the court, it was fair to say that I was angry. It had been anticipated that a jury would be empanelled that morning, then told to go home while the lawyers discussed the matter of Lizzie James's evidence – not that a jury wouldn't even be called at all. After all, the relevant paperwork had been delivered to the judge at least two months prior to the start of the trial. I well remembered all the hard work that had gone into the preparation of those papers, the desperate rush to get everything ready by the end of July.

John Nutting told us there could be as much as 10 to 14 days' delay before we would know whether Colin Stagg would even face a jury, let alone find out whether he was the man who had killed Rachel Nickell.

The trial within a trial, or *voir dire*, is a legal process carried out in the absence of the jury, because they are arbiters of the facts and not the law. At these proceedings, questions of procedure and law can be argued for days on end, simply to establish whether the police have breached the codes of practice, or acted outside the law in the way evidence was obtained. The question does not arise: 'Did the defendant do what he's accused of?' If the codes or law have been breached, then the evidence can be deemed inadmissible and the defendant goes free.

The next three days dragged by. On 8 September, we again presented ourselves at the Old Bailey to hear Mr Clegg begin his clinical dissection of the prosecution case.

This part of any criminal trial is always frustrating as you listen to the interpretation by the defence of the case that you have painstakingly put together. The adversarial system is, by its nature, argumentative and destructive; I knew what to expect, and wasn't disappointed. Mr Clegg was at the top of his profession and his performance showed why.

This police operation, asserted Mr Clegg, was a sophisticated 'sting' with the sole purpose of tricking a confession out of Colin Stagg. The Lizzie James evidence and the psychological evidence was, in his submission, inadmissible.

This, of course, would fatally undermine the prosecution case. The evidence fell into various categories: the identification evidence given by Jane Harriman, lies told by Mr Stagg in interview, the evidence gained by Lizzie James concerning Colin Stagg's knowledge of the positioning of Rachel's body, Mr Britton's evidence concerning the almost unique form of sexual deviance apparently shared by the killer and Mr Stagg and the evidence of the pathologist Dr Shepherd concerning the sequence of events at the murder scene which provided, in our submission, corroboration of Paul Britton's evidence. These elements were separate issues, but together, supported each other. The removal of any one of these elements would destabilise the whole structure of the prosecution case. Clegg knew that if he was successful in excluding the evidence of James and Britton the case would be so weakened that there would be no alternative but for the prosecution to offer no further evidence and allow Colin Stagg to be discharged.

He knew it, and so did we. The various elements of our case were independent but interdependent.

Mr Clegg briefly ran through the details of the murder. How Rachel had met her end on a summer day as she strolled with Alex and Molly; how, of the 500 people known to have been on the common that day, all but four had since been TIEd; and how, of the 30 or so men questioned about the killing, Colin Stagg had been the one eventually to be charged. Mr Stagg had always denied any involvement, he said, and had originally been freed after three days of questioning because the police had insufficient evidence.

Then Mr Clegg came to the Lizzie James undercover operation. It had been designed, he said, to trap Stagg into making a confession, taking advantage, Mr Clegg submitted, of a lonely and vulnerable young man's desperate desire to form a relationship with a woman. There had also been inducements of money, he said – small amounts, admittedly – when Stagg was known to be so strapped for cash that he couldn't find enough for a bus fare.

Mr Clegg said that he would begin to prove his argument by starting right at the beginning of the operation, with the very first letter written by Lizzie early in January 1993, and for court purposes labelled exhibit EJ1.

There was a look of consternation on the judge's face at the prospect that Mr Clegg might be preparing to wade through every one of the 700 pages of Lizzie James's evidence.

'You can assume for your purposes, Mr Clegg, that I have read them all,' Mr Justice Ognall said, 'and I believe I have the gist of them clearly in my mind – but, of course, any particular passages in any of them you must, as you please, underline. If you feel it necessary to read any out in their totality, I leave it to your discretion and judgement, but that is not an exercise which I would encourage.'

Mr Clegg took the hint. 'I certainly don't intend to read all 700 pages,' he quickly assured His Lordship, but some parts were vitally important to the defence case and must be given an airing in front of the court. For example, the very first introductory letter in which Lizzie described her supposed friend Andrea Parker as 'a little old-fashioned in her attitude if you know what I mean'. It was a clear 'come-on' from the start, he argued, and got worse as the relationship progressed.

Lizzie, he claimed, had excitedly described herself as an

attractive blonde aged 30 whose favourite record was 'Walk on the Wild Side' by Lou Reed. By the third letter, suggested Mr Clegg, Lizzie had begun turning up the heat emotionally by saying she hadn't had a relationship with a man for a very long time and longed for the company 'that only a man can give'. It was a 'very deliberate sexual undertone' to lead Stagg on, the defence claimed. It clearly implied, he said, that here was someone who was ready to become a sexual partner.

Stagg had written back saying he had never had a sex life but thrived on sexual fantasies. He enclosed an example, detailing his longings for sex in the open air in the garden. Lizzie James's response was to send Stagg a Valentine card in which she wrote, 'Roses are red, violets are blue, there will be a letter, arriving for you. Guess who?' and signed with a kiss. Mr Clegg submitted that Lizzie was now 'very obviously' trying to 'shape' the course of the relationship by portraying herself as someone sexually experienced, ready, willing and able, knowing full well that Stagg was desperate to lose his virginity. In reply to one of his fantasy letters, she had told him, 'It was so real I could almost feel you sitting astride me, pushing me into the ground.' She praised his 'brilliant' storytelling and urged him to write more.

In Mr Clegg's view, her behaviour was clearly encouraging Colin to write more extreme fantasies, controlling the relationship and setting the pace of the future contact. She told Mr Stagg that her imagination 'knew no bounds' and 'normal things' were not enough for her. Quite clearly, said Mr Clegg, she was trying to make Stagg believe she had uninhibited deviant fantasies, in a bid to get him to respond with even more lurid stories of his own which might be relevant to the Rachel murder inquiry.

Mr Clegg said that a photograph from Lizzie was given pride of place on his mantelpiece and Stagg told her, 'You are very beautiful ... I can't wait to feel your warm lips against me ... You look like a very passionate woman.'

Stagg confessed that he had never been attractive to women and had 'all the fantasies inside me, unused'.

Sometimes, said Mr Clegg, the WDC would deliberately not reply to Stagg, to keep him in suspense. 'We detect,' he said, 'that when the fantasies do not progress as the officer wishes, there is no reply, but when the fantasies increase in intensity, she replies swiftly with more encouragement.' The lawyer suggested that she then tried to tease more detail out of him by saying that there were secrets they must share with each other. The officer wrote: 'I have things to tell you that you wouldn't believe, things I need to overcome with you and, once this is done, we'll be together for ever.'

Mr Justice Ognall was quick to grasp the point. 'This is being used, if you like, as a springboard for saying to him, "Look, eventually I am going to come to deal with you about certain wicked or abhorrent things I have done, but before there can be a fruitful union between us, you must likewise unburden yourself, however shameful your conduct may have been."'

Mr Clegg replied, 'My Lord, yes.' That was exactly his point, he said – that Lizzie was dangling the carrot of romance and sex in front of Colin Stagg in the hope of a revealing confession in return.

Mr Clegg suggested that the policewoman became more and more frustrated with Stagg when he failed to produce what she wanted. She finally told him she had once taken part in the ritual slaying of a woman and the murder of a child by throat cutting, 'bringing together the woman and child elements of the Rachel Nickell murder'.

She told Stagg that after the satanic killing, she had enjoyed the best sex ever, using the phrase 'it really buzzed'.

Stagg then confessed to her of a homosexual relationship at the age of 17 when he took part in mutual masturbation with another man, but, compared with Lizzie's alleged past, this was relatively unexciting.

'It must have been very tame,' said Mr Clegg, 'and it infuriated the WDC. She had hoped he might say, "I killed Rachel Nickell." But he didn't.' Stagg's reply was to claim he had taken part in a completely fictitious murder in the New Forest. 'By confessing to a murder that never happened, the police plan was not working,' said Mr Clegg. 'So the officer said she wishes he had done the Wimbledon Common murder. But Stagg said, "I'm terribly sorry, but I didn't."'

The whole operation, argued Mr Clegg, had produced unreliable evidence which, in fairness to Colin Stagg, should not be admitted. The undercover operation was, he said, misconceived from inception and it was 'difficult to imagine an operation more calculated to result in material which a court would inevitably withhold as inadmissible. It flies in the face of the rule of self-incrimination ... one of the fundamental rules of the criminal justice system.'

Mr Justice Ognall said, 'That is the right not to incriminate himself without knowing who is the inquisitor?'

Indeed, said Mr Clegg. The undercover operation, he said, had precious little safeguard for an innocent man.

I found it incredibly difficult to sit there and listen to this diatribe against what the defence saw as the shortcomings and malpractice alleged to have been our stock in trade, and to hear our efforts to solve the murder of Rachel Nickell being so mercilessly and eloquently destroyed. No matter how many times you go through it, it never gets any easier; the only solace is the knowledge that your turn to redress the balance will come.

Mr Clegg went on to say that when Stagg and Lizzie talked about the Rachel Nickell murder, Stagg had said Rachel had been raped, and that that was why the police took DNA samples from him. Lizzie told him the police were certain to get their man. Stagg told her they couldn't take samples from every man in Britain. The conversation was significant, said Mr Clegg, because Rachel had not been raped and the real killer would have known that.

Mr Clegg continued to pour scorn on our activities. He was unnervingly impressive.

I glanced at Stagg. He seemed to listen intently as his lawyer quoted the legal precedents in support of his argument, from judgments by such legal heavyweights as Lords Scarman, Goddard, Parker, Widgery and Diplock.

Mr Clegg posed a question. Had Lizzie strayed outside the legal parameters to trick Colin Stagg? The policewoman, he said, had used lies, promises and blandishments to get her evidence, even suggesting it would be 'great' if Stagg was indeed the Rachel killer.

If he had said, 'Yes, it was me,' it would be a reliable confession – 'but I can't think of more unreliable circumstances'.

The judge agreed that, in such circumstances, he would have no choice but to disallow such a confession – yet what the Crown was saying was that because there was no actual admission, it could use the evidence.

Mr Clegg went on to suggest that Lizzie James had called the shots in the relationship, and was effectively telling Colin what she wanted him to write in his fantasy letters. The defence, he said, would be submitting a cassette tape which Lizzie James had sent to Stagg 'containing the most hard-core pornography imaginable'. He told the judge disapprovingly, 'It is happily without precedent, and is frankly a disgrace. It is the most extraordinary document for a serving police officer to send a suspect.' He assured the judge he did not intend to read a transcript of the contents.

The 'hard-core' tag was, on the face of it, true, but Mr Clegg was overlooking the fact that this unusual step had only been taken after Mr Stagg had inundated Lizzie with 'hard-core porn' over a period of many months and was beginning to smell a rat that this trafficking in filth had all been one way. He had implored Lizzie on many occasions to send him one of her fantasies. The subsequent tape was sent only after a lengthy consultation with Paul Britton, and contained only those deviant elements that had already been spontaneously generated by Mr Stagg and which had become well-established features in his prurient correspondence.

'It is our submission,' said Mr Clegg, 'that this officer, Lizzie James, subjected Stagg to quite deliberate manipulation, designed to get him to incriminate himself.'

He quoted one particular letter which Stagg began by calling her, 'My dear, beautiful, sexy Lizzie,' and saying that he now knew the sort of things 'you want me to write'. The officer also offered to lend him money – which Stagg declined – but it showed how far she was prepared to go to get him in her debt, Mr Clegg said. She had used phrases like, 'We might not be right for each other ... I've been so disappointed in other men,' and, 'If you fit my criteria, there is no going back and we will be together for ever,' in apparent attempts to prompt Stagg into making a confession about killing Rachel Nickell. This was trickery, he said, and, in the interests of fair play, should never be put before a jury.

Wickerson and I spent the lunchtime adjournment in the City canteen discussing the events of that morning.

'They're making a meal of the fantasy tape,' observed Wickerson. 'We knew they would ... but to listen to Clegg, you'd think his client was totally averse to it. He seemed to forget that Colin had been sending that sort of stuff to Lizzie for months.'

'That's what he's paid for – I mean, he's hardly likely to be pointing out to the court that out of the 65 exhibits, that tape was number 51.'

'And that the majority of those came from his client,' I said.

'You worry too much. There's nothing more we could have done. It's all in the hands of the legal eagles now.'

'That in itself is a worrying enough prospect.' I lit a cigarette and drew deeply on it. 'When I sat there this morning listening to Bill Clegg, I began to wonder what we'd been up to for the last year or so.'

'Come on, Keith. They're bound to put a different spin on things, that's the name of the game.'

'I know Mick, we've seen it enough times in the past ... but this one's different. We crossed every 'T' and dotted every 'I'. Everything done by the book, authorised and scrutinised ... and then, when the book ran out, we wrote a couple of extra chapters, and ran them by the hierarchy for their approval.'

'You know it and I know it. What's more, the judge knows it.'

'Does he? I didn't like the way he cut the defence short this morning, when Bill Clegg was going on about the letters. To my mind, if he rules in our favour there's the basis for an appeal.'

'He told Clegg he must underline any passages he thinks important.'

'He also said that reading any of the letters in their totality was not an exercise he would encourage.'

'But he qualified that by saying he would leave it to his discretion and judgement.'

'We'll see, but in any case, the way he went through the operation, taking a snippet from here and an inference from there and misinterpreting it ... things taken out of context and out of sequence ... this morning's exercise was a total misrepresentation of what we'd done.

'I don't know whether they don't understand what Paul Britton did or whether it's just a case of deliberately twisting it. Colin could just as easily have eliminated himself from the investigation – that was the whole point – but he didn't.'

'John Nutting will be on his feet this afternoon. Perhaps you'll feel a bit happier when he's had his say.'

I stubbed out my cigarette. 'Let's hope so.'

The court reconvened at 2pm, at which point Mr Nutting rose and addressed the court. A tall, slim and authoritative figure, he began by outlining the history of the investigation and how, in the view of the Crown, the circumstances of the undercover operation differed from others, and particularly the case of Hall.

He elaborated, 'In my submission, it is distinguishable, for example, from the covert operation in Hall because the object was not to trap or trick the defendant into making admissions but rather to investigate the defendant's sexual fantasies.'

Mr Nutting continued to explain the Paul Britton strategy that the defendant would, if he failed to conform to the very specific narrowing process, necessarily eliminate himself from the inquiry. 'I must stress that it was anticipated and predicted within the operation that if, at any stage, the defendant's behaviour did not conform to that which would be expected from the murderer of Rachel Nickell, then the defendant would eliminate himself from the inquiry.

'It was not a case of trapping the man who made admissions, it was as much a process of excluding him as including him, entirely in accordance with his sexual fantasy. In that sense, granted that it was controlled and interpreted at each stage not by the police but by a psychologist, the defendant had as much of an opportunity to reveal his innocence as his guilt.'

Mr Nutting then turned his attention to Mr Clegg's argument

about the operation breaching the self-incrimination rule, and the subsequent allegation that the operation had merely been a device to circumvent the law governing the conducting of interviews. 'I say it was not a case of that; it was more circular, more complicated and better designed than that.'

There was indeed an element of subterfuge, he admitted, but this was a necessarily clandestine operation and was often difficult and dangerous work. What could be used in evidence as a result of such an operation, he accepted, could also be a difficult decision to make. But each case must be judged on its own merits, with the final discretion in the hands of the trial judge.

Paul Britton, he said, had masterminded the operation following his offender profiling of the killer from evidence at the scene of the murder. It was different from other operations, he said, because it was not set up to trap or trick Stagg into making a confession but to investigate his sexual fantasies. There would come a time, Britton had predicted, where fantasy and reality would merge and he would discuss the killing. The operation was controlled and interpreted by Paul Britton at all stages, and was designed to give Stagg the opportunity to display his innocence if he was not connected with the Rachel murder. Paul Britton controlled each step on the ladder and if, at any stage, Stagg was not following the predicted path, the operation would have been stopped.

Mr Justice Ognall appeared unimpressed: 'If that be accepted as a proposition, then as one goes along the road and nowhere does there appear a portrayal inconsistent with the profile of the killer, is it not incumbent upon the police at some stage to stop because, otherwise, step by step – do you follow me – they are saying this man is fulfilling, daily or weekly, all the consistent features of the profile Mr Britton has prepared for us and we are nonetheless going to continue to exact more.'

Mr Nutting responded, 'My Lord, I make two points by way of emphasis: first, Mr Britton controlled the operation; it was not in the hands of the police. Mr Britton made the decisions about whether the defendant was continuing the process, climbing the ladder, taking the steps, whatever form of phraseology you want to use, in order to keep himself included in the narrowing process, or whether at any stage he took a step which clearly excluded him from the operation. My Lord, it would not be appropriate and I know your Lordship would not want me to attempt to fill in the scientific precision. I am certainly not competent to do it, but Mr Britton's statement and his deposition in the lower court makes it perfectly clear, firstly that he made allowance for the relationship which was developing between the defendant and the police officer, and secondly that if at any stage the defendant had not taken the next step, then Mr Britton would have been in a position to exclude him and would have done so.'

Mr Justice Ognall replied, 'That I perfectly well understand but inevitably, at any given moment, the police were the sole arbiters of how and whether the process should continue. They could have obviously said, "Well, that's it. We don't want to pursue this any further."'

'They could have done that. They could have stopped it, of course.'

'Therefore, it may be suggested that there is an element of disingenuousness about this approach, that they were merely trying to ascertain whether he demonstrated any innocent profile. As he went along with the procedure, he was, with each encounter or each expressive fantasy, betraying, you tell me, more and more of a kinship with the profile prepared by Mr Britton. Is it not at some stage incumbent on the police to say, "We are trying to achieve by the back door here what we can't legitimately achieve by the front?"'

'My Lord, that is so in every undercover operation.'

Mr Justice Ognall said, 'The fact that it was being done with a psychologist as puppet master is a vital distinction of principle.'

Things were definitely not going well. Wickerson and I exchanged glances at this turn of events.

Mr Nutting agreed with the judge, and said it underlined the fundamental safeguards programmed into the operation. 'In my submission,' he said, 'the evidence-gathering nature of this operation is best illustrated as having value only if interpreted by someone else, rather like a fingerprint obtained by a police officer only has value if evaluated by someone else.' The police, he said, decided to embark on the operation in conjunction with Mr Britton because of the gravity of the crime and the public concern it had aroused. It was sometimes good sense and good law to use alternative methods of investigation when needs be. The Lizzie James operation was a trick and was deceit, he admitted. But, in cases of really serious crime, courts had come to realise that such methods can serve the purpose of obtaining evidence and attempting to obtain the truth of matters. It was necessary for Lizzie James to have played the role she did because Stagg would certainly never have revealed his fantasies to a normal woman. That, he submitted, was why the so-called 'sting' had to be perpetrated.

Mr Nutting continued outlining the precedent and law which supported the Crown's case. Even to an experienced detective, the sheer eloquence and logic displayed by advocates of the calibre of John Nutting and Bill Clegg when propounding their respective arguments, never fails to leave you awe-struck. Even with a good working knowledge of the law and the cases to which they were referring, it was difficult to follow every nuance. To a layman listening in the public gallery, it must have been incomprehensible.

Having dealt with the law, Mr Nutting was cut short by the judge before moving on to the application of those principles. The first full day of legal debate had ended. Mr Clegg and Mr Sturman were most definitely ahead on points. There was no point in denying it; despite the best endeavours of John Nutting, it was clear that the prosecution was facing an uphill struggle.

Andrew and Monica were outside the court as Mick and I emerged, and we went to the ante-room together. There was no point in pretending that things were going well. Andrew had heard what we had heard.

'It's not going well,' he said. His tone was even, his face showed no sign of emotion.

Mick took the bull by the horns. 'Mr Clegg was very good, he scored some good points this morning. There's no getting away from it, we've got our work cut out. The judge didn't seem too receptive to Mr Nutting's arguments.'

'Yes, that's my reading of the situation.'

I said, 'I'm a bit worried that they keep on talking about offender profiling ... I thought we'd clearly explained at the committal that profiling had played no part in the UC operation and we were relying on clinical psychology for the evidence?'

'What's in a word or words, Keith?' Mick said.

'Quite a lot, really. The whole operation was based upon Paul Britton's sexual fantasy analysis of the killer, which is clinical psychology, and as such has a scientific basis. Profiling is only an investigative tool and can't have any evidential value. How many times was it emphasised at case conferences that offender profiling played no part in the operation?'

'I take your point, Keith – we'll have a word with John Nutting about it.'

Mick turned to Andrew. 'I'm not going to pretend that it's been a good day,' he said. 'But you can never tell which way a judge is going to jump. They're clinical in their decision-making and they've always got to consider the possibility of an appeal ...' He paused for a moment. 'So, not only have they got to be scrupulously fair, they have got to be seen to be scrupulously fair.'

By the end of Thursday, only the second day of legal debate, the clever money was already on the case collapsing early the following week. If that were to happen, then Stagg could walk free without ever standing trial. As the jury had never been sworn in and the trial never officially started, it would have to be a discharge by the judge, rather than an acquittal by 'twelve good men and true'.

On Friday, John Nutting resumed the case for allowing the Lizzie James evidence. The law, he said, allowed police undercover operations where they were deemed necessary to obtain evidence where no other methods were available or practical. There had been deceit in this case, he said, but it was necessary for the WDC's cover and to assist in building up a psychological profile of a suspect and it had not been conducted for the sole purpose of extracting a confession.

'What is the difference,' the judge asked, 'between police using deceit to obtain, say, a blood sample or fingerprint?'

'It is,' said Mr Nutting, 'the fact that the final analysis was always carried out by a third party, in this case Paul Britton.'

The judge remarked on the striking similarities between the Keith Hall case in Leeds and the Lizzie James operation and said he awaited Mr Nutting's observations on the matter.

John Nutting said that not every trick or deceit is inherently unfair. Stagg would only have felt able to reveal his innermost thoughts to Lizzie James because her guise had persuaded him he could trust her. The operation could not have been carried out without some element of deceit and at no stage, he argued, had Lizzie deliberately manipulated Colin Stagg. He wasn't induced to write fantasy letters for the first time – he was already involved in fantasy creations with Andrea Parker and appeared to be 'something of a compulsive fantasy writer'. If he hadn't been writing to Lizzie James, said Mr Nutting, he would certainly have been writing to someone else.

The judge gave a clear indication that he was far from happy with Lizzie James's role. If she had 'seduced or manipulated' Stagg into writing fantasy sex letters, then 'that creates problems'.

It was Mr Clegg's turn to begin his second assault on the prosecution case. Again, the subject of unfairness and, as a result, the inadmissibility and unreliability of the evidence, was expertly brought before the court. The allegations of 'shaping' Mr Stagg were forcefully put. Mr Clegg asserted that Lizzie James had been leading his client by the nose.

But what Lizzie was doing, suggested Mr Nutting, was simply creating an atmosphere of trust in which Stagg would have felt safe to reveal his darkest thoughts. He could not have written about his desires about knives and blood-letting to just any woman. Lizzie's cover was vital to the success of the operation, he said. 'She had to be a credible and sympathetic listener to anything he wanted to say, someone committed to a similar cause.' Stagg, he maintained, had been suspicious, fearing it was a journalist's trick, and she was obliged to convince him otherwise.

It was always Stagg, he insisted, who had made the first moves. One example was him writing, 'I am going to make sure you are screaming when I abuse you ...' Another was, 'I fuck you hard, my cock ramming into you, pushing you along the ground.'

He talked, too, of cutting Lizzie on her neck and breasts with a knife, drawing blood which runs down her body. 'Nothing said by Lizzie James shaped this fantasy,' Mr Nutting said. The nearest she had got to mentioning any kind of violence was to tell Stagg she enjoyed the leather belt schoolgirl fantasy he had sent her.

The next few minutes must have been unbelievably horrible for Andrew and Monica Nickell, as the prosecution quoted Lizzie's account of Stagg's reaction when he eventually began talking about Rachel and his arrest as a suspect. Stagg told her the police had shown him a photograph of Rachel's body. 'There was blood all over the grass and she was completely naked,' said Stagg. 'As they showed me the photograph I got a hard-on.' He told her he used to go over the common to masturbate afterwards, '... but it's a bit dodgy now, the police keep hanging about hoping the murderer will come back.'

There had been more talk about the murder and Lizzie, in an attempt to get him to open up, had said, 'I wish you had done it and got away with it, that would be brilliant.'

Stagg told Lizzie that he had been on the common at the time – which, said Mr Nutting, was different from what he had already told the police. Stagg had also allegedly shown Lizzie how Rachel's hands were clasped, 'as if in prayer' beside her head, when she was discovered dead on the common. He gave her a demonstration at one of their meetings in Hyde Park in July 1993. Only the killer would have known the exact position of Rachel's hands, Mr Nutting submitted; Stagg's demonstration was capable of being an admission and should be permitted as evidence. It was not something, said Mr Nutting, that Stagg could have seen in the one police picture he had been shown. 'This was a small and insignificant detail to the defendant,' said Mr Nutting, 'which slipped out unintentionally – because he forgot to differentiate between what he had seen legitimately in the police picture, and what he had seen illegitimately as the murderer.'

Not surprisingly, Mr Clegg rejected all Mr Nutting's claims over the validity of the Lizzie evidence and offender profiling 'root and branch'. There was, he maintained, absolutely no history of offender profiling ever being used as a principal plank of a prosecution case in British law. In America, in 17 cases where it had been permitted, all had subsequently been lost on appeal. 'We say Lizzie James was leading Stagg by the nose,' he said. Her evidence should be dispatched in exactly the same way as the undercover evidence in the Leeds case of Keith Hall. 'Hall cannot be distinguished from the facts in this case,' said Mr Clegg.

The legal arguments swung to and fro, but despite the fact that Mr Clegg still hadn't finished by the end of the day, the consensus was that the defence had had the upper hand as the judge rose at 3.15pm with the words: 'You will finish your submissions in the course of Monday morning, will you?'

'My Lord, yes.'

'Then you want me to rule on this aspect of the matter first?'

'Yes.'

'Well, you need not look for a ruling before Wednesday morning, for obvious reasons.'

'My Lord, yes.'

'It may even be Wednesday afternoon, but you will be the first to know. 10.30 on Monday, please.'

After the judge's departure, Mick and I made our despondent way back to the incident room in Wimbledon. Conversation on the crowded rush-hour tube would have been indiscreet, so the journey was spent with us each absorbed in our thoughts.

As we got off the train at Wimbledon, Mick suggested that a drink would be a good idea. It was the most encouraging thing anyone had said all day. We settled down at a corner table in the 'Alex', our local pub, and sought solace in a couple of pints of lager.

'Cheers!' I said with more than a little irony.

'You never know, we might be all right – John Nutting was very good.'

'And so was Bill Clegg ... and he and the judge seemed to be on the same wavelength. I grant you that John Nutting made some really good points, but I'm not so sure the judge shared the same enthusiasm.

'John Nutting couldn't have made things clearer. All that business about whether we tricked him or whether he applied himself to the trick. The simple facts are that Colin was writing sexual fantasies before Lizzie and, more importantly, he was writing sexual fantasies to the woman from Wales afterwards.'

'That's right,' Wickerson agreed, draining his pint. 'If he hadn't been writing all that stuff to Lizzie, he would have been writing it to somebody else.'

I contemplated the judge's words. 'The question is surely not whether the court is satisfied that he would, given the appropriate circumstances, have revealed these extreme fantasies in time to anybody else,' Mr Justice Ognall had said. 'The question is: in the context of his relationship with this woman, Lizzie James, he was the subject of a deliberate manipulation designed to extract from him those extreme fantasies for the purpose of determining whether or not he was the murderer. So the fact that it may be that in other circumstances he would equally have divulged these fantasies to someone is neither here nor there.'

'With respect it is,'John Nutting had replied. 'If you enquire, as I would say you are enjoined to enquire, into whether the defendant was tricked or whether he applied himself to the trick, it must, in my submission, be relevant that this was not a case of taking a man cold and trying to extract his fantasies from him which he was otherwise unwilling to reveal. This was a case of a compulsive fantasiser who had embarked on a correspondence with someone already and would do so again at the end of the operation, and in that sense Judge Macmillan's approach in R v Christou (a sting operation where the police set up a jewellery shop to catch thieves who needed to sell their ill-gotten gains), which found favour with the court of appeal, applied the test: "What would the men be doing if they hadn't gone into Stardust Jewellers?" Answer: "They would be selling the goods elsewhere." So I say, by referring to this case: "What would the defendant have been doing if he hadn't been fantasising with Lizzie James?" Answer: "Fantasising with someone else."'

Monday morning seemed to take an eternity to arrive. We settled down in the well of the court and steeled ourselves for Mr Clegg's final salvo, and it took him until 12.30pm to finish his damning criticisms.

The undercover operation was flawed, legally and morally, from start to finish, he said and, as such, inadmissible and unreliable. He rejected

Mr Nutting's assertion that the undercover evidence could be divided into sections some of which were, in his submission, admissible, and those which, in the latter stages, may have breached the rules. Mr Clegg argued that all the transcripts were either admissible or inadmissible, it was all or nothing, and that, of course, included all of Mr Britton's evidence.

From the moment Lizzie James described her so-called friend Andrea Parker as 'prudish' in her very first letter, he said, she was leading Stagg on.

'If I had strings to my bow, this would be the first,' he said, then quipped, 'or should I say the steps to my ladder.'

Lizzie James, he said, far from being passive in this strange romance, had deliberately planted the seeds for Stagg's erotic fantasies, including the scarcely veiled references to satanism, knives, domination, buggery and violence ... matters which the police knew were already contained in Paul Britton's offender profile of the killer.

Stagg, he suggested, had been encouraged, blackmailed and bribed into incriminating himself to fit that profile. He quoted extract after extract from the letters and conversations.

'Normal things are not enough' was an open invitation from Lizzie for Stagg to create wilder and more sadistic fantasies and would plant in his mind the idea of anal sex.

'You really took charge at our first meeting' hinted at her love of domination. Lizzie James had repeatedly held out the promise of sex if he fulfilled her wishes and sent her more explicit letters. And she held over him the 'very powerful inducement' that once both of them had revealed their dark secrets, then Stagg would get what he most yearned for – a loving and lasting relationship with a beautiful woman.

Lizzie said things like 'I need you to sort me out' and Stagg repeated the theme in his reply. It was Lizzie, said Mr Clegg, who introduced suggestions of the occult and black magic into the relationship when she talked of once being involved in some sort of satanic ritual. Yet it failed to extract from Colin Stagg what the police most wanted – a full confession to the murder on Wimbledon Common.

Three months into the operation, suggested Mr Clegg, the police were getting jittery. Paul Britton had predicted that, if Stagg really was their man, they would get a result within 16 weeks. The police decided to change tactics. They moved to Lizzie having direct contact with Stagg by phone, not just writing letters and hoping for a revealing fantasy among them.

Lizzie suggested that she was ready to go on holiday with Stagg. 'This was a particularly powerful inducement to a man who had never been on holiday with a pretty woman,' said Mr Clegg.

Stagg's letters clearly picked up key words that Lizzie had suggested to him, said Mr Clegg, including suggestions that he would spank her while she was dressed in a schoolgirl's or nurse's uniform. But that was not what Lizzie was aiming for, he asserted, and she was getting impatient. She tried to prompt more extreme letters by pretending to lose interest in Stagg, and by urging him to match her own bizarre and brutal experiences.

'In our submission,' Mr Clegg told the judge, 'the police had gone a long way down this road and it was still going very slowly. Lizzie James gave Stagg powerful hints that he must come up with something stronger if he was to pass muster.' Stagg still didn't respond as the police had hoped, so Lizzie James then uttered what Mr Clegg claimed had become the pivotal sentence on which the Crown case now seemed to balance: 'Frankly, Colin, it wouldn't matter if you had murdered her. I wish you had. It would make it easier for me. I've got something to tell you.' This, said Mr Clegg, was direct encouragement to Stagg; it prompted him to write the knife-point sex fantasy which followed soon after, and on which the prosecution relied as firm evidence of his sexual deviancy. 'She was saying she didn't care if his was the hand that wielded the knife that killed Rachel Nickell. He was being pushed down the Britton road,' said Mr Clegg.

Lizzie had tried to stimulate a reaction from Stagg with her satanic slaying story, said Mr Clegg, including in it gory details of how she had held a knife at the victim's throat and drawn it across, spilling blood which she and others involved in the ritual had drunk. It was followed by a full-scale orgy with 'mind-blowing' sex. Stagg's response, said Mr Clegg, had been just the opposite to what the police wanted. He told Lizzie the killing was awful, 'especially the baby'. In a desperate last gamble to elicit a confession out of Stagg, Lizzie James told him their relationship would have to end because he had become a disappointment to her. However, the threats, promises and inducements still failed to produce what the police were looking for.

'I regard the view that Lizzie James was only a listener as untenable,' Mr Justice Ognall interrupted.

The lawyers exchanged knowing glances. Colin Stagg was close to being a free man.

Mr Clegg continued his attack. The police, he said, had put pressure on a man who by now, faced with losing the woman he loved, had become depressed and lonely. He came up with the New Forest murder story in an attempt to appease Lizzie James and keep the relationship going. But his story of killing a 12-year-old girl was sneered at by Lizzie James, said Mr Clegg. She said at their next meeting that it was 'just a childish murder' – in what was clearly another bid to extract a bigger and better confession. Lizzie told Stagg she could still recall the sound of the knife going in during the ritual slaying and said they needed a 'common bond' if they were to stay together. Again, however, there was no response.

Then came the extraordinary fantasy tape that Lizzie sent Stagg in an attempt to move things along. 'I've read the transcript of this more than once,' said Mr Justice Ognall weightily.

Mr Clegg assured His Lordship yet again that he wasn't planning to read the transcript in open court, but that he felt it should be made clear that it was in this fantasy that the undercover policewoman has Stagg holding a knife during sex. Any suggestion of Stagg becoming sexually aroused over the thought of the Rachel Nickell killing, said Mr Clegg, was simply because he was trying to match the height of emotion supposedly experienced by Lizzie during her satanic ritual.

Lizzie James was, at all stages in the operation, suggested Mr Clegg, directly or indirectly interrogating Stagg. In his submission, it was impossible to separate any individual parts of the evidence: 'All the transcripts are either admissible or inadmissible,' he said, 'in order to explain to a jury the history of the relationship, the lies, the encouragements, her shaping of events, her withdrawals and the way Stagg picked up on her suggestions and reproduced them himself. It is all or nothing.'

Mr Clegg put down his notes and took his seat. There was a pause for a moment or two, then the judge announced that his ruling would be made two days later, on Wednesday. Then he collected his papers together, nodded towards the assembled lawyers, then said, '10.30, Wednesday. If not then, 2.00pm.'

Mike Wickerson gave me a dejected thumbs down as we left court. I was bitterly disappointed. There was little doubt in my mind that we had failed to convince the judge that Colin Stagg should face a jury.

I thanked Mr Nutting for his efforts and headed for Scotland Yard with Mick Wickerson. Commander Ramm, head of Covert Operations, was waiting for an update.

DCI Neil Giles was in Roy Ramm's office when we arrived.

'Come in, take a seat,' Commander Ramm invited. 'Wednesday then?'

Nothing travels faster than bad news and this particular news had beaten Wickerson and me back.

'10.30, Guv,' Wickerson answered.

'Bruce Butler's been on, and it doesn't look too promising,' Ramm said. 'I've arranged a conference for tomorrow morning to discuss the situation.'

'With whom, Sir?' I asked, sensing a distinctly frosty atmosphere.

'John Nutting, David Waters, Bruce Butler and his boss Howard Youngerwood – and I'll want you two there. In the event of an adverse ruling, we have got to protect Lizzie James and the department. We can't allow Lizzie's identity to be revealed. That would compromise her safety and place other operations in jeopardy.' Commander Ramm was reading a document on his desk and didn't bother raising his eyes from the paper work as he spoke. He pushed the file across the desk towards Giles. 'Thank you, Neil, that's OK.'

Giles took his leave and Ramm busied himself with another file. I was getting the definite impression that our presence was no longer required. We sat in silence for a minute or so. Eventually Wickerson spoke. 'Is there anything you want us to bring tomorrow?'

'No thanks, I'll see you at 11.'

We had obviously been dismissed. We left the Commander's office and made our way to the lifts.

Wickerson shrugged. 'They're distancing themselves in case it all goes horrible.'

'Yeah, success has many fathers, but failure is an orphan. Still, if we can't take a joke, we shouldn't have joined.'

The meeting the next day was short and to the point. The primary objective was to prevent Lizzie's identity coming out. It was suggested that an application be made to the judge under the Contempt of Court Act for an order to prohibit the publication of anything likely to identify Lizzie. Both Howard Youngerwood and Bruce Butler were extremely supportive, as indeed were Mr Nutting and Mr Waters. There was no doubt about it, they said, the police had done the right thing and the investigation and undercover operation had been meticulously and professionally conducted. The case had been viable in law and that was that.

It was heart-warming to listen to these words of support, and interesting to note that they seemed to boost the confidence of the other officers present. There was an undertone to the conversation which gave off very strong signals that the decision of the judge was already known and that we had lost. It wasn't a question of 'if' the judge rules against, it was more a question of 'when'.

By 2.00pm, we were back at the incident room. Nobody was in much of a mood for work and by 3.00pm I had sent the squad home.

I hung around in the deserted incident room. The emptiness and quiet was in total contrast to the first time over two years ago when I had walked into the same room and found it full of activity and noise.

I checked my correspondence tray. It was full. I picked up the bundle of papers and sorted through them. I settled down at the office manager's desk and tried to apply my mind to the pile of paper work. It was no good, the room was full of ghosts and I had no appetite for mundane red tape. I knew Andrew Nickell would deal with the disappointment in his usual dignified manner, but there was no getting away from it – privately, it would deeply wound both him and Monica. And for that fact I was truly sorry.

I knew at that moment how a condemned man must feel on the eve of his execution. I left the papers where they lay and switched off the lights. I just hoped that when the axe fell, it would be a clean blow.

Chapter 41

At 9.45am on Wednesday morning, I walked into the SO10 office on the fifth floor and was greeted by Commander Roy Ramm, who was busy typing something on his word processor.

'Morning, Keith, I'll be with you soon.'

Two or three minutes later, the printer whirred into life and disgorged a document. Commander Ramm swiftly read and signed it.

'There you are,' he said, handing me the statement for the judge. 'That should do it.' He paused. 'Do you want me to come to court?'

'No thanks, Guv – I'm a big boy now, I can deal with it.'

'If there are any problems, I'm on the end of the phone. I can be there in 20 minutes.'

'Thanks, Boss, I'll keep you informed.' I took the statement and made for the door.

'Keith,' Roy Ramm called after me. 'If it goes the way we think it's going to go, it might be an idea if you and Mick leave by the back door.'

'I don't think that'll be necessary, Guv.'

'There'll be a lot of press activity ... don't make any rash statements that you might regret later.'

I knew what he was getting at, but I wasn't about to give the press any statement and neither had it ever been part of my game plan to slink away.

'Don't worry, I won't be making any statements about the police not looking for anyone else ...' This was the phrase that police officers had used so many times in the past to indicate their concern over a court decision that had gone against them, but under new guidelines we were no longer allowed to say anything.

'One thing's for sure,' I added, 'I'll be going out the front door, right behind Andrew and Monica.'

The court was already under siege from the biggest media horde seen in years at a criminal trial. They could smell blood, and clearly wanted to be in at the kill. TV crews were setting up cameras on the pavement, photographers pushed and shoved outside the main doors and reporters jostled to get into the press seats in Court Number One – so many of them that they overspilled into seats normally used by the jury and along the rows of public seats at the back.

Andrew and Monica had been deep in conversation with Wickerson when I arrived in the small ante-room. After a brief exchange with them,we took up our respective positions in the court. Mick looked unusually tense, but I knew him well enough to realise that there was more to it than the anticipated drubbing from the judge.

'What's wrong?' I asked in a whisper as we sat down.

'Andrew.'

'What about him?' I was particularly puzzled, as Andrew Nickell throughout this whole tragic incident had never been anything other than dignified and controlled.

'He's prepared a statement for the press, but he won't tell anyone what he intends to say.'

Wickerson's concern was that Andrew might, in the highly emotionally charged situation, say something that could leave him open to a civil action for libel. 'There's nothing we can do about it now, but it would be totally out of character for him to say anything that he hadn't considered to the "n"th degree.'

'Agreed,' said Mick. 'But after everything he and Monica have been through, they don't need any more grief and aggravation. Andrew's nobody's fool but ...'

He was cut off in mid-sentence as the usher called, 'Silence and be upstanding,' and a red-robed Mr Justice Ognall made his entrance, closely followed by an American judge and his wife, on a visit to England from California.

'Here goes,' I said.

Andrew and Monica were in their usual seats, just to the right of the dock. The prosecution team looked in sombre mood. Stagg's family and supporters had gathered in strength up in the gallery. Stagg himself, wearing a black shirt and blue jeans, quickly looked round the packed court and then fixed his eyes on the judge. You could have cut the atmosphere with a knife.

Mr Justice Ognall stared at the press and said, 'Before I embark on this ruling I wish it to be clearly understood that, until its conclusion, nobody is going to leave the court. I am not having any unseemly to-ing and fro-ing. I hope the press will understand that that is both unseemly and a distraction to the court. I hope my injunction will be respected. Therefore anybody who wishes to leave should do so now.'

I thought, Shall I go?

This warning to the press was, to my mind, indicative that His Lordship was about to deliver a judgment that was going to be explosive in news terms, and I was right. I knew our cause was lost, but never in my worst nightmares had I imagined the severity of the indictment that was to follow. The next 45 minutes were to be the longest and most frustrating of my life.

'The accused, Colin Stagg, is charged with the murder of Rachel Nickell on Wimbledon Common on 15 July 1992,' said Mr Justice Ognall. 'He is, I have been told, one of very many men arrested upon suspicion of having committed this offence. He was first arrested on 15 September of that year. He was thereafter, for some three days, interrogated. He answered every question put to him. He gave a full account of his movements on the day in question. He offered an alibi for the material time. He denied being responsible.'

My blood pressure immediately rose. The judge was saying that Colin had been arrested two days prior to the broadcast of the *Crimewatch* programme. Only a small error, but one which was, to my mind, worrying. Our case was based upon a meticulous examination of the evidence. Precision was important. He had had the papers for months, for goodness' sake, and I'd have expected someone in his position to have the decency to get it right.

He'd also said that Colin had answered every question and provided an account of his movements and an alibi. Yet Colin, on evidence provided by Harriman, Gale, Avid and many others, had clearly lied and his alibi had been blown out of the water.

Things went from bad to worse. In 20 lines of judgment, he totally dismissed all of the very compelling circumstantial evidence which just fell short at the initial stage of being able to support a prosecution.

I became very concerned and passed a note to Wickerson: 'This sounds like a fascinating case, but it's not the one we spent 26 months investigating.'

Wickerson shrugged and then scribbled a reply. 'It makes you wonder what case papers he's been reading.'

I was sitting there with a growing sense of frustration, dying to shout out, 'No, that's not right!' But you can't do that; the man's a judge and you're absolutely powerless.

It was difficult to know how to occupy my mind; after about the first 20 or 30 minutes, Wickerson, who very rarely got uptight about anything, sent me a little note saying, 'I hope you're thoroughly ashamed of yourself. You are an evil bastard.'

The judge had been particularly dismissive of the tape recording sent by Lizzie to Stagg, containing what Mr Clegg had called 'hard-core pornography'. He was now openly scathing. The sending of the sex tape, he said, was 'thoroughly reprehensible' and added, 'I would be the first to acknowledge the great pressure on officers in the pursuit of this inquiry, but I'm afraid this behaviour betrays not merely an excess of zeal but a blatant attempt to incriminate a suspect by positive and deceptive conduct of the grossest kind. A careful appraisal of the material demonstrates a skilful and sustained enterprise to manipulate the accused, sometimes subtly, sometimes blatantly, and designed, by deception, to manoeuvre and seduce him to reveal fantasies of an incriminating character and to, wholly unsuccessfully, admit the offence. The prosecution said the undercover operation was the only route open to them. Well, if a police operation involves the clear trespass into impropriety, the court must stand firm and bar the way.'

In her letters, he said, Lizzie James had attempted to use bribes of sex and love to persuade him to write the kind of fantasies she wanted to hear. The early fantasy letters from Stagg, he said, were the 'not unusual' – if 'rarely expressed' – yearnings of a young heterosexual male. Stagg was clearly pressured by promises of sex and a lasting relationship into creating more exaggerated fantasies of an incriminating nature. Lizzie James, he said, had played on the emotions of a lonely and vulnerable man. 'The policewoman was acting under orders and the police, in turn, were being guided by the psychologist, but that cannot excuse the instigation of this sort of strategy.'

The murder of Rachel Nickell, said the judge, had been a 'truly terrible' crime. He called into question the use of psychology in such an investigation and said, 'I would not want to wish to give encouragement to officers to construct, or seek to supplement, investigations of this kind on this basis.'

Mr Justice Ognall said that despite the 'powerful incentives' offered by Lizzie, Stagg had consistently denied murdering Rachel Nickell.

He had been detained on the first occasion for three days, had answered all questions put to him, and had provided an alibi. In a bid to placate Lizzie, Stagg had even invented a murder which never happened.

His Lordship disputed the prosecution claim that the purpose of the undercover operation was either to elicit evidence from Stagg, or to eliminate him from enquiries. 'I believe it was not merely anticipated, but intended,' he said, 'that there should be, eventually, incriminating evidence from the mouth of the suspect. It is very important to my mind that at no stage did the accused ever admit that he was the murderer. Indeed, to the contrary, he repeatedly denied it.'

Even when, latterly, he was invited by Lizzie James to admit the crime as a condition of continuing a liaison that he was 'manifestly desperate to maintain at all costs', he had maintained that he was innocent of the offence.

On two occasions, said the judge, Stagg had given details of the killing to Lizzie which were inaccurate. He told her Rachel had been raped, when she had not, and incorrectly described the position of her body. 'Dr Britton pulled the strings,' said the judge. 'This was a desperately lonely young man, a sexual virgin, longing for a relationship. I am certain Lizzie James played upon that loneliness and those aspirations.'

The judge went on to say that, from the start of the undercover operation in mid-January 1993 until May the same year, nothing emerged from the correspondence between Stagg and Lizzie which matched the psychologist's profile. 'I accept that the increasingly extreme fantasies were the product of deliberate shaping by the policewoman. She was deliberately deceiving him by encouraging him to express his fantasies because she enjoyed them and the more extreme the better.'

A key letter, he said, was the one in which Lizzie had written, 'Each time you write I know we get closer and closer. You seem so much like me. I hope we can be soul mates. They [the letters] excite me greatly, but I cannot help but think you are showing great restraint. You are showing control when you feel like bursting – I want you to burst. I want to feel you all-powerful and overwhelming so that I am completely in your power, defenceless and humiliated. These letters are sending me into paradise already.'

The judge said that another indication of Lizzie's manipulation was the letter in which she wrote, 'My fantasies know no bounds and my imagination runs riot ... sometimes I scare myself with what I really want. Sometimes normal things are just not enough – not just straight sex.'

He had not finished yet. During the latter part of the operation, he said, Stagg had talked about slashing a woman's neck during sexual intercourse. This was highly relevant, he said, because Rachel had been stabbed 49 times. 'Lizzie James taped a cassette of fantasies for Stagg,' said the judge. 'It is a highly explicit tape covering male domination, group sex and the use of a knife by a man to heighten sexual excitement. It is scarcely surprising that, thereafter, the accused continues to speak of a knife in relation to a sexual incident.'

He found it hard to accept the prosecution's claim that Lizzie James had only asked direct questions about the murder when it was necessary to do so in order to preserve her cover. Her secretly recorded meetings with Stagg in Hyde Park had shown a 'consistent attempt' to elicit a confession from Stagg, without which the relationship would have to end. 'This serves to demonstrate the lengths to which the officer was prepared to go in this operation,' he said.

The rules covering entrapment, the judge went on, are the same where a suspect is tricked into providing evidence, such as fingerprints, as they are for someone providing material for an offender profile.

The judge ruled that all the evidence gathered in the undercover operation would therefore be inadmissible, and said that he would not consider separately the section dealing with the 'prayer-like' position of Rachel's hands, which the prosecution had submitted would be relevant and admissible on its own. 'I do not accept that this material could be construed as a confession,' he said, 'and it is so flimsy that prejudice exceeds its probative value.'

The judge eventually turned his attention to the use of such psychological evidence in the American courts. 'I have been told by the defence that their researches indicate that on some 17 occasions in the United States when criminal courts of first instance have admitted evidence of this kind at the behest of the prosecutor in proof of identity, their decisions have always been overturned on appeal.'

This latest statement came as a total surprise. I was well aware of these American cases after my time at Quantico. John Douglas, the unit head, had discussed these matters in great depth, including the case of Steven Pennell, executed by the state of Delaware on 14 March 1992. The fate of Pennell was an extreme example that the United States appeal system had not overturned all of these 17 cases. The case of George Russell Jr, sentenced to life imprisonment for three murders, without possibility of parole, was another. The Russell case had been described by Douglas as a landmark case in the use of signature analysis. It was only much later that Chris Porteous, head of the Metropolitan solicitors, visited Quantico and spoke to the FBI's legal advisers, and found that not a single one of the 17 cases quoted by the defence had been overturned on appeal.

The end finally arrived, with these words: 'The murder of Rachel Nickell was a truly terrible crime. Any legitimate steps taken by the police or the prosecuting authority in an effort to bring the perpetrator to justice are to be applauded, but the emphasis must be on the word "legitimate". I have taken, I confess, a deal longer than is perhaps usual to express my conclusions. The responsibility and implication of my task in this particular case demanded no less. For the reasons that I have given, I uphold the defence submissions that the Lizzie James material will not go before a jury.'

John Nutting got quickly to his feet. 'Your Lordship has now ruled that the correspondence and tape conversations which were the product of the undercover operation are not admissible against this defendant,' he said. 'The Crown are therefore in the same position now as in September 1992 when the decision was made that the evidence available was insufficient to justify proceedings. It follows from what I have said and in the light of your Lordship's ruling that the Crown must now offer no further evidence against this defendant. The defendant having pleaded not guilty to this indictment, would your Lordship please order that a verdict of not guilty be entered under the provisions of section 17 of the Criminal Justice Act 1967.'

The judge duly directed, at 11.45am on 14 September 1994, that Colin Stagg should now walk free.

The decision prompted an outburst of shouts and cheers from

the public gallery. 'See you outside, Colin,' somebody shouted.

I looked at Stagg, now a free man. A thin smile flickered across his face as he turned to wave at his supporters.

I turned to look at the Nickells, sitting below the cheering crowd, but whatever emotions they were feeling, their faces did not betray them.

Following a brief application to protect the identity of Lizzie James, the Court rose.

Mick immediately left to offer his condolences and apologies to Andrew and Monica, while I remained to thank Mr Nutting, Mr Waters and Mr Dennison for their efforts. It was fairly obvious that Mr Nutting was less than happy at the manner in which Mr Justice Ognall had delivered his judgment, and the extent of that discontent was to be made apparent in a phone call he made later that morning to Commander Ramm at New Scotland Yard.

I joined Mick and the Nickells in the ante-room. I was dreading the moment. What on earth could you say? There were no words that I knew which could adequately express my thoughts. After all that Andrew, Monica and Mark had been through, the words 'I'm dreadfully sorry' hardly served. But that's what I said.

Mick was trying to persuade them to leave by the judge's door. 'The press are going to have a field day, Andrew – you might want to consider going out the back.'

'No, I don't think so,' Andrew replied. 'I've prepared a statement and I want to make it. I understand your reasons for the suggestion and I thank you for your consideration, but we will be leaving by the front.'

There was absolutely no way that Mick and I were going to sneak out of the back door either, because we had absolutely nothing to be ashamed of. We emerged as a group and the massed ranks of the press surged around the Nickells, bombarding them with questions. Police horses were needed to protect them from being crushed by the sheer weight of the media pack, all wanting to know how they felt now. What could they possibly say?

Eventually, the family were escorted to an island in the middle of the road. Andrew, with Monica close by, pulled his statement from his pocket and began to compete with the traffic noise. Once again, I marvelled at his composure as his words, straight from the heart, rose above the general clamour:

'When my daughter was murdered I believed, like many other citizens, that the law was even-handed and that justice was available to all. I am afraid the last two-and-a-quarter years have been a period of disillusionment. What appears to have been lost over the last 30 years is the principle that everyone is equal under law. The pendulum has swung too far to the side of the criminal. Why has this situation arisen when society seems to care more for the criminal and less for the victim and their families? When is society and government going to redress the balance so that the scales of justice are level?'

I exchanged glances with Wickerson. I agreed with Andrew's sentiments, but I still felt uneasy that he might say something that would be actionable in law. Mick clearly shared the same misgivings and gestured with crossed fingers.

'At this point, I want to pay a tribute to the bravery of the undercover policewoman who put her life on the line. At the end of the operation, the police, the psychologist and the Crown Prosecution Service all had their own views as to whether Stagg was the murderer. Thirteen months later, having been committed for trial, Stagg now walks free. He has not been tried by a jury. His Lordship, Mr Justice Ognall, ruled that the police undercover operation broke the rules laid down to ensure a safe conviction. The ruling is well argued in law and guided by many a precedent. The effect, however, is to rule that all the evidence gained during the undercover operation is inadmissible in a court of law. The law has been upheld, but where is the justice?'

Andrew made a significant pause to reinforce his point, then went on: 'I understand that the police will now keep the file on my daughter's murder open. They are not looking for anyone else. We have an impasse, which may, and I emphasise may, put other daughters and wives at risk in the months and years ahead. The imbalance in the law allowed a defendant to stay silent during a trial without any significance being drawn to the fact. The whole of the evidence in this case, I believe 10,000 pages, is given to the defence for them to study and to find an answer. The defence must give the prosecution nothing until the trial commences. The prosecution have no appeal whatsoever against today's decision. If it was the other way round, then Colin Stagg's lawyers could have taken his case to the Court of Appeal. If the defence has the right of appeal, why not let the case be heard by a jury and not stifle the evidence? At every stage, it seems the defendant has the advantage. We, as a society, require fairness for all, not just for the criminal.'

There was one little boy in all this, he said, 'who needs the protection of us all. He is the two-year-old-boy who clung to my daughter while the killer murdered her in the most foul way. He will spend the rest of his life remembering those dreadful moments. He and his father have, with enormous courage, made a start in another country. They have survived but Alex remembers everything that happened. Alex's one hope is that you leave him alone in the peace and security he needs to grow up without the constant fear of being discovered by the media. Leave him in peace; he deserves that chance. Do not seek him out, please; leave him alone. I think that society and the law owe him some justice.'

With those last words left lingering in the air, Andrew, Monica and Mark took their leave. The emergence of Colin Stagg from the court soon distracted the attention of the press.

Having collected his personal belongings from the cells, Stagg came out holding a typed statement. Flanked by his legal team, with dozens of spare copies to distribute to the press, he delivered his message. His voice barely audible in the crush, he was smothered by camera teams as he spoke.

'I am innocent and I have always been innocent of this horrible crime, and I am pleased that this has finally been proved. I hope now the police will go out and find the real killer ...' Then he left his prepared script and added, '... the fat, lazy bastards.'

His year inside, he said, had been a nightmare. 'I have gone through a lot of emotional and physical stress. So much, in fact, that the thought of taking my own life was never far from my mind. My life has been ruined by a mixture of half-baked psychological theories and some stories written to satisfy the strange sexual requests of an undercover police officer. The judge recognised that there was never any evidence against me, no forensic evidence, no confession evidence, nothing at all. I now intend to take proceedings against the police and the psychologist Mr Paul Britton for the anguish and distress that I have suffered during the last 13 months in prison. I hope now the press will allow me some privacy over the next few days as I recover from my ordeal and I am reunited with my dog Brandy.'

He finished by thanking his legal team for their belief in his innocence, and for their strength in fighting his case.

By now, one of his team had flagged down a black cab. Stagg jumped in and was whisked away to a four-star hotel for interviews with ITN and the BBC.

I pondered Andrew's heartfelt speech as Wickerson and I made our way back to the car. I hoped that his plea concerning Alex would be respected, but at that moment watching the media, I wasn't overly confident that it would be. As for the other issues, I understood and shared Andrew's frustration, but however flawed our system may be, it is probably the best of a bad lot. Yes, the scales are tipped in the favour of the defendant, and the adversarial system is too often used to test the rules rather than the truth, but I felt it would take a long, long time before someone came up with a system that was demonstrably better.

In the side-road where our cars were parked, we met up with Sheri, Fiona, Linda and Bill Lyle. The girls were in tears. Wickerson and I were seasoned professionals; we'd been here plenty of times before, and once our disappointment had eased, the attitude of 'You win some, you lose some' would reassert itself. But these officers had come to know the Nickells well, and were taking it badly.

On the journey away from the court, the car's mobile rang. It was Commander Ramm for me. I switched on the hands-free speaker so that everyone could hear.

'Well, Keith, what happened?' Ramm enquired.

'It's not good.'

I ran through the edited highlights of how disgraceful and thoroughly reprehensible we were. There was silence for a few seconds followed by: 'Fucking hell ... I think you and Mick should come straight back to the Yard.'

My intention up to that time had been to go out and get absolutely smashed. We were by now at Vauxhall Cross, heading down through Wandsworth to go back to Wimbledon to meet the rest of the staff and drown our sorrows. But the tone of Roy Ramm's voice quite clearly indicated that his words were not a suggestion that was open to negotiation.

Wickerson and I made our journey to the fifth floor in silence. There was a frenzy of activity in the SO10 office, and Neil Giles told us to wait as he hurried past to the Commander's office. At that moment, my pager beeped into life. I examined the message. 'See you at the Yard ... and on *Panorama* ... Lizzie.' For the first time that day, a smile crossed my face. I showed the pager to Mick.

'Many a true word, Keith: was all he could say as he slipped back into his thoughts.

We stood by the reception desk for a few minutes until Giles returned and told us to follow him. Commander Ramm was on the phone as we entered, and he gestured for us to sit down. At length he put down the phone and said, 'It's a mess. The judge didn't pull any punches.'

'Too right, Guv. He went way over the top, I said with a degree of anger.

'That's just what Mr Nutting has just said ... amongst other things. He wasn't best pleased with the situation.'

'That makes at least two of us,' I added.

'If it's any consolation, Keith said Ramm, 'he was very complimentary about the professional and objective way you conducted the inquiry. In light of the judge's remarks, I think Mr Nutting was keen to redress the balance. Not to put too fine a point on things, he was furious. To use his exact words, we were shafted.'

It was very good of him to show his support, he didn't have to do that. John Nutting is nobody's fool, and if he'd thought it had been a bodged investigation, I couldn't have imagined him taking the case on. He would have found reasons for not doing it, counsel's convenience or whatever, they can always find reasons for not doing a job.

'If you'd been in court, Guv, I think you would probably be inclined to use stronger language. If the judge didn't like what we'd done, all he had to do was rule it inadmissible. For Christ's sake, as the result of that drubbing, undercover work could be put back years ...'

'That point hadn't escaped me,' Ramm said. 'Neither did it escape Mr Nutting. I think we should look at the hidden agenda.'

'The what?' asked Wickerson.

'All I'm saying,' continued the Commander, 'is that the bench, through Mr Justice Ognall, was quite clearly laying down the parameters within which undercover work is to be done.'

'Are you saying that that attack was made as an object lesson?'

'Look at the facts, Keith. If the prosecution had been successful in its application, the floodgates would have been opened. The ruling would have given every police service a very powerful tool for proactive evidence-gathering.'

'I can see that,' I said. 'So what the judge was doing was saying, "These are the rules, and if step over the line you can expect to have your legs cut off."'

'That's one way of expressing it. I believe that the judiciary have got together and set down what they are willing to accept, and were looking for a suitable case to demonstrate what's allowed and what isn't. You were just unlucky that yours was the case. He was firing a warning shot across our bows. They obviously didn't relish the prospect of the courts being inundated with undercover work, so you got a trouncing to dissuade others.'

My tone dripping with sarcasm, I said, 'Oh well, as long as we didn't totally waste two-and-a-half years' work. To listen to the judge, you would think we'd taken leave of our senses. Four Treasury counsel and a stipendary magistrate looked at that case and agreed it was viable in law. What about the victim and her family? Andrew did get it right – where is the justice?'

'It's happened and there's nothing we can do about it. We now have to start thinking about damage limitation.' Commander Ramm looked at his watch. 'Let's see what the one o'clock news says about it.'

He switched on the TV in the corner of his office. There were some fairly unpleasant things said, but at the end of the broadcast, he said, 'If that's as bad as it gets, we can live with it.'

But it wasn't, and I couldn't.

Straight after the meeting, I rang Paul and told him of the judgment. Like me, he found it hard to take in.

'But right from the beginning, the operation was scrutinised and overseen by your most senior officers. They were advised by senior Treasury counsel, and the operation was monitored by the Attorney General. None of these people ever cast any doubt over its legality, at least not in my presence.'

'He mentioned your evidence,' I said.

'But he didn't even hear legal arguments about my evidence,' Paul said, surprised.

'I know.'

'What did he say?'

'He said the Crown would have had an "even higher mountain to climb" to persuade him to accept it. And that the notion of a psychological profile being admissible as proof of identity in any circumstances was "redolent with considerable danger".'

Paul nearly exploded with anger. He had never suggested that a psychological profile or sexual deviancy analysis were proof of guilt – quite the opposite. It was Colin Stagg who chose to reveal his sexuality, but Paul had maintained all along that even though this matched exactly the original analysis he'd drawn up of the unidentified killer, it did not make Stagg the murderer. His position had always been that, only when the suspect disclosed real-world information about the actual crime, did he implicate himself.

'What happens now?' he asked. 'My phone is ringing off the hook at the office and apparently I've got journalists on the way.'

'Please don't make any comment,' I said. 'There's the possibility of further legal proceedings. I've been told the Met and the CPS are getting together to make a concerted response.'

Throughout the rest of the afternoon and evening, Paul fielded countless calls from the media, referring them all back to the Metropolitan Police. The press were infuriated. One television producer of one late-night news programme gave Paul the ultimatum: 'Either you come on our programme tonight or we're going to hang you out to dry.' When Paul declined their gracious offer, they did exactly as promised, portraying him as some sort of unsavoury mastermind of an operation designed to frame an innocent man. I watched that programme, and it included a group of people sitting in a TV studio in London all talking about Paul Britton. Behind them, a huge photograph of Paul was projected on to the wall. They hung him out to dry all right. They laid the blame for the undercover operation, the arrest of Colin Stagg, and the subsequent collapse of the trial, entirely at Paul's feet.

Colin Stagg, too, was on TV that night, telling how he had fallen for Lizzie James 'hook, line and sinker', and how utterly betrayed he had felt when she finally revealed her true identity. Stagg was asked directly if he had killed Rachel. 'No, I did not,' he said firmly. 'A crime like this is a crime against God, against the universe itself. I believe all life is sacred, from insects to human beings.'

Of Rachel's distraught family he said, 'I feel very sorry for them and very sad for them because they were seeing a man who was obviously set up by the police when they should have been seeing the real murderer.' His message to the Nickells was: 'Don't be angry with me. Be angry with the police who set me up and let the real murderer go free.'

Chapter 42

I was the first one into the incident room the next morning, holding a clutch of newspapers with headlines such as RACHEL CASE COLLAPSES, FANTASY JUSTICE, and WHO'S IN THE DOCK NOW?

WHERE IS THE JUSTICE? asked the *Daily Express*, echoing the heartfelt words of Andrew Nickell.

The *Times* said bluntly, JUDGE ATTACKS POLICE OVER MURDER TRAP and showed Stagg emerging a free man from the Old Bailey, his lawyers at his side.

The *Daily Mail* carried a photograph of Rachel playing with little Alex as a baby, beside the headline THE CHILD WHO STILL WAITS FOR JUSTICE. They quoted Andre Hanscombe as saying, 'I can't believe it. The nightmare goes on.' He said he was appalled at the inconclusive end to the murder which had so damaged his life. 'I feel so much anger, and I have two-and-a-half years of anger inside me,' he said. 'It's one blow after another. Where's the justice? Where's the sense? It's difficult to know how to go on. It's a never ending source of pain.'

NOW I'LL MAKE A KILLING said the *Daily Mirror*, referring to the massive pay-out Stagg was now apparently hoping for from Scotland Yard.

NO GIRL IS SAFE said The *Sun*'s monster headline, sandwiched between a photo of Stagg and one of Rachel. They said the 'mystery sex beast' who had murdered Rachel was now 'laughing at the law amid fears that he will kill again'.

As the team assembled over the next half-hour, we all skimmed through the papers, then gathered round the TV in the CID office to watch the morning news programme. The Stagg case seemed to dominate the airwaves.

Colin Stagg was on the BBC, tucking into a full English breakfast as he scanned the morning papers and again protested his total innocence.

Meanwhile, Andrew and Monica Nickell were on *GMTV* giving us their whole-hearted support. Once again, the dignity and courage of Rachel's parents shone through.

As was expected, the conversation very soon got around to the furore in the press caused by the judge's less than complimentary remarks about our handling of the investigation. Andrew gave very short shrift to any suggestion that the police had acted improperly. He said, 'People will listen to me and say, "OK, he will be biased," because we have obviously been close to the police over the last two years and, quite frankly, they have been magnificent.

'Are they supposed to walk away and leave society in some danger? They went to the Crown Prosecution Service, they took legal advice, as I understand it, at every stage of the operation. And yet they go to the Old Bailey and get it absolutely slaughtered. Why? They are trying to do their jobs. All I can say is that I know nothing about the law, I'm concerned about trying to find my daughter's murderer and keeping society safe.

'There are times I listened to the evidence and said, "Well, was there another way?" but I don't see there was another way. How were they supposed to do it? All the time, society want the police to protect them. We put one hand behind their back. We blindfold them and we don't support them in any way. And yet every time something goes wrong, we criticise the police. It is very easy for a judge to sit at the Old Bailey in dry surroundings when he's had a week to consider what he wants to say. He's not out there on the streets. He is not on Wimbledon Common picking up someone's body which has been cut. He's not picking somebody out of a car. They are the people who are trying to keep society safe for us and all the time we legislate against them, we make it more and more difficult for them to do their job.'

Speculation was rife that Stagg could expect to pocket damages worth anything from £60,000 to a massive £225,000, based on known compensation figures in cases of alleged unlawful arrest. His solicitors were trying to sell Stagg's story of the arrest, with full details of what was now being called his 'honey-trap' affair with Lizzie James, for 'around fifty grand'. Rumours were circulating of a deal with the *News of the World* which would involve Stagg taking a lie detector test.

Asked to comment on the prospect of Stagg reaping a fortune in compensation and newspaper deals, Andrew said, 'What value society puts on people is incomprehensible.' He said a provisional offer to Alex from the Criminal Injuries Compensation Board had worked out at £22,000, or 17 pence an hour until he reached the age of 18.

The interviewer turned his attention to Monica and the personal side of this tragedy. Monica said that she and Rachel had been especially close, and despite the fact they lived miles apart they would speak to each other every day, just for a chat. She said that every time the phone rang she answered it expecting to hear Rachel's voice. Monica admitted that she still hadn't come to terms with the fact that Rachel was dead. 'I still think of Rachel as being alive and, whenever her name is mentioned, I always respond by using the present tense – "Rachel is ..." as opposed to "Rachel was".'

Monica spoke, too, about little Alex, now living in a French village where the locals had been told his mother died in a car crash. She said, 'He talks about Rachel now. He didn't for about a year. He has pictures of her everywhere and says, "This is my mummy." In the summer, he came to stay with me and I took him swimming.

He said, "Have we been to this pool before?" and I said, "Yes, we went there with Mummy." He said, "I can remember what Mummy looks like, but I can't remember what she feels like," and from a small boy that is quite a sad thing to hear him say. But I understand that feeling because I almost forget what she feels like.'

As I looked around the little group of policemen and women glued to the set it was clear that the images and words were touching a raw nerve. I felt tears welling in my eyes and swallowed hard several times in an effort to retain my composure.

It was a very emotional time for the nine officers who were all that remained of the inquiry. The strain on us all in the hours since the collapse of the case had been tremendous. The swingeing criticism in the media and often downright misrepresentation of what we had tried to do had left us at a very low ebb. But we could take it; we were big boys and girls. The sight and sound of Monica, however, dignified and courageous as she explained her emotions at losing not only her daughter, but also her dearest friend, was too much to bear. I walked away from the TV and went to the sanctuary of my office. I closed my door and sat down, trying to make sense of it all.

My introspection was to be short-lived. The phone rang on my desk, and I took a deep breath and lifted the receiver.

The barrage had begun again. This time it was Scotland Yard, wanting copies of various documents. I felt a sudden, sick sensation deep in the pit of my stomach as Roger Lane's warning came back to me. Were we indeed going to be left holding the baby?

Mick and I didn't seem to have a friend left in the Job. I couldn't understand this apparent lack of backbone; the undercover operation had been properly authorised, and we'd enjoyed the support of the CPS, right up to the level of Director of Public Prosecutions, Barbara Mills. A senior stipendary magistrate, Terry English, had committed the case for trial, and four of the most senior prosecuting barristers in the land had considered the case to be viable – not without its problems, but viable nonetheless.

As the hours went by, it became clear that the judge's comments had sent a wave of panic through the higher echelons of the Met, where any whiff of scandal or controversy is considered detrimental.

Maybe Andrew and Monica had had a sneaking suspicion that this would be the case, because following their TV interview they had come to the incident room to thank us for our efforts and show publicly that they supported us. Their visit was greatly appreciated and was another indication that these were two very special people, who despite their own grief and heartbreak could spare the time for other people's problems.

Not much was said concerning the case. What was there left to say?

We gave Monica a bouquet of flowers, and our heartfelt sympathy. All I could say was, 'Sorry.' I wasn't sorry for adopting the method we had used, because there had been no other option. But I was sorry that Andrew and Monica had had their hopes raised that there would be a conclusion to their grief, only for those hopes to be dashed.

The rest of my conversation with the Nickells mainly centred around Alex and the new life he and Andre were making for themselves in France. The dream of living in the countryside which he and Rachel had nurtured together had come true, in part anyway. Monica mentioned the interview Andre had given to *Hello!* magazine before leaving England, and quoted part of it to me from memory. 'He said, "He only ever remembers his mother with a smile on her face. Wonderful people like Rachel leave part of themselves behind in everybody. It's staggering how normal he is now and that is a reflection of the time Rachel spent with him. She was with him all the time and we talked to him, even when he was in the womb. His personality is a lot like hers, sunny. He's only got me now and the most important thing is that he has as much of my attention as possible, because I can't bring her back for him. It's been a challenge figuring out what's for the best all the time. I was terrified at first that he would become a complete vegetable. The pressure was trying to do the right thing. When you've worked out what it is, it isn't hard. I miss talking to Rachel, but I don't find it hard making decisions without her, because I'm convinced I know what her attitude would be to virtually everything. I knew her so well."'

I remembered the article. Of the dangers of living in London, Andre had said, 'When you find out the kind of people who live in an area, how many past offenders, people out on bail, those let out after 17 years, then you realise that every street, park or area is dangerous, night or day. You can't afford to let your children out of your sight, or let anybody vulnerable be in any situation on their own. It's totally unfair on women who are the victims and children who are at risk. Rachel was very much for equality and would shrug things off and say, "Don't be ridiculous. I can go and do what I want."'

The phones were still ringing non-stop and I was certain that the ever-astute Andrew picked up on the fact that there were thunderclouds on the horizon and heading in our direction. He asked Mick and me, 'And where does this leave you?' We played down the problem by saying that the Met's reaction was merely routine, a dotting of the 'I's and crossing of the 'T's.

On Friday, the truly unexpected occurred. The Commissioner of Metropolitan Police, Paul Condon, had returned early from his holiday as a direct result of the case, and appeared on the same platform as Barbara Mills at a press conference. Both voiced their strong support for the way the investigation and the prosecution had been handled. That in itself was unusual, as the Met and the CPS, when things go awry, make uneasy bedfellows.

In a memo to Mr Etherington, a senior official at the DPP, which was immediately circulated to the Wimbledon team, Mrs Mills had written:

1. *I would like to thank you and all the staff who were involved in the prosecution of Colin Stagg. I would like to thank Howard Youngerwood and Bruce Butler, in particular, for coming with you at such short notice on Friday to help to brief me before the press conference with Sir Paul Condon.*
2. *We all knew that this was a difficult case from the start. I*

have no hesitation in saying that, in my view, the CPS made the right decisions throughout this case. No one deserves the intemperate, ill-informed criticisms which have been in the press. I have every confidence in the decisions which were made, and I am only sorry that the people who worked so hard on the case may have been upset by the press criticism.

3. *It is an inevitable part of our job that in difficult cases we are criticised whatever we do, but would you be kind enough to pass on to everyone how much I appreciated the tremendous efforts which were made to bring this case to a proper conclusion.*

Barbara Mills QC

Sir Paul Condon left little doubt in the public's mind that he stood squarely behind our actions. 'I feel no sense of shame or embarrassment at what was done,' he said. 'I have decided to comment because I feel the people of London should hear from me personally. I do not believe that my officers acted improperly or outside the law in the way they conducted the investigation, or afterwards. What do we do in circumstances where a victim has been murdered? Surely we have a public duty, in the public interest, to explore and test every legitimate avenue of evidence.

'The reason we embarked on this undercover operation was to try to do that. It was never our intention that the undercover operation should be the centrepiece of our evidence. It was always our ambition to find forensic and other detailed evidence. This was not achieved, but what did result from that operation was very properly exposed to the most exhaustive legal filters which exist in this country. The CPS had obtained independent Treasury Counsel advice who advised that in the public interest the matter should be put before a court. But, even more important, the evidence was subjected to the ultimate legal filter before a trial takes place – a contested committal.

'A stipendary magistrate said, "This case far from limps past a *prima facie* stage." An individual judge has now taken a view of the case we must respect. We will study very carefully what he said, we are always prepared to learn lessons. But what I must say is that we had a woman officer who, with a very strong sense of public duty, acted out a part in the most difficult circumstances imaginable. She deserves, and has, my thanks. Throughout the case, we have acted in the public interest and we have exposed every single thing we have done to the appropriate legal authorities. And I would like to say the CPS have given us quite excellent support throughout.'

Mick and I were elated, and the Commissioner's worried minions suddenly rediscovered their backbones. Well, for a day or two at least.

On Sunday, four days after Stagg's acquittal, the *News of the World* revealed that he had taken a lie detector test at their invitation and it had demonstrated him to be not guilty of Rachel's murder, despite the 'huge cloud of suspicion' which still hung over him. The polygraph results, said the paper, showed that Stagg was certainly sexually disturbed, 'But they clear him – almost beyond doubt – of any involvement in Rachel's murder ... These results provide an emphatic answer to the question all Britain has been asking: "Did he do it?" And they will be a further blow to the police team who were convinced they had their man.'

The paper said that Stagg had undergone a lie detector test supervised by Jeremy Barratt, Britain's 'foremost polygraph expert', who had asked 15 key questions relating to Rachel's killing and Stagg's movements on that day:

'Have you masturbated on Wimbledon Common?'

'Yes.'

'Did you ever see Rachel Nickell alive?'

'No.'

'Did you kill Rachel Nickell?'

'No.'

'Is it possible Rachel Nickell ever saw you masturbate?'

'No.'

Stagg's responses, said the *News of the World*, were the same to mundane questions like 'Is your name Colin?' as they were to the critical questions over Rachel's death. The needles on the polygraph 'didn't even flicker' they said. They quoted a former Scotland Yard officer, ex-Flying Squad chief John O'Connor, as saying, 'The results in this test would suggest that consideration be given to this inquiry being reopened with a view to looking for an entirely different suspect.'

The Commissioner was asked to comment and said, 'We live in the real world. This is not some sort of television drama.'

Stagg was now reported as saying that he didn't blame the police for suspecting him of murdering Rachel. 'I know I seem like a low-life, so I understand why the police tried to nail me,' he said. 'I let my sexual fantasies run riot, but I never put those fantasies into practice.'

He revealed, too, that his new girlfriend, Diane Rooney, had finally relieved him of his virginity when they shared a room at the Waldorf on the night of his release. Stagg said he was planning a new life with Diane, free from the shadow of the Wimbledon Common murder. Diane, a 26-year-old care worker who became acquainted with Colin after writing to him in jail after his arrest, said she hoped to move into his Roehampton maisonette soon.

On the same day that the *News of the World* claimed to 'clear' Stagg, the *Mail on Sunday*'s crime correspondent, Chester Stern, disclosed that Scotland Yard would strongly resist any claim by Stagg for compensation in a civil court. Furthermore, they would be prepared to produce all their evidence, material banned from the Old Bailey, plus everything else in their files, in what would effectively be a new 'trial'. Since no criminal charges would be involved, the police would also be allowed to put Lizzie James and any other witnesses on the witness stand. Scotland Yard sources were also quoted as saying that a civil action would not be about Stagg's guilt or innocence, but about whether the police were justified in arresting him as their prime suspect, that they had not brought a malicious prosecution against him. Stagg's reputation would stand or fall, said the *Mail on Sunday*, on how much a jury decided to award him in damages.

It seemed that the pressure on Mick and me was definitely beginning to ease.

But on the following Tuesday, apparently as the result of the intervention of a member of parliament, the Commissioner announced at a press conference that he was setting up an inquiry into the conduct of our investigation. Sir Paul promised a thorough review of the investigation by his most senior detective.

We feared nothing from an official inquiry into the way the case had been handled. The investigation had already been reviewed once by DCS Bill Hatful, who was more than happy that it was a righteous investigation.

And I would have had no problem with this new inquiry apart from two points. First, that I had been running the inquiry since JB had retired in the early part of 1993 and Wickerson had been returned to divisional duties, yet only found out about the inquiry from the national television news. Secondly, that Sir Paul Condon's most senior detective was Detective Chief Superintendent Bill Ilsley, a well-respected and a successful investigator. However, Mr Ilsley was answerable to Assistant Commissioner Ian Johnston, who had only just been promoted from Deputy Assistant Commissioner – the very same DAC, in fact, who had authorised Operation Edzell in the first place.

In all of this, however, I felt especially sorry for Paul Britton. The investigation had cost the taxpayer a considerable amount of money, and the media were looking for someone to blame. There were only three possible scapegoats – the Met, the CPS and Paul Britton. Paul had a face and a name and was by far the easiest target. He was being hounded by the media, but wasn't defending himself. Not only had I passed on the Met's message, but he had since been directly advised by Metropolitan Police solicitors that it would probably be best to keep his counsel at the moment and avoid newspaper or media publicity, in view of the potential of a civil action by Colin Stagg. So Paul did, despite the fact that he was constantly being harangued and harassed by the media, and despite the fact that when the media don't get what they want, they turn upon you and bite you. That's exactly what they did. When Paul refused to comment, they went ballistic.

He was being depicted in the press as having 'persuaded' us to launch the covert operation and then having convinced 'sceptical CPS lawyers' that they should charge Colin Stagg with murder. Of course, this was absurd and I expected that at any minute Sir Paul Condon would come out and say, 'You've got it all wrong, Paul Britton did no such thing.'

Paul, too, waited in vain for an official statement which would set the record straight. The joint press conference by the Commissioner and the Director of Public Prosecutions did nothing to remove the hounds from Paul's door. He wasn't consulted beforehand or invited to the conference, even though he appeared to be the target for most of the flak.

He told me that, as the days went by and the vilification continued, he'd been contemplating putting out his own press release and a point by point rebuttal of the claims being made in the media. 'I chose not to,' he told me, 'because I'd given you my word.'

'Things might have been so different,' I said, 'if only a judge and jury had heard the rest of the evidence we had planned to submit – if it had not all boiled down to the legal rights and wrongs of the Lizzie James testimony. If a jury had acquitted Colin Stagg after hearing all the evidence, then we would have had no complaints and none of this victimisation would be happening.'

Epilogue

I retired from the police force on 3 December 1995. Sadly, Andrew Nickell's wishes regarding little Alex's privacy were not respected and Andre was hunted down by the press as he and his son attempted to rebuild their lives in France. A year or so later, Paul was back at New Scotland Yard, having been asked to design another covert operation, this time to investigate the sabotaging of healthcare equipment. He said to a senior policeman from the covert operations team, 'I've been here before, you know. And the last time we were all at this stage, everyone said how well things were going and what a good job was being done. Come the trial when things went badly, I was the only one standing there. No one else was around.'

The policeman laughed. 'Yes, you got a fucking raw deal there. But you're a big lad, you've got broad shoulders, you can look after yourself.'

The Rachel Nickell case will go down in the annals of criminal investigations as one of the most horrific, perplexing and frustrating that any police force has ever tackled. It will surely haunt Andrew and Monica Nickell, and Andre Hanscombe and young Alex for the rest of their lives. The shadow over Colin Stagg will only be lifted, in the public's eyes, if and when another suspect is arrested, charged and convicted. The questions still of paramount importance to every decent human being in Britain are: 'Who did kill Rachel Nickell? Where is he now? Will he ever strike again?'

I am not an apologist for a legal system that keeps a murder suspect in prison for 13 months awaiting trial. We thought we had a case that should be put before a jury, and so did the lawyers. A stipendary magistrate agreed. But in any prosecution, some material will be admissible as evidence, other material will be inadmissible – it is the responsibility of the judge to decide which is which. The law is dynamic and based on precedent; what is good law one day may become bad the next and vice versa.

To illustrate this point, it is interesting to note that in the summer of 2000, Lord Justice Mance sitting with Mr Justice Newman in the High Court allowed alleged confession evidence to be admitted in the extradition case of Michael Proulx. This contentious evidence was obtained as the result of an undercover operation which bore 'striking similarities to the Stagg case'. Commenting on this decision, Mr Roy Amlot QC, Vice Chairman of the Bar Council, said the decision could be used by prosecutors to argue that evidence from similar operations should be allowed.

'Such operations were rightly described at the Stagg case as being on the cusp of what is right and wrong ... In such a situation in the future, this judgment will be examined and the prosecution will derive value from it.'

However, on 14 September 1994, Mr Justice Ognall decided that the evidence gathered by Lizzie James should not be put before a jury. The Crown withdrew and, quite properly, Colin Stagg was cleared and released.

The silver birch under which Rachel's body was discovered is dead. The oak nearby, which became known as her memorial tree, where hundreds left bouquets and wreaths, still thrives. I still go there from time to time. My visits always concentrate my mind on the tragedy of Rachel's death and always lead me to ask myself the same question: Why? I have never been able to answer it. The senseless and depraved act committed by a madman on that warm July morning defies explanation and has left a terrible legacy of suffering for Alex, Andre, Andrew and Monica. My heart goes out to them. Words cannot adequately express my sympathy for their terrible loss or my deep regret that two investigations have failed to find the man responsible.

I never stay long.